Eastern Ways to the Center

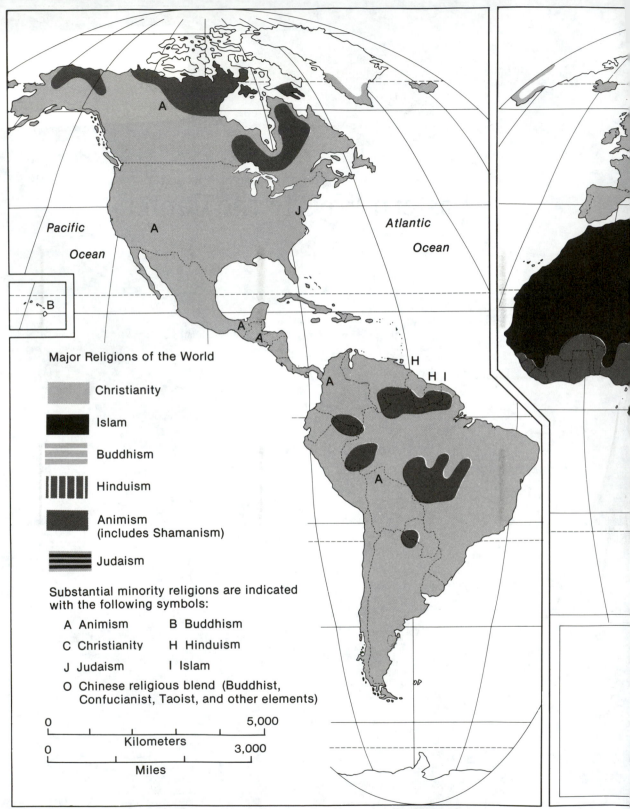

Major Religions of the World

▨	Christianity
■	Islam
▤	Buddhism
▥	Hinduism
▦	Animism (includes Shamanism)
▦	Judaism

Substantial minority religions are indicated with the following symbols:

A Animism   B Buddhism

C Christianity   H Hinduism

J Judaism   I Islam

O Chinese religious blend (Buddhist, Confucianist, Taoist, and other elements)

Pacific Ocean

Atlantic Ocean

0   5,000
Kilometers

0   3,000
Miles

Adapted from *Historical Atlas of the Religions of the World* by Isma'il R. Al Faruqi and David F. Sopher. Copyright © 1974 by Macmillan Publishing Company, Inc. Reprinted by permission of Sakhr Faruqi.

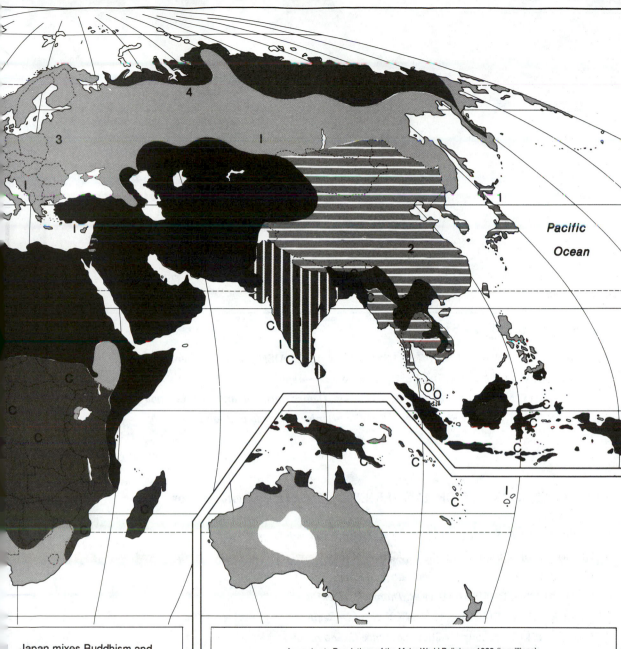

Pacific
Ocean

1. Japan mixes Buddhism and Shinto.

2. China mixes Buddhism, Confucianism, Taoism, Islam, and Marxism.

3. Eastern Europe mixes Marxism and Orthodox Christianity.

4. USSR mixes Marxism, Orthodox Christianity, and Islam.

Religion	Africa	East Asia	Europe	Latin America	North America	Oceania	South Asia	USSR	World
Christianity	283	82	413	403	233	22	133	105	1,674
Islam	254	24	9	.7	2.7	.1	560	33	883.5
Hinduism	1.5	.01	.5	.7	.9	.3	660	.001	664
Buddhism	.01	155	.3	.5	.2	.02	157	.3	313
Judaism	.3	.002	1.5	1	8.2	.09	4.2	3.1	18.3
Confucianism	—*	6.2	.001	—	.02	—	.002	—	6.2
Taoism	.01	165	.05	.05	.1	.001	8	—	173
Baha'ism	1.2	.05	.07	.6	.3	.006	2.4	—	4.5

Approximate Populations of the Major World Religions 1988 (in millions)

Source: *1989 Britannica Book of the Year.* Figures are conservative.
*— = negligible

OF RELATED INTEREST

BETWEEN TIME AND ETERNITY: THE ESSENTIALS OF JUDAISM, *Jacob Neusner*
JUDAISM: DEVELOPMENT AND LIFE, third edition, *Leo Trepp*
CHRISTIANITY: AN INTRODUCTION, second edition, *Denise Carmody and John Carmody*
WESTERN WAYS TO THE CENTER, second edition, *Denise Carmody and John Carmody*

THE RELIGIOUS LIFE OF MAN SERIES   *Frederick Streng*, Editor

UNDERSTANDING RELIGIOUS LIFE, third edition, *Frederick Streng*
THE HOUSE OF ISLAM, third edition, *Kenneth Cragg*
THE WAY OF TORAH, fourth edition, *Jacob Neusner*
THE HINDU RELIGIOUS TRADITION, *Thomas J. Hopkins*
THE CHRISTIAN RELIGIOUS TRADITION, *Stephen Reynolds*
CHINESE RELIGION, fourth edition, *Laurence G. Thompson*
JAPANESE RELIGION, third edition, *H. Byron Earhart*
THE BUDDHIST RELIGION, third edition, *Richard H. Robinson and Willard L. Johnson*
NATIVE AMERICAN RELIGION, *Sam D. Gill*
ISLAM FROM WITHIN, *Kenneth Cragg and R. Marston Speight*
LIFE OF TORAH, *Jacob Neusner*
CHINESE WAY IN RELIGION, *Laurence G. Thompson*
RELIGION IN THE JAPANESE EXPERIENCE, *H. Byron Earhart*
THE BUDDHIST EXPERIENCE, *Stephen Beyer*
NATIVE AMERICAN TRADITIONS, *Sam D. Gill*

EASTERN WAYS TO THE CENTER

An Introduction to the Religions of Asia

Second Edition

Denise Lardner Carmody
UNIVERSITY OF TULSA

John Tully Carmody
UNIVERSITY OF TULSA

Wadsworth Publishing Company
Belmont, California
A Division of Wadsworth, Inc.

Religion Editor: Sheryl Fullerton
Editorial Assistant: Tammy Goldfeld
Print Buyer: Randy Hurst
Designer: Detta Penna
Copy Editor: Mary Louise Byrd
Compositor: Weimer Typesetting Company

Cover art: Adapted from *Violet Snowflake* by Jeanette Stobie © 1992

This book is printed on acid-free paper that meets Environmental Protection Agency standards for recycled paper.

3 4 5 6 7 8 9 10—96 95

Library of Congress Cataloging-in-Publication Data

Carmody, Denise Lardner, 1935–
    Eastern ways to the center : an introduction to the religions of
Asia / Denise L. Carmody, John T. Carmody. — 2nd ed.
        p.   cm. — (The Religious life of man series)
    Includes bibliographical references and index.
    ISBN 0-534-16542-7
    1. Religions. 2. Hinduism. 3. Buddhism. 4. China—Religion.
5. Japan—Religion. I. Carmody, John, 1939–   . II. Title.
III. Series.
BL1032.C37 1992
291^1.095—dc20   91-18882
                                                                            CIP

CONTENTS

PREFACE

In this revision we have concentrated on updating the scholarly base of *Eastern Ways to the Center* and further clarifying the logic and language. To make recent scholarly trends available to undergraduate students and teachers, we have again focused on sources likely to be widely available, in this case, stressing articles in the *Encyclopedia of Religion* edited by Mircea Eliade (New York: Macmillan, 1987).

Most of our many interventions aimed at clarifying the expository prose have been small, but, in the words of an interesting article by Jonathan Z. Smith some years ago, *"Adde Parvum Parvo Magnus Acervus Erit"* ("Add a Little to a Little and there will be a Great Heap") (History of Religions, 1971, *11*:67). Teachers wishing to reduce the length of the text should note that the case studies (newly marked) are relatively independent units.

We have greatly expanded the glossary and placed the glossary items at the end of each chapter. We have also updated the annotated bibliography and the demographic data, added some schematic charts, and on occasion added historical details to clarify what had been a too concise exposition. We have expanded the questions and oriented them toward discussion (they now can serve as topics for either homework or in-class discussion). Last, we have changed important Chinese terms and names from the Wade-Giles system of Romanization to the Pinyin.

Overall, however, the basic design of the book remains a twofold exposition of the Eastern religions in terms of historical analyses and analyses of world-views. As well, the text retains a fairly demanding linguistic and conceptual level. We hope this will be less objectionable at the beginning of the 1990s, when numerous studies have lamented the decline of literacy among college students and urged a reinfusion of rigor and challenge.

There comes a point at which diluting the vocabulary, imagery, and conceptual equipment one uses to display complex phenomena such as the world religions is simply pandering to the baser educational instincts. Certainly one has to sympathize with students who have been ill-prepared for adult study in the humanities. On the other hand, one does them little

long-term good by watering down things to a level of underachievement. If a college degree is going to be worth the parchment on which it is issued, students have to have been stretched beyond the proficiency they had when entering as freshmen and have to have worked hard. In a nutshell, they have to have spent some time with an unabridged dictionary and extended the range of what they initially could name and so think about. Wittgenstein's famous epigram is remorseless: The limits of our language are the limits of our world. Having tried to clarify and sharpen the language of our text, we make no apologies for the challenges that remain. All the religions insist that there is no lazy person's way to enlightenment.

A more pleasant bit of news to deliver is our gratitude to the readers of this second edition, who have offered much useful criticism and suggestion: Arnold P. Kaminsky, California State University; Heinz C. Luegenbiehl, Rose-Hulman Institute of Technology; and Michael O'Hare, Benedictine College.

A symbol of the concentricity of the natural, the social, the divine, and the personal that religious searches for the center reveal.

(Hindu) Om: Mantra expressing the unity of reality.

Wheel: Buddhist symbol for the dharma or teaching.

Chinese character for Dao ("Way")

Torii: Gate to Shinto shrines

Eastern Ways to the Center

INTRODUCTION: ON THE STUDY OF EASTERN RELIGIONS

A symbol of the concentricity of the natural, the social, the divine, and the personal that religious searches for the center reveal.

The religious life of humanity is a vast spectacle hard to keep in perspective. Therefore, we should make our goals and methods clear from the outset. Our primary goal is to make clear how the Eastern religious traditions have oriented billions of human lives. Our primary method is to place the study of religion in the context of the humanities and approach the traditions with a consistent format. Let us explain these notions in more detail.

THE NATURE OF RELIGION

Picture yourself in New Delhi. You are outside *Rajghat,* the memorial to Mahatma Gandhi, the politician and holy man who led India to freedom from British colonial rule. Before you, squatting on the broken sidewalk, are three small boys with wooden flutes. They are piping tunes toward round wicker baskets. When they lift the baskets' covers, three silver cobras slowly weave their way out. You watch for several minutes, fearful but entranced. Then the boys shove the cobras back into their baskets and approach you for their fee. A few rupees seem fair enough—you don't want to upset those cobras.

Does this picture shine a light on the exotic East? Is it a minor revelation of Indian culture? Yes, but only if you know a little background. In India, as in many other countries with ancient cultures, serpents have been potent symbols (think of the story in the third chapter of Genesis). Perhaps because they appear menacing or phallic (penislike), they have stood for something very basic, something very close to the life force. For centuries, groups of Indians have specialized in snake handling, and the skills have been passed along from father to son. Their profession has combined show business and a bit of crude religion. It has been both entertainment and an occasion to shiver about the implications of death and life.

Now picture yourself in contemporary Tokyo. You are in the middle of a lovely park, complete with flower gardens, green space, and a teahouse. You come upon a pagoda that turns out to be a shrine. You notice a statue of a serene lady, and a bell to ring after making obeisance to her. On the walls are photographs of children and occasionally some of happy parents. You realize that you are in a place of devotion to Kannon, the *bodhisattva* (saint) whom much of East Asia treats like a Mother Goddess. The photos represent petitions for children that grateful parents believe Kannon has answered. Kannon is primarily a holy figure sought out by women, but men—prospective fathers—also show up, both at her shrines and in the photographs that celebrate her helpfulness.

Farther along in the park you sit to rest on a bench, across from a green space where children are flying kites. An elderly man clad in a kimono approaches you. He bows and asks if you are Americans. You say yes, and he proceeds to practice his English by telling you stories from the era of World War II. Then he instructs you on the significance of this park. It is a place where the kami, the Shinto deities traditionally said to number 800,000, are wont to visit. It is a place whose beauty makes it alive with the presence of helpful deities. The man says this with a gentle smile, a glint in his eyes making you wonder how much of such a tradition he believes—or perhaps the glint expresses his wonder about how much of such a tradition you could believe. Either way, he is aware of how much has changed in the twentieth century, most of which he has lived through.

Are the kami now anachronisms, or can we believe that they still function? Is the beauty of a lily pond, or the grandeur of a tall tree, or the relief that we gain from a freshening breeze a presence of divinity? What is "divinity" in a Japanese context? How can Easterners and Westerners communicate through categories such as that, which they may understand quite differently? Because questions such as these are part of your business as a student of world religions, the gentle encounter with the old man brings them to mind. But he answers none of them. Content to have exercised his English and offered you a touch of hospitality, perhaps even a bit of insight into local customs, he bows and shuffles off. Years later you still remember him and the encounter with warm feelings and gratitude.

Were we to go inside the memorial to Gandhi and look at the scene at his commemorative stone, the delicacy of Indian culture and its visions of warmth and light might rise up and parallel those of Shinto Japan. *Rajghat* blends green grass, elegant black marble, and fresh flower petals of orange and pink. They symbolize the beautiful spirit of the Mahatma, the little man of great soul. Gandhi was a politician who moved people by *satyagraha*—the force of truth. Without military arms, much money, or even much respect from British leaders, he forced the whole world to take notice. When he vowed to take no food until India's just claims were met, the world held its breath. When he led groups of nonviolent *satyagrahis* into the midst of club-swinging soldiers, he upset the conscience of the world. By the simple rightness, the sheer justice,

of his cause, Gandhi showed how his Hindu conception of God could be very powerful. His God was "Truth," and it finally shamed the British into withdrawal.

Snakes and kami, love and fertility and beauty—they have shot through India, Japan, and most other parts of the world. In contemporary America, they or their offspring live with us yet. For instance, our nuclear missiles are for many citizens and analysts eerie phallic symbols. Like cobras we are trying to get back in their baskets, the missiles give us shivers. Many people see the missiles' thrust, their destructive power, and the claims that they give us security or economic life as brutalizing and raping our culture. From Hiroshima to Three Mile Island, nuclear power muddles our wellsprings and hope.

So too with the ways that we whip ourselves for guilt, the ways that we still crave love, the ways that we search after light. Our guilt keeps psychiatrists in business. Our searches for light and beauty fill churches and schools. Clearly, we are sisters and brothers to religious Indians and Japanese. Clearly, their snakes and divine images relate to our own.

Religion is the issue of ultimate meaning that this discussion of cobras and deities spotlights. It is the part of culture—Eastern, Western, or contemporary American—that we study when we ask about a people's deepest convictions. For instance, Hinduism is the animating spirit, the soul, the way of looking at the world, that has tied snake handling and *satyagraha* together for most Indians. Buddhism and Shinto are ways of looking at the world that have oriented traditional Japanese. Religion, then, is what you get when you investigate striking human phenomena to find the ultimate vision or set of convictions that gives them their sense. It is the cast of mind and the gravity of heart by which a people endures or enjoys its time between the two great darknesses of prebirth and death.

STUDYING RELIGION

Certain attitudes should be cultivated in all study, but the study of religion demands more self-awareness and personal engagement with its materials than most other disciplines do. For instance, although reducing physical science to "objective" observing and testing is simplistic, since all knowledge is ultimately personal, physical science does not make great demands on a student's inner experiences of suffering or love. The humanities (those disciplines that study our efforts at self-expression and self-understanding) involve more of such inner experiences, because suffering and love shape so much of history and literature, yet even the humanities seldom deal with direct claims about ultimate meaning. Only in philosophy and religion does one directly encounter systems about God, evil, and humanity's origin and end. Philosophy deals with such concepts principally in their rational forms, while religious studies meet them more concretely in the myths, rituals, mysticisms, behavior patterns, and institutions through which most human beings have been both drawn to ultimate meaning and terrified of it.

More than in any other discipline, the student in a religious studies course is confronted with imperative claims. The religions are not normally warehouses where you pay your money and take your choice. Rather, they are impassioned heralds of ways of life. More than most people initially like, the religions speak of death, ignorance, and human viciousness. However, they also speak of peace and joy, forgiveness and harmony. Whatever they discuss, though, they are *mystagogic,* which etymologically means "mystery working." The religions work mystery. Their preoccupations, when they are healthy, are nature's wonder, life's strange play of physical death and spiritual resurrection, and the possibility of order in the midst of chaos. The religions say that the kingdom of God is in your midst, because you are a being who can pray, "Abba, Father." They say that the *Dao* ("the Way") that can be named is not the real *Dao.* Above all, they say that the person who lives divorced from the mysteries of rosy-fingered dawn and wintery death is less than fully human. Clearly, then, we cannot study the religions well if we are afraid of mystery or are in flight from death and life.

We also cannot study well the faiths of others if we insist on forcing them into the categories of our own faith. We must first take them on their own terms, giving their experiences and problems a sympathetic hearing. After we have listened to the wisdom of a scripture such as the Hindu *Bhagavad Gita,* we may and should compare it with the wisdom of our Western faiths. Even then, though, unless we can say with the Christians' Saint Peter, "I see now how true it is that God has no favorites, but that in every nation the person who is God-fearing and does what is right is acceptable" (Acts 10:34), we risk acting with prejudice and condescension.

A second reason for remembering life's mystery, then, is that it helps us clear away prejudice. Taken in its experiential vividness, a Zen Buddhist's enlightenment *(satori)* tears the veil of ignorance and comes as revelation and grace.[1] Therefore, it would be naive to treat Zen Buddhism as merely "natural," let alone as pagan. Any truly divine Creator has to be at work in Japan as well as in the West.

Third, it is worth pointing out that the religious studies course offered here is not theology, at least not the theology of a church. Church theology tends to be a search for an understanding of one's own faith that is directed by the particular creed or commitment of an individual or group. Spontaneously the search spreads to a probing of all life's dimensions in terms of such a commitment. So there develops a theology of art, a theology of history, and even a theology of the world religions. In these theologies, however, the main goal is to square data with one's own faith or religious group. Moreover, a church theology's ultimate goal is to promote its own faith. It studies art, history, or the world religions to beautify, advance, or defend its own vision of things, whether the "church" be Hindu, Buddhist, or Christian. The understanding that theology seeks in such study is not necessarily distorted, but it is in the service of preaching, ministering, and counseling. When it is not in such service, church theology becomes divorced from the life of its community.

In a university, however, neither students nor teachers are expected to confess their faith (or nonfaith). We, the authors, would argue that it is proper and healthy to make clear one's position on the *implications,* for thought and action alike, to which a course's studies lead. In other words, there is nothing wrong and much right with teachers and students becoming personal—dealing with concrete, practical implications. There is much wrong, however, in university courses that place their own values on other people's art, history, or religion and thereby distort them. One must listen with an open mind before judging and deciding.

So we urge you to get inside the religions' experiences and values and to compare them with your own. In fact, we very much hope that your study will enrich your appreciation of nature, will increase your wonder about life's meaning, and will increase your resources for resisting evil. But we do not set these hopes in the framework of any one faith. We are not, in other words, doing church theology. You may be Christian, Jewish, Buddhist, agnostic, atheistic, or anything else. To us such labels do not matter. What matters is that you be human: a man or woman trying to hear the Delphic oracle's "Know thyself," a person humble with the Confucian virtue of sympathy or "fellow feeling" *(ren)*.

Fourth, what benefits will this effort to study humanistically bring you? At least two spring to mind. First, you will have the chance to grapple with some of the most influential, wisest personalities of the past. Second, you will better understand the world of the present, in which all peoples on the globe are much closer than they have ever been before.

To illustrate the first benefit, let us call on the Chinese sage Confucius. In his time (551–479 B.C.E.) some people were advancing the proposition that it is better to pay court to the stove (to practicalities) than to heaven (to ideals) (see *Analects* 3:3). Confucius batted their proposition back. If you do not pay court to heaven, he said, you will have no recourse when practicalities fail to bring you good life. In other words, the mystery of life is more than food and drink, more than shelter and pleasure. Important as those things are, they do not make the truly good life. Only moving in the Way *(Dao)* of heaven makes us human beings what we ought to be, what we most deeply want to be. If we settle for the stove, we halve our human potential.

To illustrate the second benefit of the humanistic study of religion, we must comment briefly on current history. Today it is a commonplace observation that the world is becoming one. That does not mean that all peoples are agreeing on a common government, economy, or philosophy. It does mean that communications, transportation, economics, and other forces are tying all nations together. Thus, commentators speak of a "global village" or a "planetary culture." They remind us of the novelty of the twentieth century, the only time when it could have happened that when Gandhi fasted, the world held its breath; that when Mao died, his funeral reached every capital. Furthermore, in our nuclear age all curtains can be raised. In our age of escalating population and hunger, all the silos of Kansas cast shadows on East Africa. In our age of ecological pollution, the wastes of one country foul the air, water, and land of others.

The implications of this current state of affairs are too numerous to detail. We may be on the verge of a new phase of evolution; the human sciences may just be approaching their maturity. The outer complexity of human affairs may just be developing a self-consciousness among human beings so that we will be able to cope with these affairs. Or we may devastate the entire planet through nuclear war or ecological disaster. In either case, religion acquires an added significance, because we cannot learn much about the evolution or self-consciousness of the global village unless we listen to its members' deepest perceptions and convictions. We cannot understand human motivation unless we study what people have considered the highest good. Religion shows a people's deepest perceptions and convictions. Hinduism, Buddhism, Christianity, and Islam form the souls of a majority of the world's population today. To live together in the future, we human beings will have to understand the world religions very well.

SCHOLARLY METHODS

In pursuing such understanding, it is well to take note of the different methods that scholars of religion have developed. W. Richard Comstock, the author of a useful introduction to religion, once offered a list of five basic methods.[2]

First, there is the *psychological* perspective. Since the time of Freud (1856–1939), who was quite interested in religion's parallels with neurosis, Western scholars have been sensitive to the inner drives that set people to work, parenting, religion, and the many other aspects of human culture. For example, sexual satisfaction, acceptance by our peers, and a sense of control all play a part in our development of human culture. C. G. Jung (1875–1961) broke with Freud over the interpretation of sexual and religious drives. For Jung, the second half of life tends to be a pursuit of meaning (giving one's time and experience coherence). Often the symbols people use in pursuing meaning are religious, so even today psychoanalysts probing patients' dreams can come upon archetypal symbols reminiscent of ancient religious mythologies.

If we generalize the sensitivity that recent psychological studies sharpen, the main point seems to be that we must stay alert to the complexity of human motivation. For example, in studying a holy man from the Hindu tradition, such as Mahatma Gandhi, we should realize that his asceticism had a basis in his adolescent sexual traumas and that his political ambitions were forged by his experiences of racial discrimination in young adulthood. At these formative times in his life cycle, Gandhi was tested to an unusual degree. He found himself unready for the erotic aspects of marriage, and his experience as a "colored" person in South Africa told him he had to champion India's oppressed.[3]

On the one hand, if we so focus on psychological issues such as these that we neglect the history, sociology, economics, politics, and other aspects of Gandhi's life and times, we become reductionists, trying to squeeze all of reality onto the psychoanalyst's couch. On the other hand, if we neglect such inner demons and angels, we divorce ourselves from a powerful tool of understanding (perhaps because we do not want to face the similar demons and angels warring in our own souls). As usual, a balanced use is the ideal.

Just as scientific psychology is a fairly recent development, not available to scholars of religion a century ago, so is *sociology*. And just as the pioneer psychologists were quite interested in religion, so were pioneer sociologists such as Max Weber (1864–1920) and Emile Durkheim (1858–1917). In both cases, their interest was religion's role in making a group cohesive. The religious ideas of a tribe, or even a large culture, are always in part a projection of the tribe's or the culture's sense of its own identity. For example, Hindus have been people stratified by traditional wisdom into four main social classes. Chinese have been people living at the center of the world in accordance with the *Dao* they thought moved both nature and the wise ancients. Americans have been high-minded refugees come to make a place of justice and freedom in a new world. Thus neither Hindu caste nor Chinese misogyny nor American racism could be the patent inhumanity an outside observer might think it. Sacralizing the way they talked about themselves, all three peoples claimed heaven had approved their customs.

Cultural anthropologists such as Clifford Geertz and Victor Turner have tuned the interests of the classical sociologists more finely. Living in the midst of the societies they wanted to interpret, they have sought the deep structures and threshold moments through which a people reveals how it constructs its worldview. Geertz's study of the Balinese cockfight,[4] for example, is a marvel of sophisticated participant observation. Sensitive to the drama of what he calls "deep play," Geertz makes the cockfight a microcosm of the Balinese thought-world.

A third methodological orientation popular in recent religious studies is the *historical*. One of the drawbacks of the psychological and sociological approaches is that they can seem to bracket time past (and time future), as though their analyses were moved by an Archimedean lever standing outside the flowing stories of either their subjects or themselves. But such ahistoricism obviously is fallacious. The self always enacts a story, a unique version of the common life cycle, and a society is always being pushed by its past and lured by its future. Since the modern discovery of evolution, and the rise of modern retrieval techniques such as archeology, the study of religion has become more historical, and so more faithful to the traditions' ongoing changes. Even the most conservative tradition alters in at least small ways, generation by generation. Though they perform the same rituals and tell the same myths, a people of any era understands itself somewhat differently than its forebears did or its children will.

The good historian's goal is telling the story of these changes. Representing the past as it most likely was, good historians bring their readers from point alpha to point omega. Thus a Buddhist historian might muse: In the beginning, at the earliest point we can reconstruct, Buddhists understood Gautama in such and such a way. A thousand years later, when controversies inside the community had caused much debate, there were the three following major interpretations. Today, in Japanese Buddhism, the third of these interpretations prevails, due to such and such factors.

One thinks, then, of a continuum or a map. In the image of the continuum, the historian grants all centuries a certain equality, showing how Buddhism changed century by century. In the image of a map, the historian plots the journey from the Buddha's India to modern Japan, showing the geographic and cultural routes the Teaching (dharma) traveled. The result should be a sense of perspective and interrelationship. Alpha led on to beta, because of factor alpha prime, just as today omega seems to be leading on to omega-plus-one, because of factor omega prime.

Comstock's fourth methodological perspective is *phenomenological*. Referring to the work of scholars such as Geradus van der Leeuw (1890–1950), who have concentrated on the different *forms* that many religious traditions seem to share, one can emphasize the concern many phenomenologists have to find *typical* patterns that show up repeatedly across the full range of religious data. So, for example, sacred people appear in most traditions. East and West, monks or ascetics or yogis have won great veneration. One can distinguish among these three categories of holy people, but they share an orientation away from worldly affairs, toward contemplation and self-discipline. The typical Hindu holy man fits the pattern of withdrawal, as does the typical Buddhist monk. In China and Japan, both Buddhism and Daoism prized withdrawal from worldly affairs, seclusion in order to grow better attuned to the dharma or the *Dao*.

Phenomenological studies tend to stress the sameness of certain structural features, providing a basis for discussing how Hindu yogis differ from Buddhist monks in cultural details, or how Eastern ascetics differ from Western ascetics. By grouping functionaries together in general terms, we are stimulated to ask how they differ in particulars. The results of such generalizations can seldom be ironclad, since there are usually exceptions to general trends, but phenomenological inquiries can be very stimulating.

Comstock's fifth methodological perspective is *hermeneutical*. If anything, this perspective has increased in importance since the time he made his survey. Hermeneutics is the study of interpretation. It concerns processes such as that by which a teacher from Maryland tries to explain to a student from Oklahoma what it was like to live in medieval China or India. In one sense, hermeneutics applies to all parts of this communication. Even the gap between Maryland and Oklahoma can be significant, but the gap between twentieth-century America and medieval China or Japan is enormous. Thus, hermeneutics tends to be most concerned with how we can tease from texts or artifacts reliable interpretations of past or foreign cultures. The cultural anthropologists we mentioned have come to the forefront of the hermeneutical debates, but historians, psychologists, sociologists, and philosophers of language have also been prominent. These debates tend to get very technical, generating schools such as structuralism and subdisciplines such as semiotics and deconstructionism. Thus, the scholarly end of the hermeneutical "turn" is not yet in sight and its overall significance is still emerging.

For undergraduates, though, the gist of the hermeneutical perspective is clear enough: Try to be quite sensitive to the sources and ranges of the meanings you are studying. Above all, realize that in studying a text, or any other cultural artifact, you are involved in a two-way conversation. A text is not a brute object whose meanings are obvious to any beholder. Physically, a text is simply some marks on a piece of paper or some impressions in clay. To convey meaning, these marks have to "speak" from the mind of the person who set them down to the minds of people like you who are trying to pick them up. Thus, the languages and assumptions of both minds come into play, your own as much as the author's. You can assume that you and the author share a great deal, since you are both human, but you must be careful about how you use this assumption. The death of a child in ancient China was both very like the death of a child in contemporary America, and very different. Boiled down, hermeneutics is walking the tightrope between the sameness we have as members of one species and the differences we have as individuals, people of different cultures, and people of different historical eras.

THE STRUCTURE OF THIS BOOK

We begin our chapters with a sketch of the history of the tradition in question. Behind this historical section lies the conviction that one gains valuable insights into a people's sense of reality by learning the story of where they have come from, how they were formed into a people, what crucial experiences forged their deeper senses of who they are and what they believe. Such historical sections afford us the opportunity to mention many of the people's external characteristics. Sketching where they have come from and where they now seem to think they are going, we can try to move them from "once upon a time" to today.

Following on the historical section is a section on "worldview"—the tradition's view of reality. Assuming that each religion has a certain consistency, a drive to make sense out of reality as a whole, we shall indicate some of the major pillars of the adherents' worldview. The schema that we have found most adequate for this work has four headings: nature, society, self, and ultimate reality. Both the external data of the world religions and an internal analysis of human experience seem to justify using this schema as a loose working format.

For example, all peoples must contend with nature. The physical world affords all of us our food. The skies and the seas and the plains provide all of us our environment, spiritual as well as physical. Indeed, it is characteristic of most traditional peoples to strive for a close harmony with physical nature. As though they

Figure 1 *Buddha image, northwest India, Gupta period (300–620). Bronze, 14¾ in. high. This representation of the Buddha is typical in suggesting light, peace, and teaching authority. The Nelson–Atkins Museum of Art, Kansas City, Missouri (Nelson Fund).*

instinctively knew many of the lessons that scientific studies in ecology have been teaching our contemporary world, traditional peoples typically sought kinship with the plants and animals of their area, knowledge of their area's weather and terrain. Nor is it hard to find connections with our own situation as twentieth-century individuals. If we find that we tend to perform differently on a high pressure day (when the skies are open and the sun is bright) than on a low pressure day (when the skies are low and gray), we have half the stimulus we need to become interested in the ecological sensitivity of other people, in how they pictured their weather and environment.

More easily than with ourselves, we find that most traditional Eastern peoples sacralized at least portions of nature: treated them with reverence or even worship. This tended to be a rallying point for the people, whether the people was at the stage of hunting and gathering or had unified itself under an impressive king. Through their rituals and ceremonies, most people have tried to move with nature's annual flow and ebb. Spring awakening and Fall harvest, Summer heat and Winter cold, have all cried out for recognition. In giving nature such recognition, people have helped define who they were: people of the forest, or people of the mountain. Depending on the way that it has pictured reality as a whole, a people usually has appointed headmen or shamans or priests to deal with these important matters. In most religions, the people's attitudes toward nature and their own social organization have fit together, have been complementary pieces of a single puzzle.

The same with a people's attitudes toward self and ultimate reality. When religious people the world over have asked "Who am I?", their answers have reached out to include situating themselves in the physical cosmos, placing themselves in the history and social structure of their tribe, and making at least fumbling attempts to connect themselves with the ultimate power or reality they have considered the origin, destiny, or most important feature of the whole, the universe, of what human beings can see and conceive. Nature, society, self, and ultimate reality are not artificial or isolated categories, fashioned simply for the convenience of teachers and textbook writers, who must try to give the mass of data about the religions some shape. We are convinced they are interconnected dimensions of each human life that become more significant and fascinating as our exposure to human history expands and we continue our descent into the depths of our own consciousness.

So, for example, you can find in any bookstore writers telling you that: you are what you eat, your American nation is in peril, your self will flower only through physical love, and "God," a benevolent ultimate power, numbers every hair of your head. Behind each of these assertions is both knowledge and questioning. For centuries Eastern people have studied diet, national history, sex, and the mystery of the universe. Today these topics continue to imply vital questions, matters that any of us would be better for having probed. Moreover, we can use them to build bridges to other people, other eras, other faiths. That is how we plan to use them in the sections on worldview: as useful ways of presenting some of the most important aspects of Hindu, Buddhist, Chinese, and Japanese experience.

At the end of our analysis of a worldview we conclude each chapter with a short summary essay on the heart of the tradition's convictions, the center of the tradition's world. Admittedly, such essays are always just our own interpretations, but we have felt we owed students the best parting word we could write. If you use our structural analyses and summary essays comparatively, noting how a given tradition both is like the others and differs from them, you should close this textbook with a fairly adequate sense of Eastern peoples' religious beliefs.

One does not get to the center of a religious tradition by methods (controlled ways of approach) strictly so called. One works more by intuition or a sense of where the different weights of a tradition come to rest. Among the approaches that hone such intuition, however, one can mention philosophy and mystagogy. Philosophy, in the Eastern sense of the search for wisdom, involves contemplating and trying to come into harmony with the highest good a tradition reveres. Mystagogy is sensitive to the mystery (fullness and perplexing character) of existence—to ultimate reality or God. By trying to reflect back upon the coherence of a tradition with philosophical and mystogogical attunement, one often finds one's own judgments about the tradition's center emerge rather clearly.

For what should students look when they set out to study the Eastern religious traditions? Perhaps they should look especially for spirituality, beauty, and wisdom. Certainly, an interest in these matters is not exclusively Eastern. One can find adherents of Western traditions who have pursued them assiduously. Nonetheless, for people embarking upon their first encounter with Hinduism and Buddhism, Confucianism and Taoism, Shinto and the ancient underpinnings of all of the Eastern traditions, spirituality, beauty, and wisdom can serve as landmarks—sights in the new territory that the traveler should be sure not to miss.

Spirituality is lived religion—doctrine, ethics, ritual, mythology, social structure, and all the rest inasmuch as they impinge on actual lives. Hindu spirituality is what you encounter when you meet a priest offering prayers in a temple, or when a middle-aged woman fasts to safeguard the life of her husband, or when a farmer asks a god or goddess to bless the seed that he is sowing. Buddhist spirituality comes across in the peace of the yellow-robed monk seated in the lotus position meditating, or in the reserve of the mother offering her petitions at a shrine, or in the joy of little children singing songs that assure them of the Buddha's love. People who want to grow in their religious tradition, so that they approach the models of sanctity that their culture most venerates, try deliberately to improve their meditation, their detachment, their helpfulness toward their neighbors. Thus their spirituality is intentional. But all people who belong to a religious tradition and admit any significant impact from it manifest something of the spirituality of that tradition. Indeed, most of the existential, lived differences between Hindus and Buddhists or Confucians and Daoists boil down to differences in symbol, style, perception, values, hopes—differences on the common path of spirituality.

Put another way, it makes sense to ask the traditional peoples whom you are about to study to tell you about their treasures. What is it that they hold most dear, that most determines how they want to live? What is it that they are more anxious that their children should learn, or that their homes should honor, or that they think about first when they examine their consciences? These are the things that most determine the religious feel or flavor of their lives. These are the things that make their allegiance to their given tradition concrete, practical, efficacious. In a word, these are the things that express and constitute their spirituality—the values and hopes that make their space and time distinctive.

The second watchword that we suggest is beauty. This is especially important in the East, because often what a Western mentality divides into the religious and the aesthetic is undivided in the East. Perhaps East Asia preserves the unity of the sacred and the beautiful in more pronounced fashion than the cultures closer to India do, but in India, too, art, mythology, and ritual are so central to perceptions of sacredness that one cannot separate them. Does this mean that the gods, the Buddhas, the kami, and the sages who dominate traditional Eastern cultures have to be beautiful? Yes and no. On the whole, sacred figures are the ones who supply the standards for human beauty or who give ultimate meaning to natural beauty. On the whole, a holy place is a lovely place, a sacred time is one that people remember as especially clear or harmonious. But the East also uses human impressions of ugliness, violence, disharmony, of what threatens death and reminds us of the fragility of creation, to point to the sacred realm. What is ultimate, and so might explain our origins and final destiny, has to be different from what is ordinary, daily.

One way of pointing to what is ultimate is to contradict tidy human assumptions, including human assumptions about what is beautiful, fulfilling, a source of peace and joy. Thus there are Hindu goddesses who drip with blood and whose maw is the mouth of death. There are fierce Japanese spirits who remind the religious seeker to stay alert, because evil forces are always on the prowl. Even in these cases, however, the iconography can be impressive. Perhaps we would not call it beautiful, but we would have to call it artful. Watch, then, for the ways that the Eastern traditions play with harmony, beauty, ugliness, and horror. Watch for the interweaving of the sacred and the aesthetic.

Finally, watch also for the given tradition's apparent understanding of wisdom. By and large, the model that the Eastern traditions propose as the highest fulfillment of human nature is the sage. It is the person who has plumbed the human traditions long handed down, and who has used those traditions to facilitate a personal grasp of the natural order, who represents the Eastern ideal. The wisdom of such a person is much more than simply an intellectual mastery. It is an intuition about how to live a holy life, a life that integrates one's own personality, honors the sacred powers responsible for the cosmos, and makes one beneficial to other human beings—a guide, a healer, a support on life's difficult way. Again and again, the Eastern traditions sing songs to wisdom, tell stories about the ways of the sages, remind their adherents that only when they live wisely, in detachment and purity, will they find happiness. Therefore, the greatest treasure that the student of Eastern traditions can haul away is the sense of how the Hindu sage, or the Daoist sage, or the other sages who have flourished in India or China, in Japan or Thailand, has lived. What has been all-important, and how has the sage tried to

secure it? What has made life most meaningful, beautiful, able to be borne with joy despite all its sufferings and evils? That is the wisdom for which to look. That is the insight that is most likely to make your encounter with an Eastern tradition memorable.

Discussion Questions

1. What is the difference between a humanistic and a theological approach to Eastern religions?

2. Why does the interconnected character of today's international scene spotlight the significance of religion?

3. What are the main methods scholars recently have used to study religion?

4. How does "religion" relate to peoples' approaches to the mystery of human existence?

5. Briefly sketch the history and worldview of your own religious tradition.

6. How would you counsel your friends to increase their openness to people of other religious traditions?

Key Terms

ethics: study or teaching concerned with morality—right and wrong in the realm of behavior. In traditional societies ethics and religion have little separation, as metaphysics and religion have little separation. Moreover, ethics tends to be very traditional—what "our kind" have done since time out of mind. Such ethics regularly are assumed to have been encoded in the cosmos by the divine powers when they gave the cosmos birth, so the political and social orders are not secular but wholly religious.

folk religion: the beliefs and practices of the common people, in contrast to the views of the intelligentsia and religious officials. Folk religion virtually by definition is somewhat inarticulate and unreflective, but it may be no less rich or even sophisticated for that. It embraces the cult of the saints honored in a given religious tradition, the full round of paraliturgical devotions and religious practices, and the simple everyday acts of piety, prayers of petition, and other practices that get unlettered believers through the day. Some generations ago folk religion received rather short shrift from scholars, who depreciated it as un-tutored, but with the advent of anthropological inves-tigations many students of religion have realized that peasant ways often house amazingly persistent and profound views of both the particular religious tradi-tion in which they occur and the basic problematic of human existence that religious mythology regularly has kept lively, persuasive, and beguiling.

God: the supreme being, holy and creative, that West-ern religions have considered fully personal and unique. Precisely what "God" names is a question that has long exercised both theologians and philosophers, both of whom have seen that the word intends some-thing beyond the empirical or everyday order. In reli-gious perspective, the word points toward the sense of transcendence and holiness many people feel, suggest-ing that these common stirrings of human beings are best explained by there being an objective correla-tive—a Being who corresponds to them as their poten-tial fulfiller. God then becomes imagined and conceived as full of truth, beauty, justice, love, mercy, and the other qualities that human beings frequently long to meet in pure, unlimited, deathless form.

hermeneutics: the study of interpretation—how to ex-tract the legitimate meanings of a text or artifact. The hermeneutical "turn" of recent religious studies has greatly enriched our awareness of the complexity and sophistication of the exchanges among writer, text, and readers. On the other hand, sometimes hermeneu-tical works get so complicated that they seem to call impossible what manifestly has happened in many times and places: effective communication of meaning from a writer or speaker to an audience. In the case of religious communication, the mysteriousness of many of the references only heightens the need for herme-neutical scholars to test their own range of experi-ences, feelings about religious symbols, and assumptions about the ultimate construction of both reality as a whole and religious consciousness in par-ticular, asking that those who would preside over how meaning is established come clean about their own theoretical and personal prejudgments.

mysticism: experience of or direct communion with ultimate reality. Mystics come in different garbs and may be found across the religious traditions, mono-theistic and polytheistic alike. Problems of definition abound, but most commentators stress an ineffable experience that brings the person into direct contact with ultimate reality or God. How important union with ultimate reality is, or how lasting the indubitable

character of the experience must be, can be debated. What mystics commonly share is the conviction that the world open to the senses is only a fraction of total reality, as well as the conviction that direct commun-ion with ultimate reality, through gracious divine love or human enlightenment, is the most precious expe-rience any human being can have.

nature: physical reality in its totality; whatness or character. Nature in the sense of the physical world or cosmos virtually coincides with divinity in many reli-gious traditions. Not everything in nature is divine, because divinity has depths or boundaries that escape the cosmos—transcend the natural matrix. On the other hand, nature tends to be perceived as having come from a divinity stronger and less perishable than itself. Nature therefore remains mysterious, some-thing whose foundations, rhythms, purposes, and willfulness human beings cannot fathom. Nature in the sense of essence or whatness stems from rather refined philosophical analysis. When people distin-guish between the fact that something is and the char-acter of that thing (the way that it exists—as human or rabbit, tree or rock), they have begun to press be-yond commonsensical naming and started to wonder about how things give up their whatness, how mind correlates with names and essences, and so forth. Phi-losophy, poetry, and natural science differentiate from a primordial wonder about this process, taking hu-manity in several different enriching directions and then asking to be correlated again.

religion: communion with, service of, or concern for ultimate reality. The etymological origins of the term stress binding or tying, to the gods or holy forces. Religion traditionally has been little distinct from the mores of a people, naming most of what has animated its art, legal conventions, ethical expectations, role models, and senses of destiny. Religion inevitably traf-fics in mystery, contending with the Beginning and Beyond that the human mind cannot comprehend, but religious people come in various personality types, some inclining more to social service (as their expres-sion of devotion to ultimate holiness) and others in-clining more to solitary contemplation.

ritual: prescribed, formalized religious action or cer-emony. With myth, ritual constitutes the typical and basic way traditional humanity spoke to itself about the world, who it was as a people, individual destiny, and the divine forces responsible for its world and fate. Rituals tend to dramatize existence, and their appeal is holistic: to the senses, memory, feelings of social solidarity, symbolic or artistic faculties that engage people's feelings and make their experiences vivid. Few people are thoroughly convinced of truths that have not been communicated ritualistically, and instinctively most peoples have employed music, dance, special costumes, and the like to make ritualistic occasions more impressive. Rituals carry the danger of becoming overly aesthetic, ends in themselves, antagonistic to doctrinal clarity, and rubricized (legislated in all their details), but many commentators think that the renewal of myth and ritual is essential if present humanity is to reacquire the feelings necessary to have a beautiful and fully meaningful existence.

scripture: a writing thought to be especially holy and authoritative because closely connected with God, ultimate reality, or final wisdom. Literate religious traditions regularly produce scriptures, although the precision with which they define their scriptural canons varies greatly. The production and reception of a scripture involves members of the tradition in the complicated textual issues recently highlighted by literary studies: hermeneutics, reading passages against their apparent sense, altering the religious experience from something that originally generated a text to something the text now generates, and so forth. Those who revere a scripture and use it regularly tend to dwell within a world organized by the text, loving the images, cadences, and assurances which that textual world brings to mind. Scriptures need not create fundamentalist readers driven to take them literally, but they always carry that potential. They may also, however, stimulate symbolic or iconographical readings that find it richer to treat the scriptural master-images and texts as "material" presences of a holy spirituality that is bound to be dynamic, creative, alive, and so always shifting (without necessarily changing its basic identity).

tradition: teaching and practice that have been handed down. Religions generally look to the past for their standards, models, and wisdom. Indeed, many religions are nostalgic for a golden age when relations with the gods supposedly were better than they have been recently. Tradition can imply a precious connection to this better past and the way a people stays in touch with the paradigms given by the gods at the creation of the world. In religions that look back to a historical revelation, tradition tends to make that revelation its starting point and golden age. Thus Moses, Jesus, and Muhammad all launched strong traditions. Philosophically, tradition depends on and expresses the historicity of religion and the rest of human culture. Faith and morals, as well as art and scientific lore, are always evolving. As well, every people has to contrive ways to pass its culture on to the next generation. So tradition intersects with a people's ways of educating its young. The religious problems raised by traditioning boil down to finding a balance between neglecting the past, and so being condemned to repeat its mistakes, and being immobilized in the past, afraid or unwilling to make the adaptations necessary if what was believed in the past is to continue to be vital in the future.

ultimate reality: the endpoint the mind reaches when it seeks the source of the being, intelligibility, and goodness it experiences. This term may also indicate divinity in an impersonal mode. Religious traditions that shy away from calling themselves theistic sometimes are comfortable speaking of ultimate reality. Generally the term does not depend on revelation and may represent a philosophical or mystical extrapolation from the sense that finite realities do not furnish their own reason to be. The so-called proofs for the existence of God frequently amount to explorations of ultimate reality.

CHAPTER 1

HINDUISM

(Hindu) Om: Mantra expressing the unity of reality

HISTORY

Our sketch of the historical evolution of Hinduism unfolds in six chronological phases: the pre-Vedic phase; the Vedic phase; the phase of native challenges to Vedic orthodoxy; the phase when Hindus responded to such challenges by reforming, renovating, and elaborating the Vedic tradition; the phase when outside, modern Western ideas challenged reformed Hinduism, and the present phase—what we might call recent or contemporary Hinduism. Naturally, these phases overlap, since ideas and practices from early periods often have continued to exert great influence. Indeed, there is a sense in which all of the last five phases in our schema are "Vedic," since virtually all Hindus have accepted to some degree the proposition that the Vedas enshrine what we might call the constitutional beginnings of their culture (much as virtually all Christians could consider all twenty centuries of Christian history biblical, because all were informed by the New Testament).

Moreover, for an idea or practice to be challenged did not necessarily mean that it ceased or immediately was reformed. Overall, however, we find this six-phased description of how Hinduism has unfolded faithful to the historical data. The organic character of Hindu culture, which has stemmed from Indians' tendency not to discard previous ideas and practices so much as to place new ones alongside them, means that one can seldom be precise about what was waxing when and what was waning. But one can suggest the "additive" logic of the Hindu religious story by noting the new ideas and movements that slowly enlarged Hinduism into the rich and varied entity one finds today.

Pre-Vedic India

Before the first invasions of Aryans from the northwest around 2000 B.C.E., an impressive Indian culture already existed. Its beginnings stretch back to the second interglacial period (400,000–200,000 B.C.E.), and its earliest religion, if we conjecture on the basis of ancient peoples living in India today, was shamanist, focusing on the worship of nature—especially on the life force. In 1924, excavations at two sites along the Indus River, called Harrapa and Mohenjo-daro, furnished the first extensive evidence of a high ancient Indian culture. This culture, called the Harrapan, stretched over about 500,000 square miles[1] and was distributed in small towns between the two "capitals" of Harrapa and Mohenjo-daro. Other excavations in what is now Pakistan have disclosed cultures predating

Hinduism: Twenty-five Key Dates	
ca. 2750 B.C.E.	Growth of Civilization in Indus Valley
ca. 1500	Aryan Invasions; Vedic Literature
800–400	Upanishads
600–500	Challenges of Mahavira and Buddha
ca. 500	Aryans as Far South as Sri Lanka
500–200	Epic Poetry: Mahabharata (Bhagavad Gita), Ramayana
322	Chandragupta Founds Mauryan Empire
100 B.C.E.–100 C.E.	Rise of Bhakti Literature
480 C.E.	Fall of Gupta Empire
680	Flourishing of Tamil Bhakti Movement
788–820	Shankara, Leading Philosopher
800–900	Rise of Hindu Orthodoxy
1017–1137	Ramanuja, Leading Philosopher
1175	First Muslim Empire in India
1485–1533	Chaitanya, Leader of Krishna-Bhakti
1498	Vasco da Gama Visits India
1526	Beginning of Mogul Dynasty
1653	Completion of Taj Mahal
1690	British Found Calcutta
1707	Decline of Mogul Power
1818	Beginning of British Rule
1869–1948	Mahatma Gandhi
1885	Founding of Indian National Congress
1947	Indian Independence; Partition of Pakistan
1971	Founding of Bangladesh

the Harrapan, but this Indus Valley culture is the largest source of information about pre-Aryan Indian ways. Carbon dating suggests that the Harrapan culture flourished about 2150–1750 B.C.E., and some evidence suggests that the culture was remarkably stable throughout that period.

Harrapa and Mohenjo-daro seem to have had populations of 30,000 to 40,000. Both were about one mile square. That few weapons have been found suggests that their people were not very warlike. Outside each city was a citadel, which was probably used for worship rather than for military defense. There were large granaries in the cities, two-room apartments nearby for the granary workers, and high city walls. Most building was done with kiln-dried bricks, which were standardized at 3 by 10 by 20 inches. Through the city ran an excellent sewage disposal system, with terracotta pipes and manholes through which workmen could enter to clean the pipes. The houses were multistoried dwellings with thick walls and flat roofs. Outside stairways to the roofs suggest that people slept there on hot nights.

The entire city plan suggests orderliness: Streets were wide and rectilinear, houses had chutes for sliding trash down into collection bins, and apartments had bathrooms and toilets. Larger buildings included a bathhouse 108 by 180 feet, with a tank 20 feet wide by 39 feet long by 8 feet deep. If this tank was used like similar ones outside Hindu temples today, probably its purpose was ritual bathing.

Some of the most significant remains from the Harrapan culture are small sandstone seals, engraved with a pictorial script and apparently used to mark property. They are decorated with various animals, both real and imaginary, and indicate a modest economic and artistic life. Other interesting finds include a small bronze statue of a dancing girl, lithe and graceful, and a red sandstone sculpture of the torso of a young man, also artistically impressive. Some scholars hypothesize that these finds indicate creative potential that was stifled by conservative forces, but others logically suggest that these artifacts are the only remains we have of a rather vigorous art whose other products perished. The first scholars, in their interpretations of pre-Aryan culture, believed that the artistry of the Harrapans was static and even monotonous, and that it changed little over 400 years. The uniformity in the bricks and buildings suggests a strong deterrent to innovation, and the people were likely ruled by autocratic priests, who insisted on conformity to a theopolitical tradition based on worship

at the religious citadels and lavatory tanks. Since the mid-1960s, however, this interpretation has been disputed because of scholars' both finding new artifacts and learning of comparably stable groups that did not have autocratic priests. Though much of what we know of the Harrapan culture does suggest stability, it probably had its ups and downs, like most other cultures.

By about 1500 B.C.E., the Harrapan culture was destroyed, after perhaps a millennium and a half of existence. (Most scholars postulate a long growth period before the 400 years of prosperity.) The destructive Aryan conquerers were a pastoral and nomadic people who loved fighting, racing, drinking, and other aspects of the warrior life. They probably came from the north, where the cooler climate favored such vigor, and they thought of themselves as the salt of the earth—their name means "from the earth" or "noble." (This name survives in *Iran* and *Eire;* in addition, all European languages save Finnish, Hungarian, and Basque are related to the Aryans' language.)

The Aryans had fair skin and pointed noses, a fact perhaps responsible for their hostile reaction to the dark, snub-nosed Harrapans. They moved by horse, ate meat, and hunted with bow and arrow. There is no evidence that they ever learned to navigate or sail, and they produced no striking art, although they did know about iron and fashioned good weapons. Like many other warrior, nomadic peoples (for example, the Celts), they loved storytelling and singing. Indeed, their culture and religion were highly verbal. Their society was male dominated, with a primarily patriarchal family structure, priesthood, and cast of gods.[2] Above all, they were mobile, pushing through Greece, Italy, Iran, and India. After 2000 B.C.E., they were strong enough to dominate the native Indians, but they may have started trickling into India from the northwest as much as 2,000 years previously.

Troy Wilson Organ suggests that the Aryans' favorite god, Indra, whom we shall study when we turn to the *Rig-Veda,* was a projection or personification of their own sense of character.[3] He was exuberant and warlike—a boaster, a thunderbolt thrower, a big drinker, a slayer of dragons. He ruled by seizure rather than inheritance, loved action rather than stability. Thus, according to Aryan myth, Indra aggressively seized the waters of heaven, released them, and fashioned the earth. Some have suggested that Indra was first a culture hero and only later a leading god, but from their earliest time in India, the Aryans undoubtedly looked to him as the source and model of their prowess in war. Even in his fondness for drinking Indra was a great model, for what hardy people has not sanctioned its love of drink?

Two peoples thus contributed to the beginnings of Hindu culture. If the Harrapan culture was representative, the people who came before the Aryans in the Indus Valley were stable, even conservative, city dwellers who perhaps developed (or took from earlier peoples) important fertility rites. The Aryans were a rough, fighting people who had a much simpler technology than the Harrapans but whose poetry and religion perhaps were imaginative. These Aryans became the dominant force militarily and politically, imposing their will and their gods (*devas*) on the subjugated Harrapan (or Dravidian) natives. Inasmuch as the Aryans produced the Vedas, their culture always had more official status.

However, Indian culture never lost its Dravidian features, especially in the less Aryanized south. At most they were dormant for a while. After the demise of Vedic culture, Dravidian interests in fertility re-emerged (the Aryans had their own fertility interests). The complex devotionalism of later Hinduism is best explained in terms of many non-Aryan factors.

Vedic India

By Vedism most scholars mean the culture resulting from the mixture of Aryans, Harrapans, and other peoples of the Indus and Ganges valleys. This culture expressed itself in the earliest Indian writings, which are a collection of religious songs, hymns, spells, rituals, and speculations called the Vedas. It is convenient to consider them as representing the first stages of Hinduism, for although later India abandoned many of the Vedic gods and practices, the Vedas retained scriptural status throughout the later centuries, weaving themselves deeply into India's fabric.

The word *veda* means "wisdom" (cognates are the English *wit* and the German *wissen*). The Vedic pieces were originally oral. In fact, the proto-Hindus considered human speech divine, so singing and praying to the gods became sacred actions. Scholars have found that the Aryans composed some of the hymns found in the oldest Vedic literature before they entered India. The hymns honoring the sky and the dawn, for instance, are remarkably like the religious literature of other Indo-Europeans, indicating that they go back to the time before the Aryans split into their Iranian and Indian branches.

Consider, for example, the following lovely verses in praise of Varuna, the *deva* of moral order:

> He has put intelligence in hearts, fire in the waters, the sun in the sky, and the *soma* plant on the hills. . . . I will speak of the mysterious deed [*maya*] of Varuna renowned, the Lord immortal, who, standing in the firmament, has measured out the earth, as it were, with a yardstick. (*Rig-Veda* 5:85:2,5)

To the traditional Hindu, the Vedic literature represents the highest intuitive knowledge that the *rishis* (holy persons or seers) had attained.[4] The technical term denoting such a state of wisdom is **shruti,** which translators often render as "revelation." *Shruti* does not connote that divinities outside the human realm broke through the veil separating heaven and earth in order to impart light from above; as we shall see, Hinduism does not have such a remote view of the divine. Rather, *shruti* implies that the eminent holy person has heard certain things in peak experiences (often induced by the ritual drink soma). Therefore, Vedic literature, representing what the *rishis* had heard, was considered the best and holiest presentation of knowledge.

The Vedas consist of four separate collections of materials. Together, these four collections are known as the *Samhitas. Samhitas* therefore can be a synonym for Vedas. The individual collections are called the *Rig-Veda, Sama-Veda, Yajur-Veda,* and *Atharva-Veda.* The *Rig-Veda* is the oldest, largest, and most important. It contains more than a thousand *suktas,* or individual units, which are hymns to the *devas,* magical poems, riddles, legends, and the like. They show considerable learning and poetic skill, which argue against their being the spontaneous poetry of freewheeling warriors or rude peasants. More likely, they represent the work of priestly leaders—the careful creation of an educated class concerned with regulating contact with the gods and maintaining its own social status.

Most of the *Rig-Veda's* hymns have two purposes. First, they praise the god being addressed; second, they ask the god for favors or benefits. For instance, the *Rig-Veda* praises Agni for deeds that show the splendor of his status as the god of fire. (These deeds appear to be not so much mythical allusions to feats that the god performed in the beginning as similes drawn from human experience. For example, Agni's flame is like the warrior's battle rush: As the warrior blazes upon the enemy, so the god of fire blazes through the brush or woods.) Then, having admired the god, the hymn singer makes his petition. In *Rig-Veda* 6:6 he asks for wealth: "wealth giving splendor, . . . wealth bright and vast with many heroes."

Though this ritual exchange is the most usual focus, the *Rig-Veda* has other interests. For instance, it includes petitions for forgiveness of sins (such as having wronged a brother, cheated at games, or abused a stranger) which indicate a developed moral sense. Although the *Rig-Veda* may not separate itself completely from an ancient worldview, where being out of phase with the cosmic processes is almost physically dangerous, it provides solid evidence of a religion centering on free, responsible choices made for good or evil. As well, some of the hymns of the *Rig-Veda* are speculative, wondering about the source of the many phenomena of the world. A famous speculative text is 10:129, where the poet muses about the creation of the world. At the beginning there was no being and no nonbeing, no air and no sky beyond. It was, in fact, a time before either death or immortal life had begun. Then only the One existed, drawn into being by heat that interacted with the primal waters and the void. However, from desire the One started to think and emit fertile power. Thus, impulse from above and energy from below began to make the beings of the world. But, the hymn asks in conclusion, who knows whether this speculation is valid? Even the gods were born after the world's beginning, so who can say what happened? Only one who surveys everything from the greatest high heaven knows, if indeed even that being knows.

The Vedic Gods.   A study of the Vedic gods suggests what the earliest Hindus thought about the deepest forces in their world. The gods are many and complex (tradition said there were 330 million), but of course a few stand out as the most important. Indeed, for many later sages, all the gods were manifestations of a single underlying divinity: "They call it Indra, Mitra, Varuna, Agni, or again the celestial bird Garutman; the one reality the sages call by various names . . ." (*Rig-Veda* 1, 164.46). They are all *devas* (good divinities), as distinguished from *asuras* (evil divinities). (In Iran the terminology is just the reverse, suggesting that the Iranian-Indian split may have been theological.[5]) The Vedas cast most *devas* in human or animal form. Since the main feature of the *devas* was power, we may consider them functional forces: the warmth of

the sun, the energy of the storm, and so on. To express these larger-than-life qualities, later Indian artists often gave the *devas* supernumerary bodily parts. An extra pair of arms, for instance, would indicate prowess in battle; an extra eye would indicate ability to discern events at a distance. Typically, a *deva* was a male deity associated with a female consort, who represented his energetic force (*shakti*). (In developed Hindu speculation, the male principle was passive, or cool.) Later, Tantrist Hinduism focused on *shakti*, sometimes through the practice of ritual sex.

By textual analysis, scholars have uncovered different generations of the Vedic gods. The oldest group consists of the gods of the sky and the earth that the Vedas share with other Indo-European religious texts. For instance, the Vedic Father Sky (Dyaus Pitar) is related to the Greek Zeus and the Roman Jupiter. Like them, he is the overarching power that fertilizes the receptive earth with rain and rays of sun. The Vedic earth is the Great Mother, the fertile female.[6] These deities are not the most prominent Vedic gods, but they echo in the background as the oldest.

The second oldest group, whose age is confirmed by Iranian parallels, includes Indra, Mithra, Varuna, Agni, and Soma. As noted, Indra was the warrior god of the storm much beloved by the Aryan conquerors. Mithra was the god of the sun. Varuna was the god of cosmic and moral order, and Soma was the god of the exhilarating cultic drink. Known in Iran as *haoma*, soma gave visions so dazzling that it became integral to the sacramental cult (scholars dispute whether the drink was hallucinogenic). Agni, finally, was the god of fire, whose importance increased as the sacrifice focused more and more on fire. It is worth noting that most of the deities in this second generation represent earthly and especially heavenly forces. Perhaps the storm, the sun, and the sky were all originally joined in Dyaus Pitar, but later they became separate objects of devotion.

The third generation of gods includes Brahma, Vishnu, and Shiva. They arose after the Aryans arrived in India and so perhaps indicate Dravidian influences. We shall consider them more fully below.

Finally, the fourth generation, which comes to the fore in the philosophical texts called the Upanishads, comprises abstract deities such as One God, That One, Who, and the Father of Creation (Eka Deva, Tad Ekam, Ka, and Prajapati).[7] Upanishadic seers had become dissatisfied with the concrete, world-affirming outlook at the core of the *Rig-Veda* and searched for simpler, more spiritual notions.

Overall, then, we find a development within the Vedic literature from an acceptance of many divinities, to a desire for unity, and then to a focus on knowledge that culminated in the Upanishads. On the way to the Upanishads, however, Indians went through a period when rituals were all-important.

Brahmanism. In the early Vedic period, the sacrifice was quite simple. It required no elaborate rituals, no temples, no images—only a field of cut grass, some ghee (clarified butter) for the fire, and soma (some poured onto the ground for the gods and some drunk by the participants). Later the sacrifice became more elaborate, involving the chanting of magical sounds, reenacting the world's creation, and slaying a variety of animals.[8] Since this elaboration went hand in hand with the increasing importance of the priest (brahmin, or brahman), commentators often refer to sacrificial Vedic religion as Brahmanism. Always, however, the sacrifice intended to make human beings holy by giving them an operational way to please the gods.

Brahmanism reached its greatest elaboration with the horse sacrifice, a ceremony that lasted more than a year. In the first step of this complicated ritual, attendants bathed a young white horse, fed it wheat cakes for three days, consecrated it by fire, and then released it and let it wander for a year. Princes and soldiers followed the horse, conquering all territory through which it traveled. After one year, servants brought the horse back to the palace. During the next new moon, the king shaved his head and beard. After an all-night vigil at the sacred fire, the queens went to the horse at dawn, anointed it, and decorated it with pearls. A sacrifice of 609 selected animals, ranging from the elephant to the bee (and sometimes a human), followed.

The sacrifice reached its climax after attendants slaughtered the horse itself and placed a blanket over it. The most important queen then slipped under the blanket to have (simulated?) sexual intercourse with the horse, while the other queens and the priests shouted obscene encouragements. After this, participants ate the horse in a ritual meal. The entire ceremony fits the pattern of ancient celebrations of the new year, which often involved sacrifices and orgies designed to renew the world's fertility. Most of the symbolism centers on the virility of the king, in whose person the people hope to find strength like that of a lusty stallion.

Caste. When one considers the distinctive organization of traditional Indian society that goes back to the Vedic roots, the word caste comes to mind. In fact, it is a Western word, covering two distinct though related native Indian concepts and phenomena. The first native concept has been conveyed through the word *varna,* the original meaning of which is uncertain but perhaps had connections with "color." Varna mainly has referred to the division of social ranks and tasks developed by the Aryans and established by them as regulative for the India that they came to dominate. Although this social structure became more pronounced and influential in India than in the other areas (Iran, northern Europe) where Aryan ancestral stock (the proto-Indo-Europeans) prevailed, one finds that ancient Persians, Celts, Greeks, and others shared its general delineation of the main social classes. This delineation was into the three groups of priests, nobles or warriors, and commoners/farmers/merchants.

As has been true in other ancient cultures, India did not think of its social structure as designed, worked out, by human beings who might well have fashioned things quite differently. It did not think varna had arisen the way one might divide a present-day business organization into executives, managers, and secretaries, or the way one might divide an army into generals, majors, and privates. No, India thought of varna as part of the divinely ordered cosmos—part of the heavenly scheme of things. Thus the *Rig-Veda* (10:90) speaks of a primal sacrifice of a protohuman being that gave society its four varnas (India added servants). Later, the most influential law code, that attributed to Manu, repeated such Vedic justification, tying the ways Indians had come to think of their principal social classes to the divinely given order of things.

The second native Indian word usually covered by the English "caste" is *jati,* which refers to the many particular, familial, clanlike groups that have made Indian society a complex quilt of separable yet tangent entities. As one recent study of varna and jati puts it: "There are thousands of *jatis* scattered throughout the subcontinent, and they vary widely in their attributes and characteristics. Each is characterized by a set of rules governing acceptable occupations, foods, associations (that is, with members of other *jatis*), marriage rules (concerning widow remarriage, for example), and much else. European observers have long been particularly interested in three areas of *jati* regulation: the rule of endogamy [the necessity of marrying within one's own jati], the presence of a characteristic (or at least traditional) *jati* occupation, and the rules whereby *jatis* in proximity rank themselves and each other."9

In practice, this has all meant that most Indians have not grown up free to pursue what work they wished, marry as they and any with whom they established a mutual attraction might have wished, and interact with other Indians mainly on nonclannish, democratic grounds.

The simplest correlation between varna and jati, which many Hindus themselves have used, is to consider jatis subdivisions of varnas. Thus, while there might be thousands of different brahmanic jatis separating the priestly caste into various subgroups who could have only limited contact with one another, all such jatis held something in common and were more closely connected to one another than to such members of the third social echelon (the farmers/merchants) as barbers, potters, and leatherworkers. The latter three groups, although constituting different jatis that kept them apart in many significant areas of daily life, shared membership in the third social echelon and so were closer than they could be to priests, warriors, or the lower-class workers of the fourth echelon.

Most Indians have considered both varna and jati related to, indeed, derived from, their karma (a concept we discuss shortly). In other words, both aspects of social status have come under the general Indian assumption that one's movement (toward release from the painful human condition or away from such release) was a constant byplay between individual choices and outward circumstances (such as one's work, extended family, and geographic area).

The Upanishads.   Before the end of the Vedic period, Brahmanism declined for at least two reasons. First, common sense dictated that society had more to do than listen to priests chant all day. The texts imply that even during the times of the *Rig-Veda,* people were unhappy with the priests' constant prating. A satire in 7:103, for instance, likens them to frogs croaking over the waters. Second, intellectuals desired something more satisfying than an understanding of sacrifice that tended to remain on the surface. The

Upanishads reveal the intellectuals' turn to interiority, which resulted in sacrifice becoming less a matter of slaughter, ritual, and words and more a matter of soul cleansing and dedication to the divine powers.

The word *Upanishad* connotes the secret teaching that one receives at the feet of a guru. Out of hundreds of treatises (over the period from 800 to 300 B.C.E.), a few Upanishads came to the fore.10 They show that the intellectuals embraced a variety of styles and ideas and that their movement was poetic as much as philosophical. Whether poetic or philosophical, though, the movement's goal was quite religious: intuitive knowledge of ultimate truths, of the unity behind the many particulars of reality.

The Upanishads themselves do not agree on whether the unity behind everything is personal, impersonal, or a mixture of the two. However, they do tend to use two words in discussing it, both of which are more impersonal than personal. The first word is **Brahman**, which generally means the first principle, cause, or stuff of the objective world. Brahman, in other words, is the final answer for the Upanishadic thinkers who wondered about how things are founded—especially things in the material world.

The second word, **atman**, means the vital principle or deepest identity of the subject—the soul or self. Probing this reality by thought and meditation, the Upanishadic seers moved away from Vedic materiality to spirituality. The internal world, the world of atman and thought, was a world of *spirit.*

Combining these new concepts of Brahman and atman, some of the Upanishadic seers found a coincidence—the basic reality within and without, of self and the world, was the same. Atman is Brahman. So in the Chandogya Upanishad 6:1:3, the father Uddalaka teaches his son Shvetaketu that Shvetaketu himself *is,* most fundamentally, Brahmanic ultimate reality: *Tat tvam asi* ("That thou art"). The soul and the stuff of the world are but two sides of the same single "be-ing" or "is-ness" that constitutes all existing things.

In the Brihad-aranyaka Upanishad, one of the most important, an interesting discussion occurs between the thoughtful woman Gargi and the sage Yajnavalkya about the ultimate "warp" of reality (the relevant definition of "warp" is "the basic foundation or material of a structure or entity"). Gargi has pressed the sage to tell her about the weave of reality: "That, O Yajnavalkya, which is above the sky, that which is beneath the earth, that which is between these two, sky and earth, that which people call the past and the present and the future—across what is that woven, warp and woof?" The sage answers that she is asking about space. Sensing that she still has not gained the final goal of her inquiry, Gargi presses one further question: "Across what then, pray, is space woven, warp and woof?" This is the capital question, eliciting from the sage the capital answer: the Imperishable.

To describe the Imperishable, Yajnavalkya launches into a long list of negatives: "It is not coarse, not fine, not short, not long, not glowing, not adhesive, without shadow and without darkness, without air and without space, without stickiness, odorless, tasteless, without eye, without ear, without voice, without wind, without energy, without breath, without mouth . . . without measure, without inside and without outside." Only by denying the limitations implied in each of these attributes can the sage suggest the unique, transcendent character of ultimate reality.

The Imperishable does not consume anything and no one consumes it. It is the commander of the sun and the moon, the earth and the sky, and all other things. Without the knowledge of the imperishable, other religious attainments are of little worth: "Verily, O Gargi, if one performs sacrifices and worship and undergoes austerity in this world for many thousands of years, but without knowing that Imperishable, limited indeed is that [work] of his." For the Imperishable is the unseen Seer, the unthought Thinker, the only One that understands. "Across this Imperishable, O Gargi, is space woven, warp and woof."

The Imperishable, then, is the Upanishadic sage's ultimate wisdom. When pressed for the material cause of things, the "that from which" everything is made, Yajnavalkya can only say "Something that is of itself, something that does not perish." This is a characteristic answer, one that many sages, West as well as East, have fashioned. Pushing off from the perishable nature of the things of sensory experience, they have conceived of the ultimate foundation of reality as other than sensible things, other indeed than anything within the range of human experience. The best we can say of the origin of the universe, the final reason for everything that exists, is that it *is* independently, in a mode that does not perish, pass away, or suffer change. To uphold the world it must be different from the world. Either in the midst of worldly flux, or apart, it must surpass the "world," the mental construct of the material and spiritual whole that we limited humans fashion.

On the other hand, the ultimate material cause of things must be enough like us, discernible by us, to warrant our giving it negative names and seeking to know it. Were it absolutely other, completely apart from our human realm, we could not even discuss it negatively. It was by pondering this equally primordial fact that the Upanishadic seers came to focus on the human spirit or soul as the best analogue or presence of the Ultimate. This spirit or soul (atman) seemed the best candidate for the presence of the Ultimate that makes human beings exist. While they live, human beings are imperishable: something keeps them from total change and decay. Thus while they have a given identity they draw upon the Imperishable, depend upon It, and express It. Between It and them must obtain a connection, maybe even an identity. Certainly the most real part of them is the presence of the Imperishable, without which they would actually perish. So perhaps the best way to regard them (ourselves), or anything, is as a form of the Imperishable, one of its myriad extrusions or expressions. If so, one can say that, in the last analysis, only the Imperishable is real or actual or existent. Everything else at best receives a passing reality from the temporary presence to it, presence in it, of the Imperishable. For that reason, Yajnavalkya can rightly call it "that across which even space is woven, warp and woof."

For the Upanishadic thinkers, this realization was liberating because it avoided the multiplicity, externalism, and materialism that had often corroded Brahmanism. Though sacrifice and the gods continued to have a place in Upanishadic religion, they were quite subordinate to monism.

In addition, the Upanishadic thinkers felt an urgent need for liberation (*moksha*), unlike the Vedists. Perhaps echoing Buddhist beliefs, the writers of the Upanishads worked with experiences they found more dismal, depressing, and afflicting than the first Aryans had. Whereas those vigorous warriors had fought and drunk, living for the moment, these later meditative sages examined the human condition and found it sad. To express their beliefs, they fashioned the doctrines of samsara and karma, which did not appear in the early Vedas.

Samsara (the doctrine of rebirths or reincarnation) implies that the given world, the world of common sense and ordinary experience, is only provisional. It is not the ultimate existence. To take it as ultimate or fully real, therefore, is to delude oneself and thus to trap oneself in a cycle of rebirths. Only when one penetrates Brahman, the truly real, can one escape this cycle. Otherwise, one must constantly travel the scale of animal life (up or down, depending on one's advances or backslidings in wisdom).

Karma is the law that governs advancement or regression in the samsaric life of deaths and rebirths. Essentially, it is the reality that all acts have unavoidable consequences. In an almost physical way, they determine one's personality. Karma also explains one's status: A person's present life is shaped by that person's past lives. The only way to escape the round of rebirths, the pain of samsara, is to advance by meritorious deeds and be saved or freed. (Hinduism chooses to live with the illogic of a law both necessary and capable of being undercut by freedom.[11])

Case Study: The Isa Upanishad.   The Isa Upanishad, one of the shortest, offers a good specimen of the Upanishadic style. Robert Hume, a respected translator of the Upanishads into English, divides the Isa into eighteen stanzas.

The strong emotions the stanzas of the Isa display remind us that the Upanishadic seers were *religious* philosophers—people pursuing a vision that would bring them *moksha*. The Isa's passionate quest for a single principle to explain the diversity of the world's many phenomena also reinforces the impression that many of the Upanishadic seers had grown soul-sick from the complexity of Brahmanic religion.

The first stanza of the Isa announces the monistic theme: Unless we see that the Lord (Isa) envelops all that exists, we misunderstand reality. There must be a stable principle giving rest to all the moving things. Religious people renounce all these moving things and so come to enjoy human life. Such renunciation takes them away from coveting the wealth or possessions of other people, which so frequently is a cause of sadness.

Stanza two develops this basis of freedom. It is possible to live in the world, performing the duties of one's station, without being attached to one's deeds. In that case, the deed (*karman*) does not adhere to the personality or weight it down. Detachment therefore is the antidote to karma. If one is free from concern about the effects of one's actions, one can work for *moksha*.

But, as stanza three emphasizes, those who do not detach themselves receive a stern punishment after death. If they have slain the Self (the presence of Brahman within) by desirous, badly motivated deeds, they will go to dark worlds ruled by devils.

Stanza four shifts back to a positive viewpoint. The One that does not move, that stands free of the changing things of the world, is swifter than the human mind and senses. Wisdom is placing one's action in this One, reposing one's self in what is so swift it is stable.

Human life therefore faces a paradox, as stanza five shows. The principle underlying everything that exists seems both to move and not to move. Insofar as it is the inmost reality of whatever exists, it moves in all things' movement. Insofar as it gives all these things their basis, it is free of their movement, self-possessed rather then dependent on another. So, too, the One can be both far and near, both outside and within any being of the samsaric world.

Stanza six suggests a focus to bring this blur into clarity. By looking on all beings as though they reposed in the Self (the world's soul), and looking at the Self as though it were present in all things, the wise person stays close to the Brahman that is the world's ultimate significance.

According to stanza seven, the profit in this focus is the freedom from delusion and sorrow it brings. The person who perceives the unity of reality, seeing the single Self everywhere, achieves a knowledge and joy that the ignorant, mired in the world's multiplicity, never know.

This leads, in stanza eight, to an imaginative flourish. Picturing the world ruler, the human being who has realized full human potential, the Isa unfurls a flag of glowing attributes: wise, intelligent, comprehensive, self-sufficient. By dealing with what is bright, bodiless, pure, and unaffected by evil (by dealing with the Self), this person has reached the summit, come to stand close to eternity.

Stanzas nine and ten are quite mystical, probing the nature of religious enlightenment. If those who worship ignorance (who neglect the Self) go into a blind darkness, those who delight in true knowledge go into a greater darkness or mystery, a state beyond the dichotomy between knowledge and nonknowledge. The wise people who have handed down Vedic wisdom confirm this: Enlightenment and *moksha* are mysterious.

Stanza eleven adds another dimension: The wise person, holding knowledge and nonknowledge together, passes over death and gains immortality.

ĪŚĀ UPANISHAD[1] [12]

Recognition of the unity underlying the diversity of the world

1. By the Lord (*īśā*) enveloped must this all be—
   Whatever moving thing there is in the moving world.
   With this renounced, thou mayest enjoy.
   Covet not the wealth of anyone at all.

Non-attachment of deeds on the person of a renouncer

2. Even while doing deeds here,
   One may desire to live a hundred years.
   Thus on thee—not otherwise than this is it—
   The deed (*karman*) adheres not on the man.

The forbidding future for slayers of the Self

3. Devilish (*asurya*[2]) are those worlds called,[3]
   With blind darkness (*tamas*) covered o'er!
   Unto them, on deceasing, go
   Whatever folk are slayers[4] of the Self.[5]

The all-surpassing, paradoxical world-being

4. Unmoving, the One (*ekam*) is swifter than the mind.
   The sense-powers (*deva*) reached not It, speeding on before.
   Past others running, This goes standing.
   In It Mātariśvan places action.[6]

5. It moves.   It moves not.
   It is far, and It is near.
   It is within all this,
   And It is outside of all this.[1]

6. Now, he who on all beings
   Looks as just (*eva*) in the Self (*Ātman*),
   And on the Self as in all beings—[2]
   He does not shrink away from Him.[3]

7. In whom all beings
   Have become just (*eva*) the Self of the discerner—
   Then what delusion (*moha*), what sorrow (*śoka*) is there
   Of him who perceives the unity!

Characteristics of the world-ruler

8. He has environed. The bright, the bodiless, the scatheless,
   The sinewless, the pure (*śuddha*), unpierced by evil (*a-pāpa-viddha*)!
   Wise (*kavi*), intelligent (*manīśin*), encompassing (*paribhū*), self-existent (*svayambhū*),
   Appropriately he distributed objects (*artha*) through the eternal years.

Transcending, while involving, the antithesis of knowing

9. Into blind darkness enter they
   That worship ignorance;
   Into darkness greater than that, as it were, they
   That delight in knowledge.[4]

10. Other, indeed, they say, than knowledge!
    Other, they say, than non-knowledge![5]
    —Thus we have heard from the wise (*dhīra*)
    Who to us have explained It.[6]

---

[1]So called from its first word; or sometimes 'Īasāvāsyam' from its first two words; or sometimes the 'Vājasaneyi-Samhitā Upanishad' from the name of the recension of the White Yajur-Veda of which this Upanishad forms the final, the fortieth, chapter.

[2]Compare the persons called 'devilish,' *āsura*, at Chānd. 8. 8. 5. A variant reading here (accordant with a literalism interpreted in the following line) is *a-sūrya*, 'sunless.'

[3]The word *nāma* here might mean 'certainly' instead of 'called.'

[4]This idea is in apparent contrast with the doctrine of Katha 2. 19 d (and BhG. 2. 19), where it is stated that 'he [i.e., the Self] slays not, is not slain.' The word *ātma-han* here, of course, is metaphorical, like 'smother,' 'stifle,' 'completely supress.'

[5]The whole stanza is a variation of Brih. 4. 4. 11.

[6]So Com. But *apas* may refer, cosmogonically, to 'the [primeval] waters.'

---

[1]The very same ideas as in this stanza, though not all the same words, recur at BhG. 13. 15 a, b, d.

[2]This universal presence is claimed by Krishna for himself at BhG. 6. 30 a, b.

[3]The indefinite word *tatas* may mean 'from these beings,' or 'from this Self,' or 'from this time on,' or pregnantly all these. The whole line recurs at Brih. 4. 4. 15 d; Katha 4. 5d; 4. 12 d.

[4]This stanza is identical with Brih. 4. 4. 10.

[5]The point here made is that both knowledge and lack of knowledge are inadequate for apprehending the Ultimate.

[6]A somewhat more concrete, and perhaps earlier, form of this stanza occurs as Kena 3 e–h.

11. Knowledge and non-knowledge—
    He who this pair conjointly (*saha*) knows,
    With non-knowledge passing over death,
    With knowledge wins the immortal.[1]

The inadequacy of any antithesis of being

12. Into blind darkness enter they
    Who worship non-being (*a-sambhūti*);
    Into darkness greater than that, as it were,
    they
    Who delight in becoming (*sambhūti*).

13. Other, indeed—they say—than origin
    (*sambhava*)!
    Other—they say—than non-origin
    (*a-sambhava*)!
    —Thus have we heard from the wise
    Who to us have explained It.

Becoming and destruction a fundamental duality

14. Becoming (*sambhūti*) and destruction
    (*vināśa*)—
    He who this pair conjointly (*saha*) knows,
    With destruction passing over death,
    With becoming wins the immortal.

A dying person's prayer

15. With a golden vessel[2]
    The Real's face is covered o'er.
    That do thou, O Pūshan, uncover
    For one whose law is the Real[3] to see.[4]

16. O Nourisher (*pūsan*), the sole Seer (*ekarsi*),
    O Controller (*yama*), O Sun (*sūrya*, off-
    spring of Prajāpati, spread forth thy rays!
    Gather thy brilliance (*tejas*)![5] What is thy
    fairest form—that of thee I see. He who is
    yonder, yonder Person (*purusa*)—I myself
    am he!

17. [My] breath (*vāyu*) to the immortal wind (*an-
    ila*)![1] This body then ends in ashes! *Om!*
    O Purpose (*kratu*[2]), remember! The deed
    (*krta*) remember!
    O Purpose, remember! The deed remember!

General prayer of petition and adoration

18. O Agni, by a goodly path to prosperity (*rai*)
    lead us,
    Thou god who knowest all the ways!
    Keep far from us crooked-going sin (*enas*)![3]
    Most ample expression of adoration to thee
    would we render![4]

---

[1]This formula recurs at Brih. 5.15. The idea that at death the several parts of microcosmic man revert to the corresponding elements of the macrocosm is expressed several times in Sanskrit literature. With the specific mention here, compare 'his spirit (*ātman*) to the wind (*vāta*)' in the Cremation Hymn, RV. 10.16.3a; 'with his breath (*prāna*) to wind (*vāyu*),' Śat. Br. 10.3.3.8; 'his breath (*prāna*) to wind (*vāta*),' Brih. 3.2.13; and even of the sacrificial animal, 'its breath (*prāna*) to wind (*vāta*),' Ait. Br. 2.6.
[2]Compare the statement in Chānd. 3.14.1, 'Now, verily, a person consists of purpose (*kratu-maya*).'
[3]Other prayers for freedom from sin (*enas*, compare also *āgas*) are at RV. 1.24.9d; 3.7.10d; 7.86.3 a, 4d; 7.88.6 c; 7.89.5 c, d; 7.93.7 c, d; 8.67 (56). 17; 10.35. 3 a, c; 10.37. 12; AV. 6.97. 2 d; 6.115. 1,2,3; 6.116. 2,3; 6.117; 6.118; 6.119; 6.120.
[4]This stanza is identical with RV. 1.189.1, and the second line also with AV. 4.39.10b.

---

[1]This stanza occurs again in Maitri 7. 9.
[2]The sun.
[3]For the petitioner (who calls himself '*satya-dharma*') to see through; or 'For Him whose law is Truth (or, true) to be seen,' [as, e.g., for Savitri in RV. 10.34. 8; 10.139.3; or the Unknown Creator, RV. 10.121.9; VS.10.103; or Agni, RV. 1.12.7]; or, 'For that [neuter] which has the Real as its nature [or, essence; or, law] to be seen.'
[4]These lines occur with slight variations at Maitri 6.35 and Brih. 5.15.1.

[5]According to this translation the idea is entirely honorific of the effulgence of the sun. Or, with a different grouping of words, the meaning might possibly be the petition: 'Spread apart thy rays [that I may enter through the sun (as well as see through—according to the previous petition) into the Real; then] gather [thy rays together again, as normal]. The brilliance which is thy fairest form, . . .' At best the passage is of obscure mystical significance.

The "beyond" or transcendent character of true enlightenment appears even more clearly in stanzas twelve and thirteen. Both nonbecoming (changelessness) and becoming (change) can be illusory. The ultimate truth of Brahman transcends such oppositions. So too it transcends the opposition between origin (being the source of everything) and nonorigin (not being the source). The saving intuition that brings *moksha* takes the perceiver to another realm, where the dichotomies and antagonisms thrown up by ordinary human intelligence do not pertain.

According to stanza fourteen, this saving intuition also conjoins becoming and destruction. If one understands their relation, he can ride destruction across the chasm of death, ride becoming to the far shore of immortality.

The Isa concludes prayerfully, in stanza fifteen praising the sun as a cover of reality and asking divinity to uncover its face, that we might fulfill our primary human obligation, which is to grasp reality. (Note that this prayer is answered in the *Bhagavad Gita.)* Stanza sixteen calls divinity the nourisher, the sole seer, the controller of fortunes, the one who is yonder yet the inmost reality of the personality. Stanza seventeen prays that while our body ends in ashes, our breath may take us to the immortal wind. This will happen if we remember our purpose, grasp the import of our deeds. The Isa's last prayers, in stanza eighteen, are addressed to Agni: Lead us to prosperity by a godly path, you who know all the ways. Keep us from the crooked ways of sin, for we want to offer you ample adoration.

The Period of Native Challenge

From about 600 B.C.E. to 300 C.E. the Vedic religion, including its Upanishadic refinements, was seriously challenged by some Indians. We have already seen that the Upanishads represent a critical reaction to sacrificial Brahmanism.[13] However, even the Upanishads themselves, the final fruits of the Vedic tradition, were eventually contested by materialist, Jain, Buddhist, devotionalist, and other religious views. Not that "Vedism" or "Brahmanism" had ever been either a monolith or a system clearly considered official and in control. Always there had been resistance among the warrior and merchant classes, along with teachers of meditation and new philosophical views. As well, the entire Vedic tradition of revelation kept growing through commentaries and instructions. Hindus refer to these materials collectively as *smriti* (memory or tradition). Still, while some Hindus remained loyal to early Vedic gods and sacrifices, the strong challenges decisively changed the religion of the majority.

Materialistic, Jain, and Buddhist challenges to Vedism first arose in northeastern India, where warrior tribes were more than ready to contest the priests' pretensions to cultural control. By this time (600 B.C.E.), the Aryans had settled in villages, and India was a checkerboard of small kingdoms, each of which controlled a group of such villages. Some intellectuals, radically opposed to the Vedas, strongly attacked the Vedic belief that there is a reality other than the sensible or material. It is hard to know precisely what these materialists taught, because few of their writings have survived, but Buddhist literature reports that Ajita, a prominent materialist thinker, said that earth, air, fire, and water are the only elements—the sources of everything in the universe. According to Ajita, the differences among things just reflect different proportions of these elements. Human beings are no exception, and at death they simply dissolve back into these four elements. There is no afterlife, no reincarnation, no soul, and no Brahman. During the brief span of their lives, people should live "realistically," enduring pain and pursuing pleasure. Nothing beyond the testimony of the senses is valid knowledge, and what the senses reveal is what is real.

Jainism was a very different challenge that grew from the struggles for enlightenment of Vardhamana, called the Jina (conqueror) or Mahavira (great man). He was born to wealth but found it unfulfilling, so he launched a life of **asceticism**. After gaining enlightenment by this self-denial, he successfully preached his method to others. The Jina opposed both the ritualism and the intellectualism of the Vedic tradition. The only significant sacrifice, he said, is that which conquers the self. Similarly, the only worthy knowledge is that which enables the personality to gain full freedom.[14]

The Jina's followers became opponents of all forms of violence and pain. Consequently, they opposed the Vedic sacrifice of animals, calling it an assault on life that opposed true religion. Also, Jains became critical of matter. Their "karma" was a semisolid entity that attached itself to the spirit through acts involving material objects.[15] In memory of the Jina, whom they considered to be a great *tirthankara* ("crosser of the stream of sorry life"), Jains eschewed eating meat, harming anything believed to have a soul, and physical activity. Since total avoidance of these activities was practically impossible, Jains tried to balance any injury that they inflicted or bad karma that they generated by acts of self-denial or benevolence.

The popularity of Jainism and of Buddhism, which arose only slightly later, testifies to the vulnerability of Vedism that many Indians experienced during the sixth century B.C.E. At the time of the Mahavira's death (due to voluntary starvation), his followers have been estimated at more than half a million. There were more women than men, and many more laypeople than monks and nuns. For laypeople and monks alike, however, Jainism developed guiding vows, similar to commandments, which have been a principal reason for the persistence of Jainism in India to the present.

The lay vows include commitments not to injure living beings, not to lie or steal, not to be unchaste, not to accumulate large sums of money, not to travel widely or possess more than what one needs, not to think evil of others, and not to pursue evil forms of livelihood. There were also positive vows to meditate and to support the community of ascetic monks.

Today there are about two million Jains in India. Prominent centers include Gujarat in the west and Karnatuku in the south. There is also a significant Jain population in Calcutta. In Jain temples one can see pictures of nude, ascetic saints who represent an ideal of complete detachment, and the Jain doctrine of *ahimsa* (noninjury) has made a permanent impression on Indian culture.[16]

Since we discuss Buddhism at length in the next chapter, we note here only that from a Hindu perspective, Buddhism arose, much like Jainism, as an anti-Vedic protest in the sixth century B.C.E. It was another stimulus to Hindu reform, another flowering of Vedic interest in improving people's ability to cope with an often painful world, another attack on both the Vedic sacrifices and their Brahmanistic rationale. If by "Hinduism" we mean the full-bodied tradition that evolved in response to the challenges of Jains and Buddhists, then those challenges were crucial to what Hindus later believed and did.

Bhagavata. Especially in western India, movements arose that, unlike materialism, Jainism, and Buddhism, brought changes from less radical critics. A collective word for these movements is *Bhagavata* (devotionalism), which connotes an emotional attachment to personal gods such as Krishna and Shiva. Devotees *(bhaktas)* continue to claim that such devotion is a way of salvation or self-realization superior to sacrifice or intellectual meditation.[17]

In the central Indian city of Mathura, devotion was focused on the god Krishna. There has been much debate about the background of this god (his name means dark blue or black and was a common one). Some have claimed that Krishna originally was a solar god, others that he was a vegetative god, and still others that he was a mythical hero. Organ suggests that the Krishna cult may have appropriated five minor religions that flourished in the Mathura area.[18] All these religions related to a solar deity, whom the local people worshiped as a personal god and petitioned for gifts.

Whatever its origins, the Krishna cult became very popular, and it developed a wealth of legends about Krishna's birth and adventures that ultimately made Krishna the most beloved of the Indian deities.

In one legend, demons tried to kill the baby Krishna, but he was stronger than they. When the demoness Putana, who had taken the form of a nurse, tried to offer him a breast covered with poison, Krishna took it and sucked out all her milk and blood. When another demon approached him, Krishna kicked the demon so hard that the demon died. Another cluster of legends describes the child Krishna's pranks (he was always stealing his mother's butter, for which he had a great appetite)[19] and the young man Krishna's affairs with young girls. Consequently, Krishna became the object of love—the love for an infant and the romantic and sexual love for a handsome young lord.[20]

The premier work of the Bhagavata tradition is the *Bhagavad Gita,* in which Krishna is the featured god. (The contrast between the warrior Krishna of the *Gita* and the pranksters of the Bahagavata tradition reminds us that we are dealing with a complex, mythological character.) The *Gita* offers ways of salvation to all types of people, but **bhakti** (devotional love) appears to be its highest teaching.[21] This is especially so if one reads the *Gita* as the progressive instruction of a pupil (Arjuna) by his guru god (Krishna). The *Gita* is set in the context of a great battle (the subject of the epic poem the *Mahabharata*), and it deals successively with (1) the ethical problem of war (one must do one's caste duty; there is no killing of the soul), (2) the valid ways to wisdom and realization (sacrifice, meditation, and action without attachment to its results), and (3) the divinity's unveiled countenance (the dazzling vision that is recounted in chap. 11). Then, in what seems to be the work's climax, Krishna tells Arjuna that the best "way" *(marga)* is love of Krishna and that he, Krishna, loves his devotee in return. In other words, there is a divine love for humanity as well as a human love for divinity (chap. 18). This final teaching, probably even more than the *Gita's* catholic offering of many religious ways, has made it Hinduism's most influential text.

In later Hindu theology, Krishna became an avatar, or manifestation, of Vishnu, whom we discuss shortly. However, to complete our discussion of Bhagavata, we should first describe the beginnings of a devotional cult to Shiva. This cult, too, was in part a reaction against Vedism, and one of its fascinating texts is the Svetashvatara Upanishad. For the devotees of Shiva, this text serves much as the *Bhagavad Gita* serves Krishnaites—as a gospel of the personal god's love. It is unique among the Upanishads for its theism (focus on a personal god), yet it shares with the monistic Upanishads an effort to think logically.

The author begins by asking momentous questions: What is Brahman? What causes us to be born? Then the author rejects impersonal wisdom, materialism, and pure devotion as inadequate answers. His own answer is to interpret Brahman (the ultimate reality) as a kind of god who may become manifest if one meditates upon him. In the Svetashvatara Upanishad, the preferred designation for Brahman is Rudra-Shiva. Rudra probably was the Dravidian form of Indra and Shiva a god of fertility.[22] In the post-Dravidian combination of these gods, the accent was on slaying and healing, destroying and creating—Shiva as the lord of the two rhythms of life.

According to this Upanishad, Shiva is in everything. He has five faces and three eyes, which show his control of all directions and all times (past, present, and future). The devotee of Shiva therefore deals with a divinity as ultimate and powerful as Krishna but whose destructive capacities are more accentuated.

Devotion to Krishna (Vishnu) or Shiva, then, satisfies the person who wants religious feeling and a personal god with whom to interact. Probably this sort of person predominated in Hindu history. From the legends about the gods and from the epics (especially the *Mahabharata* and the *Ramayana*), the *bhaktas*

found models for religious love and for faithful living as a good child, husband, wife, and so on.

Smriti. During this period of challenge to Vedic authority, one other development merits attention because it was responsible for a great deal of Hindu religious literature. This movement was commentary on the Vedic literature that was intended to make it more comprehensible, practicable, and contemporary. The authority of this commentary movement is described by the word *smriti* (tradition). *Smriti* provided such diverse literatures as the *Dharma Shastras,* or law codes (of which the Laws of Manu are the most famous); the writings of the six orthodox schools of philosophy; legendary works such as the *Mahabharata* and the *Ramayana;* the *Puranas* (more legendary materials, often from folk or aboriginal sources); commentaries appended to the Vedas (for example, the *Ayur-Veda*—the "Life-Veda," devoted to systematic medicine—which tradition added to the *Athavara*); tantric writings on occult and erotic matters; writings ("Agamas") peculiar to sects such as the Vaishnavites and the Shaivites; and writings on logical or ritualistic forms of thought.

The basic form of the *smriti* was the sutra, an aphorism or short sentence designed to expose the pith of a position.[23] By the end of the third century C.E., the *smriti* tradition had developed some very important and common ways of understanding the Vedic heritage that greatly shaped Hindu social life.

The great social development of the *smriti* period was the caste system. The Vedas, as noted, had spoken of the creation of humanity in terms of the four ranks: priests, warriors, merchants, and workers. In the original sacrifice, Purusha, the primal man, gave his mouth, arms, thighs, and feet to make those four ranks. However, law codes such as Manu's were required to justify casteism.[24] Apparently, casteism precedes the Aryan subjugation of the native Indians, being something common to proto-Indo-Europeans, but whether it was first based on color, occupation, tribe, or religious beliefs is unclear.[25] Modern India has tried to deemphasize both varna and jati, but they remain influential. Modern India has also tried to improve the lot of the untouchables, who lie outside the caste system, but they still exist. Thus, even now, only certain groups of people carry garbage, clean homes, work in banks, and so on.

Personal Life. From the *smriti* elaboration of Vedic tradition came another influential doctrine, that of the four legitimate life goals. These were pleasure *(kama),* wealth *(artha),* duty *(dharma),* and liberation *(moksha).* *Kama* was the lowest goal, but it was quite legitimate. *Kama* meant sexual pleasure but also the pleasure of eating, poetry, sport, and so on. *Artha* was also a legitimate goal, and around it developed learned discussions of ethics, statecraft, manners, and the like.[26] Because the person of substance propped society, wealth had a social importance and was thus more significant than pleasure.

Dharma, or duty, was higher than pleasure or wealth. It meant principle, restraint, obligation, law, and truth—the responsible acceptance of one's social station and its implications. So in the *Bhagavad Gita,* Krishna appeals to Arjuna's dharma as a warrior: It is his duty to fight, and better one's own duty done poorly than another's done well. *Moksha* meant liberation, freedom, and escape. It was the highest goal of life, because it represented the term of one's existence: self-realization in freedom from karma (the influences of past actions) and ignorance. The concept of *moksha* meant that life is samsaric—precarious and illusory. It also meant that pleasure, wealth, and even duty all could be snares.

As a complement to its exposition of life goals, *smriti* also analyzed the stages in the ideal unfolding of a life.[27] For the upper classes (excluding the workers), the four stages, or *ashramas,* were student, householder, hermit, and wandering mendicant. In a one-hundred-year life, each would last about twenty-five years. In studenthood, the young male would apprentice himself to a guru to learn the Vedic tradition and develop his character. Depending on his caste, this would last eight to twelve years and dominate the first quarter of his life. Then he would marry, raise children, and carry out social responsibilities. Hindu society honored marriage, and the economic, political, and social responsibilities of the householder gave him considerable esteem. Indeed, Buddhist asceticism caused some Hindu thinkers to reemphasize the dignity of this phase of the life cycle.

When the householder saw his children's children, however, *smriti* urged him to retire from active life and start tending his soul. He could still give advice and be helpful in secular affairs, but he should increasingly detach himself from the world. Finally, free of worldly concern, seeking only *moksha,* the ideal Hindu would end his life as a poor, wandering ascetic. Thereby, he would be an object lesson in the true purpose of human life, a teacher of what mattered most.

In effect, this scheme meant an ideal development (not often realized but still influential) of learning one's tradition, gaining worldly experience, appropriating both tradition and experience by solitary reflection, and finally consummating one's time by uniting with ultimate reality. From conception to burial, numerous ceremonies have paced the Hindu through this cycle. The most important have been adornment with the sacred thread (signaling sufficient maturity to begin studying the Vedas), marriage, and funerary rites. Women have fallen outside this scheme. During most of Hindu history, their schooling, such as it was, took place at home, and they were not eligible for *moksha.*[28]

Case Study: Stories from the Mahabharata.   Two stories from the *Mahabharata* illustrate the ambivalent status to which the brahmins had fallen by the time native Indian developments were challenging and expanding the religious outlook one finds in the Vedas.

The first story might be called "The Curse of a Brahmin."[29] It shows the power attributed to brahmins and also the colorful world of supernatural forces that has long delighted Hindus.

Once the great King Parikshit went hunting. Wounding a deer, he chased it deep into an unfamiliar forest. There he came upon a hermitage with an old ascetic priest sitting near some cows. The king approached the brahmin, told him who he was, and asked him whether he had seen the wounded deer. But the brahmin gave the king no answer, for the brahmin had taken a vow of silence. The king repeated his question, and when he again received no reply, he got very angry. Gazing around, he spied a dead snake, lifted it with the end of his bow, and hung it around the priest's neck to shame him. The brahmin still did not utter a sound, so the king gave up and returned home empty-handed.

The old brahmin had a son, and when the son's friends heard of the incident, they teased the boy about his father's disgrace. The son asked his friends how his father had come to have a dead snake hung round his neck, and the friends told him the story of King Parikshit's visit. The son reacted angrily, cursing the king: "May Takshaka, the king of the serpents, kill this wretch who placed a dead snake upon the shoulders of my frail, old father."

When he returned home, the son told his father how he had cursed the king. The old brahmin was not pleased. Ascetics, he said, should not behave so impetuously. The son had forgotten that they lived under the protection of King Parikshit, who defended all the

MAJOR VEDAS	
Rig-Veda	Hymns manifesting mythology and prayers
Atharva-Veda	Materials concerning magic of special interest to Brahmins
Sama-Veda	Mantras to be chanted at various sacrifices of soma (ritual liquor)
Yajur-Veda	Priestly textbook on the Vedic ritual as a whole

MARGAS (PATHS)	
Meditation *(Dhyana)*	Experience one's unity with the ALL. Gain self-possession. Go below sensations, feelings, images, ideas, volitions to essential spirit (experience *samadhi*).
Study *(Jnana)*	Gain an intuitive understanding of religious truths. Grasp the wisdom expressed in the scriptures and tradition, through mystical insight.
Work (Karma)	Purify one's action through detachment from its fruits. Carry out one's social responsibilities blamelessly.
Love (Bhakti)	Devote oneself to a god or goddess. Make service and emotional attachment to a divinity the core of one's life and hope.

priests of his realm. The king had not known of the father's vow, so he should be forgiven much of his anger and bad behavior.

To try to repair the damage of his son's action, the brahmin promised to send a messenger to warn the king. Both the father and the son knew, though, that the curse of a brahmin could never be thwarted.

When the old brahmin's messenger told the king of the curse, Parikshit was saddened by how he had abused the priest. He was also worried about his life, so he took counsel with his ministers about how to protect himself. They advised him to build a high platform, standing on tall posts, so that no one could approach him unobserved, and to remain there for seven days. The king followed this advice and moved his living quarters to the platform.

Toward the end of the seven-day period, the serpent king Takshaka sent several of his servants to King Parikshit disguised as ascetics. Not sensing any danger, King Parikshit allowed the ascetics to mount his platform and accepted their gifts of water, nuts, and fruit. When the ascetics had departed, King Parikshit invited his counselors to enjoy the gifts with him. But just as he was about to bite into a piece of fruit, an ugly black and copper-colored insect crawled out. The king looked at the setting sun, which was ending the seventh day, gathered his courage, and dared Takshaka to assume his true form and fulfill the brahmin's curse. No sooner had he said this than the insect turned into a huge serpent and coiled itself around the king's neck. Bellowing a tremendous roar, Takshaka killed the king with a single mighty bite.

The story has several morals. First, it teaches the exalted status of priests. Dealing with holy things and marshaling great spiritual power by their ascetic practices, priests can perform marvels that ordinary humans can barely conceive. Therefore ordinary humans, including kings, ought to deal respectfully with priests.

Second, however, a brahmin's very power imposes on him the responsibility to stay above petty emotions that might lead him to abuse this power. Thus the old father was deeply disturbed by his son's intemperate curse. A brahmin's power ought to serve the people around him, improving their lives. The many Hindu stories in which priests do not act as ideally as they should suggest that the common people often found their priests wanting.

Third, the story piquantly illustrates the intimacy with nature that popular Hinduism has retained. Even though the Upanishads were pressing toward a purely spiritual conception of reality, in which a single Brahman would relativize the reality of both human beings and snakes, the popular religion that came out of the period of native challenge stayed deeply immersed in the cosmological myth. (The cosmological myth is the assumption that all things that exist live within physical nature, the span from heaven to earth. With this assumption, gods and human beings, serpents and kings, become more alike than unlike one another.) This made for a very lively and imaginative "reality," in which curses such as the brahmin's were plausible enough to teach both priests and commoners a religious lesson.

The second story from the *Mahabharata* might be called "The Well of Life."[30] It offers a dramatic picture of the dangers of samsaric existence.

Once there was a brahmin who wandered into a dark forest filled with wild animals. Indeed, so ferocious were the lions, elephants, and other great beasts of this forest that even Yama, the god of death, would only enter it when absolutely necessary. The brahmin only came to sense the wicked nature of the dark forest gradually, but then he grew more and more fearful. Panicking, he found himself running in circles, becoming more and more confused.

Finally the brahmin looked about on every side and saw that the forest was caught in a huge net held by a giant woman with outstretched arms. There were five-headed serpents everywhere, so tall that their heads nearly reached the heavens. Then the brahmin came to a clearing, with a deep well covered by vines and underbrush. Running frantically from a wild elephant that was pursuing him, he stumbled into the well, fell through the brush, and lodged halfway to the bottom, held upside down by a few vines.

At the bottom of the well was a huge snake. Above him waited the great elephant, which had six faces and twelve feet. To the side, in the vines that held him, were many bees that had built hives and filled them with honey. When the honey dripped toward him, the brahmin reached out to catch it in his mouth. The more honey he ate, the more he could not satisfy his thirst for it. Meanwhile, black and white rats gnawed at the vines holding him. Though the elephant stood guard above, the serpent stood guard below, the bees buzzed on all sides, and the rats gnawed at his lifeline, the brahmin continued to grope for more honey.

As many Hindu commentators have made clear, the story is an allegory for the human condition. The forest is the limited sphere of our life, dark and filled with dangers. The woman holding a net over the forest is the process of aging, which allows no human life to escape. The beasts of the forest are the diseases and other forces that can destroy us, while the serpent at the bottom of the well is time, which eventually receives all living things. The six-faced elephant with twelve feet is the year, with its twelve months, while the black and white rats are night and day, the devourers of our life spans. Finally, the honey is the pleasures of life, for which our thirst seems unslakable.

The allegory, then, paints human life as tragic. Despite danger on all sides, we persist in pursuing transient pleasures. This is illusion with a vengeance. It is attachment making us oblivious to the great questions of what direction we should be taking and how we ought to be battling death. If we are ever to escape the painful circle of rebirths, which ensures that life after life we will suffer fear and pain, we must realize our self-imposed bondage. Plunging heedlessly into a dangerous life, we are soon fleeing in panic. We have gotten in over our heads, and before long we are upside down in an inescapable pit. Above and below, the many forms of time wait like jailers, ensuring that we stay in terrible danger. Meanwhile, day and night nibble our life span away.

Clearly, the story wants to impress upon its hearers the fearsome nature of unreflective living. If we simply live instinctively, pursuing the pleasures of the senses and fleeing the pains, we will end up in the most trying of circumstances. Only by estimating correctly the lay of the land and refusing to get trapped in life's forests or fall into time's snares can we escape a tragic ending. Only by avoiding the whole battlefield of time can we enter into true freedom.

The Hindu keys to true freedom, therefore, are attention and detachment. We must watch where we are going, and we must stay free of worldly desires. The brahmin of the story is pathetic because his calling or station especially should have educated him in these virtues. Were he noble in substance rather than just noble in name, he would not have wandered into the forest aimlessly. Similarly, he would not have abandoned himself to the sweet honey, forgetting his mortal peril. By meditation, sacrifice, austerities within and austerities without, he would have had hold of his time and been powerful in spirit. Then the beasts would have held no terrors, the well would have gaped to no avail. But, the story implies, few priests or few people of any station are true brahmins, strong in spirit, so most people find aging a fearsome process.

The Period of Reform and Elaboration

From about 300 to 1200 C.E., the various movements that criticized or amplified the Vedic heritage resulted in a full reform and elaboration of Hinduism. Of course, it is difficult to distinguish additions, such as those of the *smriti* writings, from revisions, but we can see in the growth of the six orthodox philosophies (described below) and the rise of the major Hindu sects developments that effectively revamped Hinduism.

A convenient distinction in the discussion that follows is that between those who reject the Vedas (for example, materialists, Jains, and Buddhists), called *nastikas* ("those who say no"), and those who accept the Vedas, called *astikas* ("those who say yes"). The orthodox philosophies, or *darshanas,* originated with *astikas*. In other words, the orthodox philosophies were conceived as explanations of *shruti* (revelation). There are six such philosophies or schools: Mimamsa, Samkhya, Yoga, Nyaya, Vaisheshika, and Vedanta.[31] We can content ourselves with explaining **Vedanta,** the most celebrated *darshana*.

Vedanta. Shankara, the greatest of the Vedanta thinkers, was a Malabar brahmin of the ninth century who tried to systematize the Upanishads in terms of "unqualified nondualism" (*advaita*). In other words, he tried to explain the basic Upanishadic concepts of

Brahman and atman with consistency and rigor. To do this, Shankara first established that there are two kinds of knowledge, higher and lower. Lower knowledge is under the limitations of the intellect, while higher knowledge is free of such limitations.

The limitations of the intellect include its reasoning character, its dependence on the senses, and its dependence on the body to act. These limitations are all subjective, since they are limitations of the knower, or subject. The objective limitations to knowledge, due to aspects of the known thing, are space, time, change, and cause-effect relationships. Because of objective limitations, we tend not to see or grasp reality in itself.

Higher knowledge comes by a direct perception that is free of either subjective or objective limitations. In practice it is the direct vision that the seers who produced the Vedas enjoyed—*shruti*. Quite likely, therefore, Shankara assumed that the Vedanta philosopher practices a yoga like that of the ancient sages. If so, he assumed that the Vedanta philosopher experiences a removal of the veil between the self and Brahman (with which the self is actually identified).

Shankara then applied this theory of higher and lower knowledge to *hermeneutics,* the study of textual interpretation. According to Shankara, all passages of the Upanishads that treat Brahman as *one* derive from higher knowledge; all references to Brahman as *many* or dual derive from lower knowledge. We can paraphrase this by saying that Brahman in itself is one and beyond all limitations, while Brahman for us (as we perceive it through sensation and reasoning) appears to be multiple—to be both in the world and beyond it, both material cause and prime mover.

With the subtlety of a great philosopher, Shankara wove the two edges of Brahman-in-itself and Brahman-for-us into a seamless whole. With the religious hunger of a mystic, he sought to correlate the within and the without. Shankara's core affirmation in his philosophical construction was that reality within is identical with reality without: Atman is Brahman. In other words, when one realizes through revelation, or higher knowledge, that there is no change, no space-time limitations, no cause-effect qualifications to the real, one then discovers that there is no self. Rather, there is only the Self, the Brahmanic reality that one directly perceives to be the ground of both internal and external being.

From the perspective of lower knowledge, there is, of course, a personal, separate, changing self. In absolute terms, though, there is one indivisible reality that is both subjectivity and objectivity, that is atman-Brahman. Since we rarely perceive directly, we often live and move in **maya** (illusion). The world of maya is not unreal in the sense that there are no elephants in it to break your foot if you get in the way of a circus parade. The elephants in the world of maya are substantial, their dung is mighty, and their step will crush your foot. But this viewpoint has limited validity. From a higher viewpoint, all that goes on in maya has no independent existence. The elephants' movement is a "play" of the only reality that exists independently—that is uncaused, unconnected, sovereign, and fully real.[32]

Vaishnavism. In the period of reformation, then, keen speculative minds tried to rehabilitate the Vedic heritage by showing the reasonableness of *shruti.* It is doubtful that they directly converted more than a few intellectuals, but they did impressively demonstrate that orthodox Hinduism, through Vedic revelation, could enable one to make powerful interpretations of reality. The more popular reformations of Vedism were theistic movements that brought the energies of Bhagavata (devotionalism) back into the Vedic fold. Two principal such movements centered on Vishnu and Shiva. Although both these movements were targeted at the common person's allegiance and presented quite different versions of divinity, they both advanced Vedic tradition and made a religion that combined some intellectual clout with much emotional enthusiasm. The main determinant of why one clung to one's particular god was a combination of social factors (the religion of one's family, jati, geographic area) and personal temperament.

The theistic religion centered on Vishnu (Vaishnavism) got its impetus from the patronage of the Gupta kings in the fourth century C.E. Perhaps the most winning aspect of Vaishnavite doctrine was its notion that the god is concerned about human beings, fights with them against demon enemies, and sends incarnations of himself (avatars) to assist humans in troubled times. In one traditional list there are ten avatars, the most important being Rama (the hero of the epic *Ramayana*), Krishna, Buddha(!), and Kalki (who is yet to come).

Vishnu himself is associated with water. According to tradition, the Ganges flows from under his feet while he rests on the coils of a great serpent. He is gracious to human beings, sending them many avatars of himself to help them when they are in need. Often he rides the great bird Garuda and is pictured as blue. Like an ancient monarch, he carries a conch shell, a battle discus, a club, and a lotus. Frequently he has four arms, to signify his great power to fight evil, and his consort is the much-beloved Lakshmi.

Vaishnavism promoted itself in several ways. Two of the most effective tied Vishnu to the bhakti cult. Between the sixth and the sixteenth centuries, the *Puranas* (legendary accounts of the exploits of gods and heroes) pushed Vishnu to the fore. The *Bhagavata Purana,* perhaps the most influential, was especially successful in popularizing the avatar Krishna. In fact, the tenth book of the *Bhagavata Purana,* which celebrates Krishna's affairs with the girls who tended cows *(gopis),* mixes erotic entertainment with symbolism of the divine-human relationship. As the cow-girls were rapt before Krishna, so could the devotee's spirit swoon before god. When one adds the stories of Krishna's extramarital affairs with Radha, his favorite *gopi,* the religious eros becomes quite intense. The *Puranas* were thus the first vehicle to elevate Vishnu and his prime avatar to the status of bhakti (devotional) gods.

Vaishnavite bhakti was promoted in southern India during the seventh and eighth centuries.[33] There Tamil-speaking troubadours called *alvars* ("persons deep in wisdom") spread devotion to Vishnu by composing religious songs. However, their wisdom was simply a deep love of Vishnu, a love that broke the bonds of caste and worldly station. The constant theme of the songs was Vishnu's own love and compassion for human beings, which moved him to send his avatars. The *alvars* were so successful that they practically ousted Buddhism from India, and they were the main reason that Vishnu-Krishna became the most attractive and influential Hindu god.

Vaishnavism also had the good fortune of attracting the religious philosopher Ramanuja,[34] who is now second only to Shankara in prestige. Ramanuja lived in the eleventh century, and his main accomplishment was elaborating the Upanishadic doctrine in a way that made divinity compatible with human love. This way goes by the name *vishishtadvaita*—"nondualism qualified by difference." It opposed the unqualified nondualism of Shankara, whom Ramanuja regarded as his philosophical enemy. For Ramanuja, Brahman consisted of three realities: the unconscious universe of matter, the conscious community of finite selves, and the transcendent lord Ishvara.

Furthermore, Ramanuja held that the Upanishadic formula "This thou art" meant not absolute identity between atman and Brahman but a relationship: the psychological oneness that love produces. The highest way to liberation was therefore loving devotion to the highest lord who represented Brahman. Knowledge and pure action were good paths, but love was better. By substituting Vishnu or Krishna for Brahman or Ishvara, the Vaishnavites made Ramanuja a philosophical defender of their bhakti. For those who wanted to reformulate revealed doctrine through love, Ramanuja was the man.

Shaivism. An alternative to Vaishnavism was Shaivism—devotion to Shiva. Shankara had been a Shaivite, but his intellectualism hardly satisfied the common person's desires for an emotional relationship with divinity. Shiva was the Lord of the Dance of Life and the Destroyer who terminated each era of cosmic time. From the earliest available evidence, Shaivism was a response to this wild god. It was frequently a source of emotional excesses, and its tone always mixed love with more fear and awe than Vaishnavism did.[35]

For an extreme example, one of the earliest Shaivite sects, which the *Mahabharata* calls Pashupati, taught that to end human misery and transcend the material world, one had to engage in such rituals as smearing the body with cremation ashes; eating excrement, carrion, or human flesh; drinking from human skulls; simulating sexual intercourse; and frenzied dancing. Through such bizarre behavior, it wanted to symbolize the reversal of worldly, samsaric values that true religious devotion implied. Less defensibly, members of other sects, such as the eleventh-century Kalamukha (named for the black mark they wore on their foreheads), became notorious as drug addicts, drunkards, and even murderers.[36] Even when Shaivites were thoroughly respectable, their religion was more fiery and zealous in its asceticism than that of the love-struck but more refined Vaishnavites. Shaivite priests came from all social classes, and Shaivite followers often regarded the *lingam* as Shiva's main emblem. The *lingam* symbolized the phallus and sexual creativity in general, as well as the dedication and intensification of this power through asceticism. Parallel to the Vaishnavite *alvars* were the Shaivite *adiyars,* whose poetry and hymns were a principal factor in Shiva's rise to prominence, especially in southern India.

The Shaivite movement also received royal patronage in southern India from the fifth to the tenth centuries. During those centuries the Shaivites waged war against both the Buddhists and the Jains. After

winning that fight they turned on the Vaishnavites, singing of Shiva's superiority to Vishnu. In their theology they stressed not only the Lord of the Cosmic Dance and the god of fertility and destruction but also the hidden god. (Shiva also had such forms as the householder and the ascetic, representing several stages in the life cycle.) Even the worship of the phallus was enshrouded in mystery by placing it behind a veil. In addition, Shaivites often substituted representations of Nandi, Shiva's bull, or one of his *shaktis* (consorts) for the god himself. Finally, to stress Shiva's ability to transcend all opposites, his followers often depicted him as androgynous. Since the Shaivite often became identified with the god, Shaivism was more like yoga than was Vaishnavism, in which the worshiper and deity remained two.

The worshiper of Shiva grew conscious that he or she was a sinner through mysterious rituals and Shiva's own symbols of fire and a skull. As a result, there was less equality, less of the lover-beloved relationship, between the devotee and Shiva than what one found in Vaishnavism. The Shaivite might deprecatingly refer to himself or herself as a dog. That the god would come to such a person was pure grace. Worship, then, was essentially gratitude that the tempestuous god chose to forgive rather than destroy.

Shaktism. A last reformation of the Hindu tradition came through movements that scholars group as Shaktism or Tantrism.[37] This sort of Hinduism focused on secret lore whose prime objective was to liberate the energies of imagination, sex, and the unconscious. Insofar as Shiva's *shaktis* represented the energy of female divinity, they exemplified Tantrist powers. The general name of the ancient female divinity is Maha-Devi, whom we discuss below in her form of Kali.

It is hard to know exactly what *shakti* sects believed and practiced, because most of their rites were secret, but one of their main beliefs was that the union of coitus is the best analogy for the relationship between the cosmos and its energy flow. This belief seems to have spawned a theory of parallels or dualisms, in which male-female, right-left, and positive-negative pairings all had highly symbolic aspects. Like some of Shaivism, Tantra downplayed class distinction and violated social conventions to symbolize the reversal of ordinary cultural values implied in religious conversion and realization (of union with divine reality).

One of the many Tantrist rituals for gaining *moksha* was called *chakrapuja* (circle worship). In it men and women (Tantrist groups tended to admit members without regard for sex or caste) used a series of elements (all having Sanskrit names beginning with the letter *m*) that might facilitate union with Shakti: wine, meat, fish, parched rice, and copulation. In right-hand Tantrism these elements were symbols. Left-hand Tantrism used the actual elements [not hedonistically but with ritual discipline, to participate in maya (reality's play)]. Other Tantrist practices involved meditation to arouse the *kundalini*—the snake of energy lying dormant at the base of the spine.[38]

Overall, the reformation and elaboration of the Vedic tradition meant expanded roles for some Vedic gods and a shift of popular religion from sacrifice to devotional, theistic worship. The renovators tried to defend and extend their ancient heritage, allowing people to respond to any part of it that they found attractive. In this way they created an eclectic religion tolerant of diversity in religious doctrine and practice.

The Period of Foreign Challenge

From about 1200 C.E. on, Hinduism increasingly contended with foreign cultures, rulers, and religions. Islam and Christianity both made serious impacts on Indian life, and their presence is felt to this day. Islam, a factor in India from the eighth century on, first affected Indians of the Sind and Punjab regions in the northwestern part of ancient India, where Muslims traded and made military conquests. Invasions in the eleventh century put much of the Indus Valley region under Muslim control, and by 1206 Islam had conquered most of northern India. By 1335, Muslims controlled the south as well, and their final dynasty, the Mogul, did not end until 1858.

The policies of Muslim leaders toward Hinduism varied. Many were tolerant and allowed the Indians freedom to practice their traditional ways. Others, such as the Mogul zealot Aurangzeb (ruled 1658–1707), attempted to establish a thoroughly Muslim state and so tried to stop drinking, gambling, prostitution, the use of narcotics, and other practices that were prohibited by Islamic doctrine. Aurangzeb destroyed more than 200 Hindu temples in 1679 alone, and he discriminated against Hindus in the collection of taxes, custom duties, and various other ways.

The permanent changes that Islam made in Hinduism and that Hinduism made in Indian Islam are hard to determine because the two faiths are intertwined. Islamic architecture and learning influenced Hinduism deeply, while Hindu casteism affected Indian Muslims as well. Muslim fundamentalism, based on the belief that the Qur'an is God's final word, probably upgraded the status of the Hindu Vedas, and many Hindus found Sufism, the devotional branch of Islam, quite compatible with their native bhakti practices.

On the other hand, Muslim tendencies to regard many Hindu devotional practices (for example, reverencing cows and praying to many deities) idolatrous complicated relations between the religions. Indeed, in modern times tensions have led not only to the partition of India but to much bloodshed.

One definite result of Islam's presence in India was a new religion, Sikhism. Traces of it were found among Hindus who considered aspects of Islam very attractive, but it actually began as a result of the revelations of the prophet Nanak, a Punjabi born in 1469. Nanak's visions prompted him to sing the praise of a divinity that blended elements of the Muslim Allah and the Hindu trinity of Brahma, Vishnu, and Shiva. This God he called the True Name. The religious prescriptions for serving the True Name that he set for his followers were rather severe and anticeremonial, steering away from Hindu pilgrimages and devotions and favoring compassion and neighborly good deeds. The Sikhs developed into a small but hardy religious band, and on numerous occasions they proved to be excellent warriors. They number about six million in India today, and their great shrine remains in Amritsar in the northwest. Many of the other holy Sikh sites, however, are now in Pakistan because of the 1947 partition.[39]

Christianity has been present in India since the first century C.E., according to stories about the apostle Thomas's adventures there. It is more certain that a bishop of Alexandria sent a delegation to India in 189 and that an Indian representative attended the Council of Nicaea (325). Only in the sixteenth century, however, did the Christian missionary presence become strong, in the wake of Portuguese (and later Dutch and English) traders. The British East India Company, founded in 1600, increasingly controlled the Indian economy and trade, and after the Sepoy Mutiny in 1857 the company, which had become a sort of government, gave way to direct colonial rule. When India became independent in 1947, after almost a century of British colonial rule, it had some experience with the political ideas and social institutions of the modern West. Christianity therefore usually has had a colonial character.

The Christian impact, as distinguished from the Western impact, has not been impressive statistically.

According to 1990 census figures, only 2.43 percent of all Indians considered themselves Christians. Nevertheless, Christians opened hundreds of charitable institutions, especially schools, and were responsible for the first leprosaria. They also promoted hospital care for the tuberculous and the insane. In fact, Christianity's greatest impact was probably the rousing of the Hindu social conscience. The tradition of dharma as social responsibility had not resulted in the establishment of institutions for the poor and sickly. While Western culture opened India to modern science, technology, and democratic political theory, Western religion drove home the ideal of social concern. Mother Teresa of Calcutta continues that tradition today. On the other hand, a colonial Christianity often seemed racist and blind to native Indian genius and needs.

Modern Bhakti. The native Hindu movements during the past seven centuries have not been particularly social.[40] Perhaps in reaction to foreign rulers, the masses tended to focus on somewhat privatized, devotional religion. After the elaboration of the ancient tradition, Hinduism directed itself toward the further development of bhakti. Islamic Sufism stimulated this tendency, as we suggested above. In the religious poetry of Kabir (1440–1518), a forerunner of the Sikh founder Nanak, the love of God became the heart of a religion that ignored distinctions between Muslims and Hindus, priests and workers.[41] For Kabir this love correlated with a pure heart only.

For Ramananda, who was both the teacher of Kabir and a follower of the philosopher Ramanuja, the important thing was to adore God, whom Ramananda called Rama, with fervent devotion. Rama considered all persons equal. In southern India, especially among the people who spoke Tamil, the Lord Vishnu increasingly appeared as a god of pure grace. Self-concern is useless and distracting, the Tamils told their northern Vaishnavite brethren. Not works but love is redeeming.

In west-central India, from the thirteenth to the seventeenth centuries, a poetic movement called the Maratha renaissance carried the message of bhakti. Tukaram (1607–1649), the greatest poet of this movement, stressed God's otherness and the sinfulness of human beings. His god was not the Brahman who was identical with one's innermost self but a free agent and lover whose goodness in saving sinners was the more impressive because of their distance from him.

In these and other movements, modern Hinduism increasingly focused on bhakti, moving away from Vedic orthodoxy. The singers of bhakti cared little whether their doctrines squared with the Upanishads or the great commentators. The notions of *shruti* or *smriti,* in fact, meant little to them. They thought that the love they had found undercut traditional views of social classes, sex, and even religions. The god of love was no creator of castes, no despiser of women, no pawn of Hindus against Muslims. With little concern for intellectual or social implications, the singers and seers who dominated modern bhakti gave themselves over to ecstatic love.

Perhaps the greatest representative of bhakti was Chaitanya, a sixteenth-century Bengali saint whom his followers worship as an avatar of Krishna.[42] Chaitanya, originally a brahmin, converted to Vaishnavism and spent his days worshiping Lord Krishna in the great Bengali temple of Puri. Increasingly his devotions became emotional, involving singing, weeping, dancing, and epileptic fits. He died in delirium in the surf off Puri, where he was bathing. Somewhat typically for modern bhakti, Chaitanya repudiated the Vedas and nondualistic Vedanta philosophy as opposing a gracious god. All were welcome in his sect, regardless of caste, and he even sanctioned worship of a black stone, thinking it might help some followers' devotion. He stressed the followers' assimilation with Radha, Krishna's lover, arguing that the soul's relation to God is always female to male.

Yet Chaitanya also stressed the necessity to toil at religious love and opposed those who argued that grace was attained without effort. His followers deified him, seeing his unbounded religious ecstasy as the ideal communion of divinity and humanity. He was the major figure in the devotional surge toward Lord Krishna that produced some remarkable Bengali love poetry during the sixteenth and seventeenth centuries.[43] His movement has continued in the United States through the work of Swami Prabhupada, founder of the International Society for Krishna Consciousness and of the Bhaktivedanta Book Trust. The swami's monks in saffron robes on street corners, and his numerous publications,[44] have made "Hare Krishna" part of our religious vocabulary.

Partly in opposition to the excesses of bhakti and partly because of the influence of Western culture, a group of Bengali intellectuals in the early nineteenth century began to "purify" Hinduism by bringing it up to the standards that they saw in Christianity. The first such effort was the founding of the group Brahmo Samaj by Rammohan Roy in 1828. Roy was a well-educated brahmin whose contacts with Islam and

Christianity led him to think that there should be only one God for all persons, who should inspire social concern and criticism of any abuses, Hindu or Christian.

God should, for example, oppose such barbarism as suttee *(sati)*, the Hindu practice in which a widow climbed on her husband's funeral pyre and burned with him.[45] In 1811 Roy had witnessed the suttee of his sister-in-law, whom relatives kept on the pyre even though she was screaming and struggling to escape. He knew that in Calcutta alone there were more than 1,500 such immolations between 1815 and 1818. Roy pressured the British to outlaw the practice, and in 1829 a declaration was issued that forbade it (though it did not completely stamp it out). Members of the Brahmo Samaj thought this sort of social concern was essential to pure religion.[46]

Another movement to modernize Hinduism that originated in Bengal in the nineteenth century was the Ramakrishna Mission. Its founder, Ramakrishna, was an uneducated brahmin who became a mystic devotee of the goddess Kali, whom he worshiped as a divine Mother. After visions of Kali and then of Rama, the epic hero, Ramakrishna progressed through the Tantrist, Vaishnavite, and Vedanta disciplines, having the ecstatic experiences associated with the traditions of each. He even lived as a Muslim and as a Christian, learning the mystic teachings of those traditions. From such eclectic experience he developed the joyous doctrine that we can find God everywhere: Divinity beats in each human heart. Ramakrishna's teachings achieved wordwide publicity through his disciple Vivekananda, who stressed the theme of worshiping God by serving human beings. The Ramakrishna Mission has sponsored hospitals, schools, and cultural centers, and it keeps an American presence through the Vedanta Society, which has chapters in many American cities.[47]

Tagore and Gandhi.   In the twentieth century, these currents of domestic and foreign stimuli to religious and social reform inevitably affected the controversies over Indian nationalism and independence. The controversies themselves largely turned on the assets and liabilities of the British and Indian cultures. Not all Indians opposed the British, largely because they did not have a single national tradition themselves. Rather, Indians tended to think of themselves as Bengalis or Gujaratis or Punjabis—natives of their own districts, with their own respective languages and traditions. What the Indian tradition meant, therefore, was far from clear. This fact emerges in the lives of

two of the most intriguing modern-day personalities, Tagore and Gandhi.

Rabindranath Tagore (1861–1941), modern India's most illustrious writer, won the Nobel Prize for literature in 1913. His life's work was a search for artistic and educational forms that would instill Indians with a broad humanism. For this reason, he was leery of nationalism, fearing that it would crush individual creativity and blind Indians to values outside their own country. In the West, Tagore found a salutary energy, a concern for the material world, which seemed to him precisely the cure for India's deep cultural ills. However, he despised the Western industrial nations' stress on machinery, power politics, and democracy. In Tagore's renewed Hinduism, India would give and receive—give resources for individual creativity and receive Western energies for using that creativity to improve society.

Mohandas Gandhi (1869–1948) was a political genius who made some of Tagore's vision practical. He trained as a lawyer in England and found his vocation as an advocate of the masses in South Africa, where he represented "colored" minorities. In India Gandhi drew in part on a Western idealism that he culled from such diverse sources as the New Testament, Tolstoy's writings on Christian socialism, Ruskin's writings on the dignity of work, and Thoreau's writings on civil disobedience. He joined this Western idealism with a shrewd political pragmatism of his own and Indian religious notions, including the *Bhagavad Gita*'s doctrine of karma-yoga (work as a spiritual discipline) and the Jain-Hindu notion of *ahimsa* (non-injury). Gandhi's synthesis of these ideas resulted in what he called *satyagraha* (truth force). To oppose the might of Britain he used the shaming power of a simple truth: Indians, like all human beings, deserve the right to control their own destinies.

Mahatma Gandhi's autobiography, *The Story of My Experiments with Truth*, shows how his personal strivings for purity of spirit intertwined with his leadership of a political movement rooted in nonviolence. Gandhi fasted, followed a vegetarian diet, and practiced celibacy in order to free his spirit from bodily constraints, to prepare a vessel fit for the inspiration of God. He studied nonviolence in the intuitive conviction that this part of the Indian religious tradition held the key to humanity's future survival. Among his many reflections on *ahimsa* the following is typical:

> *Ahimsa* is a comprehensive principle. We are helpless mortals caught in the conflagration of *himsa*

Figure 2 *Rajghat, memorial to M. K. Gandhi in Delhi. Photo by J. T. Carmody.*

[violence]. The saying that life lives on life has a deep meaning in it. Man cannot for a moment live without consciously or unconsciously committing outward *himsa.* The very fact of his living—eating, drinking, and moving about—necessarily involves some *himsa,* destruction of life, be it ever so minute. A votary of *ahimsa* therefore remains true to his faith if the spring of all his actions is compassion, if he shuns to the best of his ability the destruction of the tiniest creature, tries to save it, and thus incessantly strives to be free from the deadly coil of *himsa.* He will be constantly growing in self-restraint and compassion, but he can never become entirely free from outward *himsa.*

Then again, because underlying *ahimsa* is the unity of all life, the error of one cannot but affect all, and hence man cannot be wholly free from *himsa.* So long as he continues to be a social being, he cannot but participate in the *himsa* that the very existence of society involves. When two nations are fighting, the duty of a votary of *ahimsa* is to stop the war. He who is not equal to that duty, he who has no power of resisting war, he who is not qualified to resist war, may take part in war, and yet wholeheartedly try to free himself, his nation and the world from war.[48]

Violence, Gandhi admits, is part of the evolutionary and political build of reality. Insofar as species live off one another, violence is a law of life that we cannot avoid. Nonetheless, we can strive to minimize our violence and destructiveness, not injuring any fellow creature needlessly. By a vegetarian diet, we can minimize our injury to fellow animals. By such traditions as the protection of the cow, India has long tried to focus nonviolence on a highly visible symbol of animal vitality. Such practices foster self-restraint and compassion, virtues especially needed in modern social affairs. The phenomenon of war, which for Gandhi probably reached its most tragic expression in the bloody conflicts between Indian Hindus and Muslims that followed upon independence from Britain, depends on upon our lack of restraint and compassion.

Surely a sagacious society, one that listened to the wisdom of its elders and traditions, would be able to muster the minimal spiritual power needed to keep itself from civil war. That India could not muster such minimal virtue sickened Gandhi's spirit. As a final irony, he ended his life the victim of a Hindu assassin, a fellow-religionist so unwise he thought killing a champion of peace would advance the Hindu cause.

Erik Erikson, whose psychoanalytic study of Gandhi won great praise a generation ago, has described the Mahatma as a "religious actualist":

If, for the sake of the game, I should give his unique presence a name that would suit my views, I would call him a *religious actualist.* In my clinical ruminations I have found it necessary to split what we mean by "real" into that which can be known because it is demonstrably correct (factual reality) and that which feels effectively true in action (actuality). Gandhi absorbed from Indian culture a conception of truth *(sat)* which he attempted to make actual in all compartments of human life and along all the stages which make up its course . . . while he learned to utilize craftily what was his first professional identity, namely, that of a barrister English style, and while he then became a powerful politician Indian style, he also strove to grasp the "business" of religious men, namely, to keep his eyes trained upon the all-embracing circumstance that each of us exists with a unique consciousness and a responsibility of his own which makes him at the same time zero and everything, a center of absolute silence, and the vortex of apocalyptic participation. A man who looks through the historical parade of cultures and civilizations, styles, and isms which provide most of us with a glorious and yet miserably fragile sense of immortal identity, defined status, and collective grandeur faces the central truth of our nothingness—and, mirabile dictu [marvelous to say], gains power from it.[49]

Gandhi was a genius at symbolizing truth force. In Joan Bondurant's study,[50] one can see how he worked out *satyagraha* campaigns of civil disobedience, striking, marshaling public support, and so on. In Erik Erikson's study of Gandhi at middle age, one can see the psychological roots of *satyagraha* and something of its promise as an instrument for sociopolitical change in the nuclear age. In Gandhi himself one can see the conflicts, confusion, and

riches of the Hindu tradition in the mid-twentieth century, for he called himself just a seeker of *moksha,* just a servant of the one god found whenever we harken to truth.

Contemporary Hinduism: Popular Religion

As we have already stressed, Hinduism is an umbrella for a great variety of different religious ideas and practices. Of necessity, we have concentrated on the ideas and practices that stand out when one attempts a historical overview. The outstanding ideas, however, tend to be the possession of intellectuals, at least in their reflective form. For the common people, it tends to be the many rituals of the Hindu religious year that mediate the sense of unity with the world that religion seeks to inculcate. To conclude our historical survey, we concentrate on a few of the rituals that fill popular Hinduism today. Let us begin with an anthropologist's description of how a village of central India celebrated *Naumi,* a high point of a festival devoted to nine goddesses.[51]

Naumi occurs in the fall, in either September or October. It is the ninth day of the festival of the nine goddesses—a sort of arithmetic highpoint. In the afternoon of Naumi, the main activity is a procession of men possessed by gods. Throughout the entire festival of the nine goddesses mediums are constantly making contact with the supernatural world, so the procession of possessed men is a kind of climax to their work.

In this village, the two principal mediums were a weaver and a carpenter. The weaver claimed that his tutelary spirit was the mother goddess *(Mata),* while the carpenter claimed that he was directed by the spirit of a local incarnation of Vishnu. The weaver's behavior was the more elaborate of the two. For the entire nine days of the festival, he fasted, living in a small hut adorned only with a picture of Mata, five baskets of sprouting wheat, and a few ritual objects. People visited him during these days, asking for help with their personal problems. For example, a woman asked the weaver what she should do for pains in her back. He gave her some grains of sorghum to eat and told her to offer a gift to the goddess.

The carpenter claimed that he could not afford to spend the whole nine days away from his work, so he held only limited sessions for clients. However, the carpenter's sessions had the strong support of the local headman (and so drew the wealthier people), because the headman had once consulted him about obtaining a son and had his request granted by the carpenter's guiding spirit.

On the afternoon of Naumi, at the climax of the feast, both mediums held rites in their houses. The followers of the carpenter sacrificed rice and ghee to his god, while the followers of the weaver sacrificed a goat. Both mediums then led their followers to the center of the town, where they processed to the pounding of drums. On this occasion some magicians enlivened the proceedings. Indeed, one magician continually excited the weaver, who was in trance, by sleight-of-hand tricks with limes. The magician would make the limes appear and then disappear. Since limes are thought to accompany the mother goddess, each time the limes appeared the weaver would become beside himself with expectation, thinking his special god had drawn near. The procession also had a fertility aspect, for some of the men carried seedlings which they finally sunk in a well outside the village, to "cool" them for the best growth.

In the evening the people sacrificed a goat at each of the three principal shrines, trying to assure the town's good fortune in the coming year. They also purified themselves with fire, walking between two flames and passing through the flames their tools, butter churns, swords, and the like. The anthropologist reporting these customs was advised to pass across his ever-present pen and camera.

Although the afternoon procession was the most popular part of Naumi (in large measure because it drew magicians and other showmen), the evening sacrifices, performed for the welfare of the whole village, were no less important. In fact, in the evening some people visited all forty-four of the village's shrines, praying for all the gods' help during the coming year. (Since there were only about 900 people in the village, there was one shrine for about every twenty people.) The order of visitation shows how the village ranked these shrines: mother goddess, smallpox goddess, Vaishnavite Temple, another mother goddess, lord of the south village gates, Shaivite Temple, local small god, god of the nath caste, temple where a treaty was signed with some marauders, local mother goddess, temple of the brahmin caste, another Vaishnavite Temple, and more.

The anthropologist reporting this bevy of temples did not always know precisely what function a given god was thought to perform, and his mention of so many castes shows the splintered character of Indian

village society even in recent times. The temples concerned with smallpox, cholera, and leprosy are a sad commentary on rural Indian health, while the several temples dedicated to the mother goddess show that recent folk Hinduism has continued India's millennial adoration of the Great Mother, the primal source of life and comfort.

The rituals of folk Hinduism vary from geographic area to geographic area, depending on local gods and customs. Among Hindus of the Himalayas, a strong shamanistic influence remains. Many of these people's religious ceremonies involve a shaman's possession (much like the possession of central Indian mediums such as the weaver and carpenter). More often than not, a family calls upon a shaman because of some misfortune: "Most supernatural beings make their presence felt by imposing difficulties or troubles upon people—usually disease or death to people or animals, and sometimes other troubles such as hysteria, faithless spouses, sterility, poor crops, financial loss, or mysterious disappearance of belongings."[52] When such things happen, people usually ask a shaman to hold a seance. Thus, a goodly number of ad hoc ceremonies supplement the annual cycle of ceremonies similar to Naumi.

The shaman may be from any caste, and he tends to make his living by acting as the medium of a particular god. Usually he opens a consultation by singing prayers in honor of his god, to the steady beat of a drum. As he enters into trance, often he becomes impervious to pain, as he demonstrates by touching red-hot metal. When the god has taken full possession of the shaman, the god usually uses the shaman's voice to tell the client what is troubling him and what should be done to cure it. The god may also identify thieves or harmful articles that have brought the misfortune. If the clients do not like the god's diagnosis or advice, they simply go to a different shaman.

More often than not, the treatment the god suggests is performing a *puja* (short ceremony) in honor of the being that is causing the trouble. (In the case of a ghost, the *puja* amounts to an exorcism.) Other popular treatments are making pilgrimages or removing harmful objects causing disease. If the case is impossible to cure (for example, a person deranged beyond healing), the god may prescribe an impossible treatment (for example, the sacrifice of a cow; since the cow is sacred to Hindus, sacrificing a cow is unthinkable).

If the suggested cure is performing a *puja*, other religious specialists generally enter the scene. Their job is arranging and executing a ceremony in which the god can enter a human body, ideally that of the victim, dance in it, and make known any further demands. These *puja* specialists usually come from the lower castes, and their basic method of inducing the god's possession of the victim is playing percussion instruments.

The ceremony tends to unfold in three parts: the dance, the *puja* or prayer proper, and the offering. Usually the ceremony takes place in the shrine of the god who is concerned. The shrine itself is very simple, generally consisting of one to four iron tridents about 8 inches high. The people place these in a niche in the wall, if the shrine is indoors, or at the base of a large stone, if it is outside, in effect marking off a sacred space. During the ceremonies the shrine is lighted by a small oil lamp, and often a container of rice and small coins hangs near it, as an offering to the god.

The dance, which begins the ceremony, is intended to attract the god (or any other spirit or ancestor who likes to dance in the bodies of humans). The gods are thought to like dancing because it gives them a chance to air their complaints and needs. Dancing most often occurs in the evening, but sometimes it is repeated the following day. As the drummers increase the intensity of the beat and the room fills with onlookers, smoke, and heat, the rhythms become more compelling, until someone, either the victim or an onlooker, starts to jerk, shout, and dance, first slowly but then more wildly. The possessed person is honored with incense and religious gestures, and fed boiled rice, because for the moment he or she is the god.

After the god has danced his fill, he usually speaks through the possessed person, telling the cause of his anger (the source of the misfortune) and detailing what it will take to appease him. The victimized person and his or her family then make a short prayer to the god, expressing reverently their desire to comply with his requests, after which they make the offering the god has demanded.

The most frequent offering is a young male goat. The people place the goat before the shrine and throw rice on its back, while the ritual specialist chants mantras. When the goat shakes itself, the onlookers believe the god has accepted their offering. An attendant (usually from a low caste; higher caste people tend to consider this defiling) takes the goat outside and beheads it. The attendant then places a foot and the head of the animal before the shrine, as an offering to the god, along with such delicacies as bread and sweet rice. The ritual specialist eventually gathers these up,

as part of his fee, and the family and guests share the rest of the goat.

The anthropologist describing this kind of ceremony found that the villagers strongly believed in its efficacy. Thus one teenage boy attributed his father's recovery from pneumonia to a possession ceremony, while another informant opined that the gods are like lawyers: The more you give them, the more they will do on your behalf. Clearly, therefore, the villagers of the Himalayas, as much as the villagers of central India, have continued to supplement the more official festivals of the Vedic gods with many local folk practices.

A third sort of ritual common in contemporary Indian religion deals with a stage of the life cycle, helping a person cope with puberty, marriage, parenthood, or widowhood. The *habisha* ritual performed by middle-aged women in the eastern province of Orissa illustrates this sort. To begin, the anthropologist making the report notes that the *habisha* ritual is a *brata* or vowed observance: "Historically, vows have been an important part of Hindu ritual life for centuries. People make vows mainly to secure something in this world, such as progeny, wealth, good fortune, health, fame, or long life; sometimes people make vows to secure something in the next world; and occasionally, as in the *habisha* rites, people make vows to gain something both in this world and in the next."[53] The vows may last as short a time as a day, or as long as the rest of one's life, but whatever their time, they are serious business. As the stories of the *Puranas* emphasize, failure to fulfill a vow can lead to dire consequences.

Consequently, the person who makes a vow usually prepares assiduously to fulfill it, by fasting, worshiping gods, taking frequent purificatory baths, abstaining from sexual relations, refraining from drinking water or chewing betel nuts, and not sleeping during daylight hours. From this asceticism, as well as the fulfillment of the vow itself, the vower gains spiritual power. In the case of the *habisha* ritual, the spiritual power focuses on preventing the death of the woman's husband. Most *habisha* participants, in fact, are menopausal women trying to protect their husbands from death (and trying therefore to protect themselves from the sad fate of the Hindu widow).

For the women whom our source studied, participating in the *habisha* ritual, and especially going on pilgrimage to the holy town of Puri, had been the high point of their lives. Typically, the women dedicated a thirty-five-day period in October–November to purificatory rituals and fasts in honor of Jagannatha, a local version of the young god Krishna. The imaginative context of these devotions was the legendary scene of the young Krishna among his female devotees (*gopis*). Krishna was the cow herdsman and the *gopis* were the milkmaids. The *habisha* women drew scenes from this legend in rice powder, churned milk in imitation of the *gopis*, offered coconuts and cowrie shells to a replica of Krishna, and danced ecstatically to express their great love of the god. If possible, they concluded their season of devotions with a 40-mile trip to the temple of Lord Jagannatha in Puri.

The elaborate preparations of one informant show the seriousness with which Indian women can enter upon rituals like *habisha*. This informant, a fifty-five-year-old married women named Tila, was a member of the confectioner caste. Six days before the beginning of *habisha* in 1971, she had a barber trim her fingernails and toenails. Then she took a ritual bath and summoned the brahmin who usually performed ceremonies for her family. He further purified Tila by sprinkling cow-dung water on her head. Ideally, he said, people would purify themselves for *habisha* by drinking *panchagavia*, as in the old days, but nowadays few people were so thorough. *Panchagavia*, it turned out, was the five holy substances of the cow: milk, curds, clarified butter, urine, and dung. Tila apparently forewent this treat, promising, however, that she would be the brahmin's disciple for the full month, that she would listen to his daily recitation from a sacred book, and that she would fulfill her vows of fasting, purification, and sexual abstinence.

The typical day of the votive period began with a chilly predawn bath at the village pond. Facing in each of the four directions, the women involved prayed to the gods, to their ancestors, and to other sources of help, dipping into the water and purifying themselves. Then they made mud-pictures of the god Vishnu as a child, offered prayers to the rising sun, and took burning wicks to the village temple, where they chanted and prayed. These ceremonies, as well as their common dedication, bonded the women together, so that for the *habisha* month they put aside their rivalries, jealousies, and gossip. From the village temple they retired to their individual homes, where they cooked the one meal they were allowed to eat each day at sundown. Tila was allowed to eat only rice, lentils, green plantain, taro, cucumber, ginger, and custard apple—foods considered pure. She could have no spices, but each of her meals had to contain clarified butter, a holy substance from the cow.

During the *habisha* days, Tila was especially careful to avoid such defiling contacts as stepping on animal feces or touching a person from a low caste. She would join the other women for ritual baths, prayers, drawings, and above all, dances reenacting the legends of Krishna. The psychosocial explanation for these ceremonies is the upper caste Hindu woman's fear of an early widowhood. The younger the widow, the worse her fate, because widowhood means marginal status as a financial dependent, a potential source of sexual disturbance, and a being polluted by contact with death. The religious explanation is the devotional satisfaction that immersion in the theistic cult of Krishna, loving communion with Krishna, sponsors. Insofar as Krishna becomes the center of the women's emotional lives, the chance *habisha* offers them to concentrate on Krishna intensely for a whole month is a religious delight.

Two hundred fifty miles directly south of Delhi, in the town of Bharatpur, is a famous temple, the Balaji, to which many Indians come for the cure of psychosomatic illnesses. The main assumption behind the healing rituals of the temple is that most petitioners are possessed by a destructive spirit. Usually the destructive spirit has suggested its presence through symptoms such as stomach pains, headaches, or fits of uncontrollable rage. To relieve the patient of such afflictions, the priests of the temple have developed formalized processes focused on a warfare between the offending spirit and one of the protector deities resident in the temple. The ordinary start of the formalized process or ritual is the patient's overt possession by the demon, the clearest evidence of which is a rhythmic swaying of the upper half of the body and violent sideways shaking of the head. The demon may also manifest its presence by making patients beat the floor with their hands, hit their backs against the wall, or lie down on the floor with heavy stones piled on their backs. The patients enter a trancelike state (what a psychoanalyst might call a *dissociation*). They are able to carry on a conversation but generally will not remember what went on during the ritual.

The center of the process usually is a struggle between the demon and the protector god who has been invoked. The demon shouts, curses, and makes accusations or complaints through the mouth of the patient, while the onlooking crowd (the family of the patient or other pilgrims) berates the offending spirit. Generally the demon finally agrees to leave the patient, after greater or lesser struggle, and the temple priests arrange for the continuing protection of the helpful deity by giving the patient talismans to signify the protection of a good spirit. The good spirit usually will manifest itself through a shorter and calmer trance, during which the patient will offer prayers and prostrations to the protector deity. A psychoanalyst might see most of the patient's pains as symptoms of the sexual inhibition or repressed anger that Indian ideals of self-control and family peace can cause, but the framework in which the patients and priests view the sicknesses is the folk Hindu conviction that the world is populated with many spirits, both good and evil.[54]

To balance the stress on popular religion we have made in dealing with contemporary Hinduism, we should point out that the centuries-long concern for transcendence and *moksha* certainly has continued. If the rituals we have described mainly are pragmatic, concerned with helping people in everyday life, the yogic practices, study, and asceticism practiced by the religious virtuosi have kept alive the realization that religion entails more than the pragmatic and everyday. Certainly rituals such as those we have described go back to Vedic times. Certainly in all periods Hindus would have offered anthropological observers rich materials such as those mined by observers nowadays. But throughout the ages the thirst for *moksha,* leading to withdrawal from everyday affairs, celibacy, meditation, and austerity, also has been a strong component of Hindu culture. So we are wise to think of the overall tradition as a balance—a diet that offered much to both those concerned with earthly problems and those seeking heavenly release.

Critique.   In the mid-1970s, Indira Gandhi, head of the Indian government, imposed an "Emergency" to try to get her country's political and social problems under control. V. S. Naipaul, a journalist of Indian ancestry, has ruminated on the underlying causes of such problems as follows:

> In a speech before the Emergency, Jaya Prakash Narayan, the most respected opposition leader, said: "It is not the existence of disputes and quarrels that so much endangers the integrity of the nation as the manner in which we conduct them. We often behave like animals. Be it a village feud, a students' organization, a labor dispute, a religious procession, a boundary disagreement, or a major political question, we are more likely than not to become aggressive, wild, and violent. We

kill and burn and loot and sometimes commit even worse crimes."

> The violence of the riot could burn itself out; it could be controlled, as it now was, by the provisions of the Emergency. But there was an older, deeper Indian violence. This violence had survived untouched by foreign rule and had survived [Mahatma] Gandhi. It had become part of the Hindu social order, and there was a stage at which it became invisible, disappearing in the general distress. But now, with the Emergency, the emphasis was on reform, and on the "weaker sections" of society; and the stories the censored newspapers played up seemed at times to come from another age. A boy seized by a village moneylender for an unpaid debt of 150 rupees, fifteen dollars, and used as a slave for four years; in September, in Vellore in the south, untouchables forced to leave their village after their huts had been fenced in by caste Hindus and their well polluted; in October, in a village in Gujarat in the west, a campaign of terror against untouchables rebelling against forced labor and the plundering of their crops; the custom, among the untouchable men of a northern district, of selling their wives to Delhi brothels to pay off small debts to their caste landlords.

> To the ancient Aryans the untouchables were "walking carrion." Gandhi—like other reformers before him—sought to make them part of the holy Hindu system. He called them *Harijans,* children of God. A remarkable linguistic coincidence: they have remained God's chillun. Even at the Satyagraha Ashram [community] on the riverbank at Ahmedabad, which Gandhi himself founded after his return from South Africa, and from where in 1930 he started on the great Salt March. *Son et Lumière* at night these days in the ashram, sponsored by the tourism Development Corporation; and in the mornings, in one of the buildings, a school for Harijan girls. "Backward class, backward class," the old brahmin, suddenly my guide, explained piously, converting the girls into distant objects of awe. The antique violence remained: rural untouchability as serfdom, maintained by terror and sometimes by deliberate starvation. None of this was new; but suddenly in India it was news.[55]

There are some qualifiers one should place on Naipaul's observations. First, although born in Trinidad (of Indian parents) and educated at Oxford, Naipaul brings to India the sort of special sensitivity that an American of Irish extraction might bring to "the troubles" of Northern Ireland. Because the country he is observing has shaped his own genes, he sees its failures with a special acuteness. Second, one could document the failures of other religiocultural systems as graphically as Naipaul has documented the Hindu failures. His own later work, *Among the Believers*, is a scathing indictment of the foibles and horrors of the fundamentalist Islams of Pakistan, Iran, Malaysia, and Indonesia. Nazi, Soviet, Latin American, Cambodian, Chinese, African, and other failures, atrocities, and inhumanities blot the social records of the religions that have held sway in those areas. The treatment of Amerindian tribes and black slaves in the United States raises similar hackles and cautions.

Still, it remains that Hindu caste has been a powerful ingredient in what to the outsider looks like the nearly unrelieved misery of millions of Indian poor. Simply by the accident of their birth, the majority of Indians have been assigned to the bottom levels of the social pyramid. Of course, to the traditional Hindu, birth was nothing accidental. One was born into a priestly caste, or into a caste of workers, in virtue of one's karma from previous lives. While this might provide some consolation—"my fate is what the gods have meted out to me, or what I have earned from previous existences"—it meant that Indian society as a whole could become static. If many people thought that their poverty, or their wealth, was fated, they were less likely to work hard. Certainly, talent and industry could make a difference in any individual life. On the whole, however, the tendency to think of themselves as fenced in by their caste or particular trade sapped the vitality of many Indians. In the worst cases, it also supported discrimination and outright cruelty. The upper castes had every right to think themselves superior to the lower castes, and they felt few pressures to treat lower caste people kindly. The more religious people were, the more the "impurity" of the lowest castes could vex them, leading at times to violence, even murder. So Naipaul's critique is telling. Unless one accepts a traditional worldview in which most things are dictated by birth (as the expression of divine or cosmic forces), caste seems to be a formula bound to produce pervasive injustice.

Among all classes, but especially the poor, Indian women have suffered the worst burdens. The poverty, slavery, and general abuse into which untouchable women often have fallen, simply because they had been born into a certain social stratum, call into question all the religions' tendency to justify the status quo as a matter of divine ordinance. One need not employ Marxist analyses of ideology and class conflict to clarify the self-advantage that the upper classes have pursued through the Hindu caste system. Simple common sense will do.

A good critique is aware of its own biases and tries to balance negative data with positive. For Westerners, a regular bias has been the assumption that Western technology, democracy, and higher culture have been simon-pure boons to the people colonized, missionized, or taken into trading relationships with Western powers. While often this has been true, and many Indians have taken to heart Western objections to such Indian traditions as caste, it remains equally true that technology, religious proselytizing, and trade, to say nothing of political rule by Western powers, often have upset traditional Indian culture and generated many sufferings. In addition to the humiliation and resentment caused by being forced to submit to others' rule and culture, Indians and other colonized people have had to suffer attacks on their native ways and misunderstandings that sometimes have threatened to undermine their confidence in who they were.

On the matter of positive data, scholars of Hinduism often note that bonding between women, affection between spouses, and respect for wives, mothers, and daughters regularly have softened the negative potential latent in the traditional sexual roles. Similarly, the castes and jatis often have coexisted amicably, keeping their distinctions without making them cause for disrespect, animosity, or violence. Insofar as most Hindus through the ages have accepted the caste system as simply the way things were, they have shrugged off many of the criticisms or feelings of outrage an outsider might expect. None of these positive, countervailing data ought to place Hinduism beyond criticism, but any of them can help restore balanced perspective.

WORLDVIEW

For Hinduism, as all other religious traditions, the relationship between history and worldview is dialectical—that is to say, each influences the other. What Hindus have believed about the structures of reality (worldview) has developed in the course of their history. Conversely, their worldview has directed many of the choices that have determined the patterns of their existence over time (history).

Perhaps the most significant feature to emerge from Hindu history has been pluralism. Hindus have developed such a wealth of rituals, doctrines, devotions, artworks, social conventions, and other ways of dealing with ultimate reality, one another, and nature that they could not be uniform. More than such religious traditions as the Jewish, the Christian, the Muslim, and the Buddhist, whose basic convictions have been relatively uncontested, Hindus have admitted variety and debate into the core of their religious culture. One sees this when examining the impact of such a Hindu notion as that of the four legitimate goals of life. To say that pleasure, wealth, duty, and liberation (salvation) are all legitimate ends for human beings to pursue, and then to allow numerous ways of interpreting each of these ends, has been to ensure that Hinduism would allow a vast range of options in prayer, family life, economic activity, and dealings with the natural environment.

Thus the interaction of history and worldview in Hinduism has been especially creative. The vaunted color of Hindu life, the teeming variety of sights, smells, tastes, and sounds, stems from this creativity. The tradition has encouraged people to find their own pathway, to develop the special genius of their own little group, and people have responded creatively. Even when caste or poverty seemed to limit their potential, many Hindu men and women have found a devotion that gave them hope, a god or goddess who made them feel significant, a way of finding beauty in nature or human affairs that made them smile now and then.

Nature

For the most part, Hinduism considers nature (the physical cosmos) to be real, knowable, and orderly. The cosmos is a continuum of lives; consequently, human life is seen as an ongoing interaction with the lives of creatures above and below it. Furthermore, most Hindus consider divinity to be more than physical nature and think human self-realization (*moksha*) entails release from the laws of karma. Let us develop these ideas.

The statement that the physical cosmos is real requires some qualification. Through history, the average Hindu, concerned with making a living and caring for a family, has had little doubt that the fields, flocks, and other physical phenomena are real. Also, the hymns of the Vedas that revere the sun and the storm express a vivid appreciation of nature. Even many of the philosophers spoke of the world as *sat*—having being or reality. Only the idealistic thought of the Upanishads, as the Vedanta developed and somewhat organized it, called the reality of the physical world into question.

Furthermore, because of the Vedic notion of *rita* (order, duty, or ritual) and the later notion of karma, Hinduism found the natural world quite orderly. *Rita* presided over such phenomena as sunrise, sunset, and the seasons. Karma expressed the Hindu belief that all acts in the cosmos result from previous causes or choices and produce inevitable effects. To be sure, there are various religious paths *(margas)* for escaping karmic inevitability, and we discuss those paths below. Nonetheless, *rita* and karma suggest that the world is patterned, regular, and dependable. This does not mean that flood, famine, earthquake, sickness, or war cannot occur, but it does mean that none of these calamities makes the world absurd.

Karma is connected with the notion of transmigration and rebirth. *Rita* is involved with the vast space-time dimensions in which Hindu cosmology delights. Together these concepts give nature a gigantic expanse that is replete with connections. The connections that most interested the average Hindu linked the myriad living things. Astrology and astronomy brought some people in contact with planetary forces, but the average Indian was more interested in other people and animals. Shaivites expressed this interest by venerating the powers of fertility. Ancient rites honoring the Great Mother and other rites stressing Shaktism reveal other Hindu responses to the wonders of life. The symbolism surrounding Shiva and his consorts (such as Kali) explicitly links life with death. At a level above ancient concerns with the vegetative cycle of death and rebirth and the taking of life by life, Hinduism placed the connection between death and life in the context of the universal cycles of creation and destruction: the Brahma Day and Brahma Night by which the universe pulsated, Shiva's dance of life and death, and the sportive play of illusion (maya).

The Jain notion of *ahimsa*, which many Hindus adopted to varying degrees, implied the connectedness of all lives through its practice of not harming animals. Many Indians refused to eat meat out of the desire not to harm animals. Nonviolence toward the cow, which one might not kill even to help the starving (but which might itself starve), epitomized for many Hindus a necessary reverence for life. Taking karma and transmigration (the passing of the life force from one entity to another) seriously, Hindus thought that life, including their own, was constantly recasting itself into new vegetative and animal forms. Such life was not an evolutionary accident or something that ended at the grave. The inmost life principle continued on, making nature a container of life forces.

Frequently, maya and samsara carry negative overtones. In fact, the whole thrust toward *moksha* suggests that the natural sphere is of limited value. For more than a few Indians, the natural sphere has been a prison or place of suffering. Yogis of different schools, for instance, have tried to withdraw from materiality to cultivate enstasis. Other Hindu mystics have sensed that there was something more ultimate than the ritual sacrifice, the play of natural processes, and even the emotions of the devout worshiper of the bhakti god. In this sense samsara opposed the freedom suggested by *moksha,* and *moksha* meant exit from what one had known as natural conditions.

However, it is misleading to label Hinduism as world denying or life denying, since India's culture has produced many warriors, merchants, artists, and scientists—a full citizenry who took secular life seriously.[56] Nonetheless, Hindu culture was seldom secular or materialistic in our modern senses, usually stabilizing society by referring to a god or Brahman transcending human space and time. (We may say the same of traditional premodern societies generally.) In addition, Hinduism's reference to metaphysical concepts probably held back its concern with health care, education, and economic prosperity for the masses. (Again, we could say this of many other traditional cultures.) When he argued for a secular state and a turn to science rather than religion, Premier Nehru spoke for many modern, educated Indians. Even today, the religion of the villages, which is often quite primitive, hinders the improvement of agriculture, family planning, housing, and health care.

Thus, Hinduism's Aryan beginnings, which were so bursting with love of physical life, and its Dravidian beginnings, which were tantamount to nature and fertility worship, were negated in some periods of history. The most serious blows came from intellectual Hinduism and bhakti, which found life good by spiritual exercises and thus were not concerned with social justice or transforming nature for human benefit.

In Eric Voegelin's terms, neither the early Hinduism that began close to nature nor that which withdrew from nature to focus on human spirit escaped the cosmological myth. In Israel, Greece, and European Christian culture, such a withdrawal made nature less than divine. Unlike the religions of these Western cultures and the prophetic theology of Islam, Hinduism tended to keep gods and humans within the cosmic milieu and to think of nature as a stable entity that one could little affect or change. *Moksha* is an exception, but *moksha* was seldom articulated clearly. It primarily proposed that human self-realization comes by escaping the given world.

One confirmation of the view that Hinduism did not differentiate the realms of nature, divinity, and society is that the concept of creation from nothingness never became a dominant Hindu belief. In Hindu cosmology the universe goes its rhythmic way of Brahma Days and Brahma Nights; it has always existed and always will. Insofar as the concept of *moksha* suggests that we may transcend this cosmic rhythm, it carries seeds of a doctrine of creation from nothingness. However, the usual Hindu explanation of creation involves gods molding the world from preexisting stuff.[57] Thus Hinduism differs from Western religion by considering the world divine. It always remained somewhat under the cosmological myth and so it has lessons to teach Westerners who have lost reverence for nature. The Western notion of creation from nothingness is equally mythical, but its myth was different in stressing the freedom of a single personal deity.

Society

As we have seen, Hinduism structured society by caste and numerous occupational subclasses. In addition, families traced themselves back through their departed ancestors.[58] Outside the four castes were the untouchables, and there were also instances of slavery. The basic structure of the four castes received religious sanction in the *Rig-Veda* 10:90, where the priests, warriors, merchants, and workers emerged from the Great Man's body after he was sacrificed.

The Laws of Manu, expanding the doctrine of casteism, specified the castes' social duties. The brahmin, for instance, had six required acts: teaching, studying, sacrificing for himself, sacrificing for others, making gifts, and receiving gifts. Brahmins also were to avoid working at agriculture and selling certain foods (such as flesh and salt). Were they to do these things, they would assume the character of people of other castes. In a similar way, Manu set duties and prohibitions for the warriors, merchants, farmers, and workers, giving the entire society a comprehensive dharma. As a result, Hindus considered their dharma to be something given rather than a matter of debate or free choice. Indeed, such caste obligations were the basic cement of Hindu society.[59]

Nonetheless, various religious inspirations and movements introduced some flexibility. Many of the bhakti cults rejected caste distinctions, contending that all people were equal in the god's sight. The possibility of stepping outside the ordinary organization of things to become a full-time ascetic or seeker of liberation loosened the stranglehold of both dharma and caste. Throughout history, the patchwork organization of the Indian nation also added to social flexibility. Since most of the people lived in villages, and most of the administrative units were local rather than national, local customs were very strong.

Thus, Hindu society was remarkably diverse and tolerant despite its official rigidity. The complexity of social stations and religious allegiances meant that there were many legitimate ways through life. In the family, which was usually quite large, or extended, the chief figure was the father. Family organization was usually patriarchal, as was property administration. Women had some property rights, according to some legal schools, but their position was generally inferior. In fact, the place of the female, 50 percent of Hindu society, illustrates well the overall Hindu social and religious outlooks.

Women's Status. We know little about the earliest Indian women's social status. There is evidence of fertility rites among the pre-Aryans, as we have seen, suggesting a cult of a mother goddess or a matriarchal social structure. In Vedic times women clearly were subordinate to men, but in earlier times they may have held important cultic offices, created canonical hymns, and been scholars, poets, and teachers.[60] In the Brihad-Aranyaka Upanishad, the woman Gargi questions the sage Yajnavalkya, indicating that wisdom was not exclusively a male concern.[61] It therefore seems likely that in early India at least some girls of the upper castes received religious training like the boys'.

However, between the first Vedas (1500 B.C.E.) and the first codes of law (100 C.E.), women's religious roles steadily declined. A major reason for this was the lowering of the marriage age from fifteen or sixteen years

to ten or even five. This both removed the possibility of education (and consequently religious office) and fixed women's roles to being wife and mother. In fact, in later Hinduism being a wife was so important that a widow supposedly was prohibited from mentioning any man's name but that of her deceased husband. Even if she had been a child bride or had never consummated her marriage, the widow was not to violate her duty to her deceased husband and remarry. If she did, it was thought she would bring disgrace on herself in the present life and enter the womb of a jackal for her next rebirth.

Thus, the widow was the most forlorn of Hindu women. Without a husband, she was a financial liability to those who supported her. If menstruating, she could be a source of ritual pollution. If barren, she was useless to a society that considered women essentially as child producers. In such a social position, many widows must have felt that they had little to lose by throwing themselves on their husband's funeral pyre.[62] (Even suttee, though, was not simple. If the widow did not burn herself out of pure conjugal love, her act was without merit.)

Women were sometimes admitted as equals into the bhakti and Tantrist sects. However, two circumstances in Tantrism minimized the social liberation that the open admission might have effected. First, the Tantrist sects tended to be esoteric, or secret, which made their public impact minor. Second, the Tantrist interest in tapping *shakti* energies often led to the exploitation of women by men. Thus, the males sometimes tried to gain powers of liberation *(moksha)* by symbolic or actual sexual intercourse, with the result that the females became instruments rather than equal partners. Nevertheless, the Tantrist image of perfection as being androgynous tended to boost the value of femaleness. How much this ideal actually benefited Indian women is difficult to say, but it probably helped some. Nonetheless, women were not generally eligible for *moksha;* the best that a woman could hope for was to be reborn as a man. There is little evidence that Tantrism eliminated this belief, though the *Bhagavad Gita,* 9:32, seems to contradict it.

In fact, the overall status of women in Hinduism was that of wards. They were subject, successively, to fathers, husbands, and elder sons. As soon as they approached puberty, their fathers hastened to marry them off, and during their wedded lives they were to honor their husbands without reservation. According to the *Padmapurana,* an influential text, this obligation held true even if their husbands were deformed, aged, debauched, lived openly with other women, or showed them no affection. To ritualize this attitude of devotion, orthodox Hindu authors counseled wives to adore the big toe of their husband's right foot, bathing it as they would an idol, and offering incense before it as they would to a great god.[63]

Worse than ward status, however, was the strain of misogyny (hatred of women) running through Hindu culture. The birth of a girl was not an occasion for joy. Hindus attributed it to bad karma in a previous life and frequently announced the event by saying, "Nothing was born." A girl was a financial burden, for unless her parents arranged a dowry there was small chance that she would marry, and the Vedic notion that women were necessary if men were to be complete (which the gods' consorts evidence) lost out to Manu's view that women were as impure as falsehood itself. In fact, Manu counseled "the wise" never to sit with a woman in a lonely place, even if that woman were one's mother, sister, or daughter.[64]

Consequently, Hindu religious texts sometimes imagine a woman as a snake, hell's entrance, death, a prostitute, or an adulteress. In Manu's code, slaying a woman was one of the minor offenses. In the Hindu family, the basic unit of society, woman therefore carried a somewhat negative image, although, of course, some women entered happy households. The high status of the householder did not extend to his wife or female children. India mainly honored women for giving birth and serving their husbands. (In a study of the emotional attitudes that this pattern has inculcated in modern India, Aileen Ross found the following intensity ratings for the listed relationships [the higher the number, the more intense the relationship]: mother-son, 115; brother-sister, 90; brother-brother, 75; father-son, 74; husband-wife, 16; sister-sister, 5. She gives no rating for the mother-daughter relationship.[65])

Ma Jnanananda. To show the sort of exception that relativizes general statements such as those that we have been making about Hindu women, let us briefly consider a contemporary female guru, Ma Jnanananda of Madras.

Ma is a familiar form of *mother*. Jnanananda is a spiritual mother to numerous followers in present-day Madras. She is both a *guru* and a *sannyasi*. A guru is a religious teacher. A sannyasi is "one who has taken a formal vow renouncing all worldly life, including family ties and possessions. Such a vow, in effect, means death to one's former life. This renunciation allows

full-time pursuit of spiritual goals and fosters spiritual development. Such vows have been common in India from ancient times to the present."[66]

Ma gained her lofty position as a guru because one of the leading Advaita Vedanta figures of contemporary India, Shankaracharya of Kanchipuram, recognized that she had penetrated the deepest truths of Hinduism, through mystical absorption with Brahman. Jnanananda had done this while living in the world, married and raising five children. That probably accounts for her great ability to relate the teachings of Vedanta to her disciples' daily problems at work or in family life.

Photographs of Ma taken before she became a guru show a lovely woman, well dressed and well groomed. The beauty still lingers, but now it seems a reflection of her inner peace. She has traded her fine clothes for a simple sari of ochre cloth, cut her hair short, and painted on her forehead and arms horizontal stripes of a thick paste made from ashes, to symbolize her death to vanity and worldly desires.

Ma's teaching is rooted in her profound experiences of *samadhi*. Samadhi is a state of deep trance, an experience of the basic consciousness that has no form yet relates the person to all other things. Here is Ma's description of her earliest experiences. "In that state I used to ask myself, 'Where am I?' Then I would try to think of myself at some point, but I immediately felt myself to be at the opposite point."[67] The result of such *samadhi* is a profound conviction that all things are one, that the world at bottom is a simple unity.

To help her disciples gain this perception, from which flows great peace and integration, Ma Jnanananda stresses four principles or virtues, all of which have venerable roots in traditional Hinduism. First, she insists on absolute truth, on trying always to stand in the light of conscience and the light of objective reality. One who would seriously pursue the Advaita Vedanta path toward enlightenment has to employ truthful means. Second, she urges purity. This means clearing the inner waters, letting all immoral thoughts and desires sink toward the bottom, like useless silt. Third, the disciple must develop his or her dharma, the righteousness that comes from fulfilling the duties of one's state in life. Last, Ma stresses *ahimsa* or nonviolence, the attitude of trying to do no injury to any fellow creature.

Together, these four virtues compose a spiritual program that Ma calls "action without desire." It is at least as old as the *Bhagavad Gita*, yet completely practical in the contemporary world. Essentially, it means self-surrender, so that one's life more and more stands free of either worries about the past or troubling anticipations of the future.

The end result of such a self-surrender should be a complete focus on God (ultimate reality). In the regime Ma would have a disciple follow, the day begins with some prayer or meditation to the deity of the disciple's choice. After this, the disciple turns to the work of the day, trying to perform duties in such a way that they do not distract the mind from God. The ideal is always to surrender completely to God. When distracting thoughts enter the mind, one should return to God by substituting a prayer or *mantra* (sacred sound). The goal always is "realization" of God, experiential awareness of the divinity in everything.

As this realization increases, worldly things lose their allure. Bit by bit one is skirting the dark forest of fear and desire, moving away from the powers of samsara and time. We can never control all the events of our lives, but we can control our attitude toward them. If we regard what happens to us as intended for our detachment from samsaric things, intended for our attachment to God, all things will become profitable. Such is Ma's teaching.

The final state of realization brings a great love of God. As one's union with divinity increases, one's fulfillment overflows. In this conviction, Ma Jnanananda is a sister to the great mystics of other religious traditions. East and West, they agree that union with God or ultimate reality is the greatest success a human being can attain. Ma Jnanananda therefore shows that Shankara's stress on the sole reality of Brahman is neither eccentric nor ethereal. As it works in her own life, and the lives of many of her disciples, it is a source of great fulfillment and love. She also shows that Indian women of talent can escape the limits of the image Hinduism has given them.

Conclusion. The social rewards of Hindu religion were in the hands of a relative few. By excluding most women, untouchables, and workers, intellectualist Hinduism told well more than half the population that their best hope was rebirth in a better station sometime in the future. (For the most part, only a member of a high caste could reach *moksha*.) However, in the family and the different trades, dharma gave all castes some legitimacy. Nonetheless, if the fundamental belief of Hinduism is considered to be the struggle for self-realization, these honors were rather tainted. For instance, in the ideal life cycle men of the upper three

castes were to leave their families in middle age and retire from social life. A husband might take his wife into retirement with him, but he had no obligation to do so. If anything, tradition probably encouraged him to go off alone. What a person intent on self-realization did for children, servants, or the lower classes in his city was secondary to what he did for his own atman. Thus, in the Brihad-Aranyaka Upanishad 2.4.5, Yajnavalkya praised his wife Maitreyi for wanting his help in gaining immortality rather than in gaining wealth. This made her dear to him, not because he loved her earthly self but because he loved her atman.

The smaller units of Hindu society were less honored religiously than they were in other cultures. For instance, although Hindu marriage involved a sacramental rite, it was not regarded as highly as in Judaism, where it is one of life's three great blessings (the Torah, good deeds, and marriage). The larger social organizations in India never approached the unity of a nation or empire, so one does not find the analogies between earth and heaven that one finds in Mesopotamia or Egypt, where the king was the mediator of divine substance, or *maat*—the mediator between the above of the gods and the below of the human realm. Indians may have sometimes pictured the realm of the many gods as a sort of government with superiors and subordinates, but this imagery was not so strong as it was in Greece or China. Indian society was simply too diverse and too fragmented to be considered a mirror of the macrocosm.

Thus, Hindu society is very complex. Dharma has meant that religion supported a responsible attitude toward society, and the law treatises specified these responsibilities. On the other hand, *moksha* and bhakti militated against taking worldly life too seriously. For those absorbed in religious liberation or religious love, political, economic, and even family structures could seem of negligible importance.

Understandably, many of the great religious figures of Indian history left the social scheme. The Mahavira and the Buddha both left high-caste homes (the Buddha, in fact, left a wife and small child). Shankara urged celibacy and skipping the two middle stages of the life cycle so that one could pursue liberation wholeheartedly. The wandering minstrels of bhakti clearly did little for their families' or towns' social stability. Since pleasure and wealth meant less than duty and liberation, they were less effective ties to worldly responsibilities than they have been in other cultures. Thus, Hindu society has been notably "unhistorical"—not simply in the sense that it has kept

Figure 3 *Narasimha, Madras, India, eleventh century. Bronze, 19⅜ in. high. Narasimha is an avatar of Vishnu, in which he appears as half-man and half-lion. His four arms suggest his powers to help his devotees, and his semiyogic posture suggests a masterful repose. The Nelson–Atkins Museum of Art, Kansas City, Missouri (Nelson Fund).*

relatively few records of temporal affairs but in the deeper sense that is has defined itself by a striving for something that lay outside space and time.

Self

Obviously, the average Hindu did not think about the self in isolation from nature and society. The social caste system and the cosmic samsara-transmigration system were the framework of any studious self-examination. Within this framework, however, an individual might set about the task of trying to attain *atmasiddhi,* the perfecting of human nature. This was another way, more concrete perhaps, of posing what *moksha* or the *mahatma* (the "great soul") meant.

In the *Rig-Veda, atmasiddhi* was the pious man who faithfully recited the hymns and made sacrifices to the gods.[68] The ritualistic texts called the *Brahmanas* changed the ideal to the priest who could faultlessly conduct the expanded ritual. The Upanishads shifted perfection toward the acquisition of secret knowledge about reality. The *smriti* literature such as the Laws of Manu valued more worldly achievement. There the most excellent man was he who could rule public affairs and lead in community matters. The *Bhagavad Gita* spoke of love as the highest attainment, but it described the realized human personality as being stable in wisdom and having overcome the desires of both the flesh and ambition. Recently Indian saints such as Ramakrishna and Gandhi have stressed, respectively, the mystic loss of self in God and the service of Truth. Clearly, therefore, Hindu tradition allows the self many ideals. Generally speaking, though, full success has implied emotional, intellectual, and spiritual maturity and has honored the social side of human being as well as the solitary.

The Upanishads jostled the classical life cycle for many. As we have seen, the Upanishadic self was the atman identified with Brahman. For this revered part of the Hindu tradition, then, the most important aspect of the self was the spiritual core. More than the body, this spiritual core was the key to escaping rebirth. If one was serious about escaping rebirth, why wait for the final stages of the life cycle? Why not cultivate the atman full time? Some such reasoning surely prompted those who became wanderers long before old age. Whether through study or meditation, they pursued a way that implied that the self's needs or aspirations could outweigh social responsibilities.

In the past thousand years or so, the individual Hindu has therefore had a variety of ways of viewing his or her life journey. The four stages of the life cycle, the Upanishadic or bhakti wandering, the household devotions—any of these concepts could give people's lives meaning. Hinduism explicitly recognized that people's needs differed by speaking of four *margas* (paths) that could lead to fulfillment and liberation. Among intellectuals, the way of knowledge was prestigious. In this *marga* one studied the classical texts, the Vedic revelation and commentators' tradition, pursuing an intuitive insight into reality. Shankara's higher knowledge is one version of this ideal. If one could gain the viewpoint where Brahman was the reality of everything, one had gained the wisdom that would release one from suffering.

But philosophy patently did not attract everyone, and many whom it did attract could not spare the time to study. Therefore, the way of karma (here understood as meaning works or action) better served many people. The *Bhagavad Gita* more than sanctioned this way, which amounted to a discipline of detachment. If one did one's daily affairs peacefully and with equanimity of spirit, then one would not be tied to the world of samsara. Doing just the work, without concern for its "fruits" (success or failure), one avoided bad karma (here meaning the law of cause and effect). Gandhi, who was much taken with this teaching of the *Gita*, used spinning as an example of *karma-marga* or *karma-yoga* (work discipline). One just let the wheel turn, trying to join one's spirit to its revolutions and paying the quantity of production little heed. When *karma-yoga* was joined to the notion that one's work was a matter of caste obligation, or dharma, it became another powerful message that the status quo was holy and meaningful.

A third *marga* was **meditation** *(dhyana)*, which meant some variant of the practices that Patanjali's *Yoga Sutras* sketch.[69] (This is the most popular meaning of **yoga**.) Contrasted with the way of knowledge, the way of meditation did not directly imply study and did not directly pursue intuitive vision. Rather, it was usually based on the conviction that one can reach the real self by quieting the senses and mental activity to descend without thinking to the personality's depths. In this progression, one approached a state of deep sleep and then went beyond it to nondualism. "Seedless *samadhi*" (pure consciousness) was the highest of the eight branches of yogic progress, but to enter *moksha* one had to leave even it behind. Along the way to *samadhi* one might acquire various paranormal powers (such as clairvoyance or telepathy), but these were of little account. Below even the subconscious one wished to rest without desire on the bottom of pure spirit. For the many who meditated, the way of *dhyana* usually meant peace, a great sensitivity to body-spirit relationships (through, for example, posture and breath control), and a deepening sense of the oneness of all reality.

Finally, bhakti had the status of a *marga*, and, according to the *Bhagavad Gita*, it could be a very high way. Of course, *bhaktas* ran the gamut from emotional hysteria to lofty mysticism. The *Gita* qualified the self-assertiveness that could arise in bhakti, however, by making its final revelation not human love of divinity but Krishna's love for humans. On the basis of such revelation, the *bhakta* was responding to divinity as divinity had shown itself to be. In other words, the *bhakta* was realizing human fulfillment by imitating God. (That was true of the yogi as well, which suggests that in India, as in other religious cultures, the self was finally an image of divinity.)

Case Study: The Hindu Child. We can get further glimpses into the Hindu sense of the self by considering how Hindus tended to regard their children.

The Hindu child was subjected to religious ceremonies well before birth. For devout Hindus, there were rituals to ensure conception, to procure a male child, and to safeguard the child's time in the womb. Birth itself involved an important ceremony, which ideally took place before the cutting of the umbilical cord, and that included whispering sacred spells in the baby's ear, placing a mixture of ghee and honey in its mouth, and giving it a name that its parents were to keep secret until its initiation. Birth made both parents ritually impure for ten days, which meant they were not to take part in the community's ordinary religious rites. Ten days after birth the child was given a public (as contrasted with the secret) name. Some households also solemnized both an early ear-piercing and the first time the parents took the child out of the house and showed it the sun.

A. L. Basham, from whose book *The Wonder That Was India* we are taking this description of Hindu childhood, lists some of the other rituals that devout parents included in a child's first years:

> More important [than the first vision of the sun] was the first feeding *(annaprasana)*. In the child's sixth month he was given a mouthful of meat, fish, or rice (in later times usually the latter) mixed with curds, honey, and ghee, to the accompaniment of Vedic verses and oblations of ghee poured on the fire. The tonsure *(cudakarma)* took place in the third year, and was confined to boys; with various rites the child's scalp was shaved, leaving only a topknot, which, in the case of a pious brahmin, would never be cut throughout his life. Another ceremony, not looked on as of the first importance, was carried out when the child first began to learn the alphabet.[70]

There was a pressing motive for parents to have sons, in that at least one son was thought necessary to perform the parents' funeral rites, without which they could not be sure of a safe transit to the other world. Adopted sons were better than nothing, but they were nowhere near so good as natural sons. Girls were of no use whatsoever, because girls could not help their parents in the next world, and at marriage girls passed into the families of their husbands. Although Indian history shows some evidence of female infanticide, this practice seems to have been relatively rare. Despite their lesser desirability, many girls were cared for and petted like sons.

Indeed, Indian literature shows few instances of such maxims as "Spare the rod and spoil the child," and one gathers that most Hindus had relatively happy, indulged childhoods. In Indian poetry, for example, children are often shown laughing, babbling, and being welcomed onto their parents' laps, even when it was likely they would leave those laps quite soiled. On the other hand, poor children were set to work soon after they were able to walk, and wealthier children started their studies as young as four or five. Thus boys usually were set to studying the alphabet by their fifth year. Richer families engaged tutors for their children, and through the Indian Middle Ages (before the Muslim invasions) many village temples had schools attached. The education of girls was considered much less pressing than that of boys, but most upper class women became literate. Before his initiation, when he was invested with the sacred thread and set to studying the Vedas, an upper-class boy usually concentrated on reading and arithmetic.

The initiation of brahmin boys usually occurred when they were eight. For warriors the ideal age was eleven, and for merchants twelve. The key element in this initiation was hanging a cord of three threads over the boy's right shoulder. The cord was made of nine twisted strands (cotton for brahmins, hemp for warriors, and wool for merchants). To remove this thread anytime during his subsequent life, or to defile it, involved the initiate in great humiliation and ritual impurity.

Another important element in the initiation was whispering the *Gayatri,* the most sacred verse of the *Rig-Veda* (3:62:10), in the ear of the initiate. Whereas previously he had been a child, not really a member of the Aryan people, this access to the Vedas began his spiritual, fully human life. The *Gayatri* is addressed to the old solar god Savitr, and it functions in Hindu ceremonies much as the Lord's Prayer functions in Christian ceremonies, as a basic and privileged expression of devotion. In Basham's translation it runs: "Let us think on the lovely splendour of the god Savitr, that he may inspire our minds."

In later times initiation and investment with the sacred thread became limited mainly to brahmins, but in Vedic times the other upper classes initiated their children, often including their girls. The initiation made the child an Aryan, a member of a noble people, opening the door to his first serious task, that of mastering the sacred Aryan lore. Accordingly, soon after initiation the child was apprenticed to a brahmin in order to learn the Vedas. During this period he was to be celibate, to live a simple life, and to obey his teacher assiduously. There were no sexual overtones to the initiation rite, and other ceremonies took care of the passage to physical maturity.

What was the Hindu child being taught through rituals such as these? That he or she was a being who, in addition to social responsibilities, had the potential to cope with desire and karma, thereby becoming free enough to recognize that the grounds of selfhood were divine and that full freedom lay in discovering this divinity.

Ultimate Reality

Our final consideration is how Hindus experienced and conceptualized ultimate reality. This is no less complex than the dimensions of nature, society, and the self. In the early Vedic literature, the gods are principally natural phenomena. It is the wondrous qualities of the storm or fire that elevate Indra and Agni to prominence. By the time that the Brahmanic emphasis on sacrificial ritual dominated, the gods had come under human control. The final stage of Brahmanism was the view that the ritual, if properly performed, inevitably attains its goals—it compels the gods to obey. When we couple this subordinating view of the gods with the notion of samsara, the gods become less venerable than human beings. Human beings have the potential to break with samsara and to transcend the transmigratory realm through *moksha.* The gods, despite their heavenly estate, are still within the transmigratory realm and cannot escape into *moksha.*

The Upanishads, as we saw, moved away from the plurality of gods toward monism. One can debate whether this view is atheistic or religious, but the debate turns on semantics. However, both the Upanishads and the Vedanta philosophers stated that the knowledge of Brahman or atman is redemptive. Such knowledge, in other words, is not simply factual or scientific but has the power to transform one's life—it is light freeing one from existential darkness. Therefore, from the side of the one who experiences Brahman's dominance, we can surely speak of "religious" (ultimately concerned) overtones.

As well, the place that Brahman has in the world view of the Upanishads and the Vedanta correlates with the place that God has in monotheism. Brahman is the basis of everything, if not the creator. It is the supreme value, because nothing is worth more than the ultimate being, which, once seen, sets everything else in light and order.

Attending to Brahman, Hinduism's major concept for ultimate reality, we can note finally that the two aspects of Brahman approximate what monotheistic religions have made of their God. Being beyond the human realm *(nirguna),* Brahman recedes into mystery. This parallels the Christian God's quality of always being ineffable and inconceivable. But being within the human realm *(saguna),* Brahman is the basis of nature and culture. In this way it approximates the Christian conception of the Logos, in whom all creation holds together.

Brahman, of course, is impersonal, whereas most monotheistic religions conceive their deities on the model of the human personality. Still, it is the functional equivalent of the most comprehensive realities of other religions. Like the Chinese *Dao* it cannot be named, yet it mothers the ten thousand things. Like the Buddhist suchness or buddha-nature, it must be described in both absolute and relative terms.

The bhakti cults have revered still another form of Hindu divinity. Vaishnavites do not strictly deny the reality of Shiva or Brahma, nor do followers of these other gods deny the reality of Vishnu or Krishna. The mere fact that bhakti sects devoted to different gods contend among themselves shows that they take the other gods seriously. But the emotional ardor of the devoted *bhaktas* suggests that they grant their gods the ultimate value of a monotheistic god. The same holds for devotees of goddesses, who may actually outnumber devotees of the male gods. The Devimahatmya writings, for instance, have fashioned a warrior queen who is the equal of Vishnu.[71]

In Krishna's manifestation to Arjuna in the *Bhagavad Gita,* we can see how this monotheistic value took symbolic form. Krishna becomes the explosive energy of all reality. In the *Gita,* his theophany (manifestation of divinity) is the ultimate revelation of how divinity assumes many masks in space and time.

Whatever reality is, Krishna is its dynamic source. Much like the Upanishadic Brahman, he is the one source capable of manifesting itself in many forms. But whereas the atmosphere of Brahman is serene and cool, the bhakti-prone Krishna is turbulent and hot. When J. Robert Oppenheimer, one of the developers of the American atom bomb, saw the first nuclear explosion, Krishna's dazzling self-revelation came to his mind: "If the light of a thousand suns should effulge all at once, it would resemble the radiance of that god of overpowering reality" (*Bhagavad Gita,* 11:12). Thus, the Hindu divinity, like the Hebrew divinity of the chariot or the Zoroastrian divinity of the sacrifice, could be a refining fire.

This refining fire makes the world rise from and fall back into formlessness. The Hindu trinity of Brahma, Vishnu, and Shiva stands for creation, preservation, and destruction. Shiva himself, however, presides over life and death as the Lord of the Dance of Creation. The Shaivites, in this belief, indicate more clearly than the Vaishnavites how many Hindus retain a quite ancient notion of divinity.[72] Shiva is a complex reality, to be sure, but his ascetic and destructive aspects reflect quite ancient encounters with spiritual forces.

The Problem of Evil.   The problem of evil is that so much in human experience seems to be dark and disordered. For many Western observers, Indian philosophy has seemed strangely silent about evil. In these observers' eyes, the Hindu doctrine of rebirth shifted the problem of evil away from the Western orientation, in which individuals (like Job in the Bible) can accuse God of having dealt with them unjustly, having caused them to suffer through no fault of their own. Rebirth, coupled with the notion of karma, meant that one existed through long cycles of time whose overall justice was beyond human calculation, and that one's fate in a given lifetime was the result of one's actions in a previous existence. Thus there was no unmerited punishment and consequently no "problem" of evil. The gods did not have to justify themselves before innocent sufferers and evil was not an absurd, irrational force corroding human sanity.

Wendy Doniger O'Flaherty has challenged the simplicity of these Western assumptions:

Philosophers and theologians may set up their logical criteria, but a logical answer to an emotional question is difficult both to construct and to accept. The usual example of extraordinary evil given in Indian texts is the death of a young child. If one says to the parents of this child, "You are not real, nor is your son: therefore you cannot really be suffering," one is not likely to be of much comfort. Nor will the pain be dulled by such remarks as "God can't help it" or "God doesn't know about it." It is only the ethical hypothesis that is *emotionally* dispensable: God is not good, or God does not wish man to be without evil (two very different arguments). And this is the line most actively developed by Hindu mythological theodicy.[73]

By "Hindu mythological theodicy" O'Flaherty means the effort one can find in the Hindu epics and devotional literature to justify God's ways, or the way things occur in the world. One of the early reasons why Hinduism developed an articulate response to the problem of evil was the attacks of the Buddhists, who found evil a soft spot in Hinduism's armor. Thus Buddhist texts satirically ask why the Hindu gods do not set the world straight. If Brahman, for instance, is lord of all things born, why are things so confused and out of joint? Why is there such unhappiness and deception? If we are honest, it seems as though Brahman ordained not dharma (a good working order) but adharma (chaos).

Hindu thinkers struggled to meet this challenge. In trying to understand evil, they tended to regard natural disasters, such as earthquakes, and moral wrongs, such as murder, as but two aspects of a single comprehensive phenomenon. Thus the Sanskrit term *papa* (evil) embraced both natural and moral evil. In the *Rig-Veda,* probably the moral sense prevails: People are evil-minded, committing adultery or theft. Still, the *Rig-Veda* does not necessarily see such evil as freely chosen. Moral evil or sin may occur without the sinner willing it. Therefore, one finds few prayers of personal repentance in the *Rig-Veda,* though numerous prayers for deliverance from the bad things other people can do. The *Atharva-Veda* also tends to blend natural and moral evils, and to see moral evil as an intellectual mistake rather than a culpable flaw in character. There are exceptions to these tendencies, such as the *Rig-Vedic* hymn of repentance to Varuna (5:85), but the overall inclination of the Vedic texts is to regard evil not as something we humans do but as what we do not wish to have done to us.

Although Hinduism tried out many different responses to the problem of evil, in O'Flaherty's opinion it favored myths that blamed God for evil (in contrast to the West's favorite myths, which blamed human beings). This gives Indian mythology a rather tragic tone. When it moves from the drama of creation to the pathos of creation's defects, the Indian imagination is inclined to picture reality as intrinsically misbuilt. The result is a worldview in which evil is an integral factor. In the comprehensive system of this world, as enlightened minds perceive it, there is both the purity of healthy-minded people and the dirt of sick-minded people.

We can turn to the Vedas as a source of optimism, stressing healthy-mindedness, or to the Upanishads as a source of pessimism, stressing sick-mindedness. The Vedas emphasize benevolent gods whom one can invoke as aids in attaining heaven, while the Upanishads emphasize inadequate or even malevolent gods who are a central cause of our human problems.

In the subsequent tradition, through the epics and *Puranas,* one finds an integration of both emphases, a sort of dualism or unity of opposites: "Evil is recognized as horrible, death terrifying, heresy wicked, but these are accepted and integrated with the healthy goals of the Vedic life-view."[74]

In our opinion, this traditional tendency would have enhanced the attraction of proposals to undercut the entire dualistic realm. *Moksha* would then have become an escape from a world in which tragedy was inevitable because evil was as aboriginal as good. The sages could say very little about the sort of life that *moksha* would bring, because all expressible experience was mottled by suffering. They intuited, however, that *moksha* was full of being, bliss, and awareness—was an existence beyond evil's reach.

Kali. One female deity whom scholars have studied thoroughly is Kali, the mistress of death, an important expression of Maha-devi, the ancient great goddess. In her, many of the popular ambivalences about ultimate reality come into focus. Part of the fascination Kali has evoked stems from her dreadful appearance. Usually she is portrayed in black, like a great storm cloud. Her tongue lolls, reminding the viewer that she has a great thirst for blood, and she shows fearsome teeth. Her eyes are sunken, but she smiles, as though enjoying a terrible secret. Round her neck is a garland of snakes, a half-moon rests on her forehead, her hair is matted, and often she licks a corpse. In her hand is apt to be a necklace of skulls. She has a swollen belly, girdled with snakes, and for earrings she has corpses. Her face projects a calm contentment, as if the savage realities of life, its evil and deathly aspects, suit her most loathsome, degenerate streams in Hindu culture. For example, she has been linked with blood sacrifices, including those of human beings, and she has served as the patron goddess of the Thugs, a vicious band of criminals that flourished from ancient times until the late nineteenth century and devoted themselves to strangling carefully selected victims as a way of honoring the goddess of death. (It is from this group that our English word *thug* has come.) Nonetheless, a careful study of Kali's full history as a major Hindu deity suggests that she has functioned as more than simply a lodestone for the soul's blacker passions.

First, Kali does not appear in the earliest Hindu texts, but comes on the scene fairly late. Second, throughout her history it is largely peripheral people, marginal groups, that populate her cults. In this her cult reminds one of Shavaism and Tantrism. Third, the geographic areas most devoted to Kali have been Bengal and the Vindhya Mountain region of south-central India. Fourth, when Kali became associated with the tantric cults her appearance changed, for a potential benevolence more clearly emerged.

Tantrism's concern with tapping libidinal energies led to the rise of many female deities from the seventh century C.E. on, and by the sixteenth century Kali was intimately connected with the more adventurous "left-hand" tantric sects. For some important left-hand tantric sects, religion became a dramatic effort to conquer the fractured world and gain *moksha*. An indispensable ally in this effort was the *shakti* power of female divinity.

> In his attempt to realize the nature of the world as completely and throughly pervaded by the one Sakti, the *sadhaka* (here called the hero, *vira*) undertakes the ritual known as *panca-tattva*, the ritual of the five ("forbidden") things (or truths). In a ritual context and under the supervision of his *guru*, the *sadhaka* partakes of wine, meat, fish, parched grain, and sexual intercourse. In this way he overcomes the distinction (or duality) of clean and unclean, sacred and profane, and breaks his bondage to a world artificially fragmented.[75]

Kali is a personification of the most forbidden or truthful thing, death. Therefore, the tantric hero presses on to confront Kali, trying to transform her (death) into a vehicle of salvation. Consequently, the hero is apt to go to Kali's favorite dwelling place, the

Figure 4 *The god Ganesha dancing, northwest India, tenth century. Light gray sandstone, 39 in. high. Ganesha, the elephant-headed son of Shiva, is very popular because he bestows wealth and success. The Nelson–Atkins Museum of Art, Kansas City, Missouri (Nelson Fund).*

just fine. (It is interesting that the cult of Kali flourished in areas most profoundly influenced by British colonial rule, as though to express a sense that life had turned horribly oppressive.)

Moreover, certain historic associations have besmirched Kali's name, linking her with some of the cremation grounds, meditate on each terrible aspect of her appearance, and try by penetrating her fearsomeness to pass beyond it. Translating the hero's rationale we might hear him say: "By embracing death with my every pore and synapse, I will make Kali rid me of all fear of death, all alienation from this death-infiltrated world."

It is doubtful that the average Hindu worshiper of Kali has had such an adventurous, or highly conscious, rationale as that of our tantric hero, but the devotionalism of many followers, especially those from the Bengal area, shows a similar effort to make worship of the goddess a way to come to grips with life's worst features. Thus the poetry of Ramprasad (1718–1775), one of the most influential Bengali singers of Kali's praises, speaks of a mother who makes those attached to her as mad as she is. Ramprasad begs Kali to deal with him as a mother and help him accept her wild, incomprehensible behavior. As the *Bhagavad Gita* swells the figure of Krishna, so that he becomes coextensive with the whole of mysterious creation, so Ramprasad swells the figure of Kali, so that she becomes coextensive with the whole of mysterious creation. By remaining devoted to her, despite her forbidding appearance, the poet expresses a blind faith that somehow, sometime, life will show itself to have been worth living.

Ramakrishna (1834–1886), another very influential Bengali devotee of Kali, taught much the same message, but in more ecstatic and joyful terms. Going out of himself in adoration of the goddess, Ramakrishna pointed to a realm beyond good and evil, beyond all the dichotomies we make in everyday life. This is a realm where the deepest forces of death and life intermingle, moving the world to a rhythm only divinity can comprehend.

The ordinary Hindu, man or woman, who was not a saint like Ramakrishna, tended to interact with a favorite god or goddess without understanding that this deity was merely the face of a universal divinity or ultimacy. Throughout history, most Hindus have not been literate, so their sense of the gods and goddesses has come from the oral tradition. It was the great cycle of stories about Krishna and Devi, about Rama and Sita, that filled the imagination of the ordinary person and so shaped what he or she said at prayer, thought during the religious festivals, feared in the depths of night or at the bed of a sickly child. This is not to say that the average Hindu had no sense of the unity among the different deities. In all proba-

bility, even the humblest peasant believed that the many different deities were reconciled in the realm of the gods. But for the present age, the trials of this round of the samsaric cycle, it was more helpful to focus on a particular deity than to speculate about a divine unity beyond or underneath all of the divine diversity.

A second feature of popular Hindu religion, the culture of the masses, has been a certain passivity. Sometimes Muslim ideas about the sovereignty of God (Allah) encouraged this feeling, but the Hindu notion of karma made a greater impact. Ideally, karma moved people to live on the border between acceptance and resignation. Acceptance is something positive: thinking that one's life is in God's hands, thinking that Providence must in the final analysis be benevolent. Resignation is something negative: we can't do much about our situation, in the long run, so we had best detach ourselves from foolish hopes and let happen what will.

In their prayers and rituals, Hindus tried to draw from their favorite deities a blend of acceptance and resignation fitting and powerful enough to keep them going. Popular religion certainly had its ecstatic moments, when love of a dazzling deity might move people to transports of delight, but on a daily basis Hindu piety or spirituality tended to be sober. The problems were great and the chances of solving them satisfactorily were small. The suffering was omnipresent and could easily become oppressive. Much popular piety therefore was an exercise in gaining reasons to keep going, in working out strategies for coping. The impressive thing is that it succeeded so often.

Conclusion. Indian ultimate reality thus has had many levels and many facets. In our opinion, the dimensions of nature, society, and the self are subordinate to the dimension of divinity, since the last determines the places of the first three. In other words, we suspect Hindus have arranged nature, society, and the self in view of the Agni, Brahman or Krishna who centered their lives in divine mystery. If Brahman is the ultimate reality, then nature, society, and the self are all versions of maya, are all illusion and play. If Agni, the god to whom one directs the fire sacrifice, is the ultimate reality, then nature stands by divine heat, society stands by priestly sacrificers, and the self strives after *tapas* (ascetic heat) or lives by ritual mantras (verbal formulas for controlling the divine forces). Finally, if Shiva is the ultimate reality, then ultimate reality destroys castes, is the arbiter of life and death, and reduces the self to a beggar for grace.

Nevertheless, one could begin with the view of nature, society, or the self and develop what ultimate reality and the other two subordinate dimensions meant. In other words, cosmology, sociology, and psychology all have their legitimate places in religious analysis.

However, historians of religion believe that no system of interpretation can truly substitute for the system that the religion itself implicitly uses. In other words, we cannot reduce the religions to their cosmological, sociological, or psychological factors. They must remain essentially what they claim to be: ways emanating from and leading to the divine. For this reason, the concept of ultimate reality in a religion will always be the most crucial concept. God or ultimate reality is by definition the ultimate shaper of a worldview, because divinity determines the placement of the other dimensions and thus the worldview as a whole. Having had many forms of divinity, Hinduism has had many worldviews.

SUMMARY: THE HINDU CENTER

How, overall, does Hinduism seem to configure reality for its adherents? What is the center, or summarizing pattern, that the Hindu "ways" appear to depict? It seems to us that the Hindu center is an alluring sense of unity. From the time of the Vedas, reflective personalities in India sought to put together the many disparate facets and forces of reality. Thus *Rig-Veda* hymns, Upanishads, and the later theistic cults all proposed a mystery, or ultimate reality, or god that stood behind things, promising the believer, the devout adherent, or the self-disciplined yogi, a satisfying peace. The peace would come from the order that union with Brahman or Krishna would produce. Thus the individual was not to cling to the passing multiplicity of social, natural, or even personal life. Samsara was an enemy trying to keep the individual in a state of disunion, and so of suffering. Illusion was samsara's main ally. If one broke with illusion, appropriated the wisdom of the ancient seers who had fought through to, or been blessed by a vision of, the

ultimate unity of all things, one could find being, bliss, and awareness.

Moksha probably is the watchword best symbolizing this typically Hindu cast of mind, yet *moksha* could have several different weightings. For the passionate, those either suffering with special pains or burning for being, bliss, and awareness with a special ardor, *moksha* could be an imperative. There being nothing more important than coming to right order, finding the ultimate truth and meaning of life, the passionate Hindu could pursue *moksha* wholeheartedly, opting out of India's highly structured caste and family life. For personalities either less pressured by suffering or less drawn by the prospects of fulfillment, *moksha* could carry a somewhat comforting and palliative set of overtones. If not in this life, in some future life one could hope to attain *moksha*. With such a good future prospect, the turmoils and troubles of the present life could somewhat slacken.

Theistic Hindus, bhaktas devoted to Krishna, Shiva, or one of the goddesses, tended to picture the center in terms of their beloved God. Thus the theophany or revelation that Krisha gives Arjuna in the *Gita* shows Krishna to be the center of all reality, a sort of Brahman, but more personalized, dazzling, and energetic. As the force of life and death, Shiva could have a similarly universal power to organize reality, a similarly profound religious clout. Love for such a god could give the devotee's life great meaning. Sacrifices to the god, celebrations of the god's festivals, visits to the god's temples, prayers for the god's help in time of sickness or distress—this sort of intense, personalized religion probably pictured *moksha* as an unbroken enjoyment of the god. If the god was one's lover, the Krishna who could espouse the devotee's soul, then the enjoyment beckoned as quite erotic. If the god was a mother, a goddess of comfort or even frightening command (recall Kali), then the release of *moksha* might carry overtones of a child returning to its first home or a servant hoping for the rewards of a job well done, a life of devotion well lived.

Throughout these and the other forms of Hindu religion, something beckoned Hindus to hold present times lightly, treat the things they encountered respectfully but ungraspingly. Of course, a great many Hindus disregarded this beckoning. The violence and cruelty of the subcontinent, the poverty of its so many millions, remind us that karma could be a grinding enslavement, *moksha* could be an escapist strategem of last resort. Thus V. S. Naipaul, the brilliant novelist

Figure 5 *Birla Temple, a modern Hindu temple in New Delhi, replete with statues of gods and animals. Photo by J. T. Carmody.*

and journalist, on returning to the land of his ancestors, found India to be a "wounded civilization," weighted down with a sense of the past that mottled its present and future.[76] In Naipaul's impression, karma had helped millions, both intellectuals and illiterate peasants, to accept the wretched injustices of caste, the manifold bondages of the vast majority to poverty, ignorance, and a dearth of worldly prospects.

Be that as it may (and it may be more accurate about the recent India than about the India of the pre-Muslim era), the impression remains that the Hindu center has been as ambivalent in its social effects as most other religious centers have been. By the standards of a radical contemplative wisdom that would penetrate to the core of reality's mystery and a radical social justice that would treat all human beings as equals who deserve fair dealing, the Hindu worldview emerges as more wise than just. So, of course, do most other worldviews, if only because it is usually easier to contemplate the grand source of order, the fair center of a mystery revealing itself as beautiful and healing, than it is to promote other human beings' equal access to the good life that such a mystery suggests.

The world over, religious people rightly have their proposed wisdoms challenged because their concrete social and cultural lives show continuing malignancies, ongoing patches, large or small, where they treat one another worse than wolves. Thus the critics of religion usually have plenty of ammunition, many rocks with labels such as "hypocrisy," "escapism," and "neurosis" ready to hand. That would be true for any who might want to criticize Hinduism. On the other hand, the Hindu religionist, like the adherent of most other religions, has had a simple and effective response: Where is your more beautiful, profound, or hope-inducing *moksha?* Where is your society free of caste, cruelty, and injustice?

So it goes, the dialogue or battle between religion and irreligion, anti-Hinduism and Hinduism. In our view, Hinduism's mantra of *om,* its central symbol of unity and peace, still sits on the table, awaiting from its opponents a response equally comprehensive and deep.

Discussion Questions

1. Why did Vedic religion come to stress sacrifice?

2. How could Upanishadic knowledge bring salvation?

3. Translate *moksha* into terms that your contemporaries would find attractive.

4. In what sense did bhakti personalize Hindu divinity?

5. What does the status of Indian women through the ages say about Hinduism?

6. How could we adapt the classical Hindu life cycle to the needs of Americans today?

7. Does Indian religion show that ultimate reality is as much impersonal as personal? How?

8. Explain the significance of Kali.

9. Why would you like or not like to be a disciple of Ma Jnanananda?

10. How satisfactory is the Hindu view that evil is an intrinsic part of this world? Why?

11. Explain the emotional aspects of devotion to Krishna.

12. Describe the fusion of religion and politics for Mahatma Gandhi.

13. Write a brief essay on the relations among *ahimsa,* fertility, and the cow.

14. What were your impressions when reading the accounts of possession by a god or force that required being placated?

15. What could be the positive aspects of a belief in transmigration?

Key Terms

ahimsa: an Indian term for nonviolence or noninjury. Both Hindus and Buddhists have made *ahimsa* part of their religious ideal. The liberated personality would feel no desire to hurt, abuse, manipulate, or otherwise disorder other finite beings and so would be a source of peace in nature as well as society.

asceticism: discipline; abstinence from self-indulgence. Most religious traditions have ascetical moments or streams, suggesting that when people strive to gain enlightenment or union with a holy divinity they tend to think they must discipline their desires, sensual appetites, spontaneous chatter, and the like. Asceticism should be ruled by the goal the tradition makes paramount, and so kept in the order of means to an end, but frequently it becomes a powerful if not all-absorbing interest in its own right, as people who fast, separate themselves from sexual activity, keep silence, live in solitude, and the like find they have more intense spiritual (visionary, ecstatic) experiences.

atman: Indian term for self or substantial reality. Where the Buddhists denied there was a self, many Hindu philosophers, influenced by the Upanishads, considered the atman the inmost presence of divinity. In other words, the true nature of the self could not be separated from that which made everything else exist and be what it was: Brahman.

bhakti: an Indian term for devotional religion centered on love. Bhaktas, devotees of a Hindu deity, usually conceive of their relationship with the deity in question on the model of a love affair, or at least an intense friendship. Thus women have tended to associate themselves with the cow-herding girls featured in legends about the young god Krishna, or they have associated themselves with one of the wives of a god celebrated in the epic literature. Men devoted to a god such as Shiva have tended to picture themselves as servants, even slaves, of the god, while both men and women devoted to one of the forms of the mother goddess have generally approached her on the model of a child seeking maternal help or comfort.

Brahman: Hindu term for ultimate reality. Brahman carried overtones of being the ultimate basis of nature and the cosmos, somewhat in contrast to the psychological overtones of atman. Both effable and ineffable, Brahman existed within human experience as the ground of what people felt and knew, but it also transcended this realm and stood for the basis of all that existed beyond human perception.

brahmin: a member of the highest, priestly Hindu caste. Brahmins traditionally have had responsibility for ritual, sacrifice, and religious knowledge. Some interpretations of caste made being a brahmin a prerequisite for *moksha,* and even when this interpretation did not hold, brahmins tended to enjoy great social prestige. They could expect being protected by warriors, having available the goods of traders, and being able to call on workers to care for their mundane needs.

caste: the Hindu social system that grouped people into four main ritualistic classes (priests, warriors, merchants, and workers) and innumerable occupational groups (jatis). Scholars debate the origins of caste, many now being less confident than past generations that color was the dominant motivation. Caste received cosmic sanctions in the Hindu accounts of the birth of human society from the sacrifice of a gigantic original human being and so came to be thought encoded in the way the universe had been born. Modern, secular India legally abolished caste, but it continues to exert a considerable cultural influence. Those who have fallen outside the caste system and become known as untouchables—people ritually impure—have suffered great alienation and been forced to support themselves by carrying out the most abhorred tasks (sewage disposal, garbage collection, animal slaughtering, and the like).

dharma: an Indian term for teaching and duty. Buddhists have stressed the idea of teaching, speaking of the dharma of the Buddha as one of their three great treasures (Buddha, dharma, community). Hindus have more vaguely spoken of dharma as a Truth rooted in their tradition (most notably in the Vedas). The word has had a more precise set of Hindu connotations when used in a social context, pointing to the responsibilities attendant on one's caste and the teachings of the famous law codes (such as that of Manu) that regularized social relationships.

karma: an Indian term for the relations among past deeds, present character, and future fate. Indian thought was intrigued by the problem of why people are what they are and do what they do. It related this problem to the basic problematic summed up in samsara: Why are people immersed in webs of relationships that bring them suffering, death, and rebirth? The doctrine of karma postulated that each choice or action shaped one's character, and that what one's character had become at death shaped what one's next existence would be like. Most Indian thinkers wanted to leave individuals the freedom to choose their acts, and so their characters, and so their future fates, but the overall weight of taking karma seriously was to make one's fortune seem predetermined. Still, Indians

felt urged to live virtuously by the general consensus that one would only gain release from samsara by having gained a good karmic condition, which in turn could only be gained by virtuous living.

maya: a Hindu term for reality taken to be so marvelous that it proves incomprehensible and thus unreliable. Human beings tend to be seduced by maya and so live unrealistically, in illusion. Maya can be understood to be a divinity, wooing the mind away from what is really so, playing with human beings for the sport of seducing them. To combat maya, one must attend to the scriptures and root out one's desires, on which maya trades. Insofar as maya predominates in most situations, it becomes a synonym for unenlightened living and so quite cognate to samsara and the wheel of rebirths.

meditation: mental exercises aimed at clarifying one's sense of the truth, advancing one toward enlightenment, and actualizing one's best spiritual potential. The term varies in connotation from context to context, in the East having yogic overtones while in the West suggesting either simple rumination or the first stages of mental prayer. Yogic meditation can be quite contemplative, trying to undercut the discursive mind and exercise the holistic powers of the basic spirit or heart. All meditation carries the danger of overmentalizing reality and religion alike, so many meditational regimes self-consciously require complementary manual labor or devotional prayer that engages the senses. A further question is the relation between meditation and social life, or even ecology, which some traditions solve by requiring common meditation halls, or communal prayers in a more devotional (liturgical) style, or walks and works calculated to make one's purifying mind penetrate the spiritual significance of nature and society.

moksha: the Hindu term for release, liberation, salvation from the bondage of samsara. *Moksha* necessarily must be approached "negatively," by way of denying the limitations afflicting daily human experience. So it implies what is not limited, mortal, bound to the cycle of births and deaths, afflicted with desire, deluded, and the rest. Positively, Hindu thinkers have spoken of being, awareness, and bliss. *Moksha* is lasting, self-sufficient, truly real, in contrast to the fragility, passingness, and dubious reality of ordinary existence. It is full of the light of knowing and the joy of loving. As such, it can symbolize a good sufficient to justify the asceticism and toil necessary to escape samsara.

puja: a Hindu term for ceremonial prayer or worship, especially that which occurs in the home or local temple. The many small offerings, prayers of praise, prayers of petition, sacrifices, vows, and festival celebrations that punctuate the traditional Hindu year suggest that *puja* carried the Hindu spirit along from day to day. What the grand myths and ceremonies did on a great scale, the humble species of *puja* did in the home, for the small group, or for the individual concerned with personal problems. Women were prominent in *puja,* their many devotions to local goddesses, prayers for the health of their families, reverences to Lord Krishna, and the like being a prominent strand in the Hindu tapestry.

reincarnation: the notion that the vital force survives after death and returns to animate a new body, usually in a nearly endless, cyclical way. Theories of reincarnation flourish within the orbit of the cosmological myth, which justifies thinking of the many different creatures in the cosmos as democratic sharers in a single basic stuff. Then the movement of the vital aspect of such stuff from one temporary housing to another poses little imaginative difficulty. Some advocates of reincarnation point to psychic experiences (for example, that of déjà vu) as evidence for reincarnation, and philosophers as diverse as Plato and the Buddha have promoted it. A corollary question usually is how one merits incarnation up or down the scale of creatures and how one ought to treat other creatures, in view of their probably being reincarnations of other forms of being.

samadhi: an Indian term for the highest state of meditation or yoga. *Samadhi* usually is described as an imageless trance, an experience of pure human spirituality. Mircea Eliade has explained *samadhi* in terms of a yogic goal of defeating time and space. The yogi who realizes *samadhi* has such control over the body and spirit that the usual constraints of space and time seem broken. Insofar as yoga is trying to defeat samsara and lead the person (or the atman) to an unconditioned state (*moksha*), *samadhi* is a sort of down payment on *moksha,* much as mystical experience serves many theistic traditions as a down payment on heavenly communion with the deity. The philosophical question *samadhi* sharpens is whether humanity can be perfected by withdrawing from ordinary dependencies on the body. Incarnational religious systems tend to dispute the claim that it can, although any adequate comparison of traditions' views on this matter would involve many further questions and distinctions.

satyagraha: an Indian term meaning "the force of truth." Mahatma Gandhi employed the term and made it famous as the rationale for his various strikes, demonstrations, and efforts to arbitrate grievances between the British and Indian communities. Coupled with Gandhi's dedication to nonviolence and his conviction that God was the ultimate foundation of all truth, *satyagraha* undergirded the remarkable discipline of Gandhi's followers. *Satyagrahis* frequently were brutally clubbed, if not exposed to rifle fire, but Gandhi consoled them that the truth of their cause one day would bring them justice. So *satyagraha* stands in the modern world as a challenging proposition: If one nonviolently demonstrates the truth of one's situation, the justice of one's cause, one will preserve one's own integrity and will shame or encourage one's adversaries into hearing their own better voices of conscience.

shakti: the generative energy of divinity or ultimate reality, often represented as the wife or consort of a Hindu god. In Hindu typology, the male gods were accounted cerebral, passive, and detached. The female consorts were the bodily, active, involved, creative side of the divine dimorphism. The *shaktis* needed the control of their male counterparts if they were not to run amok. Many folktales depict the awesome power of a mother goddess or wife of a powerful god on the verge of annihilation. The notion of *shakti* undergirded tantric attempts to tap into ultimate creativity, and it helped make the Hindu female an ambivalent figure. No doubt *shakti* has roots in ancient Indian awe about female fertility, as well as in philosophical speculation about the relationship of spiritual and sexual energies.

shruti: a Hindu term for revelation or scriptural truth, the highest sort of wisdom, found in the Vedas. *Shruti* came from ancient seers (*rishis*) who saw ultimate realities in deepest trance or spiritual transport. Hinduism has maintained a flexible sense of revelation, tending to be inclusive rather than exclusive. Nonetheless, it reserved the highest official respect for the Vedic scriptures, which have included the principal Upanishads one finds at the end of the Vedas. On the testimony of the Upanishads, the ultimate reality grasped by the *rishis* was a simple unity of being, bliss, and awareness—a Brahman with the features one attains by escaping samsara and achieving *moksha.*

smriti: a Hindu term for traditional truth, such as that found in commentaries on the Vedas or traditional law codes like Manu. *Smriti* therefore has less dignity than *shruti* and is considered less revelatory, more the product of human reasoning. Where the *rishis* intuited in mystical vision, the makers of tradition studied and reasoned. On the other hand, *smriti* had great influence in Hindu culture, because any elaboration of the social responsibilities of the different castes (their dharmas) involved such traditioning. Hinduism was sufficiently this-worldly, patient with space and time, to honor the station of the householder, which in turn meant thinking about family life, business, law, the arts, military matters, and political science. All of this fell to the conservers and developers of tradition.

tantra: a Hindu and Buddhist term for a ritual manual; by extension, the term has come to mean the effort to gain liberation that uses rituals, the imagination, and libidinal energies. The tantras—texts and adepts alike—were holistic, sensing that only by getting mind, body, and psyche to pull together could they generate the maximal force and enlist it in the service of enlightenment. Tantric Buddhism predominated in Tibet, where it sponsored a tradition of one-to-one instruction from a guru. The guru would supervise one's practice, and many of the most famous gurus developed dramatic, even hyperbolic, personas. Tantric Hinduism sometimes has flouted convention, to make disciples realize that convention alone can be a dead letter. Thus it has played with sexual and dietary taboos, even urging the eating of meat or the drinking of alcohol, to stimulate the insight that the ultimate reality itself undercuts all such distinctions as those between the socially approved and the socially forbidden.

transmigration: the passing of the life force from one entity to another. Transmigration assumes a distinction between soul (life force) and body, such that the soul does not perish along with the body. It further assumes an interaction among the various forces of the natural world, such that the soul can come to animate another body, whether that of another human being or that of a nonhuman animal. Some defenders of transmigration point to experiences of reminiscence and déjà vu, which they think suggest previous lives.

Others speak of a collective unconscious, a sort of racial memory encoded in the genes, that carries the sum of human experience. The Indian systems of karma and samsara imply something like transmigration, though the Buddhists deny there is any soul to migrate.

Vedanta: one of the six orthodox Hindu philosophical schools. Vedanta is associated with the sage Shankara (about 788–820), who taught a strict monism. To his mind, reality is nondual and all variety and change should be attributed to illusion. Vedanta may be said to have systematized and deepened the teachings of the monistic Upanishads, taking their equation of Brahman and atman to its logical consequence. Vedanta has had considerable influence in the West, and often (wrongly) has been considered the sum or best representative of Hindu spirituality. In fact, Indian history has furnished numerous other respectable schools, such as Shamkya, which have allowed for duality (matter and spirit, for example). The philosopher Ramanuja (eleventh century C.E.) attacked Shankara's system, arguing for a qualified nonduality that would permit love between the deity and the disciple.

yoga: an Indian term for discipline. Both Hinduism and Buddhism fostered several different yogas, most of which ideally were in the service of liberation from samsara. Yogas focused on the body aimed at achieving better tone, relaxation, digestion, suppleness, and the like. A discipline focused on the breath might try to unify the matter-spirit composite. The most prestigious yoga was the *jnana* discipline aimed at gaining an intuitive understanding of reality and so liberation. The yoga of trance and meditation sought to gain *samadhi*, or at least much better mental concentration. *Karma-yoga* was geared to purifying action, by bringing people to work and strive without desire. *Bhakti-yoga* was a discipline for emotion and love, by which one might unify one's heart and focus it entirely on one's favorite deity. Overall, yoga testified to India's conviction that to escape pain and gain enlightenment one had to marshal one's energies and put oneself under discipline.

CHAPTER 2

BUDDHISM

Wheel: Buddhist symbol for the dharma or teaching

HISTORY

Overview

The term *Buddhism* derives from Western scholarly efforts to organize the movements, ideas, and practices that appear to have been spawned by the Buddha (ca. 536–476 B.C.E.). As well, it covers the diverse things done and thought by followers of the Buddha, who in the early centuries of the Common Era spread from India throughout Asia and recently have established roots on other continents.

Buddhism began as an Indian sectarian religion—a way of seeking release from life's problems that clashed at some points with the prevailing Indian (Hindu) patterns. Gautama, the Buddha, drew followers because of his remarkable insight and compassion, which he claimed were based on an experience of enlightenment that others minimally could find helpful for improving their own lives and in some cases could replicate. It appears that the Buddha's authority over those who came to follow his way and comprise his community at times was contested by more ascetic disciples, such as his cousin Devadatta. After the death of the Buddha, his disciples began to collate his teachings, but they also began to go separate ways, depend-

Buddhism: Twenty-five Key Dates	
536–476 B.C.E.	*Buddha*
519	*Gautama's Enlightenment*
473	*First Buddhist Congress*
363	*Second Buddhist Congress*
273–236	*Reign of Buddhist Emperor Asoka*
236	*Rise of Mahayana Tradition*
160	Prajna-paramita *Literature*
80	Lotus Sutra
ca. 200 C.E.	*Nagarjuna, Leading Philosopher*
220–552	*Missions to Vietnam, China, Korea, Burma, Java, Sumatra, Japan*
430	*Buddhaghosa, Leading Philosopher*
594	*Buddhism Proclaimed Japanese State Religion*
749	*First Buddhist Monastery in Tibet*
805–806	*Foundation of Japanese Tendai and Shingon Sects*
845	*Persecution of Chinese Buddhists*
1065	*Hindu Invasions in Sri Lanka*
1175	*Honen; Japanese Pure Land*
1193–1227	*Rise of Japanese Zen Sects*
1260–1368	*Tibetan Buddhism Influential in China*
1360	*Buddhism Becomes State Religion in Thailand*
1543–88	*Final Conversion of Mongols*
1603	*Tokugawa Government Begins Domination of Japanese Buddhism*
1646–94	*Basho, Great Japanese Buddhist Poet*
1868–71	*Meiji Persecution of Buddhism in Japan*
1954–56	*Sixth Buddhist Council in Rangoon, Burma*

ing on their interpretations of what he had taught. Thus the meetings (councils) that took place in the fourth century B.C.E. failed to keep the community completely intact. Indeed, the split between Hinayana (small vehicle) and Mahayana (great vehicle) Buddhists that had become perceptible by the beginning of the Common Era had its beginnings in the aftermath of the early councils.

During the reign of Asoka (ca. 270–232 B.C.E.) Buddhism received imperial favor. Asoka wanted to reject the violence that prevailed in his early years of conquest and establish a regime consonant with Buddhist nonviolence. Within fifty years of his death, however, the Mauryan dynasty to which he had belonged collapsed and was replaced by one more sympathetic to Hinduism.

From the second century B.C.E. to the first century C.E., Buddhism was a powerful force throughout the whole Indian subcontinent, from the northwestern areas influenced by Greek ideas to Sri Lanka in the south. Buddhist influence also spread into Central Asia. Scholars sometimes speak of the transition during this period from an imperial to a civilizational impact—that is, Buddhism no longer depended on the favor of a king but had become a widespread influence throughout Indian culture (even when its power at the royal court had declined).

	THERAVADA	MAHAYANA
Monks	Makes the *sangha* the center	Considers compassion for others the best way to nirvana; monks especially compassionate
Buddha	Stresses the historical figure Gautama	Develops a wealth of devotional and metaphysical buddhas
Saint	One detached and highly ethical (*arhat*)	One noted for great compassion toward all living things (*bodhisattva*)
Geography	Sri Lanka, Burma, Thailand	East Asia
Philosophy	Rather scholastic and tied to meditation and ethics	Boldly speculative and tied to Zen and devotional schools

The 700 years from the second to the ninth century C.E. were a time when Buddhism enjoyed great cultural vitality, flourishing in Sri Lanka, India, and Central Asia. As well, it became firmly established in both north and south China, and also in Southeast Asia. After 500 C.E., it had taken root in both Tibet and Japan. Between 400 and 700 C.E., there was great traffic between China and India, much of it due to Chinese Buddhist monks seeking contact with the origins of their faith. By 500 C.E., a new branch of tradition, called the Vajrayana (thunderbolt vehicle) and stressing esoteric techniques, had developed out of Indian Mahayana insights and come to have great allure. During the eighth and ninth centuries C.E., it spread to Tibet and Japan.

After 900 C.E., the rise of Islam was disastrous for Buddhist interests in both India and Central Asia. As well, the intensification of Hindu bhakti movements gave it problems. Thus, by the end of the first millennium C.E., the influence of Buddhism had waned in both India and Central Asia. Although it continued to be significant in Sri Lanka, the future lay with such lands as Burma, Thailand, China, Japan, Korea, and Tibet. During the second millennium C.E., those have been the great Buddhist cultures, although usually there have been notable adversaries (Confucianism and Shinto, for instance) that have kept the Buddhists from gaining complete control. The wealth, vigor, and influence of the Buddhist monasteries have waxed and waned, new schools and reinvigorations steadily appearing but slack periods of laxity and stultification also occurring rather regularly. In the twentieth century Buddhism has suffered greatly from the spread of Communism in East Asia, but it has somewhat been compensated by a significant penetration of North America. Our historical treatment will assume this chronological skeleton and concentrate on the complex of ideas and ritualistic practices that gradually created the rich Buddhist system.

The Buddha

The Buddha was born about 536 B.C.E. outside the town of Kapilavastu in what is now a part of Nepal just below the Himalayan foothills. His people were a warrior tribe called Sakyas and his clan name was Gautama. The religious climate in which he grew up was quite heated. Some objectors were challenging the dominance of the priestly brahmin class. As we saw in

KEY SUMMARIES OF BUDDHIST BELIEF	
Three Jewels	The Buddha, dharma, *sangha*
Three Pillars or Main Concerns	Wisdom, morality, meditation
Three Characteristics (Marks) of All Reality	Painful, fleeting, selfless
Four Noble Truths	All life is suffering. The cause of suffering is desire. Removing desire removes suffering. The way to remove desire is to follow the noble Eightfold Path.
Five Ethical Precepts	Not to kill, lie, steal, be unchaste, take intoxicants
Eightfold Path	Right views, intention, speech, action, livelihood, effort, mindfulness, concentration

Chapter 1, the writers of the early Upanishads reveal the dissatisfaction with sacrifice that was burning among intellectuals, while the accounts of the Mahavira are evidence of the ascetic movement that also challenged the priestly religion of sacrifice. In secular culture, the sixth century B.C.E. saw a movement from tribal rule toward small-scale monarchy, a growth in urban populations, the beginnings of money-based economies, the beginnings of government bureaucracies, and the rise of a wealthy merchant class.[1] Thus, the Buddha grew up in a time of rapid change, when people were in turmoil over religion and open to new teachings.

Religious faith heavily embellishes the accounts of the Buddha's birth and early life, so it is difficult to describe this period accurately. Legend has it that his father, Suddhodana, was a king, and received a revelation that his son would be a world ruler if the child stayed at home but a spiritual savior if the child left home. According to other legends, the Buddha passed from his mother's side without causing her any pain, stood up, strode seven paces, and announced, "No more births for me!"[2] In other words, the child would be a spiritual conqueror—an Enlightened One.

As the Buddha grew, his father surrounded him with pleasures and distractions, to keep him in the palace and away from the sights of ordinary life. When the Buddha came of age, the father married him to a lovely woman named Yasodhara. So Sakyamuni ("sage of the Sakyas") lived in relative contentment until his late twenties. By the time of his own son's birth, however, the Buddha was restless. (He named the child Rahula [fetter].)

What really precipitated Sakyamuni's religious crisis, though, were experiences he had outside the palace. On several outings he met age, disease, and death. They shocked him severely, and he became anxiety ridden. How could anyone take life lightly if these were its constant dangers? Meditating on age, disease, and death, the young prince decided to cast away his round of pleasures and solve the riddle of life's meaning by becoming a wandering beggar concerned only to gain enlightenment. Renouncing his wife, child, father, and goods, he set off to answer his soul's yearning. (Indian tradition allowed renouncing the world after one had begotten a son.)

The teachers to whom the Buddha first apprenticed himself when he started wandering in pursuit of enlightenment specialized in meditation and asceticism. Their meditation, it appears, was a yogic pursuit of enlightenment through *samadhi* (trance). From them the Buddha learned much about the levels of consciousness but was not fully satisfied. The teachers could not bring him to dispassion, tranquillity, enlightenment, or **nirvana** (a state of liberation beyond samsara). In other words, the Buddha wanted a direct perception of how things are and a complete break with the realm of space, time, and rebirth. He sensed that to defeat age, disease, and death he had to go beyond ordinary humanity and tap the power of something greater.

To try to attain his goal, Sakyamuni turned to asceticism—so much so that he almost starved himself. The texts claim that when he touched his navel, he could feel his backbone. In any event, asceticism did not bring what Sakyamuni sought either. (Because of this, he and his followers have always urged moderation in fasting and bodily disciplines. Theirs, they like to say, is a Middle Way between indulgence and severity that strives to keep the body healthy, as a valuable ally should be, and to keep the personality from excessive self-concern.) The Buddha was learning key lessons for the conquest of self—key stratagems for getting the body, mind, and spirit to agree to seek liberation wholeheartedly.

What liberated the Buddha, apparently, was recalling moments of peace and joy from his childhood, when he had sat in calm but perceptive contemplation. According to the traditional accounts, Mara, the personification of evil or death, tried to tempt Buddha (who sat meditating under a fig tree) away from his pursuit.[3] First, he sent a host of demons, but the Buddha's merit and love protected him. Then, with increased fear that this man sitting so determinedly might escape his realm, the evil one invoked his own power. However, when Mara called on his retinue of demons to witness to his power, the Buddha, who was alone, called on mother earth, which quaked in acknowledgment. As a last ploy, Mara commissioned his three daughters (Discontent, Delight, and Desire) to seduce the sage. But they, too, failed, and so Mara withdrew. (Psychological interpretation can illuminate the details of this legend, considering them as symbols of dramatic changes in the personality — the challenges, fears, resistance, and final breakthrough one experiences when pursuing liberation. Then Mara would stand for the dread the personality feels at having to be converted to a radically new path.)

Enlightenment.   The enlightenment (realization of the truth) itself occurred on a night of the full moon. According to tradition, Buddha ascended the four stages of trance. In later times these four stages were considered as a progressive clarification of consciousness: (1) detachment from sense objects and calming the passions; (2) nonreasoning and "simple" concentration; (3) dispassionate mindfulness and consciousness with bodily bliss; and (4) pure awareness and peace without pain, elation, or depression.[4]

According to tradition, then, the Buddha progressed in his contemplative sitting by moving from confusion and sense knowledge to pure, unemotional awareness. The assumption was that this progress facilitated his direct perception of reality—seeing things as they really are. Enlightenment might bring in its train magical powers (the ability to walk on water, to know others' minds, or to remember one's previous lives, for instance), but its most important result was to eliminate desire, wrong views, and ignorance, the bonds that were tying Gautama to samsara. To break these bonds was to free his consciousness for nirvana.

Another traditional way of describing the Buddha's enlightenment is to trace his progress through the night. During the first watch (evening), he acquired knowledge of his previous lives. This is a power that some shamans claim, so it is not Buddha's distinguishing achievement. During the second watch (midnight), he acquired the "divine eye" with which he surveyed the karmic state of all beings—the cycle of dying and rebirth that is their destiny. With this vision he realized that good deeds beget good karma and move one toward freedom from samsara, while bad deeds beget bad karma and a deeper entrenchment in samsara. This second achievement made Buddha a moralistic philosopher, one who saw the condition of all beings as a function of their ethical or unethical behavior.

During the third watch (late night), the Buddha reached the peak of perception, attaining "the extinction of the outflows" (the stopping of desire for samsaric existence) and grasping the essence of what became the **Four Noble Truths**: (1) All life is suffering; (2) the cause of suffering is desire; (3) stopping desire

Figure 6 *Head of Buddha, Afghanistan, third century* C.E. *Polychrome stucco, 7 in. high. The half-closed eyes suggest the Buddha's repose, while his trace of a smile suggests his cool joy. The Nelson–Atkins Museum of Art, Kansas City, Missouri (Nelson Fund).*

Dependent Coarising, also came later. It explains the connections that link all beings.

Enlightenment seems to have been the dramatic experience of vividly perceiving—seeing, understanding, feeling—that life, which Sakyamuni had found to consist of suffering, had a solution. One could escape the terror of aging, sickness, and death by withdrawing one's concerns for or anxieties about them—by no longer desiring youth, health, or even life itself. By withdrawing in this manner, one could lessen the bad effects of karma, since desire was the means by which karma kept the personality on the wheel of dying and rebirth. Removing desire therefore took away karma's poison. To destroy desire for karmic existence, though, one had to penetrate and remove the illusion of its goodness. That is, one had to remove the ignorance that makes sensual pleasures, financial success, prestige, and so on, seem good. Buddha designed the Eightfold Path and the doctrine of Dependent Coarising to remove such ignorance and rout desire.

The picture of the Buddha sitting in repose after having gained enlightenment has always been a great consolation to his followers. With the pictures and stories about his kindness as a teacher, his affection for his disciples, his wisdom in instructing kings, and the like, it has given the Buddha the human qualities most followers of a religious leader seem to need if they are to follow the path with enthusiasm. The general rule seems to be that followers must love the leader if they are to love the path. Admiring the clarity of the leader's teaching and experiencing the benefits of the path are not enough. The leader inevitably becomes the model, the prime evidence, the proof that the teaching indeed is wholly wise, that the path in fact is fully efficacious. So Muhammad became the prime Muslim, beloved of all who confessed Allah, while Jesus became not only the way, the truth, and the light but the personal face of a God who was love to the core. The teaching of Krishna that we found in the *Bhagavad Gita,* where he finally revealed that bhakti was the great way and he himself loved those who loved him devotedly, applies in many other religious contexts. The Buddha was an effective teacher because his students loved him. They did not find his detachment something cold and forbidding. They found it just the far side of the compassion, the kindness, the charm that made him seem to reach into their very beings and loosen the bonds in which ignorance and fear had kept them tied.

will stop suffering; and (4) the Eightfold Path (explained below) is the best way to stop desire.

The **Eightfold Path** outlines the life-style that Buddha developed for people who accepted his teaching and wanted to pursue nirvana. As such, it is more detailed than a description of what he had directly experienced in enlightenment—something that he probably elaborated later on. The explanation of reality that Buddha developed out of his experience of enlightenment, which became known as the doctrine of

The Dharma (Buddhist Doctrine)

Buddhists have seen in Sakyamuni's enlightenment the great act centering their religion. The Buddha is worthy of following because in enlightenment he became shining with knowledge *(bodhi)*. What he saw under the bodhi tree in the third watch was nothing less than the formula for measuring life and curing its mortal illness. The Four Noble Truths and Dependent Coarising are two favorite ways of presenting the essential truths of Buddha's knowledge.

Dependent Coarising and the Eightfold Path. Often Buddhists picture the doctrine of Dependent Coarising, which provides their basic picture of reality, as a wheel with twelve sections or a chain with twelve links (the first and the last are joined to make a circuit).[5] These twelve links explain the round of samsaric existence. They are not an abstract teaching for the edification of the philosophical mind, but an extension of the essentially therapeutic analysis that the Buddha thought could cure people of their basic illness.

The wheel of Dependent Coarising turns in this way: (1) Aging and dying depend on rebirth; (2) rebirth depends on becoming; (3) becoming depends on the appropriation of certain necessary materials; (4) appropriation depends on desire for such materials; (5) desire depends on feeling; (6) feeling depends on contact with material reality; (7) contact depends on the senses; (8) the senses depend on "name" (the mind) and "form" (the body); (9) name and form depend on consciousness (the spark of sentient life); (10) consciousness shapes itself by samsara; (11) the samsara causing rebirth depends on ignorance of the Four Noble Truths; and (12) therefore, the basic cause of samsara is ignorance.

One can run this series forward and back, but the important concept is that ignorance (of the Four Noble Truths) is the cause of painful human existence, and aging and dying are both its final overwhelming effects and the most vivid aspects of samsara. Thus, the chain of Dependent Coarising is a sort of practical analysis of human existence. It mingles concepts of physical phenomena (for example, aging and dying depend on rebirth) and concepts of psychological phenomena (for example, appropriation depends on desire). The result is called Dependent Coarising (or origination) because it is a doctrine of coordinated influences—of how the basic factors shaping reality impact on one another.

In the Buddha's enlightenment, as he and his followers elaborated it, there is no single cause of the way things are. Rather, all things are continually rotating in this twelve-stage wheel of existence. Each stage of the wheel passes the power of movement along to the next. The only way to step off the wheel, to break the chain, is to gain enlightenment and so detach the stage of ignorance. If we do detach ignorance, we stand free of karma, karmic consciousness, and so on, all the way to aging and rebirth.

The result of enlightenment, then, is no rebirth, which is the implication of nirvana. Nirvana is the state in which the chain of existence does not obtain —in which desire is "blown out" and one escapes karma and samsara. Thus, nirvana begins with enlightenment and becomes definitive with death. By his enlightenment, for instance, the Buddha had broken the chain of Dependent Coarising; at his death his nirvana freed him from rebirths.

The Eightfold Path (which is the Fourth Noble Truth) details how we may dispel ignorance and gain nirvana by describing a middle way between sensuality and extreme asceticism that consists of (1) right views, (2) right intention, (3) right speech, (4) right action, (5) right livelihood, (6) right effort, (7) right mindfulness, and (8) right concentration.[6] "Right views" means knowledge of the Four Noble Truths. "Right intention" means dispassion, benevolence, and refusal to injure others. "Right speech" means no lying, slander, abuse, or idle talk. "Right action" means not taking life, stealing, or being sexually disordered. "Right livelihood" is an occupation that does not harm living things; thus, butchers, hunters, fishers, and sellers of weapons or liquor are proscribed. "Right effort" avoids the arising of evil thoughts. In "right mindfulness," awareness is disciplined so that it focuses on an object or idea to know its essential reality. "Right concentration" focuses on a worthy object of meditation.

The first two aspects of the Eightfold Path, right views and right intention, comprise the wisdom portion of of the Buddhist program. If we know the Four Noble Truths and orient ourselves toward them with the right spiritual disposition, we are wise and come to religious peace. Tradition groups aspects three, four, and five under morality.[7] To speak, to act, and to make one's living in wise ways amount to an ethics for nirvana, a morality that will liberate one from suffering. Finally, aspects six, seven, and eight entail meditation. By setting consciousness correctly through right effort, mindfulness, and concentration, one can perceive the structures of reality and thus personally validate the Buddha's enlightened understanding.[8]

The three divisions of the Eightfold Path compose a single entity, a program in which each of the three parts reinforces the other two. Wisdom sets up the game plan, the basic theory of what the human condition is and how one is to cope with it. Morality applies wisdom to daily life by specifying how one should speak, act, and support oneself. Regular meditation focuses one on the primary truths and the reality to which they apply. In meditation the Buddhist personally appropriates the official wisdom, personally examines the ethical life. As a result, meditation builds up the Buddhist's spiritual force, encouraging the peaceful disposition necessary for a person to be nonviolent and kindly.[9]

The Buddha's Preaching. Buddha himself apparently debated what to do after achieving enlightenment. On the one hand, he had this dazzling light, this potent medicine, to dispense. On the other hand, there was dreary evidence that humanity, mired in its attachments, would find his teaching hard to comprehend and accept.[10] Legend says that the god Brahman appeared to the Buddha and pleaded that the Enlightened One teach what he had seen for the sake of wayward humanity. Out of compassion (which became the premier Buddhist virtue), the Enlightened One finally agreed to Brahman's request.

According to tradition, his first sermon occurred in Deer Park near Benares, about five days' walk from where enlightenment took place. He preached first to some former ascetic companions who had rejected him when he turned away from their harsh mortification, and his calm bearing won them over. What Buddha first preached was the Four Noble Truths, but he apparently prefaced his preaching with a solemn declaration of his authority as an immortal enlightened one. From this preface Buddhists have concluded that one must have faith in the authority behind the **dharma** (the teaching) if the dharma is to have its intended effect.

Opening ourselves to the Buddha's authority, let us imagine that we are listening to his famous Fire Sermon, preached after the sermon in Deer Park. He was following his customary pattern, dwelling in one place as long as seemed profitable and then moving on to the next. So, having finished a stint in Uruvela, he

set out for the town of Gaya Head. With him went a great band of monks. When they got to Gaya Head, the Blessed One addressed the monks as follows:

O priests, [monks], all things are on fire. The eye is on fire, as are the forms the eye receives, the consciousness the eye raises, the impressions the eye transmits, the sensations—pleasant, unpleasant, or indifferent—that the eye's impressions produce. All that has to do with our seeing is on fire.

And in what does this fire consist? It consists in the flame of passion, the burning of hate, the heat of infatuation. Birth, old age, death, sorrow, lamentation, misery, grief, and despair are all expressions of the fire that comes into us through our eyes.

In the same way, the ear is on fire with burning sounds. The nose is on fire with burning odors. The tongue is on fire with flaming tastes. The whole body is on fire with flaming touches. Even worse, the mind is on fire; hot ideas, burning awareness, searing impressions, smoldering sensations. Again I say, the fire of passion, birth, old age, death, sorrow, lamentation, misery, grief, and despair is burning you up.

What, then, should you do? If you are wise, O priests, you will conceive an aversion for the eye and the eye's forms, the eye's consciousness, the eye's impressions, and the eye's sensations, be they pleasant, unpleasant, or indifferent. If you are wise, you will conceive an aversion for the ear and its sounds, the nose and its odors, the tongue and its tastes, the body and the things it touches, the mind and all that passes through it.

If you conceive this aversion, you will divest yourselves of passion. Divesting yourselves of passion, you will become free. Being free, you will become aware of your liberation and know that you have exhausted rebirth. This will prove that you have lived the holy life, fulfilled what it behooved you to do, and made yourselves subject to this world no longer.

When the Buddha finished his sermon, many of the monks' minds became free from attachment and they were delivered of their depravities.[11]

What, though, about ourselves, twentieth-century hearers of the Buddha? Can the Fire Sermon carry across 2,500 years? Many Buddhists think it can.

After all, we are still possessed of eyes, ears, nose, tongue, and hands eager to touch. We are still the strange animals possessed of minds flowing with ideas, reflex awareness, sensations to drive our days and bedevil our nights. As with the Buddha's contemporaries, unless we have these faculties under control, we are burning with useless passions. If our senses lead us, instead of our leading them, we are bound hand and mind.

Look around you. See how many of your contemporaries rush like lemmings to the sea. Some rush after money. Others rush after pleasure. A third group hustles to gain power. From dawn to midnight, their brains teem with schemes, images of success, numbers adding up to bigger and bigger bank accounts. Do they not seem feverish? Is there not within them a fire wisdom would have to douse?

And how could wisdom go about dousing this fire? Could it not scoop up the old Buddhist verities, the millennial lessons in detachment? "If you want peace," Buddhist wisdom continues to say, "you must gain control over your senses and your mind. To gain control over your senses and your mind, you must detach yourself from their blandishments. Not every image that floats before your mind is profitable. Not every lissome limb or attractive scheme brings you good. Indeed, few images, limbs, or schemes conduce to your peace and freedom. Unless you have conquered your passions, most visitors to your soul will do you harm."

How pressing is this teaching? That depends on how seriously you take human death. If you think your basic task before death is gaining enlightenment, wisdom to free you from death's hold, you will find the Buddha's teaching pressing. If you do not think your basic task is gaining enlightenment, you will let the Buddha's teaching pass by. The Buddha's own criterion for evaluating your state likely would focus on your degree of inner pain. If you find your current circumstances depressing, and you long deeply to change who you are, you are apt to be open to the dharma. The Enlightened One gained his wisdom through struggles with sadness and discontent; so can you. His wisdom means little to those content with their lot, happy to eat, drink, and be merry. For them the wheel must turn again. They need a deeper experience of life's burning.

The Buddha's preaching won him innumerable converts, men and women alike, many of whom decided to dedicate their lives to following him and his way. A great number entered the *sangha,* or monastic order, assuming a life of celibacy, poverty, and submission to rules of discipline.[12] Other followers decided to practice the dharma while remaining in their lay state, and they frequently gave the Buddha and the Buddhist community land and money.[13] In both cases people became Buddhists by taking "refuge" in the three jewels of the Enlightened One's religion: the Buddha himself, the teaching (dharma), and the community (*sangha* can mean either the monastic community or the entire community of Buddhists, lay and monastic, past and present).[14]

By uttering three times the vow of taking refuge, one became a follower in a strict, official sense. (This act reflects the special, almost mystical effect that words had in ancient India. When the Buddha preached, just as when the Vedic priests uttered sacrificial formulas, an active force was believed to be released. When one took refuge, the words effected a binding to the Buddha, the teaching, and the community.)

Buddhist Catechetics.   In time a catechism developed to explain the Buddha's teaching. One of the catechism's most important notions was the "three marks" of reality. Together with the Four Noble Truths and Dependent Coarising, the three marks have helped countless Buddhists hold the dharma clearly in mind. According to this conception, all reality is painful, fleeting, and selfless (*dukkha, anicca, anatta*). This formula adds something to the insights of the Four Noble Truths. That all life or reality is painful is the first truth: the reality of suffering. By this Buddhists do not mean that one never experiences pleasant things or that one has no joy. Rather, they mean that no matter how pleasant or joyous one's life, it is bound to include disappointment, sickness, misunderstanding, and finally death. Since the joyous things do not last, even they have an aspect of painfulness.

Second, all life is fleeting, or passing. Everything changes—nothing stays the same. Therefore, realistically there is nothing to which we can cling, nothing that we can rely on absolutely. In fact, even our own realities (our "selves") change. On one level, we move through the life cycle from youth to old age. On a more subtle level, our thoughts, our convictions, and our emotions change.

Third, there is no self. For Buddhists, the fleeting-ness of our own consciousness proves that there is no atman—no solid soul or self. In this the Buddhists directly opposed Hinduism as well as common belief. All people, it seems, naturally think that they have personal identities. Buddhists claim that personalities consist of nothing solid or permanent. We are but packages of physical and mental stuff that is temporar-ily bound together in our present proportions.

The tradition calls the component parts of all things *skandhas* (heaps), which number five: body, feeling, conception, karmic disposition, and con-sciousness. Together the *skandhas* make the world and the person of appearances, and they also constitute the basis for clinging to existence and rebirth. To cut through the illusion of a (solid) self—Buddhists do not deny that we have (changing) identities—is therefore the most important blow that one can strike against ignorance. This is done by being open to the flowing character of all life and decisively pursuing nirvana.

The early teachers described the realms of rebirth to which humans were subject and in so doing devel-oped a Buddhist version of the Indian cosmic powers and zones of the afterlife. Essentially, the Buddhist wheel of rebirth focuses on six realms or destinies. Three are lower realms, which are karmic punishment for bad deeds. The other three are higher realms in which good deeds are rewarded. The lowest realm is for punishing the wicked by means befitting their par-ticular crimes. However, these punishments are not eternal; after individuals have paid their karmic debt, they can reenter the human realm by rebirth. Above the lowest realm is the station of the "hungry ghosts," who wander the earth's surface begging for food. The third and least severe realm of the wicked is that of animals. If one is reborn in that realm, one suffers the abuses endured by dumb beasts.

The fortunate destinies reward good karma. The human realm is the first, and in it one can perform meritorious deeds. Only in the human realm can one become a buddha. The two final realms are those of the demigods (Titans) and the gods proper. Both include a variety of beings, all of whom are sub-ject to rebirth. Since even the Buddhist gods are subject to rebirth, their happiness is not at all compa-rable to the final nirvana. Better to be a human being advancing toward enlightenment than a divinity liable to the pains of another transmigratory cycle. Perhaps for that reason, the Buddhist spirits and divinities, as

well as the Buddhist ghosts and demons, seem inferior to the human being. Apparently Buddhism adopted wicked and good spirits from Indian culture without much thought. In subjecting these spirits to the pow-ers of an *arhat* (one who achieves nirvana), however, Buddhists minimized their fearsomeness.

Despite its sometimes lurid description of the six realms, the dharma basically stated that each individ-ual is responsible for his or her own destiny. The future is neither accidental, fated, nor determined by the gods. If one has a strong will to achieve salvation, a day of final triumph will surely come. As a result, karma is less an enslavement than an encouragement. If one strives to do good deeds (to live by the dharma in wisdom-morality-meditation), one cannot fail to progress toward freedom. At the least, one will come to life again in more favorable circumstances. Thus, Buddhism ousts the gods and the fates from control over human destiny. This is interesting sociologically, because Buddhism has been most appealing to people who have wanted control over their own lives, such as warriors and merchants.

The simpler folk, who might have had to spur themselves to such a sober and confident state of mind, drew encouragement from Buddhist art, which illustrates the delights of heaven and the torments of hell. Many renditions of the wheel of life, for instance, show Mara (Death) devouring the material world and those who cling to it. In the center of the wheel are such symbolic animals as the cock (desire), the snake (hatred), and the pig (delusion), who work to keep the wheel turning.[15] "Break with these," the art shouts. "Rise up. You have nothing to lose but your chains."

The dharma, therefore, began as a proclamation of diagnosis and cure. Likening himself to a doctor, the Buddha told his followers not to lose themselves in extraneous questions about where karma or igno-rance comes from. Furthermore, he told them not to concentrate on whether the world is eternal or how to conceive of nirvana. To ponder such issues, said the Buddha, would be like a man severely wounded with an arrow who refuses treatment until he knows the caste and character of the man who shot him. The point is to get the arrow out. Similarly, the point to human existence is to break the wheel of rebirth, to slay the monstrous round of suffering, fleetingness, and emptiness.

For about forty-five years after his enlightenment, the Buddha preached variants on his basic themes: the

Four Noble Truths, Dependent Coarising, and the three marks. His *sangha* grew, as monks, nuns, and laypeople responded to his simple, clear message. He had to suffer painful threats to the unity of his group, but on the whole he did his work in peace. At his death he had laid the essential foundation of Buddhism —its basic doctrine and way of life. Thus, his death (*parinirvana*) came in the peace of trance. The physical cause of his death was poisoning by either pork or mushrooms (depending on which commentator one reads), but in the Buddhist view the more profound cause was the Buddha's sense of completeness. When he asked his followers for the last time whether they had any questions, all stood silent. So he passed into trance and out of this painful realm. According to legend, the earth quaked and the sky thundered in final tribute.

Early Buddhism

After the Buddha's death his followers gathered to organize the dharma (which for some centuries remained largely oral) in part because he had said it should be their leader after him. According to tradition, they held a council at Rajagraha during the first monsoon season after the *parinirvana* to settle both the dharma and the **Vinaya** (the monastic rules). The canon of Buddhist scriptures that we now possess supposedly is the fruit of this council. Today the **Pali canon** (the authoritative collection of materials in the Indian vernacular that the Theravadins use) consists of five *nikayas,* which are collections of discourses (**sutras**) that the Buddha supposedly preached. Just one of these collections, the middle-length *Majjhima Nikaya,* runs to 1,100 pages in modern printing.

In addition to these sutras and the monastic rules, early Buddhists added to the canon the *Abhidhamma* treatises of the early philosophers, who tried to analyze reality by correlating the Buddha's teaching with the experiences of meditation. Therefore, the Buddhist tendency in forming a canon (etymologically, a ruler) by which to measure faith and doctrine was to be as comprehensive as possible.

However, within 100 years of the Buddha's death, dissensions split the *sangha.*[16] These were the precursors of the major division of Buddhism into the Theravada and Mahayana schools, which we consider below. The apparent forerunners of the Mahayana schools were the Mahasanghikas, who seem to have considered the Vinaya adaptable, while the Sthaviras (Elders), the precursors of the Theravadins, stressed the importance of the letter of the monastic code. About 200 years after the Buddha's death the Pudgalavadins branched off from the Sthaviras. They taught that there is a person or self (neither identical with the *skandhas* nor separate from them) that is the basis of knowledge, transmigration, and entrance into nirvana.

These first schisms prefigured later Buddhist history. New schools have constantly arisen as new insights or problems made old views unacceptable. As a result, the *sangha* has not been a centralized authority and Buddhism has not kept a full unity. Nonetheless, the *sangha* has given all Buddhists certain essential teachings (almost all sects would agree to what we have expounded of dharma so far). Also, it has fostered a very influential monastic life. The monastic order, which has always been the heart of Buddhism (monks have tended to take precedence over laity as an almost unquestioned law of nature), has been a source of stability in Buddhism. Let us therefore turn to the lives of Buddhist monks and nuns.

Monasticism. A major influence on the Buddhist monastic routine has been Buddha's own life. According to Buddhaghosa, a Ceylonese commentator in the fifth century C.E., the Buddha used to rise at daybreak, wash, and then sit in meditation until it was time to go begging for food. He stayed close enough to a village (wandering from one to another) to obtain food, but far enough away to obtain quiet. Usually devout laity would invite him in, and after eating lightly he would teach them the dharma. Then he would return to his residence, wash, and rest. After this he would preach to the monks and respond to their requests for individual guidance. After another rest he would preach to the laity and then take a cool bath. His evening would consist of more individual conferences, after which, Buddhaghosa claims, he would receive any deities that came for instruction. [17]

The Vinaya established rules that would promote such a steady life of meditation, begging, preaching, and counsel. Originally the monks always wandered except during the rainy season, but later they assumed a more stable setting with quiet lands and a few simple buildings. From the Vinaya's list of capital offenses, though, we can see that a monk's robe did not necessarily make him a saint.

The four misdeeds that merited expulsion from the order were fornication, theft, killing, and "falsely claiming spiritual attainments." Committing any of thirteen lesser misdeeds led to a group meeting of the *sangha* and probation. They included sexual offenses (touching a woman, speaking suggestively to a woman, urging a woman to gain merit by submitting to a "man of religion," and serving as a procurer), violating the rules that limited the size and specified the site of a monk's dwelling, falsely accusing other monks of grievous violations of the rule, fomenting discord among the monks, or causing a schism. With appropriate changes, similar rules have governed the nuns' lives.

There are hundreds of other things that monks and nuns cannot do, and all of them suggest something about the ideals of the *sangha*. Prohibitions against lying, slander, stealing another's sleeping space, and "sporting in the water" testify to an ideal of honest and direct speech, mutual consideration, and grave decorum. Similarly, prohibitions against digging in the ground and practicing agriculture reflect the ideals of not taking other creatures' lives and of begging one's food. Rules for good posture and table manners indicate that an ideal monk has stood erect, kept his eyes downcast, refrained from loud laughter, and not smacked his lips, talked with his mouth full, or thrown food into his mouth. The refined *bhiksu* (monk) also cannot excrete while standing up or excrete onto growing grass or into the water. Finally, he is not supposed to preach the dharma to monks or laypeople who carry parasols, staffs, swords, or other weapons, or wear slippers, sandals, turbans, or other head coverings.

The *sangha* accepted recruits from all social classes, and many of them were youths. From this circumstance one can understand the concern for the rights of the growing grass and the water. In addition, historians regularly note that the Vinaya is remarkably free from taboos (irrational proscriptions of contact with certain items labeled dangerous, such as menstrual blood, corpses, hair, or fingernails), although Buddhism has developed its share of irrationalities. Monks often carried their two principal fears (of taking life or being sexually incontinent) to extremes. Especially regarding matters of sex, the monastic leg-islation was quite strict. (This is also true of Christian monastic legislation.)

The Laity. From earliest times, Buddhism encouraged its laity to pursue an arduous religious life. Though his or her white robe never merited the honor that a monk's colored robe received, a layperson who had taken refuge in the three jewels and contributed to the *sangha*'s support was an honorable follower. From early times Buddhism has specified morality (*sila*) for the laity in five precepts. The first of these is to refrain from killing living beings. (Unintentional killing is not an offense, and agriculturalists have only to minimize their damage to life.) The second is to refrain from stealing. The third precept deals with sexual matters. It forbids intercourse with another person's wife, a nun, or a woman betrothed to another man. It also urges restraint with a wife who is pregnant, nursing, or under a religious vow of sexual abstinence. Apparently relations with courtesans were licit. The commentators' explanation of this precept assumes that it is the male's duty to provide control in sexual matters (because females are by nature wanton). The fourth precept imposes restraint from lying, and the fifth precept forbids drinking alcoholic beverages.

This ethical code has been the layperson's chief focus. Occasionally he or she received instruction in meditation or the doctrine of wisdom, and later Mahayana sects considered the laity fully capable of reaching nirvana. (In the beginning only monks were so considered; nuns never had the status of monks, in part because of legends that the Buddha established nunneries only reluctantly.) The principal lay virtues were to be generous in supporting monks and to witness to Buddhist values in the world. The financial support, obviously enough, was a two-edged sword. Monks who put on spiritual airs would annoy the laity who were sweating to support them. On the other hand, monks constantly faced a temptation to tailor their doctrine to please the laity and so boost financial contributions. The best defenses against such abuses were monasteries in which the monks lived very simple, poor lives.

Other practices that devout laity might take up have included regular fasting, days of retreat for reading the scriptures, praying, hearing sermons, giving up luxurious furniture and housing, abstaining from singing, dancing, and theater, and decreas-

Figure 7 *Temples of the Imperial Compound, Bangkok. Photo by J. T. Carmody.*

ing their sexual activity. Clearly, such practices have further advanced the pious layperson toward a monastic sort of regime and have sometimes smacked of puritanism.

Scholars suggest that early Buddhism did not develop many new ceremonies or rites of passage; instead it integrated local celebrations and customs into its practices. To this day, birth and wedding ceremonies do not involve Buddhist priests very much, but funeral services do. In early times, the Indian Buddhists likely celebrated the New Year and a day of offering to the ancestors, both of which were probably adopted from Hinduism. In addition, Indian Buddhists commemorated the Buddha's birthday and the day of his enlightenment. Robinson and Johnson suggest that cults of trees, tree spirits, serpents, fertility goddesses, and funeral mounds all came from preexisting Indian religious customs.[18] However, the bodhi tree under which the Buddha came to enlightenment

prompted many Buddhists to revere trees. Such trees, along with **stupas** (burial mounds) of holy persons, were popular places of devotion.

The worship of statues of the Buddha grew popular only under the influence of Mahayana thought after 100 C.E., but earlier veneration of certain symbols of the Buddha (an empty throne, a pair of footprints, a wheel or lotus, or a bodhi tree) paved the way. These symbols signified such things as the Buddha's presence in the world, his royal renunciation, and the dharma he preached. The lotus became an especially popular symbol, since it stood for the growth of pure enlightenment from the mud of worldly life.

Meditation.   A central aspect of early Buddhist life was meditation, which has remained a primary way to realize the wisdom and inspire the practice that lead to nirvana. Meditation (*dhyana*) designated mental discipline. For instance, one could meditate by practicing certain devotional exercises that focused attention on one of the three jewels—the Buddha, the dharma, or the sangha. These would be recalled as the refuges under which one had taken shelter, and the meditator's sense of wonder and gratitude for protection would increase his or her emotional attachment. Thus, such meditative exercises were a sort of bhakti, though without sexual overtones.

Indeed, both the saints (*bodhisattvas*) and the Buddha could become objects of loving concentration. However, such devotion was not meditation proper, for *dhyana* was a discipline of consciousness similar to yoga. As is clear from the story of his own life, Buddha's enlightenment came after he had experienced various methods of "mindfulness" and trance. It is proper, then to consider Buddhist meditation a species of yoga.[19]

From early times the mindfulness of Buddhists has usually been a control of the senses and imagination geared to bringing "one-pointed mental consciousness" to bear on the truths of the dharma. For instance, one fixed on mental processes to become aware of their stream and the *skandhas*, and to focus on the belief that all is fleeting, painful, and selfless. In addition, meditation masters sometimes encouraged monks to bolster their flight from the world by contemplating the contemptibleness of the body and its pleasures.

Buddhaghosa, for example, proposed lengthy exercises concerning the repulsiveness of food. To help monks control eating, he suggested that they consider (1) that they have to go get food and thus leave their solitude; (2) that they have to search it out through muddy streets and often suffer abuse from villagers; (3) that chewing food crushes it to a state of repulsiveness, "like a dog's vomit in a dog's trough"; (4) that the four effluvia (bile, phlegm, blood, and pus) go to work on the ingested food; (5) that the food goes into the stomach, which "resembles a cesspool that has not been washed for a long time"; (6) that the food has to pass through this cesspool and its malodorous regions, which are traversed by the stomach's winds; (7) that digested food is not like gold or silver but gives off foam and bubbles, becoming excrement and filling the abdomen like yellow loam in a tube; (8) that digested food brings forth various "putridities," such as hair and nails, and that poorly digested food produces ringworm, itching, leprosy, eczema, and dysentery;

(9) that excreted food is offensive and a cause of sadness; and (10) that eating and excreting soil the body.[20]

This master has similar proposals for meditations on corpses and even beautiful women. A beautiful woman, for instance, is really a bag of bones and foul odors. In a few years she will be a corpse, and like all dead corpses she will be full of worms and maggots. Only a fool would risk nirvana for illusory pleasure with her.

However, wisdom was more than just attacks on hindrances to freedom and nirvana. In careful meditations, Buddhist adepts tried to replicate the Enlightened One's experience during the night of vision, cultivating first his one-pointedness of mind and then his dispassionate heightening of awareness. Adepts also composed meditations focusing on doctrinal points such as the Four Noble Truths or the three marks in order to see their reality directly. This was similar to the insight practices or the way of knowledge (*jnana-marga*) that Hinduism offered, though of course Buddhist beliefs often differed from Hindu.

Case Study. The Theravada tradition, which claims ties with pristine early Buddhism, has stressed the importance of meditation for gaining freedom from the illusions of the self, and this teaching has experienced a vigorous renaissance in contemporary Burma. By and large, most of the recent Burmese meditation masters have emphasized attaining insight into the true nature of reality, in contrast to meditation masters in other eras or lands who have emphasized attaining a formless yogic trance. Since they claim that insight was the original Buddhist emphasis, while trance was the Hindu emphasis, the recent Burmese masters have rather self-consciously striven to give preference to the Buddhist, rather than the Hindu Brahmanistic, influences that Indian history bequeathed them.

For most contemporary Burmese practitioners of meditation, the goal is improving one's karmic state and so gaining a fortunate rebirth. In contrast to the Hindu yogic tradition, which pays close attention to body-mind control, the Buddhist insight tradition pays close attention to *observing* the body-mind unity in its actions, thoughts, and feelings. Control is secondary and less important.

The preferred Burmese focus for observing the human unity is the breath or the body's tonus (feeling). By cultivating a regular breathing that integrates the body-mind components and stressing feeling, the Burmese masters have shifted away from the visual emphasis of the yogic tradition. They urge that one try to grow more sensitive to the touch of the breath at the nostrils or the rise and fall of the abdomen. Then, with practice, one can expand this tactile awareness to other dimensions of experience, for example the pleasures or pains one is experiencing. The result should be a heightened attention to what seems most real— stimulating, pleasing, or irritating—to the body-mind unity at a given moment. Behind the efforts to gain this heightened attention lie the conviction that the three marks, if vividly experienced, will bring one great progress.

The descriptions of a European Buddhist who learned Burmese meditation may concretize some of these theoretical remarks. The man was in Rangoon on a business trip in December of 1952. He had been a practicing Buddhist for eighteen years, had grown interested in meditation while spending a year in monasteries in Mongolia and Tibet, and therefore contacted Guru Sithu U Ba Khin, a prominent Burmese meditation master. Guru Sithu put him on a regime of insight-meditation (*vipassana*), beginning with two half-hour introductory sessions. These were all the man required to see clearly within himself a remarkable light. He took this light to be the powerful and bright illumination the mind gives off when we free it from disturbances and let it be pure and serene. The basic method the man used to come to this illumination was concentrating on his breath, which allowed him to still and focus his consciousness to "one-pointedness."

The man continued meditating, shifting his concentration to his bodily sensations. The first sensation that preoccupied him was his body's burning or suffering. As he focused on his bodily temperature, a burning within him grew to the point that he felt like steam on the surface of boiling water. As he stayed with this sensation, it expanded to the point that it seemed to envelop the core of his being. The suffering he felt was almost unbearable, since all of him seemed on fire.

At the last moment, when I felt myself about dying, it was as if my heart was pulled out of my body and at the same moment—wanting eagerly to be freed from Dukka [suffering]—with a sudden but a small flash of light, I was out of it and

felt a refreshing coolness and delight, which words cannot describe. It is an escape and a refuge from all daily trouble, too great to be understood, when not experienced. And the great bliss is that every one can achieve this state; provided he has a pure mind at least for the time of concentration, has the right intentions, attentiveness and concentration, and anyhow tries to live as pure as possible.[21]

Guru Sithu glossed this account of the man's meditational experiences with the following remarks: (1) He and the European Buddhist had agreed that morality, meditation, and wisdom were the three indispensable steps to Buddhist development. (2) He had found the man morally sound and already well advanced in meditation, as the man's quick access to the light of the mind revealed. (3) The man understood theoretically the Buddhist (and contemporary scientific) notion that everything in the universe is in flux. By developing his insight-meditation, he would soon be able to realize the true nature of the forms and names under which ever-changing reality appears. (4) The man's experience of heat was a breakthrough on the way to realizing the fluctuating and painful character of all reality. (5) He assured the man that experiencing suffering is one of the best ways to extinguish suffering. (6) The coolness the man experienced was a sort of rebirth, showing that he had burned up a significant portion of the impurities that cause our human suffering.

So, we find in this Burmese example the traditional truths of suffering and transiency. Drawing on centuries of meditators' experience, many contemporary Buddhists are hard at work trying to change their body-mind condition, so that one day, one lifetime, they may experience no-self and be ready for nirvana.

Mahayana

In the development of Buddhist sects, which reached its most important point in the years 100 B.C.E. to 100 C.E. with the rise of Mahayana Buddhism, wisdom, meditation, and mortality were important to all parties. However, the saintly ideal and the place of the laity differed among Theravadins and Mahayanists. Even more, the notion of the Buddha and the range of metaphysics varied considerably. The rise of Mahayana was the first major change in Buddhism.[22] Before its emergence, early Buddhism was fairly uniform in its understanding of Buddha-dharma-sangha and wisdom-morality-meditation. (Theravada has essentially kept early Buddhist beliefs, so the description of Buddhism thus far characterizes Theravada.)

Of course, Mahayana was not without forerunners. We have indicated the liberalizing orientation of the Mahasanghikas, and also the split among the Sthaviras that occurred when the Pudgalavadins advocated the reality of the person. However, the hallmark of Mahayana was its literature, which placed in the mouth of the Buddha sutras describing a new ideal and a new version of wisdom. *Mahayana* means "great vehicle," symbolizing a large raft able to carry multitudes across the stream of samsara to nirvana. *Hinayana* is the term of reproach that Mahayanists used to characterize those who rejected their literature and views. It means "lesser vehicle," symbolizing a small raft able to carry only a few persons across the samsaric stream. Theravadins, pointing with pride to the antiquity of their traditions and claiming to have preserved the original spirit of Buddhism better than the innovating Mahayanists, do not refer to themselves as Hinayanists.

Why did Mahayana conceive the need for a greater vehicle? The answer seems to be twofold: the sense that the career of the Buddha showed him to be so full of compassion that one could not limit Buddhist doctrine or practice in any way that confined the outreach of the Enlightened One's mercy, and the sense that people everywhere, indeed all living creatures, needed such compassion—were burning with desire and could only be saved by the wisdom of Gautama. Thus the Mahayanists came to think that the ideal follower of the Buddha, the saint they call a *bodhisattva* (one who had the knowledge and being of a Buddha, who essentially was an Enlightened One), would so extend compassion that any notion of self-concern would fall away. Somewhat in contrast to the *arhat,* the holy person whose concentration on self-perfection had brought deep wisdom, goodness, and peace, the *bodhisattva* would postpone entrance into nirvana (postpone gaining the fruits of his or her perfection) and stay in the samsaric world to labor for the salvation of all living human beings.

In Mahayana, therefore, the self-giving symbolized by Gautama's decision to return to the world and preach the dharma empowered a considerable outreach. Emotionally, horizons expanded to include all

beings in need. In terms of missionary impulse, the Mahayanists felt impelled to preach to people everywhere. Culturally, Mahayanists sensed that all aspects of life ideally would be colored and enriched by the Buddha's compassion. As well, they realized that laypeople had to be better appreciated and shown how any state of life, married life and work in the world as much as monastic living, could be a means to enlightenment and a place where one could do good. Finally, the Mahayanists put great effort into developing Buddhist wisdom so that it could accommodate the large-heartedness they found in the Buddha's career. Thus their metaphysics came to look for traces of *bodhi,* liberating wisdom, everywhere, and they soon came to question any facile distinction between nirvana and samsara.

Historically, Theravada spread to southern India and Southeast Asia, while Mahayana became the "northern" tradition, spreading to Central Asia, China, Korea, and Japan. Today Theravada Buddhism dominates Sri Lanka, Thailand, Burma, and Laos. Other Asian countries are dominated by Mahayana Buddhism. Tibet has been dominated by Vajrayana, as we shall see.

In focusing on Mahayana doctrine, let us deal first with two innovative teachings of the Mahayana schools, emptiness and mind-only, and then consider the Mahayana views of the Buddha himself.

Emptiness. Emptiness *(sunyata)* is a hallmark of Mahayana teaching. In fact, the Mahayana sutras known as the *Prajna-paramita* ("wisdom-that-has-gone-beyond") center on this notion. By the end of the Mahayana development, emptiness had in effect become a fourth mark of all reality. Besides being painful, fleeting, and selfless, all reality was empty. Thus, further rumination on the three marks had led Mahayana philosophers to consider a fourth mark, emptiness, as the most significant feature of all beings. No reality was a substance, having an "own-being." Obviously, therefore, none could be an atman, be constant, or be fully satisfying.

The Heart Sutra, a short specimen of the *Prajna-paramita,* exemplifies the dialectical reasoning with which Mahayana worked on emptiness. In this sutra, we can also perceive the paradoxical result of such reasoning: Nirvana and samsara are not two. The sutra begins with an act of reverence (which reminds us that this is religious wisdom, not arid speculation): "Homage to the Perfection of Wisdom, the Lovely, the Holy."[23] "The Lovely" (*Bhagavati*) is feminine, indicating that Buddhism conceives of wisdom as a goddess or maternal figure, out of whom issues the light of knowledge.[24] Next the sutra speaks of the *bodhisattva* Avalokitesvara (who in East Asia became known as Kuan-yin) moving in the course of the wisdom that has gone beyond (that has reached the shore of nirvana) and looking down compassionately on our world. He beheld but five heaps (the *skandhas*), and he saw that they were in their own-being (their substance) empty (*sunya*).

The word *sunya* conveys the idea that something that looks like much is really nothing. Etymologically it relates to the word *swelled*. As a swelled head is much ado about nothing, so things that are *sunya* appear to be full, solid, or substantial but actually are not. The spiritual implication of emptiness (*sunyata*) is that the world around us should not put us in bondage, for it has nothing of substance with which to tie us. Philosophically the word implies *anatman* (no-self): nothing is independent of other existents. For the Mahayana, all dharmas (here meaning items of existence) are correlated, and any one dharma is void of classifying marks—characteristics that would give it a distinctive independent being.

Dialectics. Having recalled these staples of Mahayana tradition, the Heart Sutra then employs dialectics (the act of playing both sides of an issue) in analyzing the five *skandhas:* Form is emptiness, and this very emptiness is form. Feeling, perception, impulse, and consciousness are all emptiness, and emptiness is feeling, perception, impulse, and consciousness. This identification, the sutra emphasizes, can be seen by anyone "here"—from the viewpoint of the wisdom that has gone beyond. Therefore, reminiscent of Shankara's two levels of knowing Brahman, the *Prajna-paramita* says that there are several ways of looking at ordinary reality. From the lower point of view, feeling, perception, impulse, consciousness, and form are all "something." From the higher viewpoint of enlightenment or perfect wisdom, however, these terms all designate something that is empty, that has no solid core or own-being. A third, middle viewpoint, is that both of these truths are true.

To deal with any dharma as though it were full, therefore, would be to deal with it at least erroneously and possibly desirously—thus, karmically. If, however,

we see that *nothing* is pleasant, stable, or full, then we will deal with all things in detachment, moving through them toward nirvana. So, according to the sutra, a *bodhisattva* sees things without "thought coverings," does not tremble at the emptiness that this attitude reveals, and thereby attains nirvana. That is what all buddhas (Gautama is not the only one) have done, and it shows that the *Prajna-paramita* is a great spell of knowledge (the sutra concludes with a mantra, a chanting of a wisdom spell: "Gone, gone, gone beyond, gone altogether beyond, O what an awakening, all-hail—this completes the Heart of perfect wisdom").[25]

Case Study: The Diamond Sutra. Another good example of the *Prajna-paramita* literature that Mahayana Buddhism developed is the Diamond Sutra, which probably originated in India in the fourth century C.E.[26] This sutra begins by setting the stage for a dramatic discourse. Once when the Buddha was dwelling in the garden of a person named Anathapindika, with a group of 1,250 monks, he rose, went on his round of begging, returned, washed his feet, and sat down to meditate. Many monks approached him, bowed at his feet, and seated themselves to await his teaching. One of them, a monk named Subhuti, ventured to ask the Enlightened One how a son or daughter of good family, having set out on the path toward enlightenment, should stand, progress, and control his or her thoughts. The Buddha graciously replied that such a person ought to entertain the thought that although the Enlightened One has led many beings to nirvana, in reality he has led no being to nirvana. How can this be? Because, as any true *bodhisattva* or enlightened person understands, the notion of "being" or "self" or "soul" or "person" is actually an illusion.

With various subtleties, examples, and further inferences, this is the sutra's main teaching. Thus somewhat later the Buddha repeats the message: *Bodhisattvas* are those who do not perceive a self, a being, a soul, or a person. They do not perceive a dharma (individual item of reality), or even a no-dharma. They neither perceive nor nonperceive. Why? Because they have reached a realm beyond the dichotomies that perception usually entails, beyond our ordinary tendency to organize things in terms of beings, persons, or selves. Such a tendency seizes on individuals and turns aside from the whole. By concentrating on beings it neglects nirvana. Nirvana is not a thing, nor an entity. Those who think in terms of things or entities cannot enter nirvana. Only those who have gone beyond, to the higher knowledge that is unified, intuitive, and comprehensive, can enter nirvana.

To try to jar the hearer from ordinary consciousness, the sutra even moves to outright paradox: "The Tathagata [Buddha] has taught that the dharmas special to the Buddhas are not just a Buddha's special dharmas. That is why they are called 'the dharmas special to the Buddhas.'" If we try to make sense of this, we find ourselves straining at the edge of logical reason. The dharmas — realities or teachings—applying to buddhas (fully enlightened beings) and making them buddhas are not just peculiar to buddhas. They are what enlightenment finds intrinsic to all reality, the way things are. For that very reason, however, grasping them makes one a buddha. In other words, buddhahood consists in grasping what is so for everyone, for all beings. The special, distinguishing feature of buddhas is that they *realize* what the rest of us only experience or are. The rest of us, in the final analysis, deal with the same (empty) reality as the buddhas do. The rest of us are potentially enlightened, potentially *bodhi-* (knowledge) beings. But only the buddhas realize or actualize this knowledge. Only the buddhas become what they are, illumine their full selves (which are no-selves) with the light of nirvana or emptiness. One can see how this viewpoint could encourage all people, laity as well as monks, to find their true, *bodhi* being, and how it could inspire the development of Mahayana schools such as Zen, where meditation aims at triggering insight into the enlightened being one already is.

Because he understood this line of discourse, Subhuti could reply to the Buddha in kind.

I am, O Lord, an arhat [saint] free from greed. And yet, O Lord, it does not occur to me, "an Arhat am I and free from greed." If, O Lord, it could occur to me that I have attained Arhatship, then the Tathagata would not have declared of me that "Subhuti, this son of good family, who is the foremost of those who dwell in Peace, does not dwell anywhere; that is why he is called a dweller in Peace."

Once again, the key to moving this statement from the column marked "gibberish" to the column marked "wisdom" seems to be to take it as a paradox,

the uneven sort of speech that comes when we have one part of our mind on the level of superior knowledge and the other part on the level of ordinary, worldly knowledge. In terms of ordinary knowledge and discourse, Subhuti is an *arhat* free of greed. That is how the man in the street rightly would describe him. In terms of ultimate knowledge and discourse, however, this view of the man in the street is seriously flawed, because it assumes that "Subhuti," "arhat," "greed," and the like are solid things. Ordinary discourse tends to reify what it deals with, to invest it with the solidity of a "thing." Forgetting that everything is painful, fleeting, and possessed of no-self, ordinary speech withdraws from the interrelational field of mutual influence, the wheel of Conditioned Coarising, that, on deeper analysis, shows everything to be without an "own-self."

As one who has passed beyond ordinary speech, Subhuti does not allow himself reifications. Not for him such expressions as "an *Arhat* am I and free from greed." He would not be dwelling in the peace of enlightenment, the fulfilling realm of nirvana, were he still pervaded by such substantial and dichotomizing thinking. Indeed, for him truly to be an *arhat* is for him to appreciate the omnipresence of emptiness. *Arhat* and emptiness therefore coincide. Emptiness defines the outlook of an *arhat,* and the outlook of an *arhat* discloses everything to be empty. How very important, then, are the exercises of meditation that cut below the ordinary mind, the exercises of morality that root out normal egocentricity. Without them, we will never reach the state of wisdom, never will become an *arhat* (that is, a no-*arhat*). Even less would we become *bodhisattvas,* determined to help all beings realize their (empty) buddha-nature.

Mind-only. Emptiness was the special concern of the Madhyamika Mahayana school.[27] The second major Mahayana school, the Yogacara, which became influential from about 300 C.E. on, proposed another influential teaching on ultimate reality, mind-only.[28] Like the teaching on emptiness, it went beyond early Buddhist teaching, and the Theravadins rejected the sutras that attributed this teaching to the Buddha. The teaching of mind-only held that all realities finally are mental. There were antecedents to this viewpoint in the morality literature that Mahayana shared with the Theravadins, such as the *Dhammapada,* and the proponents of emptiness implied it in their belief that all phenomena are illusory, because we do not grasp them in their ultimately empty reality. The *Dhammapada*'s interest, however, was practical, not speculative: "What we are today comes from our thoughts of yesterday, and our present thoughts build our life of tomorrow: our life is the creation of our mind."[29] The Yogacarins wanted a fuller explanation of mental reality, probably because their intuitions grew out of meditational or yogic practices (whence their name).

One of the principal Yogacarin sutras, the *Lankavatara*,[30] described a tier of consciousness in the individual culminating in a "storehouse" consciousness (*alayavijnana*) that is the base of the individual's deepest awareness, the individual's tie to the cosmic. The storehouse consciousness is itself unconscious and inactive, but it is the repository of the "seeds" that ripen into human deeds and awareness. Furthermore, Yogacarins sometimes called the storehouse consciousness the Buddha's womb. Thereby, they made the Buddha, or Tathagata (Enlightened Being), a metaphysical principle—a foundation of all reality.

From the womb of the Buddha issued the purified thoughts and beings of enlightenment. The symbolism is complex (and interestingly feminine, suggesting a Buddhist version of androgyny or primal wholeness). Its main point, though, is clear: The womb of the Buddha (*Tathagata-garbha*) is present in all living beings, irradiating them with enlightenment. Like the feminine *Prajna-paramita,* then, the ultimate reality of the Yogacarins "mothers" the many individual things (that are themselves empty). It is the great mental storehouse from which they issue, the matrix that holds them all in being. It stimulates their dancing flux.

Mahayana Devotion.   Both major Mahayana schools developed sophisticated theories to correlate the many beings of experience with the simple finality of nirvana. It was not philosophy that brought Mahayana popular influence, though, but its openness to the laity's spiritual needs, its devotional thought. Early Buddhism held monks in great regard, considering them the only true followers of Buddha. They were the teachers, the determiners of doctrine, and the guardians of morality. They were the stewards of tradition who made the *sangha* a jewel alongside the Buddha and the dharma. Consequently, the laity considered themselves to be working out a better karma,

so that in their next lives they might be monks (or, if they were women, so that they might be men). The central lay virtue, as we have seen, was giving financial support to the monasteries, and the *sangha* seldom admitted laity to the higher occupations of philosophy or meditation.

Mahayana changed this view of the laity. As we have seen, by stressing the Buddha's compassion and his resourcefulness in saving all living creatures, it gradually qualified the Theravadin ideal of the *arhat* (saint) and fashioned a new, more socially oriented ideal, the *bodhisattva*. Mahayana thereby prepared the way for later schools that were in effect Buddhist devotional sects, such as the **Pure Land** sect. Such sects believed that through graceful compassion, a buddha or *bodhisattva* only required that one devoutly repeat his name and place full trust in him for salvation. In this "degenerate age," the difficult paths of wisdom and meditation were open only to the few. Therefore, the Enlightened One had opened a broader path of devotion, so that laity as well as monks might reach paradise and nirvana.

Mahayana did not destroy monastic dignity. Rather, it stressed the social side of the ideal. The Mahayanists saw the Hinayana *arhat* as too individualistic. To pursue one's own enlightenment and salvation apart from those of other living beings seemed selfish. Out of great compassion (*mahakaruna*), the full saint would remain in the samsaric world, for eons if need be, content to put off final bliss if that would help save other living beings.

Mahayanists stress six great "perfections" (*paramitas*) in becoming a *bodhisattva,* and these effectively summarize Mahayana religious living. First is the perfection of giving: giving material things to those in need, but also giving spiritual instructions, one's own body and life, or even one's own karmic merit. In a life of compassionate generosity, everything could be given over to others. Mahayanists understand the five other perfections of morality, patience, vigor, meditation, and wisdom in a similarly broad fashion. Thus, they have applied the traditional triad of wisdom-morality-meditation in more social ways. Giving, patience, and vigor have meant that one became selfless in more than a metaphysical way. For the love of others, for the grand vision of a totally perfected world, the saint may cheerfully donate his goods and talents, suffer abuses, and labor ceaselessly.

Finally, Mahayanists began to contemplate the Buddha's preexistence and the status he had gained as a knowledge being. In this contemplation, his earthly life receded in importance, so much that some Mahayanists began to say that he had only apparently assumed a human body. Then, linking this stress on the Buddha's metaphysical essence with the Indian doctrine of endless kalpas of cosmic time and endless stretches of cosmic space, Mahayanists emphasized the many buddhas who had existed before Sakyamuni and the buddhas who presided in other cosmic realms. All became potential objects of adoration and petitionary prayer.

In this way the notion of buddhahood greatly expanded. First it was the quality shared by many cosmic beings of wisdom and realization. Later, in East Asian Mahayana, buddhahood became the metaphysical notion that *all* beings are in essence enlightenment beings. As we have seen in the *Prajna-paramita* sutra, enlightenment implies grasping how all beings are empty of individual solidity. Enlightenment, therefore, is just realizing one's buddha-nature, the knowledge and light that dawn when the grasp of emptiness allows true human nature to show itself. It is the beginning of nirvana, the break with samsara, and the achievement of perfect wisdom all in one.

Buddhahood thus became complex and many-sided. The Buddha came to have three bodies: The dharma body, in which he was the unmanifest aspect of Buddhahood or Enlightenment-being; the human body, in which he appeared on earth; and the glorification body, in which he was manifest to the heavenly beings, with all his marks and signs. Moreover, the distinction between buddhas and great *bodhisattvas* blurred and largely dissolved in the popular mind, giving Buddhist "divinity" a full spectrum of holy beings. Citing the Mahayana understanding of divinity, therefore, is a sure way to refute claims that Buddhism is not a religion. By the fifth or sixth century after the Buddha's death, Mahayana Buddhists were venerating a variety of divine figures. This was especially true in East Asia, where Mahayana devotionalism built on pre-Buddhist traditions (for example, many Japanese kami became *bodhisattvas*).

Tantrism

We have seen the Hindu mixture of occult and erotic practices called Tantrism or Shaktism. Indian Buddhism helped create this trend and incorporated many of its notions. Buddhist Tantrism in India seems to have originated around the sixth century C.E., flourishing first in the northwest. From the eighth century on it prospered around Bengal, combining with *Prajna-paramita* philosophy and native symbolic practices. It later reached Sri Lanka, Burma, and Indonesia.[31] Often it merged with Shaivism, but in Tibet it combined with native Bon (shamanist) practices and became the dominant Buddhist faith.[32]

Tantrism had antecedents in both Buddha's teaching and in the surrounding Hindu Brahmanism. Buddha appears to have allowed spells, and the canon contains reputed cures for snakebite and other dangers. *Prajna-paramita* sutras such as the Heart often ended with spells, transferring certain key ideas and words from strictly intellectual notions to mantras. In Brahmanic sacrifices, as we noted, the prayers were understood so literally that they became mantras; if a priest recited a prayer properly, it was sure to accomplish its end.

Buddhist Tantrists took over such sacred sounds as *om,* as well as esoteric yogic systems, such as *kundalini,* which associated sacred syllables with force centers (*chakras*) in the body. They also used mandalas (magic figures, such as circles and squares) and even stupas (shrines). The Buddhist Tantrists were thus hardly bizarre or innovative, mainly developing ancient Hindu esoteric practices in a new setting.

What novelty the Tantrists did introduce into Buddhism came from their creative use of rites that acted out mandalas and esoteric doctrines about bodily forces. Perhaps under the influence of Yogacara meditation, which induced states of trance, the Tantrists developed rituals in which participants identified with particular deities. If it is true that many meditation schools, such as the Yogacara, employed mandalas for the early states of trance in order to focus consciousness, then the Tantrists probably built on well-established practices. In their theoretical elaboration, however, they retrieved certain ancient cosmological notions.

For instance, they came to see the stupas as replicas of the cosmos. The railings that separated the stupa precinct from secular ground divided the sacred from the profane. The edge of the moving mandala that the Tantrist troupe would dance or act out had a function similar to that of the railings. Often Tantrism strove to symbolize the entire cosmic plan. Indeed, the

Tantrists tried to draw heavenly worlds (*bodhisattva* realms) and gods into their meditations and rituals.

A principal metaphysical support of Tantrism was the Madhyamika doctrine of emptiness, which the Tantrists interpreted to mean that all beings are intrinsically pure. Consequently, they used odd elements in their rituals to drive home the truths of emptiness, purity, and freedom. For the most part, these ways did not become public, since the Tantrists went to considerable pains to keep their rites and teachings secret. In fact, they developed a cryptic language that they called "twilight speech," in which sexual references were abundant.[33] For instance, they called the male and female organs "thunderbolt" and "lotus," respectively. As with Hindu Tantrism, it is not always possible to tell whether such speech is symbolic or literal. Some defenders of Tantrism claim that it tamed sexual energy in the Indian tradition by subjecting it to symbolization, meditative discipline, and moral restraints. Other critics, however, view Buddhist Tantrism as a corruption of a tradition originally quite intolerant of libidinal practices. For them the Tantrist explanation that, since everything is mind-only, the practice of erotic rites means little is simply a rationalization.

In a typical Tantrist meditation, the meditators would begin with traditional preliminaries such as seeking refuge in the three jewels, cleansing themselves of sins (by confession or bathing), praying to past masters, or drawing a mandala to define the sacred space of the extraordinary reality that their rite was going to involve. Then the meditators would take on the identity of a deity and disperse all appearances of the world into emptiness. Next, using their imaginations, they would picture themselves as the divinities whose identities they were projecting.

So pictured, a man and his consort would sit on the central throne of the mandala space and engage in sexual union. Then they would imagine various buddhas parading into the sacred space of the mandala and assimilate them into their bodies and senses. In that assimilation, their speech would become divine, they could receive offerings as gods, and they could perform any of the deities' functions. So charged with divinity, they would then return to the ordinary world, bringing back to it the great power of a buddha's divine understanding.[34]

The relation of the master (guru) and the disciple was central in Tantrism, because the master represented the tradition. (Zen has maintained this stress on the master. The Tantric guru was the authority needed to help the striver receive the original enlightenment disclosed by the Buddha. Texts were too pale and ambiguous.) The Tantrist gurus occasionally forced their pupils to engage in quite bizarre and painful practices, to teach them to examine the mirror of their minds, to learn the illusory character of all phenomena, and to stop the cravings and jealousies that clouded their mirror.[35] Pronouncing the death of old judgments and the birth of new ones of enlightenment, the guru might confuse pupils, punish them and push them to break with convention and ordinary vision. When Buddhism had become vegetarian, some Tantrist masters urged eating flesh. When Buddhism advocated teetotalism, some urged intoxicating spirits. In such ways, Tantrist wisdom could become paradoxical and eccentric.[36]

Tibet. Perhaps the best place to examine the Tantric tradition full-blown is Tibet. Tantrism was welcomed in Tibet and came to dominate in the region between India and China. Our first historical records date from only the seventh century C.E., when Chinese historians started mentioning it. Under King Srongsten Gampo in 632, Tibet borrowed both writing and Buddhism from Kashmir. Toward the end of the eighth century, two notable Indian figures came to Tibet, Santaraskita and Padmasambhava, who founded a lasting Tibetan *sangha*. Tradition credits Padmasambhava with inaugurating the influential Nying-ma-pa Tantrist sect, while Santaraskita apparently was responsible for the triumph of Indian traditions over challenges from Chinese schools (especially Chan). Since that triumph, Tibet has owed more to Indian scholarship and philosophy than to Chinese.

Indian academic structures greatly influenced Tibetan Buddhism.[37] During the Indian Gupta dynasty (320–540 C.E.), great monastic universities became the pillars of Buddhism. The "curricular Buddhism" of these schools encompassed all the arts and sciences. Furthermore, meditation integrated with scholasticism, assuring that the academic efforts to correlate Buddhist beliefs with existing knowledge never divorced themselves from practical religion. The Tibetan adoption of an Indian rather than a Chinese religious style correlated with this union of study and meditation, for the Indian schools favored a gradual penetration of enlightenment, in which study could play an important role.

One characteristic of Tibetan Buddhism has therefore been its line of scholars based in monastic universities. They have produced voluminous translations and commentaries for the canonical scriptures, as well as a tradition that learning should inform ritualist life. Learning and ritual, in fact, became the primary foci of the Tibetan monastic life. The king and the common people looked to the monastery for protection through ritual against evil powers, while individual monks utilized both meditation and ritual in their pursuit of enlightenment.

The typical day of a traditional Tibetan monk began with a private ritual contemplation (Tantrist) before dawn for an hour and a half. During the morning, the monk regularly participated in the community's prayers for two hours and then worked in the monastic library. He devoted the afternoon to more work and public ceremony and again meditated in the evening.

Many monks spent a lifetime in this regime, coming to the monastery at the age of nine or ten and receiving a thorough training in the scriptures, meditation techniques, and ceremonial details. As suggested above, the king supported this life-style, because ritual could prop his authority. (Pre-Buddhist Tibetan culture thought of the king in ancient sacred terms, as the tie between heaven and earth. Something of this ancient view continued when monks prayed and conducted rituals for the king's good health.) The common people, whose shamanist heritage emphasized many malevolent spirits of sickness and death, saw in the ritual spells and ceremonies a powerful defense. As a result, the monasteries were quite practical institutions for them, too.

By emphasizing ritual in both public ceremonies and private meditations, Tibetan Buddhism created its own version of the Tantrist belief that the imagination, senses, and psychological and bodily powers are all potential sources of energy for enlightenment and wisdom. When we discussed Indian Tantrism, we considered how the adept tried to identify with divine forces and gain control over a *cosmion*—a "little world" that represented universal space and time. The Tibetan Tantrist cult acted out many such identifications, so that the common people could indwell something comfortably universal. The worship of the goddess Tara, for instance, which monasteries and popular festivals promoted, gave the world a motherly and protecting aspect. Monks and laity both prayed personally to Tara for help, while many of Tibet's musical and dancing arts developed through festivals devoted to her.

The success that Buddhism enjoyed in Tibet may also be linked to its ability to capitalize on native shamanist themes and political institutions. The ancient Tibetan Bon ("he who invokes the gods") was a shaman very like the archetypal Siberian shaman. Beating his drum, whirling in dance, weaving his spells, he fought against the demons of sickness and death.[38] In addition to developing its own Tantrist rituals to cover these interests of the older religion, Tibetan Buddhism also produced a type of wandering, "crazy" saint who drew much of the awe and respect that the older shamans had.

The prototype of this ascetic, visionary holy man in Tibet was the much beloved Milarepa (1040–1123).[39] After a harsh initiation by family suffering and a cruel guru, he took to the mountain slopes and gained a reputation for working wonders. In his songs he poetically expressed profound insights into both the nature of dharmic reality and the psychology of the ascetic life. Other famous saints, such as Tilopa and Naropa, were similarly poetic. They show that for personal religious life, Tantrism could cast all conventional values and assumptions in doubt in order relentlessly to pursue enlightenment.

Buddhism capitalized on the demise of kingship in Tibet in the ninth century to establish a theocratic regime with the monastery at its heart. Despite early persecutions during a period of kings' intrigues and assassinations, by the eleventh century the monasteries were strong. Until the Communist takeover, in fact, the monasteries and the Dalai Lamas (religious leaders) dominated Tibetan politics (often with much intrigue and sectarian strife).[40] The Mongol emperor Kublai Khan granted the abbot 'Phags-pa (1235–80) temporal power over all Tibet, firmly establishing a theocratic rule. By the fourteenth century, however, Tibet was a cauldron of various Buddhist sects vying for power. The Nying-ma-pa sect that Padmasambhava had founded claimed a certain primacy because of its antiquity, and it also kept close ties with the ancient shamanist loyalties.

Of the sects that developed after the demise of the Chinese Tang dynasty in the ninth century, the most important was the Ge-lug, which shrewdly employed the idea of reincarnation. Consequently, the Mongols both recognized the Dalai Lama as a spiritual leader and considered him a grandson of the Mongol chief.

From the sixteenth century onwards, the Ge-lug wielded great political clout. The Dalai Lamas, for the most part, have been men of considerable spiritual and political acumen, and their rule has meant a vigorous *sangha*. The fourteenth, and current, Dalai Lama (b. 1935) was exiled by the Chinese Communists, but he is still the spiritual leader of tens of thousands of Tibetan Buddhists, working for the day when Tibetans will again govern their own lives and be free to practice their religion.

Tibetan Buddhism thus stands out for two things: its Tantrist bent and its especially knotted political history. Few cultures have so absorbed one version of Buddhism as Tibet has absorbed the "thunderbolt vehicle" (Vajrayana or Tantrism). Perhaps the most famous Tibetan religious text to reach the West is the Tibetan *Book of the Dead*,[41] which purportedly describes the experiences of the deceased during the forty-nine days between physical death and entry into a new karmic state. By employing vivid imagery and specifying rituals designed to help the deceased to achieve nirvana, the *Book of the Dead* exemplifies the Tantrist mentality well. It is a journey through the imagination and unconscious that severely challenges most notions of reality, since it maintains that the period right after death is the most opportune time for liberation.

Recent Trends. Much of the Tibetan tradition continued a vigorous life well into the twentieth century, as one learns from travelers such as Alexandra David-Neel, whose *Magic and Mystery in Tibet*,[42] originally published (in French) in 1929, makes fascinating reading. Neel was not long into her travels through Tibet when she had the opportunity to meet the Dalai Lama. Watching him bless a large crowd (one by one), she was struck by the people's manifest belief that physical contact with the Dalai Lama would put them in touch with a magical beneficent power. Indeed, great throngs gathered in Kalimpong, where the Dalai Lama was staying, seeking to benefit from his power.

However, not all the onlookers shared the general faith, and Neel's contact with one skeptic opened a door to Tibet's Tantrist past. She noticed that a man wearing dirty, much torn monk's robes seemed to be watching the crowd cynically. His matted hair wound around his head like a turban, and he had the small traveling bag of a wandering ascetic. In fact, Neel's interpreter described him as a *naljorpa,* an ascetic possessing magical powers. Upon inquiry, the interpreter found that the man was a wandering monk from Bhutan, who usually lived here and there—in caves, empty houses, or under the trees. He just happened to be passing through Kalimpong when the crowds gathered for the Dalai Lama's blessing.

Reflecting on the monk's strange behavior, Neel decided to seek him out at the local monastery, where he had said he was headed. She and her interpreter found him finishing his meal in a room containing the holy images before which the monks prayed. When Neel and her interpreter tried to begin a conversation, the monk only grunted through a mouthful of rice. Then he began to laugh and mutter. "What is he saying?" Neel asked. The interpreter was embarrassed, explaining that he did not know whether he should translate the monk's rough speech. Neel urged him to translate accurately, since she was in Tibet precisely to capture the local color. So licensed, the translator said that the monk had asked him, "What is this idiot here for?" To Neel this was the sort of insult Indian yogis frequently threw out, so as to put off or test those who approached them. She told the interpreter to tell the ascetic she wanted to know why he had mocked the crowd that had come to seek the blessing of the Dalai Lama.

The *naljorpa* muttered, "They are insects fluttering in dung, puffed up with their own importance." Once again, this seemed the sort of iconoclasm Neel had witnessed in India. "Are you yourself free of all taint?" she asked. The monk laughed noisily and then launched into a speech worthy of Milarepa, Naropa, or one of the other ancient Tantrist saints. "The person who tries to get out of the dung only sinks in deeper. Therefore I roll in it like a pig. I swallow it, trying to turn it into golden dust, into a brook of clear water. That is the great work: to turn dog dung into stars." He said this with great delight, evidently enjoying himself.

Neel decided to press him. "What was wrong with the people approaching the Dalai Lama? They are simple folk, unable to study the high doctrines. Why should they not take what blessing they can?" The ascetic broke through her little objection. "The only efficacious blessing is that given by a person who truly possesses the power he professes. If the Dalai Lama were genuine, he would not need soldiers to fight the Chinese or his other enemies. He would be able to drive all his enemies out of his country, surrounding Tibet with an invisible barrier no enemy could penetrate. Padmasambhava had such power, and his blessing still reaches those who worship him twelve centuries later, though he now lives in the heavenly land of the sages." The ascetic then suggested that he himself had experienced Padmasambhava's genuine blessing.

Neel tried to extricate herself from the situation gracefully, feeling that the ascetic was perhaps a little crazed, but she made the mistake of having her interpreter offer the ascetic some money. Insulted, he refused the money, and when the interpreter tried to insist, the interpreter was hurled backwards and doubled over in pain, as though he had received a terrible blow in the stomach. He was convinced the monk had loosed a spiritual force against him, and none of Neel's Western, commonsense efforts to explain the incident would appease him.

Throughout her journey, Neel found Tibetan Buddhism undergirt with a great respect for the occult. Ordinary people thought meteorological phenomena were the doings of demons or magicians. A hailstorm, for instance, was one of the demons' favorite ways of preventing pilgrims from journeying to the holy places. It was also the way magicians kept intruders from their hermitages and tested would-be disciples. Many mediums found steady employment communicating with the dead or transmitting messages of the gods. In the Himalayas, the centuries-old tradition that sages and ascetics have to battle powerful forces of darkness was alive and well.

The Demise of Indian Buddhism

Buddhism declined in India after the seventh century, only in part because of Tantrist emphases. Invaders such as the White Huns and the Muslims wrecked many Buddhist strongholds, while the revival of Hinduism, especially of Hindu bhakti sects of Vishnu and Shiva, undermined Buddhism. Mahayana fought theistic Hinduism quite fiercely, not at all seeing it as equivalent to the Buddhist theology of *bodhisattvas* and buddhas, but Hinduism ultimately prevailed because of its great ability to incorporate other movements. Indeed, Buddha became one of the Vaishnavite avatars.

By the seventh century the Indian *sangha* had grown wealthy and held much land—facts that contributed to a decline in religious fervor and to antipathy among the laity. From the time of its first patronage under Asoka (around 260 B.C.E.), Buddhism

had enjoyed occasional support from princes and kings, and its ability to preach the dharma, to enjoy favor at court, and to influence culture depended on this support. The Kusana dynasty (ca. 78–320 C.E.), for instance, was a good time for Buddhists, while the Gupta age (320–540 C.E.) revived Hinduism. When the Muslims finally established control in India, Buddhism suffered accordingly. Early missionary activity had exported it to the south and east, however, and Buddhism proved to be hardy on foreign soil. So Hinduism, which has largely been confined to India, became the native tradition that opposed the Muslims, while Buddhism became an internationalized brand of Indian culture.[43] We deal with the East Asian version of Buddhism in the next two chapters.

Contemporary Buddhist Rituals

The austere meditational focus of Zen and the continuing challenge of lofty Buddhist philosophy have captivated most Western observers of Buddhism, perhaps preventing them from properly appreciating Buddhist ritual. To fill out our historical account, let us focus on how contemporary Buddhist piety actually functions in such disparate locales as Burma and California, remembering that a similar ritualism has been important throughout all of Buddhist history.

Melford Spiro's informative anthropological study, *Buddhism and Society*,[44] includes a chapter on the ceremonial cycle of Burmese Buddhism that he witnessed. Of special interest are the devotions that paced the individual through the day. Although participation in these devotions was voluntary, and those who did not participate neither sinned nor lost merit, most Burmese took part (children being observers until they reached their teens).

The pious Burmese Buddhists whom Spiro met in the late 1950s and early 1960s began and ended the day with devotions performed in front of a small household shrine. This shrine usually consisted of a shelf for a vase of fresh flowers and a picture of the Buddha. It was always located on the eastern side of the house (the most auspicious side) and placed above head level (to place the Buddha below head level would be insulting). During the time of devotions, householders would light candles and place food offerings before the Buddha.

Coming before this shrine, the householders would begin by saying: "I beg leave! I beg leave! I beg leave! By act, by word, and by thought, I raise my hands in reverence to the forehead and worship, honor, look at, and humbly pay homage to the three gems—the Buddha, the Law, and the Order—one time, two times, three times, O Lord." Then they would petition to be freed from the four woes (rebirth in hell, as an animal, as a demon, or as a ghost), from the three scourges (war, epidemic, and famine), from the eight kinds of unfortunate birth, from the five kinds of enemy, from the four deficiencies (tyrannical kings, wrong views of life after death, physical deformity, and dull-wittedness), and from the five misfortunes, that they might quickly gain release from their pains. They would end the morning prayer by reciting the five precepts, renewing their commitment to abstain from taking life, from stealing, from drinking intoxicants, from lying, and from sexual immorality.

Clearly, therefore, the Burmese Buddhists sought to orient each day by honoring the Buddha, begging his protection against misfortune, and rededicating themselves to the Buddhist ethical code. In the evening many Burmese, especially the elderly, would conclude a similar session of homage, petition, and rededication by praying a rosary. The Buddhist rosary consisted of 108 beads, one for each of the 108 marks on the feet of the Buddha (which, in turn, represented his 108 reincarnations). While fingering a bead the devotee usually would say either "painful, selfless, fleeting" or "Buddha, dharma, *sangha*" three times.

In addition to these devotions held in the home, the villagers whom Spiro studied held a public ceremony every evening after sunset in the village chapel. This was located in the center of the village and consisted of a shed open on three sides. The fourth side enclosed an ark containing a statue of the Buddha. Attendance usually was sparse, except in special periods such as the Buddhist Lent, and more sophisticated believers, who thought meditation was the central expression of a mature Buddhist faith, spoke disparagingly of the chapel services as magical or superstitious.

Nonetheless, the village service was interesting because it was led by laypeople, rather than monks, and because it used the Burmese vernacular, rather than Pali, the formal liturgical language. Thus, it was a place where common folk and Burmese youth could experience their religion in a form easy to understand.

The ceremony usually began with an invocation of the gods, and then an invocation of the Buddha, before whose image fresh cut flowers had been placed. The worshipers asked permission to reverence the Buddha and prayed that their worship might bring them to nirvana or the higher abodes (the states near to nirvana). Other prayers followed, asking the Buddha to grant the petitioners strength to fulfill the five precepts and understand the three marks.

The central portion of the village ceremony began with an offering of flowers, candles, and water— symbols of beauty, reverence, and purification. Following this, the faithful expressed their veneration of the Buddha, the teaching, the order, their parents, and their teachers. Next came recitations of parts of the scriptures, a profession of love for all creatures, a recitation of the doctrine of Dependent Coarising, a recitation of the Buddha's last words, a recitation of the five "heaps" (*skandhas*) of which human individuality is composed, a prayer to the eight planets, and a confession of faith.

The ceremony concluded with a water libation that called the merit of the worshipers to the attention of an ancient earth goddess, the release of the gods who had been called into attendance, and an enthusiastic "sharing of merit" (of the benefit the participants had gained from the service) with the participants' parents and all other beings. Overall, the ceremony reinforced the main points of Buddhist teaching, reminding the participants how to orient their lives and encouraging them to express both their reverence for the Buddha and the main concerns for which they wanted the Buddha's aid.

Since 1970 there has been a successful Buddhist monastery near Mount Shasta in northern California. It has seventeen buildings (a Zendo or meditation hall, a founder's shrine, a shrine to the *bodhisattva* Kannon, a sewing room, a laundry, a tool shed, a store room, a library, eight residences, and a common room). The monastery was founded by an Englishwoman named Peggy Kennett (Jiyu Kennett-Roshi), who is a guru in the Soto Zen tradition. (Soto and Rinzai are schools that began in China but underwent a further development in Japan.) While maintaining traditional Soto teachings, the Shasta monastery has tried to adapt to American cultural forms. Thus members eat their meals American style at a table rather than Japanese style sitting on the floor, they chant in Gregorian tones rather than Japanese tones, they usually wear Western clerical garb rather than Japanese robes, and they serve English rather than Japanese tea.

The central occupation of the monastery is *zazen*, or sitting in meditation. Most members of the monastery spend two to three hours in meditation each day. Charles Prebish has described the daily schedule of all the monastic duties as follows:

5:45 A.M.	Rising Bell
6:15	Zazen
7:00	Morning Service
7:45	Community Tea
8:15	Breakfast
8:45	Community Clean-up
9:15	Trainees' Class
11:00	Community Tea
11:30	Junior Trainees' and Laypeople's Class
1:00 P.M.	Lunch
1:30	Rest
2:00	Priests' Class (Work Period for Others)
3:00	Community Tea
3:30	Work Period
5:00	Zazen
6:00	Dinner
6:30	Choir Practice
7:30	Evening Service
7:45	Zazen
8:30	Tea
9:00	Return to Residences[45]

During the morning service, the trainees make three bows and offer incense to the celebrant, Kennett-Roshi. The community then intones and recites portions of the Buddhist scriptures. There are three more bows, and then the community processes to the founder's shrine, where they recite more scriptures. During the evening ceremony, in addition to the scripture recitations, there is a reading of the rules for *zazen*. At meals someone recites portions of the scriptures while the food is passed, to help community members increase their sense of gratitude for what they are about to receive. Since the meditation hall is closed on any day of the month having a four or a nine (for reasons Prebish does not disclose), six times in most months there is a "closing ceremony." Vespers finish the evening service, and through the day monks say prayers before such activities as shaving their heads and putting on their robes.

If this schedule inculcates the same dispositions that the similar schedules of strict Christian monasteries do, the result is a great focusing of attention. The day passes largely in silence, for speech is allowed

Figure 8 *Standing Buddha, Kashmir, tenth–eleventh century. Bronze; 10⅜ in. high. This statue blends the styles of north-central India with Hellenistic influences. The upraised right hand is a gesture of protection. The Nelson–Atkins Museum of Art, Kansas City, Missouri (Nelson Fund).*

only at stated times, and most community members expend much effort in meditation. At Mount Shasta there are regular periods throughout the year when the monks concentrate on meditation almost full-time, making a strong effort to come closer to enlightenment. Yet the Soto conviction that buddha-nature should emerge peacefully tempers such effort.

The recitation of the Buddhist scriptures potentially has the effect of creating mantras, for when sounds enter consciousnesses that have been purified by discipline and made alert by meditation, they can develop almost mesmerizing cadences. The ritual bows, use of incense, use of flowers, and the like help to engage all the senses and focus all the spiritual faculties, so that the prayer or meditation to be performed can be wholehearted.

A major difference between the monastic ritualism of Mount Shasta and the lay ritualism of the Burmese Buddhism we described is the stress the lay ritualism placed on petitioning the Buddha for protection against misfortune and help with worldly needs. Part of this difference stems from the greater stress that Theravada lay doctrine places on gaining merit. Whereas the monastic doctrine of Soto Zen stresses the enlightenment nature of all reality, the Burmese Buddhists live in a thought-world filled with ghosts and gods that constantly make them aware of a need to improve their karmic state. Consequently, Burmese ritual seems more anxious. While the Burmese stress the merit one must attain for a better future, the Soto ritual stresses the grace, harmony, and peace that enlightenment brings. (Of course, Soto ritual is also an effort to inculcate the dispositions that conduce to enlightenment, such as inner silence, gratitude, and a sense of harmony with all of creation.)

As we saw, Burmese ritual also tends to be a constant reminder of staple Buddhist doctrine. It has an important place for honoring the Buddha, and for expressing the worshipers' needs, but a great deal of its energy goes into reviewing, or trying to deepen the worshipers' hold on, the five precepts, the three jewels, and so on. Mount Shasta appears to take care of doctrine in the classroom.

In both cases, however, Buddhist rituals encourage believers to worship, the central religious act, as other religions' rituals bring adherents to worship. At worship, members of quite different religious traditions appear to draw much closer to one another. Despite massive doctrinal differences (which, of course, shape what the worshipers understand themselves to be doing), the members of the different traditions all seem to be trying to collect themselves, praise what they take to be ultimate reality, and gain the spiritual aid they need. Not surprisingly, therefore, some of the most fruitful comparative study of religion occurs when scholars try to enter the inner dispositions of the worship and sense what the different rituals are trying to bring about.

WORLDVIEW

We have stressed the intellectual aspects of Buddhist history, the development of key notions and important philosophical schools, because Buddhism is a tradition that has stressed enlightenment: grasping experientially the structures of reality. Often, this "grasp" has involved a lot of un-knowing—realizing ways in which spontaneous, commonsensical views of reality are erroneous. Such views are not innocuous, because they keep people chained in samsara. The Buddha's personal experience was that he broke the chains of samsara only when he had the insight that gave rise to the Four Noble Truths. Ever since, attaining a personal understanding of the Four Noble Truths—replicating something of the Buddha's genetic insight—has been very important. The Buddhist *sangha* has existed to facilitate gaining such an understanding. The monastic life has been geared to putting aside desire and preparing the spirit for nirvana. Laity have venerated monks and nuns because these spiritual athletes have striven for experiential wisdom.

Naturally enough, Buddhism has made accommodations for the laity, since they were bound to be the majority of the members of the community. The Japanese holy man Shinran (1173–1262) made explicit what many other Buddhist leaders have done implicitly, adapting the dharma to the needs of married people, unlettered people, people who have to work in the world. Shinran went farther than most others, stressing faith in the Buddha more than a grasp of the dharma, but whenever it allowed rituals and devotions to multiply, the *sangha* accommodated the Buddha's Way to the needs of ordinary people.

Thus, the worldview that we now study has usually come to ordinary laypeople through ceremonies, festivals, traditional stories, and Buddhist culture at large. Music, poetry, views of sickness, views of good fortune—all aspects of a popular religious culture carry parts of the core religious message. If the core religious message has always been the Four Noble Truths, young people have heard it differently from old people, women have heard it differently from men, the wealthy are bound to stress one side of the message and the poor bound to stress another. That is how popular culture works. It is never straightforward, completely clear, univocal. It is always complex, many-layered and many-voiced.

Thus, you have to imagine the intellectualism that we have stressed working its way out in terms of images and feelings—thoughts and hopes that the average Buddhist seldom brought to clarity or full articulation. For example, you have to imagine the typical devout Buddhist family centering its religious life on the little altar in its home. When family members decorated the altar with flowers and fruit and incense, they expressed concretely their love of the Buddha, their trust that Buddhist tradition would make their lives meaningful, their inclination to go to the Buddha and tradition in time of trial. We should not despise religious traditions for being most powerful in time of trial. We ought to accept the fact that, the world over, most human beings only think completely seriously when suffering, death, injustice, evil, and other trials or hardships force them to. Paradoxically, and mercifully, that is how the bad things that happen to good people sometimes turn out to have brought a blessing. The blessing does not remove the badness, but it can become a solid consolation.

In the same way, we have to accept the fact that the majority of Easterners, like the majority of Westerners, have gone beyond what a restrained orthodoxy might have preferred and sought human faces in which they might concretize the ultimate reality that they needed to worship. For example, a great many Buddhists have worshiped Gautama, even though some schools of Buddhism have taught that he was only a man who embodied a universal wisdom. The distinction between venerating a holy man and worshiping a truly ultimate, divine reality escapes many laypeople in many different traditions. The popular treatment of the Virgin Mary in Christianity and of Muhammad in Islam are cases in point. Rather than debate about the propriety of the cultus that grew up around Gautama, as around central figures in other religious traditions, we do better to appreciate the human needs that the cultus expresses.

In the case of the Buddha, the people who have bowed, offered gifts, chanted verses from the scriptures, and in various other ways given flesh to their vow to place their trust in the Buddha (as in the dharma and the *sangha*) have expressed their need for a center—a holy place of refuge. The Buddha has functioned for most Buddhists as such a place, just as Christ has functioned that way for Christians. The Buddha has meant that reality is not chaotic, life is not meaningless, suffering and defeat are not the final

word. More positively, the Buddha has meant that, in the ultimate analysis, human existence is blessedly good and carries a wonderful potential. That is what human beings most need to hear. That is the sort of "place" the human heart most needs to be able to go, if it is not to feel like a motherless child—an orphan in an uncaring, hostile world.

So, as you consider the Buddhist worldview, think of how it probably played itself out in a Buddhist of your own age, sex, and socieconomic situation. Think of what the Buddha might have meant to a person in the equivalent of our modern business, or art, or science, or family life. If one studies the world religions with a sympathetic eye, it is easy to find an equivalence among their different symbolisms. All have been faced with the same basic problems: survival, justice, hope for a meaning that goes beyond the grave. All have tried to bless love and creativity, stand against untruth and cruelty. And so all have invited people to do the same things: reflect, reform their lives, detach themselves from destructive private and social behavior, commit themselves to what brings light and peace. That has been the reason-to-be of the Buddhist worldview and so the key to Buddhist history.

Nature

Stepping back from the historical view of Buddhism, we find that Buddhist attitudes toward nature do not fit together neatly. From its Indian origins, Buddhism assumed much of Hinduism's cosmological complexity. That meant taking up not only a world that stretched for vast distances and existed for immense eons (kalpas) but also the Aryan materialism and yogic spiritualism that lay behind such a cosmology. However, Buddhism came to contribute its own world views. Its numerous "buddha-fields," for instance, are realms with which our earthly space-time system shares the boundless universe.

Buddhism has had few equivalents to Vedic materialism, but Buddhism used the doctrine of samsara early in its history to justify acceptance of one's worldly situation and working only to improve it (rather than to escape it for nirvana). On the other hand, the ancient Indian yogic practices impressed the Buddha and his followers deeply. Since Gautama had in fact become enlightened through meditation, and since this enlightenment expressed itself in terms of the antimaterial Four Noble Truths, Buddhism could never settle comfortably in the given world of the senses and pleasure.

Initially, therefore, Buddhism looked on nature or physical reality as much less than the most real or valuable portion of existence. Only consciousness could claim that title. Certainly the belief that all life is suffering reflects a rather negative attitude toward nature, and it indicates that what the eyes see and the ears hear is not the realm of true reality or true fulfillment. Also, to analyze physical reality in terms of three negative marks (pain, fleetingness, and selflessness) further devalues nature. At the least, one is not to desire sensory contacts with the world, because such desire binds one to illusory reality and produces only pain. Thus, Indian Buddhists separated themselves from nature (and society and self).

Philosophy and Popular Buddhism. Because the great interest of early Buddhist philosophy was an analysis of dharmas (elements of reality) based on probings of consciousness sharpened by intense meditation, the material aspects of the natural realm fell by the way. At best they were background realities and values. The scholastic Abhidharmists did not deny nature, for they were acutely aware of the senses, but they did deflect religious consciousness away from it.[46] Far more impressive than natural phenomena were the states of consciousness that seemed to go below the gross phenomena to more subtle phenomena. They were the places where the Indian Buddhists preferred to linger.

In considering the Buddhist view of nature, we must distinguish between the inclinations of the meditators and scholars, who were interested in nonphysical states of consciousness, and the inclinations of the laity, who saw the world more concretely and less analytically. As we might expect, the laity were more worldly than the monks. When they heard that all life was suffering, they probably thought of their family burdens, their vulnerability to sickness, and the many ways in which nature seemed out of their control. The comforts they received from Buddhist preaching, therefore, lay in the promise that right living would take them a step closer to the kind of existence where their pain would be less and their enjoyment greater.[47]

Thus, it is no surprise that the most popular Buddhist movements were built on the Indian traditions of devotion. Just as popular Hinduism fixed on Vishnu, Krishna, and Shiva, popular Buddhism fixed on **Amitabha, Avalokitesvara,** and **Vairocana.** These celestial buddhas or *bodhisattvas* drew the popular religious imagination away from the historical Buddha and the commonplace world of the here and now to the realm of future fulfillment. In that way, popular Buddhism lay in between the deemphasis of the physical realm that the monks and scholars practiced and the simple acceptance of physical life that a worldly or naturalist outlook (such as that of the early Vedas) produced. Emotional Buddhism influenced the sense perceptions of the laity so that this world became just the preliminary to the Western Paradise.[48]

Samsara and Nirvana. We have seen that as the intellectuals and contemplatives worked further with immaterial consciousness and its philosophical consequences, they changed the relationships between samsara and nirvana. In the beginning, Buddhism thought of samsara as the imperfect, illusory realm of given, sense-bound existence. Nature, therefore, was part of the realm of bondage. The Buddha himself exemplified this view when he urged his followers to escape the world that was "burning" to achieve nirvana. His original message regularly said that spontaneous experience makes one ill, and that health lies in rejecting attachments to spontaneous experience. With time, however, the philosophers, especially the Mahayanists, came to consider the relations between nirvana and samsara more complex. From analyzing the implications of these concepts, the philosophers determined that nirvana is not a thing or a place. The Buddha realized this, for he consistently refused to describe nirvana in detail. But while the Buddha's refusal was practical (such a description would not help solve the existential problems of being in pain), the refusal of the later philosophers, such as Nagarjuna, was largely epistemological and metaphysical. That is, they thought that we cannot think of such a concept as nirvana without reifying it (making it a thing), and that the reality of nirvana must completely transcend the realm of things. Therefore, nirvana could be the deepest reality of nature.

To follow this line of thought is no easy task, so only the elite grasped the philosophy of the *Prajnaparamita,* with its concepts of emptiness and transcendence. That philosophy influenced the devotional life of Mahayana and the ritual life of Tantrism, however, because even the simple people could grasp its positive implications as presented by the preachers. These positive implications, which blossomed most fully in the East Asian cultures, amounted to seeing that all reality is related. The other side of saying all dharmas are empty is to say that the buddha-nature (or nirvana, or the other ways of expressing the ultimate totality) is present everywhere. This belief gave religion a very positive tone. For instance, if all things contain the buddha-nature, then the natural and social worlds can become glowingly fresh and beautiful, as one realizes their potential.

Tantrist Buddhism, finally, shared the belief in the nonduality of samsara and nirvana that Indian Mahayana developed but differed in its expression of this belief through ritualistic imagination. Tibetan practices, for example, played with the world, both loving nature and kicking it away, through sights (mandalas), sounds (mantras), and ceremonies (symbolic intercourse) that engaged the participant both psychologically and physically. All of this, of course, implied using nature as a somewhat sacramental way to gain liberation. Insofar as physical nature reaches into the human being through the subconscious and unconscious, Tantrism has both honored and provided for nature's "depth psychology."

Society

The Indian society of the Buddha was divided into castes, which were religiously sanctioned as a way of maintaining social order. Moreover, casteism was part of Vedic India's cosmological myth, since according to legend human society's order resulted from the sacrifice of Purusha, the primal human being. In Brahmanism, the priests merited their primary status because they derived from Purusha's mouth.

Buddha, himself a member of the warrior class, brought a message that clashed with this hierarchy. His dharma taught that beings are to free themselves from painful worldly life. Since this invitation was from human nature, from what we are, it was more compelling than the call to accept the caste tradition. At least, Buddhists could strongly refute the cosmological myth that legitimated casteism. Many warriors and merchants no doubt also found Buddhism a convenient weapon in their struggles with the brahmins for power. So they and others who wanted to change the status quo gave Buddhism a close hearing.

There was great liberation potential in the Buddha's message. Indeed, there was considerable social radicalism. Buddha did not concern himself very much with politics as such, but his stress on enlight-

enment, nirvana, and the human calling to conquer karma and samsara challenged the politics of his day, as did the decision to admit people of all castes into the *sangha* and to include women. This decision was a logical application of the belief that all humans were in misery and might gain enlightenment.

In application, though, Buddhism never fully realized these ideals of liberation and radical equality. Caste was too much a part of Indian society to be exorcised without great difficulty. For instance, the *Dhammapada* (vv. 383–423) uses the brahmin as a figure of perfection. The "true Brahmin," it is at pains to show, is not he who is born into a priestly bloodline but he who gains a noble character through morality, meditation, and wisdom. Nonetheless, the *Dhammapada* does not choose to reinterpret the sudra (lowest class worker). It is the brahmin who continues to denote nobility.

Women's Status.   Buddhism offered Indian females considerably more than had been available to them previously.[49] Women were capable of enlightenment and could join the monastic community as nuns. This was in stark contrast to the classical Hindu view, which held that women had to be reborn as men to be eligible for *moksha*. By opening religious life to Indian women, Buddhists gave them an option besides marriage and motherhood—a sort of career and chance for independence. No longer did a girl and her family have to concentrate single-mindedly on gathering a dowry and arranging a wedding. Indeed, Buddhists viewed Hindu child marriage darkly, and they thought it more than fitting that women should travel to hear the Buddha preach. In later times, women could preach themselves, but from the beginning they could give time and money to the new cause.

Moreover, by offering an alternative to marriage, Buddhism inevitably gave women more voice in their marriage decisions and then in their conjugal lives. In fact, Buddhism viewed spouses as near equals. The husband was to give the wife respect, courtesy, faithfulness, and authority, while the wife was to give the husband duties well done, hospitality to their parents, faithfulness, watchfulness over his earnings, skill, and industry. One concrete way in which a Buddhist wife shared authority was in choosing their children's careers. For instance, to enter a monastery, a child needed both parents' consent. Married women could inherit and manage property without interference. Buddhism did not require or even expect that widows be recluses, and suttee was abhorrent to a religion that condemned animal sacrifice, murder, and suicide. Finally, Buddhist widows could enter the *sangha,* where they might find religious companionship, or they could stay in the world, remarry, inherit, and manage their own affairs.

Still, Buddhism never treated women as full equals of men. Though the logic of equal existential pain and equal possession of the buddha-nature could have run to equal political and educational opportunities, it seldom did. Nuns had varying degrees of freedom to run their own affairs in the monasteries, but they were regularly subject to monks. Women never gained regular access to power over males, either in Buddhism's conception of the religious community or in its conception of marriage. Insofar as celibacy became part of the Buddhist ideal, marriage could become a second-class vocation and women could become a religious danger.[50]

Politics. In its relations with secular political powers, Buddhism had varying fortunes. The Buddha seems to have concerned himself little with pleasing public authorities or worrying how his spiritual realm related to the temporal. No doubt his assumption was that if people became enlightened they would relativize social problems and solve them fairly easily. At the time of Asoka, however, the importance of royal patronage became clear. Much of Buddhism's influence outside India began when Asoka dispatched missionaries to foreign lands, and his efforts to instill Buddhist norms of ethics and nonviolence in his government became a model for later ages. As Christianity rethought Jesus' dictum about rendering unto Caesar the things that are Caesar's when it found a potentially Christian Caesar in Constantine, so after Asoka Buddhism longed for a union of dharma and kingly authority, thinking that such a union would beget a religious society.

Historically Buddhists tried to gain favor at court.[51] In Sri Lanka, Burma, Thailand, and the rest of Southeast Asia, this effort often succeeded, and temporal rulers played a large role in Theravada's victory over Mahayana and Hinduism. In China, Buddhism's fortunes depended on whether it fared better or worse than Confucianism in getting the emperor's ear. During the worst periods, it became the object of imperial persecution. The same was true in Japan, where such persecution had much the same rationale: Buddhism was not the native tradition. Overall, how-

ever, Buddhism fared well in East Asia. It had to co-exist with Confucian and Daoist cultural forces, but it regularly dominated philosophy, funeral rites, and art. Tibet realized the theocratic ideals that Asoka had sparked: Throughout most of its history religious leaders doubled as temporal powers. However, the intrigue, murder, and moral laxity that this binding of the two powers produced during certain periods of Tibetan history suggested rethinking the relation between the religious and the secular powers.

As with Christianity, there is a built-in tension between the Buddhist religious community and any temporal state. The *sangha* and the church both make claims upon their followers that can bring them into conflict with secular powers. Since these claims are made in the name of dharma or God, they carry an aura of sacredness or of coming from a higher authority. To be sure, Buddhism took pains to establish an ethics that urged peaceful citizenship.[52] But the proviso always lurking behind these sincere efforts was that secular rulers not order things unjust, evil, or irreligious. The things that rightly are Caesar's are limited. So long as there is a Christ or a Buddha, a God or a nirvana, Caesar cannot claim everything.

One ploy that Caesar can develop, however, is to claim that he, rather than the priests or monks, is the representative of God or dharma. In other words, employing the aspect of the cosmological myth by which the human ruler is the link between heaven and earth, the king can claim a sacredness of his own. Many Christian successors to Constantine claimed this, and in effect many Buddhist rulers after Asoka did also. Eric Voegelin has sketched the preparation for this sort of claim that a society such as the Mongol had. According to his hypothesis, Kublai Khan gave the Buddhists authority over Tibet as an administrative extension of his own sacred power.[53]

Despite its focus on otherworldly matters, then, Buddhism remained knotted in secular-religious controversies. Since it did not clearly establish an authority outside the cosmos (for instance, by coming to a doctrine of creation from nothingness), it was always liable to attack from kingly Buddhists who wanted to make doctrinal dharma serve the state.

The Sangha. The *sangha* alternately raised and dashed hopes that most human beings might live together in harmony and peace. Energetic monasteries, run by learned and holy monks or nuns, were models of what human society could be. Living simply, obeying a common rule and a common authority, such Buddhist professionals acted out a vision of equality and cooperation. When a monastery was in good spiritual fettle, one survived there only if one's motivation was religious. Meditation, hard work, austerity in diet and clothing, long periods of silence, celibacy—these staples of Buddhist monastic life offered little to the worldling. However, monasteries of the devotional sects could be quite different. Often people entered them rather grudgingly and briefly, to learn the minimal ritual and doctrine necessary to function at the inherited family temple. Meditation-centered monasteries also differed from the pampered, court-favored centers of learning, art, and intrigue frequently spawned by East Asian Buddhism. Still, as long as the genuine articles existed, Buddhism was alive and well.

The life of Buddhist laity has always reflected the state of the monastic *sangha*. When the monasteries were spiritually active, the laity tended to support them generously. In return, the monks usually served the laity spiritually. During these periods, the notion that the layperson's vocational obligation was primarily to support the monks evoked no cynicism. The monastery was embodying the social ideal and so encouraging the whole *sangha* to think that dharma could be an effective social philosophy. On the other hand, when the monks were lax, the reaction of the laity was ambivalent. The laity enjoyed seeing clay feet under yellow robes, but they missed the examples and teachings that might have dissolved some of their own clay. Ideally, then, the monks and nuns and the laity have provided mutual support. [54] Mahayana and Tantra have acted on this ideal by relating nirvana and samsara in such a way that vocational differences between the laity and the clergy are lessened. Even for these schools, however, the monasteries have symbolized idealistic places of retreat, meditation, study, and ritual devotion.

Buddhist Ahimsa. In an appendix to his study of Theravada ethics,[55] Winston King has some interesting remarks about recent Buddhist attitudes toward killing. Perhaps they will somewhat bridge the way from the Indian tradition of *ahimsa* to our present age, with its pressures from nuclear weapons, ecological disorders, and dietary researches, to rethink our modern aggression. If so, it may suggest the perennial power of Buddhist social thought.

Traditionally, Buddhism laid great stress on the precept of nonkilling, not only because this precept inculcates a respect for all living things, but also because carefully observing it leads to great self-control and promotes peace. For example, if one is to stay away from killing or injuring other creatures, one must control anger, greed, hatred, and the other vices that usually spur our injurious actions and inhibit social justice.

Nonetheless, in countries such as Burma, where many political figures profess to be faithful Buddhists, the question of how to apply the precept of nonkilling in public policy has grown quite vexing. Thus, one candidate in the 1959–60 elections pointed out the difficulty of adhering to strict interpretations of nonkilling while trying to suppress rebel insurgents or run such important government industries as fishing and mutton production. This dilemma differs little from that of the Christian pacifist, but nonviolence probably has been closer to the core of Buddhist tradition than to the core of Christian tradition. Leading Buddhist politicians, such as U Thant, who became head of the United Nations, therefore have had to make some distinctions. Generally they have tried to moderate public policies in the direction of nonkilling but have conceded that a thorough application of *ahimsa* (for example, prohibiting all military action) is not always practical.

Capital punishment is another problem that the precept of nonkilling heightens. Ideally, most Buddhists probably would oppose a law of capital punishment, urging sentences of life imprisonment for capital crimes. Not only would this honor *ahimsa,* it would also offer the criminal an opportunity to repent and be converted to Buddhist convictions. Still, through history to modern times most Buddhist countries have practiced capital punishment. This has caused some analysts to speak of a conflict between the mundane morality of the state and the ideal morality of the Buddhist religion. In their view, the state needs capital punishment to maintain order, so one must reluctantly kill the worst social offenders. This might seem to relegate Buddhist ideals to complete impracticality, but further reflection has led some ethicians to a more dialectical notion of nonkilling.

For these dialecticians, there are circumstances in which *not* slaying heinous offenders would be a great violence. Those charged with protecting the common good would seriously fail their charge were they to allow murderers to continue operating without fear of capital punishment. So the dialecticians come to the conclusion that committing the lesser evil is doing a species of good. In other words, they justify capital punishment as a necessary evil, a means public officials must employ if they are to honor the precept of noninjury in more general, far-reaching terms. To prevent great injury to the public at large, one must injure some criminal offenders. Once again, it would not be hard to draw parallels to Western debates over capital punishment.

Still another implication of the precept of noninjury is that one must avoid contributing to the *conditions* that lessen or warp the span of living things, especially human beings. This is parallel to the Latin American theoreticians' discussions of *violencia blanca*. *Violencia blanca* is the white or invisible violence that an unjust system perpetrates through its inequitable distribution of wealth and power. Thus, when they are accused of corrupting their revolutionary cause by resorting to military violence or violence against the property of the rich, some Latin Americans argue that the prevailing *violencia blanca* in the slums, poverty, shortened life spans, bloated stomachs of little children, illiteracy, and the like, is a greater evil, though of course one to which most people have grown accustomed.

The Buddhist parallel quoted by King is quite exact. In it a contemporary Burmese ethician urges his fellow countrymen to apply the precept of nonkilling to "crowded and ill-ventilated buildings, workshops and factories; slum conditions in big cities and towns; the overworking of children as well as adults; careless driving of steam boats, rail engines, planes, motor and other vehicles and engines; sale of spurious and other adulterated foodstuffs; unskilled use of syringes with or without license; treatment of sick people by quacks; sale of foodstuffs not fit for human consumption," and so forth. Anything that violates human health or dignity can be subsumed under the precept of nonkilling. When taken radically, this precept approximates the Christian and Confucian commandment to treat one's neighbor as oneself.

King contrasts this radical social ethics with the fatalistic, somewhat self-centered views of karma that too often obtain in Buddhist countries, offering the radical view as a hopeful sign. Were Buddhism to apply its imagination to developing a social ethic that carried noninjury down to concrete details, it could develop the dharma into a powerful social message. Caring for the well-being of all living things, it might make greater strides toward enlightened health care, education, economics, and the like.

Self

The practical accent of Buddha's original preaching made the issues related to self paramount. Yet, paradoxically, a capital thesis in that preaching was that self is an illusion, "the most pernicious of errors, the most deceitful of illusions."[56] Consequently, Buddhist religious experience and doctrine concerning the self have been complex. On the one hand, Buddhism has directly addressed individuals, insisting that only the individual can change his or her life. On the other hand, Buddhism has counseled that to escape samsara and achieve nirvana, we have to rid ourselves of the notion that we have or are an atman, a soul, or self. This belief has prompted some of Buddhism's central meditational practices and philosophical doctrines.

Historically, the teaching of *anatman* most distinguished the Buddha's way from that of his Hindu predecessors. As we have seen, a staple of Upanishadic wisdom was that the self is part of the great Atman (the interior aspect of Brahman). In yogic meditation, the Hindu tried to realize this ultimate identity, to experience the oneness of everything in Atman. When Buddha turned away from this teaching, calling human identity just a bundle of elements (*skandhas*) temporarily fused, he laid down a philosophical challenge that Hindu and Buddhist philosophers seldom neglected in later centuries. What motivated this new conception of the human being?

The principal motive, it appears, was Buddha's conviction that the key to human problems is desire. If pain expresses the problem ("All life is painful"), then desire expresses its cause ("The cause of suffering is desire"). These, we have seen, are the first two Noble Truths. The Third Noble Truth ("The removal of desire leads to the removal of suffering") extends the first two, and when Buddhists pondered its meaning and implications, they came to the doctrine of no-self (*anatman*).

The Third Noble Truth itself is psychological. For instance, we may analyze the suffering in human relations in terms of desire. Parents desire their children's success and love. When the children choose paths other than what the parents have dreamed, or when the children demand distance in order to grow into their own separate identities, the parents suffer pain. They feel disappointed or rejected, or that their toil and anxiety have gone for naught. Buddhists would tell such parents that their relations with their children have been unwise or impure. Because they have desired success and love, instead of remaining calm and free, they have set karmic bonds that were sure to cause pain.

But to cut the karmic bonds, the Third Noble Truth implies, one must get to the root of the desire. At this point one must turn psychology into metaphysics—one must realize that the self from which desires emanate is neither stable, fixed, permanent, nor, ultimately, real. In our distraction and illusion, we gladly accept the fiction that we have stable selves. Under the prod of analysis and meditation, however, we start to see what Alfred North Whitehead (the Western philosopher currently touted as the most "Buddhist" of our metaphysicians)[57] called the "fallacy of misplaced concreteness."

In simple terms, the prime reality in our interior lives is flux. At each moment we are different "selves." True, some continuity exists in that we remember past events and project future ones. But this continuity hardly justifies clinging to or relying upon a permanent self.

What Buddhists stressed, therefore, was the change and coordination of the "self's" components, just as they stressed the interconnectedness and flux of the entire world (through Dependent Coarising). They developed a view of both the interior realm of consciousness and the exterior realm of nature that became quite relational. Their metaphysics focused on nature's coordinated interdependencies, its continual movement. The self could not be the exception to such a worldview. Humans were too clearly a part of the total natural process to violate the process's fundamental laws. And just as analysis showed all the natural elements to be empty, so, too, analysis showed the self to be empty.

Therefore, Buddhists directly denied what Western philosophers such as Aristotle called a "substance." To live religiously, in accordance with the facts of consciousness, one had to cast off the naive assumption that the human person is a solid something—one had to slide into the flux. In so doing, one could both remove the basis for desire and open up the possibility for union with the rest of coordinated reality.

This movement toward coordination with the rest of reality became the positive counterweight to the Buddhist negative view of the self. That is, as people advanced in their meditation and understanding, they started to glimpse what Mahayana saw in enlightenment: the realization that all buddha-nature is non-

dual. According to the *Prajna-paramita,* ultimately only buddha-nature existed. All multiplicity or discreteness resulted from a less than ultimate viewpoint. Yogacara texts such as the Chinese *Awakening of Faith*[58] explicitly correlated this view of ultimate wisdom with meditation. Stressing the centrality of mind, the *Awakening of Faith* tried to lead the reader toward the realization that his or her own consciousness reflected the ultimate connectedness. Such a realization, of course, meant the death of the illusion that one was an independent atman.

We have belabored this teaching of *anatman* (no-self) because it seems most important to the Buddhist attitude toward the individual. It is also the key to the Buddhist view that nature flows together and that society should strive for ultimate reality by means of enlightenment. Because of no-self, the individual could move toward greater intimacy with nature. There were no barriers of separate identity, no walls making him or her isolated. For those who attained enlightenment through the dharma, this nonseparation of self, nature, and society was a personal experience. As a contemporary account of enlightenment puts it, "The big clock chimes—not the clock but Mind chimes. The universe itself chimes. There is neither Mind nor universe. Dong, dong, dong! I've totally disappeared. Buddha is!"[59]

Buddhism regularly counseled the individual to regard the body, the family, society, and even a spouse or a child with detachment. One was to revere and discipline the body according to the Middle Way. Clearly, though, the body was only a temporary station on the way to nirvana or one's next incarnation. Wealth and pleasure were not, as they were for Hinduism, worthy life goals. The family was a necessary unit, biologically and socially, but frequently it was also an impediment to spiritual advancement, as the Buddha's own life showed. Society would ideally be a context for mutual support in realizing enlightenment. Personal bonds, therefore, could not be passionate and karmic, and even a spouse or a child came under this law.

The love proper to a Buddhist was "great compassion"—desire for the other's good in nirvana. This became no-desire in worldly terms. So alcohol, sex, clothing, and other items affecting the body were governed by the ethical rule of detachment (and came under the "Buddhist economics" that E. F. Schumacher made a cornerstone of his book *Small Is Beautiful*).[60] So business, politics, and art ideally sprang from a free spirit. East Asian painting, poetry, and calligraphy, for instance, ideally occurred in a state of no-mind.[61] Contrary to the regular Western view of the artist, in which the person agonizes through his or her work to produce a vision (and a self), the East Asian artist was to let art flow out of a meditative experience. Its hallmark was to be spontaneity, and the major stumbling block to spontaneity was self-concern.

Tantrism seems to qualify the Buddhist view of the self, since it allowed a more intense connection with food, alcohol, sex, and material ritual items. However, according to its own masters, the watchword in Tantrist rituals was still discipline and detachment. To use alcohol or sex licentiously was just a quick way to attachment and bad karma. The point to Tantrist ritual was to master these items and retain the energies that would have flowed out to them.

Even if not carried out, the doctrine of *anatman* (no-self) shaped Buddhist culture. Wherever Buddhist religion was vigorous, the doctrine of *anatman* was influential. In fact, we often can sense its effects in the peace and humor of Buddhist texts. Many texts, of course, are complicated and complex. However, some raise serenity, irony, paradox, and wit to a high religious art. For instance, in one story two monks meet a fetching damsel by a rushing river. One charitably hoists her and carries her across. Later the second monk chastises the first for such sensual contact. The first monk replies, "I let the girl down when we crossed the river. Why are you still carrying her?" The Buddhist ideal was to carry nothing, to have a self utterly free.[62]

Case Study: Nagarjuna. Nagarjuna gained such a lofty reputation in later Buddhism, especially that of Tibet, that he deserves special consideration as an example of the wise Buddhist personality, the ideal Buddhist "self." He probably lived between 150 and 250 C.E., most likely in south India, and his style of argumentation, as well as his analyses of his opponents' positions, suggests that he was trained as a Hindu brahmin before he converted to the budding movement of Mahayana Buddhism.

Although Nagarjuna is known as the most acute of the Mahayana dialecticians, Tibetan tradition also reveres him as a guru who offered his disciples sound ethical advice. Some verses from the "The Staff of Wisdom," a work attributed to Nagarjuna, suggest his ethical style.[63]

Figure 9 *Head of a Buddha image, northwest India, first–second century. Stone; 19¼ in. high. The topknot, long ears, mark of knowledge on the forehead, and half-closed eyes are marks of authority, vision, and peace. The Nelson–Atkins Museum of Art, Kansas City, Missouri (Nelson Fund).*

First, Nagarjuna insists that the only way to gain the real meaning of the dharma, the Buddhist sciences, and the holy mantras is directly to experience them. Those who merely analyze the meaning of words never come to the core. This insistence expresses the conviction of all Buddhist gurus that words can be deceptive. If we allow words a life of their own, detached from the experiences they are trying to describe, words can distract us from reality. To grasp the dharma or the treatises of wisdom, we must both meditate on the realities to which they point and practice the virtues they extol. The same with the holy mantras that the tradition urges us to pray. Unless we experience the states from which they flow, the realities to which the saints have spontaneously directed them, the mantras will be but nonsense sounds.

Nagarjuna then reflects on the sort of knowledge that is truly valuable. We only know what this knowledge is in time of need, when we are hard-pressed. Then it is clear that the knowledge contained in books is of little use. Unless we have made an insight our own, it will give us little light or peace. In this, knowledge is parallel to wealth. Time of need shows us that wealth we have borrowed from others is no real wealth. It is nothing on which we can depend, for it can be taken from us at a stroke. Whether it be a matter of knowledge or of wealth, need, pressure, or suffering shows us the stark contrast between what we truly own and what we have merely borrowed. Thus hard times can have a silver lining. If they strengthen our resolve to gain our own wisdom, possess our own (incorruptible) wealth, they can advance us toward fulfillment.

We should consider our work in the same vein. The accomplishments of a teacher of ants, as Nagarjuna describes a person concerned with trivial affairs, are but ways of earning a living. Even the master baker, carpenter, or clerk deserves only the praise we can accord worldly skills. But suppose we meet a person studying liberation. Helping us terminate our earthly incarnation, such a person deals with heavenly affairs, the only things truly necessary. Were we wise, we would turn our admiration from masters of trivial affairs to those few masters who teach the only things truly necessary. Thereby, we would clarify our own essential task, making the study of how to terminate our earthly incarnation *the* great accomplishment to which we aspired.

Even master-teachers wander off the track at times, and Nagarjuna's next verse seems a tangent to his main line. If you have a chosen truth, a pearl of special wisdom, he says, be careful to whom you give it. Make sure that you scrutinize the character of any person to whom you would impart the dharma. Unscrupulous people can turn the best of teachings to injurious use. Remember the legend of the man who took compassion on a monkey and gave him a small

place to live. Before long the monkey had taken over the whole house and the man was out in the street. The same can happen with careless teachers. Unscrupulous disciples can turn the dharma against their teachers, making an act of charity into a shambles.

Bending back to the main stream of his thought, Nagarjuna turns to two kinds of teaching. Some people teach with words; others instruct silently. This is reminiscent of the reed-flower, which has no fruit, in contrast to the walnut, which has both fruit and flower. It is also reminiscent of the kataka tree, the fruit of which clears mud from the water. If you only mention the name of the kataka tree, you will not remove the mud. You must make your teaching bear fruit, make it deal with more than words. You must extend it to the realm of action, instructing by silent deeds as well as wordy lectures. Indeed, if you do not apply your knowledge, you are like a blind man with a lamp. Though you have in hand a source of great illumination, you do not shed it on the road, do not light the way for others to travel.

Stanza after stanza, Nagarjuna tosses out aphorisms like these. Line after line, his advice is poetic, symbolic, image-laden. From deep meditation and reflection, he finds emptiness a font of great illumination. For one who sees, the spiritual life is paradoxical and parabolic. As we come close to enlightenment, the main structures of the holy life stand clear, but these structures (meditation, wisdom, and morality) are capable of endless application. The key is having the experience, grasping the center, knowing emptiness directly. When we realize that reality is a seamless cloth, we can enjoy all its various designs. At that point, Buddhist selfhood will be properly achieved (and empty).

Ultimate Reality

Debate has raged over the question of whether Buddhism is a theistic religion. For instance, the late Chogyam Trungpa, a Tibetan master living in the United States, complained, "It is especially unfortunate that Buddhism has been presented as a theistic religion, whereas in fact it is a nontheistic spiritual philosophy, psychology, and way of life."[64] On the other hand, there is a good reason why scholars have frequently presented Buddhism as a theistic religion: It has frequently seemed to be such.[65] Devotional Buddhism has venerated a variety of buddhas and *bodhisattvas,* treating them as other religions treat gods and saints. Also, the Buddhist concepts of nirvana, buddha-nature, and emptiness have on occasion evinced the sacred aura of divinity, generating language that can only be called, by its difference from ordinary language, religious. In its perceptions of nirvana, Buddhism has made ultimate reality the touchstone of all wisdom. While this reality has been judged ineffable, all the meditation-masters imply that it is wholly positive. One cannot speak about it because it is too full, whole, basic, and brilliant for human language to describe. It is impersonal and reached by meditation more than by words. Therefore, Buddhism frequently has seemed to be both theistic or religious and matter-of-factly nontheistic.

To be sure, the Buddha himself does not appear to have claimed divinity. For example, he cast no speeches in the "I am" form that the Jesus of John's Gospel assumed. Rather, Gautama seems to have been a human being who thought that he had found the key to living well. The key was enlightenment, whose expression was the Four Noble Truths. In the enlightenment experience, Gautama encountered ultimate reality. The overtones to this encounter gleaned from the texts are not those of meeting a personal God. Whether that differentiates Gautama's ultimate reality from the God of Western religion is another question, the answer to which depends on careful analysis of peak experiences and conceptions of ultimate reality. The personal character of the Western God is not so simple as many Westerners assume, and the impersonal quality of Gautama's encounter with nirvana is less absolute than many assume.

Images of the Buddha. We may suggest the status of the Buddha by drawing on some of the images in which the sutras have delighted. A first image, of the Buddha's dharma as a raincloud, comes from the Lotus Sutra, a scripture very influential in such Mahayana sects as the Chinese Tien-t'ai and the Japanese Nichiren.

The sutra puts the image of a raincloud in the Buddha's own mouth: "The King of Dharma I am, who arose in the world to crush becoming; Dharma I teach to beings, after I have discerned their dispositions. . . . It is like a great cloud which arises above the earth, which covers up everything and overshadows the firmament. And this great cloud, filled with water, wreathed with lightning, resounds with thunder, and refreshes all the creatures."[66]

A few verses later, the Buddha says that he has arisen in this world like a raincloud. And when he has arisen, "the World's Savior" speaks, to show all living beings the true course they ought to travel. For this he is honored by the whole world, with all its gods. He is the Tathagata, the one who has gone over to enlightenment, a conqueror who has arisen in the world like a raincloud. He refreshes all living beings, whose bodies are withering away because they cling to the lower worlds. The Buddha will ease the pains that are withering them. He will give them pleasures and the final rest of nirvana.

Moreover, he preaches the dharma to all beings, always making enlightenment the foundation of his teaching. This teaching is the same for all hearers. There is no partiality in the Buddha's message, no alteration of voice, for he is beyond hatred and love. Once again, this makes him like a raincloud, which releases its rain evenly on all. Enlightenment applies equally to the noble and the mean. It is the message the Blessed One offers the immoral as well as the moral. The depraved are no different in their need for enlightenment than those whose conduct is good. In all cases, final fulfillment depends on grasping, realizing, the dharma. Thus people who hold false views and people who hold right views, people who hold unsound views and people whose views are pure all stand in need of the Buddha. Prescinding from their merit or demerit, enlightenment presses on all of them as a fierce imperative. Without enlightenment, they are equally needy, equally bereft of the truth that saves. The Buddha is the one doctor dispensing the medicine needed by all the world's sickly souls.

For that reason, the Buddha spends himself, preaching dharma to beings of inferior intellect and beings of superior intellect, to beings whose faculties are weak and beings whose faculties are strong. Setting aside his own fatigue, he rains down dharma on them all. Feeling this rain, the world is well refreshed. Each being who comes under the shower of truth benefits, according to its own capacity. Each finds the well-preached teaching to its taste. In this the dharma is again like the rain, which falls on shrubs and grasses, bushes and smaller plants, trees and great wooded tracts, doing good to each. Throughout all the realms, earthly and celestial, the Buddha's teaching makes beings glow with refreshment and satisfaction.

Thus, the sutra concludes, it is the nature of dharma always to exist for the good of the world, offering a continual refreshment. From this refreshment the world should, like a well-watered plant, burst forth in blossoms of insight, purity, good behavior, and compassion.

If we step back to analyze this imagery, it is clear that the sutra pictures the Buddha and his teaching as the heavenly dew that makes the world green. Without the Buddha's dharma, the world would be a desert, arid and joyless. In the empty wastes of suffering, there would be no cause for hope. But the words of the Blessed One are so powerful and creative they make what was barren burgeon with sturdy growth. Cool, detached, above all the world's tribulations, the Buddha serenely makes the rain of truth fall on just and unjust alike. Only the sun moving in its heavenly circuit, or the clouds drifting high above, can symbolize the Buddha's equanimity and evenhandedness. To him all creatures are in need of the truth, so all have a claim on his enlightened compassion. Whatever their station or disposition, his message is apt and helpful.

The sutra depends on the conjunction of natural imagery with a conviction of Buddha's "skillfulness in means." In this phrase the tradition epitomized its belief that the Enlightened One could find a way into any heart, no matter what that heart's condition. Possessing the light of salvation in all its effulgence, the Buddha knows how to make the light shine into every corner of the world. So deeply does his wisdom go, it is always relevant, always able to clarify the hearer's condition. Just as all creatures need the rain of the skies, so all rational creatures need the heavenly truth. The Buddha was so closely associated with heaven, the supervising powers that rule the world, that the Lotus Sutra instinctively expressed his compassionate aid in terms of heavenly phenomena. Taking up the awe and gratitude human beings have always directed toward the heavens, the sutra focused them on the teaching, the Buddha's way out of this vale of tears.

Consequently, in a comparative perspective he was the great Buddhist divinity. Although at times *bodhisattvas* such as Kuan-yin drew more attention, often because they projected a maternal mercy, the core tenets of Buddhism ran toward placing Gautama, man and primary manifestation of enlightenment, at the center of the bull's-eye. As human, he modeled the pious life. As the primary manifestation of enlightenment, he brought nirvana into the midst of samsara. So his dharma became *the dharma*, the teaching that ran the world. So all enlightened people grew in his lineaments (though Zen masters and others fought any tendency to a literalist aping; for them the essential following of the Buddha was doing what he did, realizing one's own enlightenment-nature). For the common people, reverencing the Buddha was a main way to a better life, in which they might win release from suffering and gain the bliss of nirvana.

If Gautama has represented the personal aspect of Buddhist ultimate reality, putting into human form the truth that might free the human mind, heart, soul, and strength from the sufferings of samsara, it remains to be said that both Gautama himself and many subsequent Buddhists have considered nirvana, or the state of liberation, to be impersonal, a kind of no-thingness that both psychologically and ontologically (that is, in both the shifts in consciousness it denoted and what it suggested about being or the build of reality itself) did not fully square with either theistic or religious terminology.

Buddhist masters often explained that nirvana was something positive, as we have mentioned. Yet both etymologically and in terms of some of the classical descriptions of it, nirvana implied the denial of the limitations humanity presently suffered. So it would be like the state of the flame when the candle of desire had blown out. It would be an unconditioned—unfettered, unbound—way of being. When ignorance, pain, mortality, and disease (both physical and moral) had passed away, or had been escaped, one could speak of nirvana. When the last residue of karma, the final traces of debt to dying and being reborn, had been erased, one would be at the nirvanic far shore. Sometimes Mahayana thinkers translated this sort of thought into terms that seemed to equate it with a shift in consciousness: Think in nondesirous terms, live free of karmic impurity, and you could experience the substance of nirvana. Often such translations used the calm, the peace, the compassion of Gautama as emotional and behavioral anchors: That is what nirvana looked like in the life of the Enlightened One. Moreover, such a focus tended to make light of, if not ignore, the question of whether there was a nirvanic realm of being—a place or state to which one went, or into which one entered, when one died as an enlightened being. The result was a peculiarly Buddhist form of secularism: a stress on the here and now that urged a nongrasping, fluid, sort of harmony. One was not to exploit the beauty, or even to flee the outward pain, of life in the here and now. Neither was one to take the here and now as an icon of eternity or God's other-worldly grace. Rather, one was to accept and join the flux of all beings, enjoying their being, light, and change. This was the way things were, and from the supreme realism of agreeing to the way things were one would both gain ultimate wisdom and enact it. Certainly one was to be compassionate toward the sufferings woven through most unenlightened people's perceptions of the way things were, but this compassion need not rouse one to anger at natural disaster or social injustice, need not shake one's deep-seated peace with agonies over evil, worries that reality itself had cancerous lesions.

The ontological correlative of this psychologically impersonal appreciation of ultimate reality largely traded in negation and silence. One could not define or describe nirvana as a state, a thing, a realm without falsifying it. Nirvana was in the midst of samsara. It was true being in contrast to mottled, desire-ridden, mortal being. Yet it was so whole, so basic, so pure that the human mind, intrinsically given to dichotomies and partialities, was bound to distort it. So the best approach was simply to let nirvana be, treating it as the wonderful, even the gracious partner to the wholeness, freedom, and delight one had entered upon with enlightenment. It was primary and human awareness of it was secondary. It was true or real, while most metaphysical schemes, like most human lives, were illusory—because they did not stem from the center of a healed, enlightened personality. One might use the Buddha to exemplify this appreciation of nirvanic ultimate reality; one might even sanction devotions such as reading the sutras or praying at the shrines of the *bodhisattvas*. But these were instrumental things, limited to the order of means. If they helped people, especially the common people, to sense the grandeur of what the Buddha had discovered and nirvanic reality always offered, fine. In itself, however, nirvana simply was, grounding all of samsaric existence and offering a perennial basis for hope, yet never yielding itself up to human control, never becoming less mysterious or less paradoxically both the treasure that might fulfill human longing and something so transhuman it could never be tamed, it would always remain somewhat alien.

SUMMARY: THE BUDDHIST CENTER

The Buddhist center seems to us to lie in enlightenment. This is the experience that gives the religion its name; this is the experience from which the Middle Way proceeds, to which it conduces. At various times we have spoken about enlightenment. In these last lines we would speak about it summarily, epitomizingly, in a final effort to cut to the heart of the Buddhist matter and find therein a lotus of peace.

Historically speaking, enlightenment made Gautama the Buddha. He became the person who knew the way to happiness, the secret of good living, by bringing his meditations under the bodhi tree to fruition. Flooded with light, realizing how things were and always had been, the Buddha solved the problem of suffering, broke the chains of samsara, gained a light and peace that made him compassionate, able and willing to succor all beings in need. Come to rest and insight himself, he could give order to the flux of human existence, see the implications of the light that he had found this flux to bear. So he became the great promulgator of the Teaching, the Noble Middle Way. He became the guide who was sufficiently skillful in means to mediate the Truth to any who would hear. As one of the devotional texts that we saw put it, his teaching "is like a great cloud which arises above the heart, which covers up everything and overshadows the firmament. And this great cloud, filled with water, wreathed with lightning, resounds with thunder, and refreshes all creatures."[67]

A center, however, should be perspicuous to most beholders. However much a full appreciation of it depends on a deep immersion in its presuppositions and implications, a center of a living, well-tested faith should have some allure for outsiders, should sparkle with the possibility of becoming their center, reorienting their lives for the better. Can we gain a sufficient appreciation of Buddhist enlightenment for this to happen to us? Can we see ourselves, in our mind's eye, becoming flooded with light like the Buddha's and so gaining the Buddhist sense of reality, the Buddhist feel for the world? Let us try.

For many Buddhists, what Gautama experienced or discovered was neither new nor unique. Other enlightened beings had preceded him, and enlightenment is a possibility for all human beings. Why? Because reality itself is lightsome, knowing and knowable. To exist is to be mind-oriented, making sense, taking one's place in a scheme of things. Thus Yoga-cara Buddhists could come to the position that only Mind exists. Becoming greatly impressed with the mental or knowing aspect of all reality, they could put brackets around any nonknowing remainders, push them to the side of reality's essential definition. Zen Buddhist masters often speak in similar tones. For them reality itself is intrinsically perfect, complete and undefiled. It is only our ignorance or illusion that prevents us from seeing reality's perfection. As we grow more accustomed to right views and the rest of the Eightfold Path, through study, meditation, and good living, reality will grow brighter and brighter for us. At the lightsome center of the mind that has meditated well, the reality that has been well studied, there is only a coruscant emptiness, a brilliant lack of fixity, stolidity, desire.

When the Buddha realized this, he broke free of suffering. There was nothing to desire, and so nothing to suffer from. He and the rest of reality were not two or many. They were not one, in the Hindu sense of atman and Brahman. Their relation was ineffable, impossible to fix in clumsy human language. Only one who had come to understand this relation, to enjoy the light of being itself, could fully sense, feel, and profit from it. The best advertisements for enlightenment were the wisdom, freedom, and compassion that it generated. The serenity of nonattachment was like a breeze that blew out samsara, a dawn that unveiled nirvana. Were human beings to relate to nature, one another, and themselves in the light of such freedom, all things might go well. With humor and humility, intense presence to the given moment and great common sense, human beings might make their own organization a place of refuge. Then the *sangha* would indeed be a jewel, a worthy object of trust.

The humility and joy of enlightenment make it a very attractive center. Perhaps for that reason, William Johnston, one of the best translators of Buddhist spirituality to the West, has reminded his readers of a famous koan (a puzzling Zen saying meant to break down commonplace approaches to understanding). "A monk asked Ummon, 'What is the Buddha?' Ummon replied, 'A dried shit-stick.' A shit-stick was used in China instead of toilet paper. And Ummon, asked about the wonderful buddha-nature that is the true self, makes this shocking and iconoclastic answer. What does he mean? He means that however noble our aspirations, we must remember that we are (in the words of one commentator) 'a bag of manure.' Nor is it sufficient to give an intellectual assent to this proposition. One who would solve the koan must live it, realize it, act it out with his or her body, demonstrate to the master that one has identified with this ugly shit-stick . . . [yet] the Buddhist realization that the one is a dried shit-stick is also accompanied with great joy. There is no gnawing guilt in this koan but a great emancipation from anxiety together with the overflowing joy that always accompanies the recognition of the truth."[68] At the Buddhist center, we may find the liberating truth of our nothingness. Not all traditions would express this truth so graphically, but all would agree that humility makes one free, emptiness is fulfilling.

Discussion Questions

1. What was the essence of Gautama's enlightenment?

2. Is wisdom-morality-meditation a comprehensive, fully adequate religious regime? Why? Why not?

3. In what sense was Mahayana both more popular and more speculative than Theravada?

4. How did Tantrist Buddhism utilize the imagination?

5. Does Buddhism merge nature and divinity?

6. How would you try to persuade your best friend that he or she has no self?

7. Explain the Buddhist symbol of the lotus.

8. What do the various images of the Buddha seem to be saying?

9. What would you expect from a session with guru Nagarjuna?

10. How attractive do you find the daily routine of Mount Shasta Monastery?

11. What sense do you make of nirvana?

12. How can Buddhism be both religious and non-religious?

13. What is the significance of Buddhist compassion?

14. What would be the main thesis of a Buddhist social ethics?

15. How has Buddhism regarded sexuality?

16. What did the Buddha's acceptance of women into the *sangha* say about his views of contemporary Indian culture?

Key Terms

Amitabha: the Buddha of light, who presides over the Pure Land. Known in Japan as Amida, this buddha has been a prime object of veneration among such devotional groups as the followers of Shinran, who preached that faith in the mercy of Amida would suffice for salvation, due to the religious difficulties of his time.

anatman: the Buddhist doctrine that there is no substantial self and so nothing to which desire actually can cling. Buddhist philosophers have analyzed all the realities human beings experience as empty of either duration or permanent significance, trying to enlist disciples' minds in the pursuit of a complete detachment from the karmic allure of anything finite or conditioned.

arhat: a Buddhist term for one who has reached nirvana. In contrast to the *bodhisattva,* the *arhat* usually is considered to have been a rather solitary pursuer of enlightenment and full release, not much interested in the social side of liberation, where one would take up the burdens of other people, indeed of all living things, who also suffer from ignorance and desire.

Avalokitesvara: one of the greatest of the *bodhisattvas* reverenced by Mahayana Buddhism. Avalokitesvara is noted for his great compassion, and one finds in the *Prajna-paramita* sutras an indication that he presides over the philosophical way to enlightenment, being associated with Lady Wisdom herself in the effort to get believers to realize the emptiness of all dharmas and the coincidence of nirvana and samsara.

bodhisattva: a Mahayana Buddhist term for the enlightened one or saint who is a buddha-to-be. Typically, the *bodhisattva* postpones entrance into nirvana to labor for the salvation of other living beings, and generally the *bodhisattva* becomes a figure of help and mercy. Thus Kuan-yin, the *bodhisattva* most influential in the popular Buddhist religion of East Asia, has functioned as a kindly maternal figure, ever-available to help people with their worries about sickness, having a child, business problems, and the like.

buddha: one who comes to enlightenment and so becomes a knowledge-being, full of light and compassion. Gautama therefore has been only one of the many buddhas, but his making clear in earthly, historical terms the requirements for enlightenment has kept him central in Buddhist faith. Some Buddhist schools urged freeing oneself from overdependence on Gautama, under the conviction that each person was a potential buddha and had to develop this potential by self-reliance.

Dependent Coarising: the Buddhist doctrine about the structure of reality as a chain of mutually connecting influences. This chain straddles what we might call the physical and the moral realms, linking desire with death and rebirth but also specifying how desire works through the senses and intellect. One result of the doctrine of Dependent Coarising was to distance Buddhists from Hindus who thought in terms of a Brahman behind the phenomenal world and responsible for its patterns. Dependent Coarising meshed with the Buddhist view that all reality is empty and processive—moving along like a dance or even a flux.

dharma: an Indian term for teaching and duty. Buddhists have stressed the idea of teaching, speaking of the dharma of the Buddha as one of their three great treasures (Buddha, dharma, *sangha*). Hindus have more vaguely spoken of dharma as a Truth rooted in their tradition (most notably in the Vedas). The word has had a more precise set of Hindu connotations when used in a social context, pointing to the responsibilities attendant on one's caste and the teachings of the famous law codes (such as that of Manu) that regularized social relationships.

Eightfold Path: the Buddhist program of right views, right resolve, right speech, right action, right livelihood, right effort, right mindfulness, and right concentration. This is the fourth of the Buddha's Four Noble Truths, and traditionally Buddhists have understood it as undergirding wisdom, morality, and meditation, the three principal foci of their religious enterprise. Of course one could only learn what was "right" in each of these areas from the Buddha, the dharma, and the *sangha,* but the Eightfold Path laid out the principal things on which one was to concentrate when thinking about the outlook, ethics, and reflective life necessary for enlightened living.

emptiness: an important concept in Mahayana Buddhist philosophy, stressing that no reality is substantial and that reifying language is misleading. Emptiness does much of the work in a Buddhist scheme accomplished by "contingency" in some of the Western religious schemes. By pressing hard on the limitations of the things we experience, on the mortality of human beings, on the ignorance of all living beings, and the like, Buddhist philosophers could show that none of these beings grounded or explained itself and so that all were "empty" of both fixed reality and ultimate significance. Practically, this meant good reasons for not clinging to any such entities in desire and so not being ensnared in samsara through their influence.

enlightenment: In Buddhist circles enlightenment names the experience that made Gautama the Buddha and that could take any human being out of the vicious circle of death and rebirth, onto the path toward nirvana. Enlightenment usually came with a flash of understanding, mainly that most of the dualisms we propose are illusory and most of the desires we have are misguided. In addition to light, enlightenment therefore also suggested liberation from bondages that had taken away one's peace and joy.

Four Noble Truths: the epitome of the Buddha Gautama's preaching and teaching, which says that all life is suffering, that the cause of suffering is desire, that by removing desire one can remove suffering, and that the way to remove desire and travel freely through human time is to follow the Noble Eightfold Path. The Four Noble Truths, therefore, have served Buddhists as an easy reminder of the heart of their religion's matter, although when one starts to investigate any one of the four one finds things considerably more complicated than they first appeared to be.

Hinayana: a somewhat pejorative term (meaning "the smaller vehicle") used by Mahayana Buddhists for the groups that opposed their liberalizing policies. "Theravada" (referring to the traditions of the elders) is the term these groups themselves prefer. The Mahayanists claimed to be providing a greater vehicle or raft, which would carry more living beings across the stream of samsaric existence to the far shore of nirvana. The Hinayanists objected to the liberties taken with the image of the Buddha, to the proliferation of sutras professing to be authoritative, to making laity more equal with monks, and to other such tendencies. They also resisted a certain supernaturalizing of Buddhist faith and practice, preferring a more sober, humanistic focus on Gautama's basic teachings about the need to root out desire and come to a clear understanding of reality.

Kuan-yin: the female form of the *bodhisattva* Avalokitesvara, who became the great savior figure in much of East Asia. Kuan-yin is the Chinese name, which in Japan became Kannon. In both countries an East Asian desire for a motherly divinity seems to have been responsible for the change of sex. Kuan-yin was the special refuge of women seeking children, a healthy birth, or help for family problems. She became a great favorite in East Asian art, often personifying the compassion and serenity of Buddhahood (enlightenment). Like the *Prajna-paramita,* the Wisdom-That-Had-Gone-Beyond, she softened the potential harshness of Buddhist discipline and probably linked up with the Daoist sense that the ultimate Way runs by a motherly love.

Lotus Sutra: a Mahayana scripture that pictures the Buddha Amitabha and the Western Paradise over which he presides. This sutra became one of the texts most influential in devotional Buddhism, especially that of Japan. Thus, the Jodo and Nichiren schools have made the Lotus Sutra central to their faith and practice, the latter chanting homage to the Lotus Sutra, which it has seen as an epitome of all Buddhist teaching. The Lotus Sutra is seen as a condescension to the moral weakness of modern times, when people can hardly be expected to accomplish more than to believe in the mercy of the Buddha and throw themselves upon it in faith. Thus reverence of the Lotus has gone hand in hand with a lay orientation and a stress on faith (a sort of Buddhist bhakti) rather than intellectual or meditational attainments.

Madhyamika: a moderate school of Mahayana Buddhist philosophy, founded by the famous dialectician Nagarjuna in the second century C.E.. The Madhyamika stressed the teachings of the *Prajna-paramita* sutras on emptiness, and through its dialectical analysis of the relations between nirvana and samsara justified a this-worldly focus. That in turn supported later Mahayana developments such as Zen, which assumed one could find nirvana in the midst of samsara and sought to give emptiness full impact in meditation, aesthetics, the martial arts, and other aspects of Japanese life. The Madhyamikas contrasted with the Yogacarins as moderate realists to idealists, because they did not subscribe to the Yogacara position that all reality is mind-only. Rather, they stressed that the ultimate is inexpressible, must be present to give any existent thing its existence, and appears differently depending upon whether one speaks of it as an enlightened person does or as one still immersed in samsara.

Mahayana: a branch of Buddhism that arose in controversies during the second century after the Buddha's death. Mahayana became opposed to Hinayana or Theravada, as the "great vehicle" to the "lesser vehicle." It paid more attention to the spiritual needs of the laity, broadened the saintly ideal from that of the individualistic *arhat* to that of the *bodhisattva* filled with great compassion for all enslaved creatures, and developed many metaphysical systems, some of which involved an extensive Buddhology that greatly advanced the simple appreciation of the man Gautama. Mahayana came to predominate in East Asia, whereas Theravada came to predominate in Sri Lanka, Burma, Thailand, and other countries between India and China.

nirvana: the Buddhist term for the goal of liberation or fulfillment. Nirvana has been likened to the state of the flame when the fire has gone out. In that figure, the implication is that nirvana is what one gets when desire has been fully extinguished. Other similes stress unconditionedness: what one gets when the various lets, hindrances, barriers, limitations that afflict everything of present experience have fallen away, when one has existence pure and simple, without qualifications or dependencies. Insofar as enlightenment opens the door to nirvana, and enlightenment is fully positive, one can think of nirvana as like the Hindu *moksha:* full of being, awareness, and bliss. The Buddha was leery of philosophizing about nirvana, thinking that talking about the ineffable soon was profitless and that it was more important to cure the disease than to speculate on the qualities of the postdisease state.

Pali canon: the collection of the scriptures (Tipitaka) judged authoritative by the Theravada Buddhists and written in Pali, one of the Prakrit languages associated with Sanskrit. The three baskets of the Pali canon contain discourses associated with the Buddha, as well as other early, foundational writings. Some of them were only recorded generations after their first utterance, having been preserved in the community's memory. The early Buddhist conciliar meetings that discussed right doctrine and monastic practice perhaps inevitably also discussed canonical texts and so were a stimulus toward making official collections.

Prajna-paramita: a group of Mahayana sutras concerned with the perfection of wisdom. Some of these sutras are very long, but others (such as the Diamond and the Heart) are able to put the perfection of wisdom quite concisely. Usually it boils down to grasping the emptiness of all dharmas. From the standpoint of enlightenment, nothing has an own-being. The *Prajna-paramita* has built on such staple Buddhist notions as that of the three marks (painful, fleeting, selfless) of all realities and Nagarjuna's dialectics of emptiness. One should remember that the point of this literature is not an academic analysis of ontology, much as ontology may be involved. It is, rather, to clarify the nature of reality and so develop the right thinking necessary for enlightenment.

Pure Land: the world of bliss (Sukhavati) pictured by the Lotus Sutra as the place in the West where Amitabha Buddha dwells and the devout will be reborn. The Pure Land became the focus of much East Asian devotional Buddhism, which frequently taught that the mercy of Amitabha was sufficient to bring his devotees thence with more regard to their faith than their merits. On the other hand, those Buddhists absorbed with karmic merit could think that they were building a dossier capable one day of winning them entrance to the Pure Land. The colorful descriptions of the Pure Land in the Lotus Sutra and other devotional texts greatly influenced popular Buddhist imagination, providing much of the sense of "heaven" that kept the common people hoping one day to enjoy a better world.

sangha: the Buddhist community. The term may refer to either the entire community or just the monastic part, in reflection of the paramount role monks played in the formation of the Buddha's community. Tradition records Gautama gathering disciples through his preaching and offering them spiritual direction. Laity were enrolled as supporters of the monastic ventures and from quite early times women were admitted into the monastic life. The *sangha* is placed alongside the Buddha and the dharma when the faithful enumerate the jewels of their faith. One formally becoming a Buddhist takes refuge in these three, which implies that the *sangha* will provide not just a haven from the samsaric world but also help with coming to know the Buddha and the dharma. As well, it should provide companionship along the Eightfold Path and instruction. The *sangha* has not been so unified or institutionalized as has the Christian church. Like the Jewish and Muslim communities, local variations have been tolerated, without giving up the sense that all the faithful are members of one overarching or organic community.

sila: a Buddhist term for morality—the ethical precepts incumbent on all members of the *sangha*. In briefest compass, these have been five: not to kill, not to lie, not to steal, not to behave unchastely, and not to take intoxicants. More broadly, *sila* has added further precepts proportioned to the lives of monks and nuns, to the lives of laity, and drawn from such key doctrines as *ahimsa*. Along with wisdom and meditation, Buddhist morality has been a basic component of the Middle Way, so *sila* has been as significant as meditation and philosophical study—perhaps more so in most lay lives. Characteristically, Buddhist ethics has focused much more on the individual's actions than on social questions, in part due to Buddhist convictions that the key to proper social behavior is enlightened individual consciousness.

skandhas: a Buddhist term for the "heaps" thought temporarily to comprise the human "person." The *skandhas* give the human being what integrity or identity it has as it passes through time. Traditionally they have been enumerated as five: form (or bodily shape), sensation (or feeling), perception, the aggregates of consciousness, and consciousness (or the faculty of consciousness). None of these should be pictured as static, independent, or substantial. Each is in flux and is empty. But Buddhist psychologists realized that if they wanted to analyze consciousness they had to make distinctions and namings such as these five, so the *skandhas* figure in most discussions of how to purify consciousness or gain a wise view of what happens in consciousness. Buddhists say the *skandhas* dissolve at death and are not carried over to the next existence; only karma links one life to another.

stupa: a mound of earth or stone that serves as a shrine to a Buddha or *bodhisattva* and so becomes a focus of Buddhist piety. The stupas, along with the devotional use of statues, flowers, incense, and other material objects, give Buddhism its sacramental side. They make it analogous to Islam, Catholic and Orthodox Christianity, and Hinduism in honoring saints and thinking the body, the material world, and the lives of fellow pilgrims all capable of being endowed with sacredness. Stupas become points of pilgrimage, giving Buddhists access to some of the religious effects pilgrimage regularly produces (entrance into a zone free of ordinary, profane, concerns, divisions, and sulliedness). Like the shrines that have developed in East Asian Buddhism, they provoke observers to consider the geography of Buddhist faith: where the faithful tend to find their convictions refreshed and revivified.

sunyata: a Buddhist term for emptiness. This term appears most significantly in the Mahayana *Prajnaparamita* literature and was developed by the philosopher Nagarjuna into a keystone of his understanding of both nirvana and samsara. To the traditional three marks—painful, selfless, fleeting—emptiness added a metaphysical conclusion: insubstantial. *Sunyata* has had the ethical and devotional implication that one should not cling to anything one experiences, because there is no-thing really there to justify one's grasping. It can be developed into a profound appreciation of the mysteriousness of existence: a Buddhist variation on the basic Western problem of the one and the many, or a Buddhist version of the Western question about why there is something rather than nothing.

sutra: a Buddhist text or discourse, especially one attributed to the (or a) Buddha himself. The sutras arose shortly after the death of Gautama, first in oral traditions, then in written texts. They appear to have been a blend of memories of what Gautama himself actually taught and what devoted disciples imagined Gautama might or would have taught on other given occasions. The Mahayana Buddhist movement spotlighted Buddhas other than Gautama and sparked the creation of sutras, such as the Lotus, that purported to be discourses from heavenly places such as the Western Paradise (Pure Land). The Buddhist canon (Tipitaka) collects a great number of sutras. The Mahayana sutras include discourses by famous *bodhisattvas* such as Avalokitesvara and may be quite metaphysical. Different Buddhist sects have favored different sutras, sometimes (as in the case of Nichiren Buddhism's absorption with the Lotus Sutra) relegating most others to irrelevance.

Tathagata: a title of the Buddha, usually taken to mean "One who has fully realized thusness or suchness," the state of ultimate, unconditioned perfection. The title suggests Buddhist realism: desire to be what one ultimately is, to see what ultimately is there just as an incontrovertible reality. Enlightenment, therefore, is just dispelling illusion, letting unfold what always was true or so, was always waiting to be allowed to show itself. The Tathagata is close to the *dharmakaya,* the body of the Buddha that makes reality be as it is, although probably the accent of the former is more on the subject Gautama whose enlightenment made him objective. In using the title as a term of praise, Buddhists in effect praise the wisdom of the Buddha, his utter realism, implying that association with him may make them similarly realistic.

Theravada: the older, conservative school of Buddhism that contrasts with the Mahayana schools. Theravada sometimes is described as the sole present survivor of the several Hinayana schools in existence at the time of the divergence of what became the Mahayana. It predominates in the Asian lands closest to India—Sri Lanka, Burma, Thailand—and has tended to be less metaphysical and lay-oriented than the Mahayana. The Buddhist scriptures of the Tipitaka have been the textual authority in Theravada, and such beloved texts as the *Dhammapada* express that school's ethical cast. Yet Theravada has also sponsored a full cultural development—art, political theory—as well as distinctive contributions to Buddhist views of meditation and the monastic life.

three jewels: the mainstays of Buddhist faith—the Buddha himself, the dharma, and the *sangha*. By "taking refuge" in Gautama, his teaching, and his community, Buddhists could save themselves from the pains of samsara. They could follow the path to liberation. As "jewels," these three foci of trust seemed to adorn or beautify the Buddhist way of life. They called to mind, and comprised, most of what was attractive. Gautama had been a model of wisdom and liberation, as well as its prime spokesman. His teaching was the font of everything good that his followers had experienced. And his community provided the context, tradition, and further modeling that a living religion required.

three marks: the Buddhist view that all of reality is painful, selfless, and fleeting. The three marks may be considered elaborations of the First Noble Truth, carried out under the influence of the Buddha's insight into how to solve the human problem. By elaborating why one should not desire ordinary existence—why one should flee a life that is intrinsically painful—the three marks gave Buddhist students intellectual ammunition, for themselves even more than others. No rational person would cling to something so illusory as an item of ordinary life. Developing Buddhist detachment therefore became an eminently sane thing to do.

Vajrayana: a development of Mahayana Buddhism that came to stress tantric methods and to predominate in Tibet. Known as the "thunderbolt" vehicle, Vajrayana

combined the scholastic interests of Indian Buddhism with the East Asian desire to vest authority in lineages of gurus. Its own special contribution was an interest in the psychology of enlightenment that led to experiments with psychosomatic influences and symbols that might engage the whole personality. The psychosomatic influences included social conditioning, through inculcation of accepted mores, and sexual desire. By challenging convention and rousing the libido contained in both of these psychic areas, Vajrayana often was able to work dramatic changes in the personality of the disciple striving for enlightenment. The mandalas, mantras, *chakras* (ritual circles within which the gods could be encountered or impersonated) furthered the Vajrayana experiments in enlightenment, while such texts as the *Tibetan Book of the Dead* expressed the Vajrayana sense that the end of a given existence was an especially propitious time for escaping from the wheel of karma.

Vinaya: the code of Buddhist monastic discipline. The Vinaya developed in the first centuries after the death of the Buddha, as monks and nuns tried to work out the discipline under which they would live. While there have been points of dispute and minor variations between Theravadin and Mahayanin monks, on the whole the Vinaya has been a force unifying Buddhism. In addition to obeying the basic precepts of *sila,* monks and nuns have been expected to obey the detailed rules regarding their clothing, admission into the order, housing accommodations, diet, and interactions with other monastics. They have been guided by the Buddha's Middle Way between austerity and laxity toward a sparse but healthy diet, have been expected to obey the directions of the abbot or head of the monastery, frequently have begged their food, have offered counsel and good example to laypeople, have kept the festivals traditional in their area, have participated in the special periods of increased meditation, and so forth, in all cases trying to eliminate desire and concentrate single-mindedly on following the Buddha's path.

Yogacara: a school of Mahayana Buddhist philosophy, founded by Asanga and Vasubandhu in the fourth century C.E., that taught that only consciousness is real. As the name suggests, Yogacara speculation had debts to the experience of yoga (meditation). In teaching that only consciousness was fully real, it amounted to being an idealism that doubted the reality of matter. The implications of Yogacara included the need to purify one's mind and the conviction that as one thought, so would one be or become. Yogacara speculation took up such topics as the functioning of consciousness and the debts of human consciousness to a matrix of cosmic consciousness. It influenced such practical schools as Zen and in general was a greater prop to meditation than to wisdom or morality, although it did not deprecate either.

Zen: the Japanese name for the school of Buddhism that has most stressed meditation. In China this school went by the name Chan and was attributed to Bodhidharma, a meditation-master come from India. Zen has considered meditation to epitomize the Enlightened One's teaching and methodology. Historically it had great influence in Japanese culture, shaping the ideals of the samurai and undergirding such practices as swordsmanship, floral arrangement, the tea ceremony, and gardening. Rinzai Zen has tended to seek sudden enlightenment, urging disciples to strive hard and keep up a firm discipline of work, silence, and obedience. Soto Zen has been more relaxed, thinking that enlightenment should come gradually, as the ripening of an overall maturation in Buddhist faith and practice. Soto has also lessened the distinction between meditation and the rest of life, thinking that as one's practice developed one would always be cultivating one's innate buddha-nature and helping it manifest itself.

CHAPTER 3

CHINESE RELIGION

Chinese character for Dao ("Way")

HISTORY

Preaxial Chinese Religion

The philosopher Karl Jaspers has spoken of an "axial period" of human civilization, during which the essential insights arose that spawned the great cultures.[1] In China the axial period was the sixth and fifth centuries B.C.E., and the two most important figures were Confucius and Laozi, whose Confucianism and Daoism, respectively, formed the basis for all subsequent Chinese culture. Before them, however, were centuries, perhaps even millennia, of nature- and ancestor-oriented responses to the sacred, when the prehistoric mind dominated the Chinese people. In China, for instance, divination mixed with the Confucian ethical code, so that the prime divinatory text, the *Yi Jing*, became one of the Confucian classics. As the popular Chinese folk novel *Monkey*[2] shows, other ancient attitudes were alive well into the sixteenth century C.E. So the preaxial worldview that we now sketch was a constant feature throughout Chinese religious history.

First, though, we must qualify the concept of Chinese religion. China, like most ancient cultures, did not develop religion as a separate realm of human

Chinese Religion: Twenty-five Key Dates	
ca. 3500 B.C.E.	Earliest Chinese City
ca. 1600	Shang Bronze Age Culture
551 – 479	Confucius
520	Traditional Date for Death of Laozi
403 – 221	Warring States Period
206	Han Dynasty Reunites China
ca. 200	Rise of Religious Daoism
ca. 112	Opening of "Silk Road" Links China with West
ca. 150 C.E.	Buddhism Known to Exist in China
304 – 589	Huns Fragment China
607	Beginning of Chinese Cultural Influence in Japan
658	Height of Chinese Power in Central Asia
700	Golden Age of Chinese Poetry
ca. 730	Invention of Printing in China
845	Great Persecution of Non-Chinese Religions
1000	Flourishing of Painting and Ceramics
1130 – 1200	Ju Xi, Leading Neo-Confucian Thinker
1234	Mongols Destroy Dynasty
1275	Marco Polo in China
1585	Matteo Ricci in China
1644	Manchu Dynasty; Confucian Orthodoxy
1850	Taiping Rebellion
1893 – 1977	Mao Zedong
1900	Boxer Uprising
1949	Communist Victory

concern. The rites, sacred mythology, ethics, and the like that bound the Chinese people were simply their culture. These cultural phenomena were not distinguished from the daily routine. So, what we underscore for our purposes is not necessarily what the Chinese underscored. Second, the Chinese attitude toward ultimate reality stressed nature—the physical world. Nature was the (sacred) essential context of human existence, and there was no clear Creator outside nature.

Of course, nature appeared to be both constant and changing. The cosmos was always there, but it had seasons and rhythms, as well as unexpected activities such as storms and earthquakes. To explain this tension between stability and change, the Chinese of the Han period (206 B.C.E.–220 C.E.) thought in terms of a union of complementary basic forces. **Yang** was the force of light, heat, and maleness. **Yin** was the balancing force of darkness, cold, and femaleness. The changes in the relations between yang and yin accounted for the seasons, the moon's phases, and the tides.

Another aspect of nature was the mixture or proportions of the five vital forces (water, fire, wood, metal, and earth) at any given time. They were the qualities that activated nature—that gave particular things and events their character. Together, the yin-

	CONFUCIANISM	DAOISM
Key Figures	Confucius (Kongzi) Mencius (Mengzi)	Laozi Zhuangzi
Key Texts	*Analects*	*Dao De Jing*
Key Ideas	1. Humaneness 2. Ritual 3. Subordination of younger to elder and women to men 4. Good ethical example the key to political prosperity	1. Active not-doing (*wu-wei*) 2. The Uncarved Block (presocialized human nature) 3. Following the way of nature (*Dao*) 4. Resisting convention and routine
Key Influences	Government, family life	Private life, arts, philosophy, meditation

yang theory and the theory of the five vital forces formed the first Chinese explanation of nature.[3]

Above the system, not as its Creator from nothingness but as its semipersonal overlord, was the heavenly ruler. His domain was human and natural behavior. The heavenly ruler probably was the first ancestor of the ruling dynasty. That is, the Chinese first conceived of him as the clan head of the ancient ruling house of Shang.[4] Later they modified this anthropomorphic conception to heaven, a largely impersonal force. Then the emperor became the "Son of Heaven," not in the sense that he was the descendant of the first ancestral leader of the ruling clan but in the sense that he represented the force that governed the world.[5]

Another name for the director of the natural system was *Dao*. Essentially, *Dao* means "way" or "path." The Confucians spoke of the *Dao* of the ancients—the customs or ethos that prevailed in the golden beginning times. Similarly, the Chinese Buddhists described their tradition as the "Way of the Buddha." However, the Daoists most directly appropriated the naturalistic overtones of *Dao* and focused on nature's

directing path. For them, the *Dao* was an ultimate reality, both within the system and beyond it.

We shall see how the *Dao* was characteristic of the different Chinese religious traditions. The point here is that they all assumed the ancient view that nature is sufficiently orderly to suggest an overseer and a path. Within the natural system, however, the prehistoric Chinese stressed harmony. That is, they tended to think that trees, rivers, clouds, animals, and humans compose something whole. As a result, natural phenomena could be portents, while human actions, whether good or evil, influenced both heaven and earth. As the Native Americans identified closely with their forests, so the oldest Chinese were citizens of nature, not a species standing outside and apart from it. Consequently, they did not consider human beings apart from the other creatures of the cosmos.

When the Daoist philosopher Zhuangzi spoke of reentering the Great Clod,[6] he spoke from this ancient conviction. To die and return to the material world, perhaps to be a tree or a fish in the next round, was natural and right. With some qualifications that we shall mention, the Chinese have favored long life

Figure 10 *Animal spiral, western Zhou dynasty, early ninth century* B.C.E. *Bronze; 13½ in. high. This spiral was made to be fitted to a pole, perhaps for protection or use in shamanistic rituals. The Nelson–Atkins Museum of Art, Kansas City, Missouri (Nelson Fund).*

ers developed prescriptions for both social and individual life. In that way, ancient reflection helped form the rational framework of classical Chinese culture. More influential, though, was the nonrational heritage of the preaxial days. The vast majority of China's billions have been peasants, who, with relatively few changes, continued to stress animistic forces, amulets, and divination rites up to the beginning of the twentieth century (if not right up to the present).

Folk religion is always an effort to explain nature, but it employs a logic that is more symbolic than that of yin-yang, the five dynamic qualities, or *Dao*. Rather, it emphasizes similarities and differences, whether in shapes, sizes, or names. As close to dreaming as to science, folk religion easily allows the subconscious great influence. So, for instance, diviners thought they had a key to nature in the cracks of a baked tortoise shell, or the flight patterns of birds, or the broken and unbroken lines that the ancient text called the *Yi Jing* interpreted as ratios of yin and yang. It was but a small step to use these interpretational techniques to control nature—to use them as magic.

One functionary who has specialized in this symbolic magic is the practitioner of *feng-shui*.[7] *Feng-shui* is the study of winds and water, or geomancy. Essentially, it involves how to position a building most auspiciously. In a convoluted symbolism employing dragons and tigers, it has tried to make the living forces of nature yield good fortune by figuring out the spiritual lay of the land. What nature disposed, according to *feng-shui*, architecture could oppose or exploit. For instance, straight lines were believed to be evil influences, but trees or a fresh pond could ward them off. Consequently, the basic design of Chinese villages has included trees and ponds for protection. Similarly, a winding approach to a house has diverted evil forces. The *feng-shui* diviner would plot all the forces, good and evil, with a sort of compass that marked the different circles of power of these forces. *Feng-shui* has prevailed well into modern times, a fact attesting to its perceived importance.

Other important ancient functionaries were the mediums and the shamans. As Waley's translations suggest,[8] the shaman's song frequently called on a personal spirit to come down and enlighten him. Perhaps, then, the Chinese shaman (or shamaness) was more a subject of possession or a medium than a traveler to the gods.[9] More importantly, the existence of the shaman shows that ancient China believed in a realm of personified spirits.[10] These spirits could come

rather than immortality, enlightenment that polishes worldly vision rather than enlightenment that draws one out of the world. Chan Buddhism's transformation of the Mahayana philosophy of nirvana owed much to Daoist philosophy and this ancient worldliness.

The Peasant Heritage. The preaxial views of nature, therefore, provided the axial thinkers with basic beliefs about nature's patterns, elements, and the consubstantiality (substantial sameness) of humans with other forms of life. From these beliefs, the axial think-to susceptible individuals with lights and messages or be the spirits of departed ancestors speaking through a medium who was in trance. If one did not revere them, speak well of them, and give them gifts of food, the ancestor spirits could turn nasty.

In later times, ordinary people thought that the ancestor spirits lived in a spiritual equivalent of the human world, where they needed such things as food, clothing, and money. Thus, pious children would burn paper money to send assistance to their departed parents.[11] In fact, one's primary obligation of a religious sort was just such acts of commemoration, reverence, and help. This reverence for ancestors so impressed Western missionaries that they fought bitterly among themselves about its meaning. Some missionaries found ancestor rites idolatrous, while others found them praiseworthy expressions of familial love.[12]

Exorcism. Another feature of ancient Chinese religion was the personification and exorcism of evil. In historical times, the Daoist priesthood dominated exorcism, but the roots of exorcism go further back. Peter Goullart has given an eyewitness account of a modern Daoist exorcism,[13] complete with descriptions of weird phenomena like those enacted in the American film *The Exorcist*. The assumption behind exorcism, of course, is that evil forces invade and possess a person. In part, this assumption is just the logical conclusion of a thought-world in which shamanism is possible. If the Chinese shaman could be invaded by his helping spirits, and if evil spirits existed, then other people could be invaded by evil spirits. Along another line of interpretation, demon possession is just the development of ancient fears of evil, while exorcism is just the development of ancient ways of combating such fear.

Goullart's description of the "energumen" (demoniac), however, renders the evil most concrete. The possessing power curses, threatens, and pours out hate (in a terrifying distortion of the demoniac's own voice). It bloats the demoniac's body, pushing the bedspring on which he rests down to the floor. The demoniac howls like an animal, gives off horrid smells, and empties his bladder and bowels repeatedly. Onlookers are terrified, and the Daoist priest strains to the utmost in his spiritual struggles with the evil one. The reader senses something absolutely primitive: human shock before the possibility of naked evil. Exorcisms were not daily occurrences, but they open a window onto the recesses of the Chinese psyche.

In his summary of the religious beliefs of the Chinese Neolithic age,[14] Mircea Eliade sketches the general context for such shock, as well as for shamanism, divination, and other ancient features that we have discussed. There was from earliest times a connection between life, fertility, death, and afterlife that took the form of a regular cosmic cycle and gave rise to annual religious rites. Furthermore, the ancestors were a source of magical and religious power, and all natural forces had an aura of mystery—the mystery of the conjunction of opposites: of life and death, good and evil, rational and irrational. Possession and exorcism, then, are but vivid instances of a generally volatile mix. The ancient Chinese world was thoroughly alive, and one never knew precisely where its power would go.

Confucianism

Inasmuch as it furnished many Chinese with the ideas about order and ultimate reality that directed their lives, Confucianism fulfilled many of the functions of a religious tradition.

Confucius (551–479 B.C.E.) became the father of Chinese culture by transforming the ancient traditions into at least the beginnings of a code for directing social life. More than two centuries passed before his doctrine became the state orthodoxy (during the Han dynasty, 206 B.C.E.–220 C.E.), but from the outset it had a healing effect on Chinese society. Confucius lived during a warring period of Chinese history, an epoch of nearly constant social disorder. For Master Kong (the Chinese name of Confucius), the way from such disorder toward peace could be obtained from the ancients—the venerable ancestors who were closer to the beginning and wiser than the people of the present age. What the ancestors knew, what made them wise, were the decrees of heaven. As we have seen, heaven meant nature's overlord. Thus, Confucius accepted the ancient, preaxial notion that nature has some order. In his view, the way to a peaceful and prosperous society was to adapt to that order. People could adapt externally through sacrificial rites and hierarchical social relationships. Internally, one had to know the human mind, and the human mind had to be set in *ren* (fellow-feeling or love).[15]

For external order, the emperor was paramount. As the Son of Heaven, he conveyed heaven's will to earth. In other words, the China of Confucius' time held to the cosmological myth. With many other ancient societies, it shared the notion that the king was the sacred intermediary between the realm of heaven and the realm of earth modeled upon it. What the king did for human society, then, was both priestly and exemplary. By officiating at the most important rites, through which his people tried to achieve harmony with heaven, the king represented society before the ultimate judge of society's fate. By the example that he set at court and by the way that he directed imperial policy, the king not only served as a good or bad model for his followers, he also led the state in following or defying heaven's intent. The king achieved his power simply through his close connection to heaven.[16]

Confucius approved of the model leadership of the legendary kings, and he also approved of the notion that ritual makes what we might call a sacrament of the vital flow between heaven and earth. One focus of his teaching, then, was historical: He concentrated on how the ancients reportedly acted. Another focus was liturgical. He was himself a master of court ritual, and he thought that proper sacrifice and etiquette were very important. Probably Confucius' most profound impact on Chinese culture, though, was his clarification of human virtues, or spiritual qualities.

Having had little success in public affairs (he never obtained high office or found a ruler willing to hire his counsel), he turned to teaching young men about politics and the way to private virtue. In other words, he became the center of an academic circle, like that of Plato, which had ongoing dialogues about the good life, political science, private and public morality, and so on. Confucius consistently stressed practicality in his tutoring. The wisdom that he loved built up the good society, the commonweal. It was not a yogic or shamanic regime dedicated to a single individual's spiritual development.

The *Analects* are a collection of fragments from the Master. In them we can see why Confucius impressed his followers, who finally made him the model wise man. (After his death, Confucius gained semidivine status and became the center of a religious cult.)[17] Especially in the third through ninth books, the Confucians preserved sayings that seem to be original, although Confucius himself claimed no originality. In fact, he did not even claim divine inspiration. His Way was nothing novel; he only studied the past and then transmitted the ancients' customs.

"The Master said, At fifteen I set my heart upon learning. At thirty, I had planted my feet firm upon the ground. At forty, I no longer suffered from perplex-ities. At fifty, I knew what were the biddings of Heaven. At sixty, I could hear them with docile ear. At seventy, I could follow the dictates of my own heart, for what I desired no longer overstepped the boundaries of right" (*Analects,* 2:4).

It is clear, then, that the mystical union with the Way that consummated the Master's life was the fruit of many years' labor. This example reminds us that wise or holy people tend to become identified with the models, texts, or rituals that they use to interpret ultimate reality. We become what we study, meditate upon, and establish as the treasures on which our hearts are set. Perhaps that is why Confucius was so insistent on hard study—constant effort during one's youth and maturity to master the wisdom of the past.

For Confucius, the Way manifests itself as a golden mean. It opens a path between punctiliousness and irregularity, between submissiveness and independence. Most situations are governed by a protocol that will produce graceful interactions if it is followed wholeheartedly. The task of the *junzi* (true gentleman or superior person) is to know that protocol, intuit how it applies in particular cases, and have the discipline to carry it out. The death of a parent, for instance, is a prime occasion for a *junzi* to express his love and respect for his parent. According to the rites of mourning, he should retire from public affairs, simplify his living arrangements, and devote himself to grieving (for as long as three years).

As that example suggests, filial piety was a cornerstone of Confucianism. If the relations at home were correct, other social relationships would likely fall into line. The **Confucian classic** *The Great Learning*[18] spells out this theory, linking the individual in the family to the order of both the state and the cosmos. Moreover, the family circle was the training ground for a *junzi*'s lifelong dedication to humanity (*ren*) and ritual propriety (*li*). When a man developed a sincere love for his parents and carried out his filial duties, he rooted himself firmly in both *ren* and *li*. (We consider the place of women below.) Confucius' own teaching, therefore, called for a balance between interior goodness and exterior grace. He thought that if people knew their inner minds (grasped at "inwit," in Ezra Pound's translation)[19] and manifested their knowledge through social decorum, society would have both the substance and the appearance of humanity.

Different followers developed different aspects of Confucius' teaching. Mencius, for instance, softened the Master's view of *ren,* drawing it down from the lofty status accorded it by Confucius and making it a possibility for everyman.[20] For Mencius, human nature was innately good. We are evil or disordered only because we forget our original nature. Like the deforested local hill (Mencius 6.A.8), the typical human mind is so despoiled by abuse that we cannot see its spontaneous tendency toward altruism and justice. If we would stop deforesting it with vice, we would realize that virtue is instinctive. Just as anyone who sees a child at the edge of a well rushes to save the child (Mencius 2.A.6), so anyone educated in gentlemanliness will rush to solve civic problems.

Thus, Mencius centered Confucius' teaching on the goodness of human nature. Living two centuries after the Master, Mencius tried to repeat Confucius' way of life. He searched for an ideal king who would take his counsel, but he had to be satisfied with having a circle of young students. Mencius, though, somewhat lacked Confucius' restraint in discussing heavenly things (Confucius considered the human realm more than enough to master). According to Lee Yearley,[21] Mencius practiced a disciplined religion to increase physical vigor by acting with purity of heart, and he was willing to die for certain things such as justice and goodness. So, just as one can consider some of Confucius' sayings quite religious (for example, "It is not better to pay court to the stove than to heaven"), one can view Mencius as having transcendent beliefs. Both Confucian thinkers, we believe, appealed to more than human prudence.

Mencius also proposed an ultimately religious theory that history moves in cycles, depending on how a given ruling family handles the *de* (the power to govern well) that heaven dispenses.[22] The sharpest implication of this theory (which clarified some traditional notions) was that an unjust ruler might lose the mandate of heaven—that a revolutionary might be justified in establishing a new regime. Furthermore, Mencius advanced the view that the king brought prosperity only when he convinced the people that the things of the state were their own. This view was in part shrewd psychology: A people who have access to the royal park will think it small even if it is 100 miles square; a people denied access to a royal park one mile square will complain that it is far too vast. As well, however, this view brought Confucius' stress on leadership by example and virtue up to date: Only if the king demonstrated virtue could he expect the people to be virtuous.

A legalistic wing among Confucius' later followers, led by Xunzi, opposed both Mencius' teaching that human nature is essentially good and the non-Confucian Mozi's doctrine of universal love.[23] Xunzi taught that only strong law can confine human nature to right action; for lack of strong law, a great many states flounder. Furthermore, Xunzi connected this belief with Confucius' own stress on ritual, arguing that law and etiquette have the pedagogical function of showing the inner spirit what goodness and justice really mean. Unfortunately, later apologists for the state took some of Xunzi's ideas as a warrant for government by compulsion. In themselves, however, his ideas perhaps complemented Mencius' program as much as they opposed it, since they clarified the place for external codes. Arthur Waley, at least, has tried to show that Xunzi mainly reacted against possible abuses of Mencius' views on human nature.[24]

In summary, then, the hallmarks of the original Confucians were a reliance on ancient models, a concern for the golden mean between externalism and internalism, a stress on filial piety, and a deep respect for the ruler's connection with heaven. These socially oriented thinkers emphasized breeding, grace, and public service. Their goal was harmony and balance through a hierarchical social order.[25] They gave little attention to the rights of peasants or women, but they did prize ethical integrity, compassion, and learning. Against the blood and violence of their times, they called for a rule through moral force. This was their permanent legacy: Humanity is fidelity to virtue.

Neo-Confucianism

During the Song dynasty (960–1279 C.E.), the seminal Confucian thought that lay in the teachings of Confucius, Mencius, and Xunzi grew into a full-fledged philosophy that included metaphysical interpretations of nature and humanity. That was largely in response to the impressive systems that Buddhism, with its Mahayana doctrines of emptiness and the Buddha's cosmic body *(dharmakaya),* and to a lesser extent Daoism, had developed, and it produced a new synthesis known to scholars as neo-Confucianism. To Confucius' ethics the neo-Confucians added an explanation of all reality. They accepted the ancient worldview, granting an important place to sacrifices for the state and the family. As well, they accepted the moral supremacy of the sage, whose virtuous power might move society or even nature. But they went on and reasoned about the sort of reality that nature must be if the sacrifices or the sages were to be efficacious. This neo-Confucian development gave the Song rulers and their successors a doctrine that buttressed their practical preference for Confucian ethics.

The neo-Confucian philosophy of nature that gained the most adherents involved the interaction of two elements, principle and ether. Ether, or breath, was the basis of the material universe. All solid things condensed out of ether and eventually dissolved back into it.[26] In the dynamic phases of this cycle, ether was an ultimate form of yang. In the still phases, it was the ultimate form of yin. The neo-Confucian view of material nature therefore preserved the tension of bipolarities—of, for example, hot and cold, male and female, light and dark—that had always fascinated the Chinese. One reason for the acceptance of neo-Confucianism, in fact, was that it appeared to be just an updated version of the ancient patrimony. The second element in nature's dualism, principle, etymologically related to the veins in jade or the grain in wood. It was the *pattern* running through all material things, their direction and purpose. If you opposed principle (went against the grain), all things became difficult. In terms of cognitional theory, the neo-Confucians invoked principle to explain the mind's ability to move from the known to the unknown. They also used it to ground the mind's appreciation of the connectedness of things. Principle was considered to be innate in human beings—it was nature's inborn guidance. The main task of human maturation and education was to remove the impediments that kept people from perceiving their principle. This task implied a sort of asceticism or moral diligence, sometimes involving meditation and self-denial.

Finally, the neo-Confucians tried to assimilate the folk aspect of Confucianism by finding a place for the spirits. They preferred not to venerate the ancestors' ghosts, but they allowed that *shen* and *kuei* (the two traditional kinds of spirits) could be the stretching and contracting of ether. In that way, they could agree that the "spirits" worked the planets, the stars, the mountains, the rivers, and so on. Once again, neo-Confucianism was less personal than the earlier traditions, but its new, rather rationalistic system stayed in touch with the old roots.

Ju Xi (1130–1200 C.E.) was the master thinker who systematized these neo-Confucian ideas.[27] His predilection was sober analysis, a sort of scientific philosophy, and he concentrated on physical nature. Another more idealistic wing of the neo-Confucians took to the Chan Buddhist stress on mind and tended to place principle in the context of a meditative, as well as an analytic, cultivation of reason. Because Ju Xi's ideas became authoritative in such government-controlled areas as the civil service examinations, neo-Confucianism inculcated in the educated classes a realistic, affirmative view of material nature. As well, it accepted meditation enough to stay competitive with Buddhism,[28] and it tried to stay open to such artistic movements as the magnificent Song dynasty landscape painting.

Despite these metaphysical developments, neo-Confucianism retained a commitment to the traditional Confucian virtues associated with character building. The paramount virtue continued to be *ren*. The ideogram for *ren* represented a human being in relationship: *ren* is humaneness—what makes us human. We are not fully human simply by receiving life in a human form. Rather, our humanity depends upon community, human reciprocity.[29] *Ren* pointed in that direction. It connected with the Confucian golden rule of not doing to others what you would not want them to do to you. Against individualism, it implied that people have to live together helpfully, even lovingly. People have to cultivate their instinctive benevolence, their instinctive ability to put themselves in another's shoes. That cultivation was the primary education task set by Confucius and Mencius.

The neo-Confucians also kept the four other traditional virtues: *yi, li, zhi,* and *xin. Yi* meant duty or justice, and it signified what is right, what law and custom prescribe. Its context, therefore, was the Chinese culture's detailed specification of rights and obligations. Where *ren* undercut such formalities, giving justice its heart, *yi* took care of contractual exactitudes.

Li, which meant manners or propriety, was less exact than *yi.* To some extent it depended on learning, so Confucius tried to teach by word and example what a gentleman would do in various circumstances, but it also required instinct, breeding, or intuition. Handling authority over household servants, men in the fields, or subordinates in the civil service involved *li.* So, too, did deference to superiors, avoidance of ostentation, and a generally graceful style. *Li* therefore was the unguent that soothed all social friction. In a society that prohibited the display of hostile emotion, that insisted on a good "face," *li* was very important.

Zhi (wisdom) was not a deep penetration of ultimate reality like the Buddhist *Prajna-paramita;* it depended on neither enlightenment nor mystical union with *Dao.* Rather, it was the prudent sense of right and wrong, decent and indecent, profitable and unprofitable that one could hope to gain by revering the ancients and living attentively. *Xin* meant trustworthiness or good faith. It was related to *ren* insofar as what one trusts in another is his or her decency or humanity, but it pertained more to a person's reliability or dependability. A person of *xin* was not flighty or capricious.

Case Study: The Cult of Confucius. Although the intelligentsia resisted efforts to deify Confucius, the Chinese people at large long reverenced the Master with rituals and cult. To communicate the flavor of this cult, let us briefly describe some of the ceremonies that regularly took place at Confucius' shrines in the southwestern part of Shandong Province. Before the Communist revolution, such ceremonies were an important part of the Chinese ritual year.

A Western visitor who witnessed the rites at Confucius' ancestral temple in Chufu in 1903 was first received by the Yeng-sheng Kung ("the Duke who propagates"), as the head of Confucius' clan officially was known. The duke took the visitor around the temple grounds, which covered about 35 acres well-wooded with old cypress, yew, and fir trees. Tradition said that one of the trees was planted by Confucius himself and that two others were planted during the Tang and Song dynasties. The temple proper was divided into six courts, the innermost of which was venerated as the area where Confucius had lived. In front of this innermost precinct were various tablets with inscriptions of praise by various Chinese emperors.

Inside the central area stood an altar, commemorating the spot where Confucius had received people who came for his instruction. Behind this altar lay a great hall containing a statue of the Master. The statue was 16 feet high and portrayed the Master seated on a throne. Near it were screens, embroidered with dragons, that could be arranged as a shield. Magnificent pillars of white and black marble supported the great hall, its floor was lined with black marble, its roof was covered with yellow tiles, and its ceiling consisted of 486 square panels gilded at the edges and ornamented with dragons.

Two of the principal festival days for worshiping at the Confucian temple were the Ting days of spring and autumn, when the stems and branches of the foliage were supposed to be flourishing. The minister of music would open the ceremonies, which featured music used in Confucius' own day (but composed even earlier, supposedly about 2000 B.C.E.). The entire ritual employed symbols and artifacts considered to come from the ancient days, when the model heroes whom Confucius had revered had led Chinese society wisely by faithfully following the dictates of heaven. The dominant cloth, for instance, was a pure white silk, which ancient chiefs used to give people they wished to take into their employ. Other symbols of the Ting ceremony included the head of an ox (chief of the domestic animals, who leaves broad, permanent footprints); a pig (an animal with a will of its own, as its bristles suggest); and a sheep (plump for food and useful for wool). The incense used suggested the fragrance of virtue, while the wine and food typified the abundance of a virtuous kingdom. The boys performing the ceremonial dance dressed in ancient costumes, bearing in one hand a flute and in the other a pheasant feather. The flute represented the refinement music produces, while the feather stood for the adornment of learning.

Obviously, this ceremony, like most of the others that took place in Confucius' temple throughout the year, was meant to convey elegantly the benefits of virtue and breeding. In tune with the cosmic rhythms, the dancers suggested how any diligent student of virtue might hope one day to live, how any well-ordered state might hope to flourish.

Some of the hymns sung during the sacrifices to Confucius suggest the respect, veneration, and religious need his cult expressed. In one hymn, the choir begins, "Great is Confucius!" Why is Confucius great? Because he perceives all things accurately, knowing them before they even arise. Because he stands in the realm of heaven and earth, the primal realities, and so can teach the ten thousand ages. Because his power brought lucky portents: The unicorn's horn gained a tuft of silk. Because he unveiled the sun and the moon, making heaven and earth fresh and joyful.

During the offering of the gifts to Confucius the choir members would sing: "I think of thy bright virtue." Never had there been a human being equal to the Master. His teaching was in all respects complete. The vessels people offer today are filled as vessels have been filled through thousands of years. From time immemorial, the Ting days have been sweet with the smell of sacrifice, adorned with clear wine.

Later in the ceremony, the choir referred to the traditional sounds of the drum and the bell. Echoing as the celebrant offered the ritual wine, the drum and bell expressed the reverence and harmony at the heart of the ceremony. The rites proceeded, the music cleansed the participants' hearts, and the liturgy reached a point of perfection—let all rejoice!

Then the choir would remember how people had performed these holy rites since antiquity. Even primitive people performed them, wearing rough skin hats. Though these ancient ancestors had only the fruit of the ground to offer, their music was orderly. Only heaven has ever guided any people well, and only a sage of Confucius' stature could have suited his instructions to the needs of any given hour. Following him, present-day people could carry out their moral duties properly, reverencing the emperor and their elders. Confucius taught his followers the link between sacrifice and happiness. Who would dare not be reverent in his hall? In their joy, all who prosper remember him as the source of their culture. Like the mountains of Fu and Yi, the rivers of Zhu and Si, Confucius' beautiful acts have spread his influence high above and all around. The sacrifice reminds all of his great virtue. He renovates thousands of the people. He fosters their schools and instruction halls.[30]

As elements of the cult to Confucius suggest, Confucianism built on Chinese customs that had long antedated the Master. Indeed, sacrifices such as the one we have described can be traced as far back as the Shang dynasty, which is the limit of current archeological research. Insofar as most emperors gravitated toward Confucianism rather than Buddhism or Daoism, because Confucianism offered social thought more likely to produce docile subjects, they found it useful to involve themselves in the Confucian sacrifices. Thus the emperor himself would officiate at the major ceremonies, as clan heads had since earliest times, while Confucian bureaucrats would officiate at lesser ceremonies in the capital and at state occasions in the provinces. This meant that there was no special caste of Confucian priests. In Confucianism, state official and religious priest merged, becoming but two faces of one public functionary.

Characteristically, the Confucian public functionary opposed innovation, both in the cult and at the government bureau. The party line was that the Confucian literati merely handed on the wisdom and customs of the venerable ancestors, as Confucius had definitively interpreted them. Thus Confucius was in effect the patron saint of the literati. As other clans had their divine protectors, so the literati had Confucius. The difference was that the literati headed the corps of civil servants. Their "clan" staffed the government offices, transmitted the imperial will. As teacher, cult figure, and model, Confucius gave civil servants the sanction of tradition and sober wisdom. Through him came the *Dao* of the ancestors, the basis of good order in his or any time.

By the seventeenth century C.E., the diverse elements of the Confucian tradition had been merged into a rather unwieldy official cult. According to an official list of those to whom imperial worship was due in the seventeenth century, there were three classes of worthies. First came the Empress Earth, the imperial ancestors, and the guardian spirits of the land and the harvest. Second came the sun, the moon, the emperors of the preceding dynasties, the patrons of agriculture and sericulture (raising silkworms), the spirits of the earth, the planet Jupiter, whose revolution around the sun regulated the Chinese calendar, and Confucius. (In 1907 Confucius was moved up to the first class.) Third came the patron saints of medicine, war, and literature, the North Star, the god of Beijing, the god of fire, the dragons of several pools in Beijing, the god of artillery, the god of the soil, the patron saint of the mechanical arts, the god of the furnace, the god of the granary, the gods of the doors, and many official patriots.

This list illustrates the amalgamating tendency of the Confucian tradition. On the list's map of reality are the imprints of ancestor veneration, veneration of the deities of the earth, veneration of the patron gods or saints of particular clans, and veneration of Confucius, the mortal whose interpretation of the past was most congenial to the crown. Some of the deities in this list are very ancient, going back to the Shang and Zhou dynasties, at the very beginnings of Chinese history.

During the Qing dynasty (1644–1911), the government instructed its officials in the particulars of worshiping the cult figures of the several ranks. The official was to bathe, fast, prostrate himself, and offer prayers. He was to make thanksgiving offerings of incense, lighted candles, gems, fruits, cooked foods, salted vegetables, wine, and other gifts. For special occasions sacrifices of whole oxen, sheep, pigs, deer, or other game were appropriate, as was a burnt sacrifice of a whole bullock. Music and dancing were to accompany these sacrifices. If the sacrifice was to a deity of the first rank, the official had to "fast" for three days before it. For sacrifices to deities of the second rank, two fast days sufficed. Fasting meant refraining from flesh, strong-smelling vegetables (such as leeks and onions), and wine.

Moreover, officials were to see to it that during important ceremonial seasons there were no criminal proceedings, no parties, no visits to the sick, and no mourning of the dead. They were especially to forbid entering the chamber of a dead woman, sacrificing to spirits, and sweeping a tomb. The government commissioned inspectors to check on the officials delegated responsibility for the Confucian cult, to make sure that they followed these prescriptions scrupulously. Behind this concern that the officiants be properly prepared lay the Confucian conviction that a province follow the moral character of its officials. If the officials were scrupulous in performing the rites, the people would be orderly. As Confucius was reputed to have said (*Analects,* 2:3): People led by laws and restrained by punishments will avoid laws and punishments without qualm. People led by moral example and restrained by social ritual will develop a sense of shame and become good.[31]

Daoism

The classical, axial-period Daoists responded to the troubled warring period quite differently from the Confucians. They agreed that the times were disordered and that the way to set them straight was by means of the ancients' *Dao.* But the great Daoist thinkers, such as Zhuangzi and Laozi, were more imaginative and mystical than the Confucians. In their broad speculation, they probed not only the natural functions of the Way and the interior exercises that could align one with it but also the revolt against conventional values that union with *Dao* seemed to imply. Of the two great Daoists, Zhuangzi is the more poetic and paradoxical. His stories stress the personal effects of living with *Dao.* Laozi's orientation is more political. For him, *Dao* gives a model for civil rule, lessons in what succeeds and what brings grief. Insofar as Zhuangzi is more theoretical and less concerned with political applications, he enjoys a certain logical

priority over Laozi.[32] Thus, even though he probably came after Laozi historically, we treat him first.

Zhuangzi. What impressed Zhuangzi most was the influence of one's viewpoint. The common person, for example, can make little of the ancients' communion with nature, their unconcern for human opinion, and freedom. Such things are like the great bird flying off where the sparrow has never been. Yet if one advances in the "fasting of the spirit" that the ancients practiced, their behavior starts to make sense. Apparently such "fasting of the spirit" was a meditative regime in which one laid aside distractions and let simple, deep powers of spiritual consciousness issue forth.

Zhuangzi pictured those powers rather dramatically: They can send the sage flying on the clouds or riding on the winds, for they free the soul so that it can be directed by *Dao* itself. *Dao* is the wind blowing on the ten thousand things, the music of the spheres. With little regard for petty humankind, it works nature's rhythms. The way to peace, spiritual ecstasy, and long life is to join nature's rhythms. But by joining nature's rhythms, one abandons social conventions. *Dao* throws off our human judgments of good and bad, right and wrong. Thus, the true Daoist becomes eccentric with respect to the rest of society, for he (or she, though women seldom predominated in Chinese society) prefers obscure peace to troubled power, leisurely contemplation to hectic productivity.

In rather technical terms, Zhuangzi attacked those who thought they could tie language directly to thought and so clarify all discourse. If *Dao* touches language and thought, he showed, they become highly symbolic. Moreover, Zhuangzi made his attack on conventional values and language into simple good sense. It is the worthless, cast-off, unpopular trees and people that survive. Those who would be prominent, who would shine in public, often end up without a limb (as punishment for crime or disfavor). When he was asked to join the government, Zhuangzi said he would rather drag his tail in the mud like a turtle. When his wife died, he sang and drummed instead of mourning. She was just following *Dao,* just taking another turn in the process by which matter keeps changing. Puncturing cant, deflating pomposity, excoriating our tendency to trade interior freedom for exterior position, Zhuangzi ridiculed the sober Confucians. They, like other prosaic realists, seemed too dull to be borne— too dull for a life of spiritual adventure, for a *Dao* as magnificent as the heavens and as close as the dung.

Laozi. Thomas Merton has published a delightful interpretation of Zhuangzi that relates him to the contemplative spirit of Western poets and monks.[33] No one has done quite the same thing for Laozi or the *Dao De Jing,* perhaps because Laozi's style is more impersonal. The *Dao De Jing (The Way and The Power),*[34] like the *Zhuangzi* (the book left by Zhuangzi and his school), is of undetermined origin. Indeed, its author's very existence is less certain than that of Confucius. But the book itself has become a world classic, in good measure because of its mystic depth (and vagueness). In it a very original mind meditates on *Dao*'s paradoxical qualities, gleaning lessons about human society. Interpreters vary in the weight they give to the mystical aspects of the *Dao De Jing,*[35] but in any interpretation it is clear Laozi thought that *Dao* held the secret to good life.

Consequently, a major concern of the *Dao De Jing* is to elucidate just how nature does operate and how society should imitate it. The text's basic conclusion, presented in a series of striking images, is that *Dao* moves nature through *wu-wei* (active not-doing). Three of the principal images are the valley, the female, and the uncarved block. Together, they indicate *Dao*'s distance from most human expectations. The valley symbolizes *Dao*'s inclination toward the lowly, the underlying, rather than the prominent or impressive. Laozi's female is a lesson in the power of passivity, of yielding and adaptability. She influences not by assault but by indirection, by nuance and suggestion. The uncarved block is human nature before society limits it. These images all show *wu-wei.*

Wu-wei is also shown in the power of the infant, whose helplessness can dominate an entire family. It is in the power of water, which patiently wears away rock. Wryly Laozi reminds us of the obvious: A valley resists storms better than a mountain, a female tends to outlive a male, an infant is freer than a king, and a house is valuable for the space inside it, not the furniture or the wall hangings. Such lessons underscore a reality that common sense tends to ignore because common sense tends to notice only what is prominent. In contrast, *Dao* moves nature by a subtle, elastic power. Were rulers to imitate *Dao,* moving others by *wu-wei* rather than *ba* (violent force), society might prosper.

Wu-wei, it follows, tries to short-circuit the law of the human jungle, the round after round of tit for tat.[36] But to gain *wu-wei,* human nature must become like an uncarved block, which is perhaps the most important of Laozi's symbols. (Holmes Welch, who argues that we can read the *Dao De Jing* on several levels, makes the uncarved block its key.[37]) It symbolizes the priority of natural simplicity over social adornment. A block of wood or jade, before it is carved, has infinite potential, but once we have made it into a table or a piece of jewelry, its use is fixed and limited.

Impressed by the limitless creativity of nature, Laozi wanted to recover human nature's originality. In his eyes, the Confucians tended to overspecialize human nature. A society with fewer "modern" advances, less technology, and more spontaneous interaction with nature and fellow humans would be much richer than the Confucians'.[38] The Daoists, who took their lead from Laozi and Zhuangzi, tried to show how less could be more, how neglect could be cultivation. If people would shut the doors of their senses and thus cut off distractions, how less can be more would be obvious. The good life was not to be found in having but in being. By being simple, whole, alert, and sensitive in feeling, one could find joy.

Throughout history, many commentators have criticized Laozi and his followers for both naivete and obscurantism. They have especially jumped on the Daoist precept that a good way to promote peace and simplicity is to keep the people ignorant. Daoists believed that by not knowing about a wide range of possibilities, and therefore not having many desires, a populace would be quite docile. Critics have maintained that it is but a short step from such docility to sheephood and being at the mercy of evil rulers. The commentators have a point: The ideas expressed in some of Laozi's sayings invite easy abuse. For instance:

> Heaven and Earth are ruthless;
> To them the ten thousand things are
> but as straw dogs.
> The sage too is ruthless;
> To him the people are but as straw
> dogs.[39]

However, a close reading of the *Dao De Jing* shows that *wu-wei* is quite different from mindless docility or even complete pacifism. Rather, it includes the regretful use of force to cut short greater evil. As well, *wu-wei* is not sentimental, which further distinguishes it from most Westerners' views of the "the people." As easily as nature itself, *wu-wei* discards what is outworn, alternating life with death. Because of this objectivity, Daoism can seem inhumane. For a people close to nature, though, humaneness is a less anthropocentric virtue than it is for ourselves. It is less personal and more influenced by the belief that self-concern or forgetting how nature and death dwarf human existence leads to folly.

"*Dao* is empty, but it never exhausts itself through use. Fathomless, it seems to be the genesis of all things. It dulls its sharpness, unties its tangles, dims its luster, and mixes with the dust. Hidden as it is [it] exists. I do not know whose son it is. It seems to have existed before the emperor of heaven" (*Dao De Jing*, 4).

In this passage Laozi is working in his usual oracular fashion. Again and again, he makes the *Dao* the opposite of what human beings expect and honor. For example, *Dao*, the ultimate reality, is more like emptiness than fullness. The fertility that it lavishes upon the world comes from something unstructured, something rich in the mode of an infinite treasure house, too vast or simple for us human beings to grasp. Where our minds crave clarity, sharpness, it is dull. Where we love complexity and sophistication, it unravels itself to appear completely plain. It has no polish or vanity. It is so real, so elementary, that it mixes with the dust of ordinary creation. Yet, though it is hidden in all of these ways, it is the most real thing we could know. If we doubt its reality, we miss the point of our human condition. We cannot know the lineage of the *Dao,* because it is at the very beginning of any world that we could grasp. So we have to make do with unknowing.

Like many mystics, Laozi finds that his encounters with ultimate, primary reality leave him in the dark. He has to yield to the *Dao*. He cannot bend the *Dao* to his understanding or will. So the practical message of Daoism is both obvious and radical: Submit yourself to what is greater than you are. Organize your reality in terms of what is objectively so: an Other has all of the priority.

Religious Daoism and Aesthetics.   Two great consequences of the school in which Zhuangzi and Laozi predominated had considerable influence through subsequent Chinese history. One consequence was religious Daoism, which was considerably different from the philosophical Daoism of the founding fathers.[40] The other was a Daoist aesthetics.

Religious Daoism owed as much to Chinese folk beliefs and practices as it did to the reflective, mystical, ironic musings of Zhuangzi and Laozi. Scholars call this use of the *Dao* "religious" because it deals with myth, ritual, faith, and even superstition and magic—in contrast to the poetic but still rational accents of philosophical Daoism. In fact, religious Daoism owed a great deal to Laozi and Zhuangzi, but it tended to interpret their poetry literally, becoming preoccupied with their oblique remarks about extraordinary powers and immortality, so that it actively pursued such gifts through chemical experiments and yogic techniques. In addition, religious Daoism had a considerable influence on Chinese art, furnishing it many themes and sometimes suggesting that artistic work could occasion an experience of the *Dao* that would yield special power or even immortality.

The religious Daoists formed a "church," generated a massive literature complete with ritualistic and alchemical lore, and earned the wrath of modern educated Chinese, who considered religious Daoism a bastion of superstition. Also, religious Daoists sometimes became embroiled in politics and sponsored violent revolutionary groups.[41] Their rituals and revolutionary politics went together, because from their rituals they derived utopian visions of what human society ought to become.

The religious Daoists sought physical immortality by diverse routes.[42] Some sponsored voyages to the magical islands in the East, where the immortals were thought to dwell. Others pursued alchemy, not to turn base metal into gold but to find the elixir of immortality. A third Daoist interest was hygiene. The two favorite regimes were breathing air and practicing a quasi-Tantric sexual yoga. Along with dietary oddities, some religious Daoists counseled trying to breathe like an infant in the womb, so as to use up vital force as slowly as possible. Adepts would lie in bed all day, trying to hold their breath for at first a hundred and eventually a thousand counts. Perhaps some became euphoric through carbon dioxide intoxication. The yogis of sex practiced retention of the semen during intercourse, thinking that this vital substance could be rechanneled to the brain and thereby enhance one's powers and longevity. In these exercises, the proximate goal was prolonging physical life, and the ultimate goal was a full immortality.

Religious Daoism also developed regimes of meditation, which it coupled with a complicated roster of gods. The basic assumption behind this venture was that the human body is a microcosm—a miniature world.[43] Within it, certain gods preside over particular organs and functions. By visualizing one of these gods, Daoists thought, one could identify with its powers of immortality.[44]

Daoism had as strong an impact on Chinese aesthetics as it did on Chinese popular religion.[45] As a guide to creativity, it stressed spontaneity and flow. Largely because of Daoist inspiration, calligraphy, painting, poetry, and music ideally issued from a meditative communion with the nature of things. In what Chan Buddhism popularized as "no-mind," artists worked spontaneously, without calculation or design. Their products were the outflow of a fullness far more comprehensive than logic or method. In fact, the artists were supposed to render both the stream of nature and the way that particular items suddenly focus that stream. So a bird alighting on a tree, a rush of wind, the striking colors of persimmons at daybreak—these were typical themes of poetry and art. Daoist artists owed a great deal to the "retirement" that Daoism advocated as a respite and counterpoint to Confucian "office."[46] Mixed with Buddhist aesthetics, Daoism provided China most of its artistic depth. Nature, art, and the spirit so came together for the traditional Chinese that they considered their Way superior to the rest of the world.

Buddhism

Buddhism may have entered China as early as the beginning of the first century B.C.E. and almost certainly established itself by the middle of the second century C.E.[47] Buddhist missionaries traveled along the trade routes that linked northeastern India and China, probably entering at Dunhuang in the west. By 148 C.E., monks such as Anshigao had settled at Luoyang, considerably to the east, and begun translating Buddhist texts. The first interests of these translators and their audiences appear to have been meditation and philosophy, which suggests that the Chinese first considered Buddhism similar to Daoism. However, as the translating progressed through the Han dynasty (ended 220 C.E.), sutras on morality became popular, too.

From this beginning, Buddhism slowly adapted to Chinese ways. Most of the preachers and translators who worked from the third to the fifth centuries C.E. favored Daoist terminology. This was especially true in the south, where the intelligentsia had created a market for philosophy. In the less cultured north, Buddhism made progress by being presented as a powerful magic.[48] By the middle of the fifth century, China had its own sectarian schools, comparable to those that had developed in India. Thus, by that time most

of the major Buddhist philosophies and devotional practices had assumed a Chinese style, including the *Abhidhamma* (a system that employed erudite philosophy and psychology in interpreting the scriptures) and the Indian Madhyamika and Yogacara schools. In general, Mahayana attracted the Chinese more than Hinayana, so the native schools that prospered tended to develop Mahayana positions.

The Chinese brought to Buddhism an interest in bridging the gap between the present age and the age of the Buddha by constructing a line of masters along which the dharma had passed intact. The Master was more historical than timeless scriptural texts were, and the authority-minded Chinese were more concerned about history than the Indians had been.

Indeed, conflicts over the sutras were a sore problem for the Chinese, and in trying to reconcile seemingly contradictory positions, they frequently decided to make one scripture totally authoritative. A principal basis for the differences among the burgeoning Chinese Buddhist sects, therefore, lay in which scripture the sect's founder had chosen as most authoritative. (The notion of sects is distinctively Chinese, since it is based on the old concept of the clan. Chinese culture venerated its ancestors, and each Chinese Buddhist school accordingly had its dharma founder or patriarchal teacher.)

Buddhist Sects. The most popular sects were the Chan and Jingtu, which devoted themselves to meditation and the Pure Land, respectively. The Chinese took to meditation from the beginning of their encounter with Buddhism. There are evidences of yogic practices in the Daoist works attributed to Laozi and Zhuangzi, and certainly Daoist imagery of what the sage who knows the "inside" can accomplish had made many Chinese eager to tap interior powers. Chan capitalized on this interest, working out a simple regime and theory that focused on meditation.[49] (Chan is the transliteration of the Indian *dhyana;* the Japanese transliteration is Zen.) Its principal text was the *Lankavatara Sutra,* which the Yogacarins also much revered, because that text stressed the mentality of all reality.

According to legend, Bodhidharma, an Indian meditation-master devoted to the *Lankavatara,* founded Chan in the fifth century C.E. Paintings portray Bodhidharma as a fierce champion of single-mindedness, and he valued neither pious works nor recitations of the sutras. Only insight into one's own nature, which was identical with the dharma-nature of

all reality, was of significance; only enlightenment justified the Buddhist life. Tradition credits Bodhidharma
with developing the technique of "wall gazing," which
was a kind of peaceful meditation—what the Japanese
later called "just sitting" *(shikan-taza)*.

Probably the most eminent of the Chan patriarchs
who succeeded Bodhidharma was the sixth patriarch,
Hui-neng. According to the *Platform Sutra,* which
purports to present his teachings, Hui-neng gained his
predecessor's mantle of authority by surpassing his
rival, Shenxiu, in a demonstration of dharma insight.
To express his understanding, Shenxiu had written:

> The body is the Bodhi Tree
> The mind is like a bright mirror and
> stand.
> At all times wipe it diligently,
> Don't let there be any dust.

Hui-neng responded:

> Bodhi really has no tree;
> The bright mirror also has no stand.
> Buddha-nature is forever pure;
> Where is there room for dust?[50]

This juxtaposition and evaluation of the two rivals' verse reflects the beliefs of the southern Chan
school, which looked to Hui-neng as the authoritative
spokesman for its position that enlightenment comes
suddenly. Because all buddha-nature is intrinsically
pure, one need only let it manifest itself. The northern
school held that enlightenment comes gradually and
thus counseled regular meditation. (Hui-neng himself
probably would have fought any sharp distinction between meditation and the rest of life. In wisdom all
things are one and pure.) The southern school finally
took precedence.[51]

Pure Land Buddhism (Jingtu) derived from Tanluan (476–542). He sought religious solace from a
grave illness, and after trying several systems, he
came to the doctrine of Amitabha Buddha and the
Pure Land. Amitabha is the Buddha of Light, devotion
to whom supposedly assures one a place in the Pure
Land or Western Paradise. Tanluan stressed faith in
Amitabha and the recitation of Amitabha's name as
ways to achieve such salvation. This, he and his successors reasoned, was a doctrine both possible and
appropriate in the difficult present age. The Pure Land
sect greatly appealed to the laity, and it developed
hymns and graphic representations of paradise to fo-

cus its imagination. In stressing love or emotional
attachment to Amitabha (called A-mi-to fo in China),
it amounted to a Chinese Buddhist devotionalism. By
chanting "na-mo a-mi-to-fo" ("greetings to A-mi-to fo
Buddha"), millions of Chinese found a simple way to
fulfill their religious needs and made A-mi-to fo the
most popular religious figure of Chinese history.[52]

Case Study: Medieval Buddhism. "For the first two
hundred years of the T'ang, Buddhism flourished as
never before. Supported by the lavish donations of the
devout, guided by leaders of true piety and brilliance,
graced by the most gifted artists and architects of the
age, Buddhism was woven into the very texture of
Chinese life and thought. These centuries were the
golden age of an independent and creative Chinese
Buddhism."[53]

The Tang dynasty (618–907) followed on the Sui
(589–618), under which north and south China had
been reunited. Buddhism had made steady gains in
China even before this reunification, but after reunification it grew by leaps and bounds. A major reason for
this growth was the perception of both the Sui and the
Tang rulers that Buddhism could help them knit together the northern and southern cultures. Thus the
founder of the Sui dynasty presented himself as a universal monarch who was both a pious Buddhist believer and a generous patron of the *sangha.* He likened
his wars to campaigns to spread the ideals of Buddha,
calling his weapons of war incense and flowers offered
to the Enlightened One. It is hard to see how this
squared with Buddhist nonviolence, but the popularity
of Buddhism among the emperor's subjects led him to
associate himself with the dharma as much as he
could.

On the other hand, both the Sui and the Tang
rulers feared the power of the *sangha* and took steps
to limit its influence. Thus they insisted on regulating
the admission, education, and ordination of the
Buddhist clergy and on licensing the Buddhist temples. As well, the emperors put pressure on the *sangha*
to enforce the Vinaya strictly, for its rules governing
monastic life tended to restrict the clergy's economic
enterprises. Such imperial efforts to control Buddhism were only partly successful, for many medieval
empresses and wealthy merchants saw to it that
temple wealth grew. The merchants' support of Buddhism is an interesting example of fitting a religious
rationale to economic goals. For the merchants, the
Mahayana notion that money gifts should be put to
productive use became a justification for widespread

commercial enterprise. Since the prevailing economy was, by imperial design, focused on agriculture, the Mahayana notion in effect buttressed the merchants in their conflict with the state comptrollers.

The government did its best to limit the ways that Buddhist doctrines might become politically subversive, guarding against the revolutionary implications of Mahayana dharma. For example, potential rebels had available to them the Mahayana belief that Buddhism would pass through three ages. In the third age, religion would come close to extinction and no government would merit the full allegiance of the Buddhist faithful. A wealthy and powerful sect called the Sanchieh chiao seized on this notion and tried to use it to undermine the imperial authority, but the Sui and Tang rulers reacted vigorously and had the sect suppressed. The Mahayana teaching about Maitreya, the future buddha, was similarly dangerous. Enough Buddhists believed that the advent of Maitreya was close at hand to present the government a sizable problem. The popular understanding was that when Maitreya came, a new heaven and a new earth would begin. Thus both the Sui and the Tang emperors had to battle rebels moving against them under banners of white (the color associated with Maitreya).

Still, the golden age that Buddhism enjoyed in these dynasties flowed from the positive support the emperors gave it. For all their care that Buddhist fervor not become subversive of their own rule, the Sui and Tang leaders made Buddhist ritual an important part of the state ceremony. Thus the accession of a new emperor, the birth of a prince, and the ceremonies in honor of the imperial ancestors all incorporated Buddhist sutras, spells, and prayers. When the emperor ritualized important occasions, the monasteries and temples received handsome donations, which of course increased their patriotic loyalty and pliability.

At the great capital of Changan, Buddhist art dominated a vibrant cultural life. The architecture of the pagodas and temples gracefully blended Indian and native Chinese elements, producing a distinctively Chinese Buddhist appearance. The images and paintings that adorned the temples drew on the full range of sources with which the great Chinese Empire came in contact. Thus there were not only native Chinese art forms but also Indian, Persian, Greco-Roman, and Central Asian. With sufficient freedom married to sufficient imperial support, Chinese Buddhist artists enjoyed a period of great prosperity and created a distinctive new style.

This sort of syncretism—a core of Chinese Buddhist inspiration in touch with many other sources of inspiration—extended to literary art. The Tang dynasty was a high point in the history of Chinese poetry, and the moving forces behind this poetry were the two congenial streams of Buddhist and Daoist philosophy. Thus the celebrated poet Bozhui was representative in filling his work with references to the Buddhist rituals and temple grounds that gave him and his contemporaries spiritual nourishment. In one poem he remembers visiting a great hall called the Jade Image, in which rows of white jade buddhas sat like serried trees. He and his fellow journeyers shook the dust from their clothes and bowed to worship the buddhas, whose faces were like frozen snow. The buddhas' white cassocks hung like folded hoarfrost, and their crowns glittered like a shower of hail. So perfect were these white images that the journeying poets scrutinized them in wonder, feeling that here was a work of heavenly spirits, a work more exalted than any earthly chisel could have managed.[54]

The following lines from the renowned Du Fu (712–770) show the moving humanism that Tang art could achieve. The poet is speaking of his absent wife:

Tonight, the moon over Fu-chou,
From her room she can only watch alone.
Far away, my poor little children
Don't know they should remember the capital.
Fragrant mist moistens her hair, dark as clouds.
Clear rays chill her arms, fair as jade.
When shall we lean against the empty curtain,
With the moon drying the tears of us both?[55]

Medieval Buddhism also permeated the life of the common people, including the village peasantry, for the government developed a network of official temples that linked the provinces to the capital. On official feast days, ceremonies held throughout the land reminded the people that they shared a uniform religious faith. The provinces also used the Buddhist temple grounds for their fairs, thereby making them the centers of the local social, economic, and artistic life. The great feast days were the Buddha's birthday and the Feast of All Souls, when large crowds would gather to honor the Buddhist deities, listen to the sutras, or hear an accomplished preacher expound the dharma.

When local organizations met for vegetarian dinners, clergy and laity had a fine chance to socialize. Fashioning close bonds of mutual interest, these dinners became a great source of fund raising for the monasteries and blessings for the mercantile and personal interests of the laity. The village clergy usually were not well educated, but they tended to know the laity intimately and to provide them considerable solace at such important times as weddings and funerals. Many of the village Buddhist clergy also functioned as healers and mediums, as well as storytellers and magicians.

The state and the *sangha* therefore had a symbiotic relationship throughout the Sui and the Tang dynasties. Whether pulling in the same direction or wanting to go opposite ways, they were mutually influential. One place where Buddhist views considerably modified traditional Chinese customs was the penal codes. The traditional customs were quite cruel, so the Buddhist ideals of compassion and respect for life served as a mitigating influence. Both the Sui and the Tang rulers granted imperial amnesties from time to time, and when the rulers remitted death sentences they often justified their actions in terms of Buddhist compassion or reverence for life. Specifically, both dynasties took up the custom of forbidding executions (indeed, the killing of any living thing) during the first, fifth, and ninth months of the year, which were times of Buddhist penance and abstinence.

The emperors also converted Buddhist notions of the soul to their own ends, using them for the psychological conditioning of the imperial armies. Whereas the traditional Chinese cult of filial piety had weakened martial fervor, teaching that a good son should return his body to the earth intact, out of gratitude to his parents, the Buddhist stress on the soul (or spiritual aspect of the "person") downplayed the importance of the body. The traditional cult had also taught that immortality depended on being buried in the family graveyard, where one's descendants could come to pay tribute. Thus a soldier buried far from home would have no continuing significance. The Sui and Tang dynasties made it a practice to build temples at the scene of foreign battles and endow these temples with perpetual services for the souls of those slain in military service. In this way, they lessened the conflict between a generous service in the army and a generous filial piety.

Medieval Buddhism also increased the charitable helps available in Chinese society. Monks were the first to open dispensaries, free hospitals (supported by the Tang government), and hostels for travelers. They built bridges, planted shade trees, and generally broadened China's ethical sensitivity. Whereas the na-

Figure 11 *Sakyamuni Buddha, northern Wei dynasty, 494 C.E. Gray stone; 21¼ in. high. This statue shows Gautama as the sage of his tribe (the Sakyas). The* mudra *or gesture of his right hand is a symbol of his protection. The nimbus behind him emphasizes the peace and power of buddhahood. The Nelson–Atkins Museum of Art, Kansas City, Missouri (Nelson Fund).*

tive ethic seldom took much charitable interest in affairs outside the clan, Buddhism encouraged an interest in the welfare of all living things. For example, it said that giving alms to poor people outside one's clan was a fine way to improve one's karma. This Buddhist universalism never displaced the formative influence of the Chinese clans, but it did move many Chinese to great magnanimity.

Finally, it was during the medieval flourishing that Buddhist philosophy became fully Chinese. A hallmark of this domestication was the rendering of the abstractions in which Indians delighted into the concrete images the Chinese preferred. For example, the Indian "perfection" became the Chinese "round," while the Indian "essence" became the Chinese "pupil of the eye." Chan, the school that most stressed meditation, carried the Chinese spirit to the heart of Buddhist spirituality, distrusting abstract words and stressing metaphors, paradoxes, gestures, or direct, person-to-person intuitions. Chan and the other native schools also stressed living close to nature, in the conviction that nature held many of the secrets of enlightenment. This had great appeal for medieval Chinese artists, poets, and philosophers, many of whom would refresh themselves in retreats at Buddhist monasteries.

The Traditional Synthesis

Confucianism was the most influential religious tradition for the public functions of the Chinese family and the state, and in that sense the most official. For private worship, philosophy, and art, however, Buddhism and Daoism were quite influential. Buddhism and Daoism contended for influence at court and sometimes gained dominance. After the fall of the Han dynasty (third century C.E.), for instance, Confucian influence waned, and Buddhism gained great influence that lasted well into the ninth century. Nonetheless, in most periods the state bureaucracy hewed to the Confucian line.

Buddhism's major impact in the public sphere was its control of burial rites. In time, China associated funerals with monks. Partly out of envy at such influence and partly out of its own searches for enlightenment, Daoism established monastic communities in the fourth century C.E. Along with the rituals of the Daoist priesthood and the Daoist political parties, these communities were strong sources of Daoist public influence.

However, in their struggles against Confucian dominance, Buddhism and Daoism primarily depended on their greater appeal to individualist and artistic sentiments. In comparison, the sober Confucians offered relatively little to nourish a private, meditative, philosophical, or aesthetic life, although they were not completely lacking resources for meditation,

self-improvement, and aesthetics. The Master's love of music, for instance, though he set it in a traditional and public context, could have inspired personal creativity in the arts. However, such inspiration tended to fall to Buddhists and Daoists.

In addition, the Buddhist and Daoist texts seemed richer and more mysterious to middle-aged people seeking meaning in their existence. Few Chinese could live fifty years and not suffer some surfeit from rules, laws, ceremonies, or traditions. At such point, the lean paradoxes of Zhuangzi, Laozi, the *Prajnaparamita,* and Chan could be very attractive. So could the *Dao* that could not be named, the Buddhist emptiness that one had to attend to in silence.

Peasant Religion. Only the educated upper classes, of course, had the opportunity to immerse themselves in any of the high three traditions. For the majority of the population, the influence of these traditions only vaguely affected a world dominated by family loyalties and naturalistic animism, largely because the Chinese population was always overwhelmingly composed of peasants. Close to nature, these people filtered Buddhist and Daoist ideas through a primal reverence and fear of nature's powers.

For instance, the Chinese peasants incorporated Buddhist demonology, Daoist demonology, and both traditions' concern with saints into their ancient world of ghosts and helpers, which was home to the ancestors. This world was real because it affected the peasants each day, as the family sacrificed or tried to avert bad luck. The world of the spirits was alive. Daily the phenomena of the sky and the fields expressed that world's mysteries, and the wind and the sea carried great swans and dragons. The cities and the imperial court had their influence on the hamlets, but real life there confronted nature with little polish or form. What we might call an instinctive Confucianism about family relations blended with an instinctive Daoism about nature and human destiny to produce a curious mixture of formality and fear.

Moreover, the peasants had not separated, either through study or through deep meditation, rationality from mythical or pragmatic hopes and fears. Getting enough food, sheltering one's family, warding off sickness, continuing the family line—those were the concerns of the villagers. To meet them, different gods were honored at festivals for the New Year and for the changing seasons. As well, the Buddhist Goddess of Mercy drew those seeking easy births and strong children, and the Daoist cult of the immortals attracted a few who wanted longevity or knowledge of the rulers of their bodily organs. Tradition sanctioned these quests for meaning, but it was a tradition with many cracks. Daily life was shadowed by a greater need to avoid the wrath of the ancestors or the evil spirits.

Mercantile Religion.   By the fourteenth century C.E., guilds of artisans and businessmen had developed, and folk religiosity in China had become more mercantile. The guild became a sort of family or clan and had its patron gods and rituals. People now invoked the spirits who were the patrons of good selling, and a folk mentality affected the examinations that were part of the way to civil office. For instance, masters of the Confucian classics who did well in the examinations and secured good jobs took on an aura of religious power. As well, numerous stories were told of scholars who had received miraculous help from a patron deity, and these scholars gave the Confucians their own measure of magic and mystery.[56]

The common people could go to a great variety of shrines and temples to find out their futures. In addition, students prayed for success in their examinations, travelers prayed for safe journeys, and young people prayed for good marriages. Popular Chinese religion thus became almost economic. Gods and powers were the foci of business—the business of getting along well with an unseen world of fate and fortune. Confucianism, Daoism, and Buddhism all were mixed into this economic popular religion, but its base was preaxial closeness to nature. Few Chinese were so far from nature or so safe from adverse fortune that "secularism" was a live option. The state somewhat controlled religion by keeping the Buddhist and Daoist clergy in check, but the religious life of the family and the individual ran all the traditions together in a form that was largely outside the government's control.

The Communist Era

For more than two millennia, the ideas and beliefs that we have described prevailed in China with amazing stability and consistency. (Indeed, Hans Steininger has said of Confucianism, "It is these ethics which even today we meet all over East Asia."[57]) Despite new dynasties, wars, changing artistic styles, and even dramatic new religions such as Buddhism and Christianity, the general culture perdured. In the family, the government bureaucracy, and the villages, the folk/ Confucian tradition was especially solid.

However, that changed in the early twentieth century. From without, Western science and Western sociopolitical thought dealt it heavy blows; from within, the decay of the imperial government led to the birth of the republic in 1912. Belatedly, China entered the modern world. In the twentieth century, its ancient culture showed cracks and strains everywhere. As a result, Chinese religious traditions, especially Confucianism, came under strong attack. Identified with the old culture, they seemed out of place in the modern world. Since the "cultural renaissance" of 1917, China has tried to cast off its Confucian shackles; since the Communist takeover of 1949, it has espoused a program of ongoing socialism and modernization.[58]

The paramount figure in this program, of course, was Mao Zedong. Mao was born in 1893 in Hunan (a south-central province) of a "middle" peasant family (that is, not one of abject poverty). His father had little culture or education, and his mother was a devout Buddhist. Mao himself received a traditional primary school education, whose core was memorizing the Confucian classics. (As a result, he developed a profound distaste for Confucius.) He had to leave school when he was thirteen to work the land, but prompted by his desire for more education, he ran away and enrolled in a modern high school. There he first encountered Western authors who challenged traditional Chinese culture. (At that time many educated Chinese felt humiliated by their defeat by the British in the Opium War of 1839–42, their defeat by the Japanese in 1895, and the repression of their Boxer uprising in 1900 by a coalition of mainly Western powers. In the opinion of biographer Stuart Shram, Mao probably saw China's need to gain respect in the international community more clearly than he saw its internal needs.[59])

Slowly Mao adopted a more positive program as a result of increased engagement with the developing Chinese Communist party, increased knowledge of developments in Russia, and then years as a guerrilla soldier. Before long, Mao was a convert to Marxism-Leninism. He joined the Chinese Communist party in 1921, took part in the Communist collaboration with Jiang Kai-shek's Guomindang party until 1926, and then led Communist forces that opposed Jiang. By 1935 Mao was in charge of the Communist party and engaged in what became his legendary "Long March." Through World War II the Communists and the Guomindang collaborated uneasily against the Japanese; after the war the final conflict with Jiang led to the Communist takeover in 1949. Throughout this period

Mao pursued the twofold career of military general and political theoretician. While gaining power he collaborated with the Russians, but he eventually decided that China had to go its own way. The result was a massive experiment in agrarian reform, enfranchising the lower classes, and trying to control economics by Marxist-Leninist and Maoist dogma.

The reason for this brief biographical sketch of Mao is that he was the most important figure in China's break with tradition and plunge into modernity. Influenced by the Confucian classics and Buddhism, he nevertheless repudiated both. On the surface at least, Maoism took shape as a secular humanism—a system that referred to nothing more absolute than "the people." Some of its doctrines and programs dramatically changed the life of the people. The women's movement, for instance, and the related changes in the marriage law raised an entire segment of the population from subjection to near equality.[60] By stressing agricultural production, local health care, and "cellular" local government, Chinese Communism has become an even more grandiose socialist experiment than the Soviet.

As part of the program instituting these changes, Mao's party denounced religion. Instead of gods and sacrifices, it offered self-reliance, hard work, and the mystique that the people united are invincible. Temples became government property, religious professionals were persecuted, and religious literature was derided or proscribed. The party likewise attacked the Confucian classics, virtues, and traditions. Throughout, its goal was to destroy the old class society and make a new people with one will and one future.

However, as one might expect, religion and tradition died harder than the Communists had hoped. In the rural regions, peasant traditions continued to have great influence. Among the intellectuals, conforming to the party line resulted in rather wooden, if not second-class, philosophy, science, and art. According to R. J. Lifton,[61] Mao himself ruminated on immortality in his last years, for he saw the problem of keeping the revolution "green"—retrieving for a new generation the experiences of the Long March and the other peak events that had united the wills of the founding generation.

Something of that concern comes through in the last of Mao's poems.[62] "Two Birds," supposedly written in 1965, contrasts a sparrow, concerned only with beef-filled goulash, with a soaring roc that sees how the world is turning upside down. The options, Mao seems to say, are settling down in material comfort and keeping the revolution green. Many commentators saw in Mao's sporadic activism (periods of stability followed by upheavals such as the Cultural Revolution) an effort to ward off stagnation.

Since the death of Mao Zedong, China has opened to the West. The "four modernizations" (in industry, science and technology, agriculture, and military affairs) urged by Mao's successors aimed at bringing China into the modern world. "To 'handle the problem of religion' correctly, the regime has recently convened 2 major study conferences: the China Atheistic Seminar (Nanking, December, 1978) calling for scholarly research on atheism, and the National Planning Conference on Religious Studies (Kunming, February, 1979) calling for scholarly research on religions from the Marxist standpoint. On 15 March 1979, the regime promulgated a new policy statement entitled 'Religion and Superstition,' re-establishing the pre-1966 religious policy as 'correct.' The Religious Affairs Bureau in Beijing formally resumed operation the next day. Open persecution of believers is now expected to decline, but authentic legal toleration remains unlikely."[63]

Before 1966, the policy, expressed in article 88 of the Constitution of 1954, had been that the people of the People's Republic enjoy freedom of religious belief. During the Cultural Revolution of 1966–69, the policy was to promote atheism. The Constitution of 1975 stipulated in article 28 that citizens have the freedom to practice a religion, and the freedom not to practice a religion and to propagate atheism. In mid-1980, the demographic results of these policies were estimated as follows: nonreligious Chinese, 527 million people, or 59 percent of the population; folk religionists, 179 million people, or 20 percent of the population; atheists, 107 million people, or 12 percent of the population; Buddhists, 53 million people, or 6 percent of the population; Muslims, 21 million people, or 2.4 percent of the population; Christians, 1.8 million people, or 0.2 percent of the population.[64]

The upheavals in China in the late 1980s called the future of all individual liberties seriously into question. By putting down the movement among students and intellectuals for democracy, the regime, headed by elderly successors of Mao, ensured that a Communist orthodoxy would continue to dominate official culture, at least for the short run. While some religious groups had made progress and seemed to be on the verge of gaining a considerable following, the suppression of free speech and criticism by the government caused all such groups, along with all other

Chinese coalitions seeking reforms and greater freedoms, to hold their breath. At the time of this writing (April 1991), the future of religion in mainland China remains very unclear.

WORLDVIEW

The history of religion in China is a story of the interaction of many forces and traditions. The oldest and deepest stratum, which reveals a folk religion much concerned with fertility and various supernatural forces, always predominated for the great numbers of Chinese who were peasants. The "higher" indigenous traditions, expressed in Confucian and Daoist ideas and convictions, assumed this deepest stratum and labored to clarify the stances that educated people, people of reflective awareness and refinement, ought to take toward it. The Confucians dominated social attitudes, inasmuch as education could shape them. Confucian convictions about how the wise people of the fortunate past had lived and thought established a preference for ritual, ceremony, class consciousness, the rule of men over women, and above all, reverence for one's elders and ancestors.

Certainly all of these features of Chinese culture owed much to folk convictions, but the Confucians gave them an anthropocentric focus. Inasmuch as sages such as Confucius and Mencius experienced themselves to be living repositories of tradition, existential awarenesses of the Way, they felt powerful enough to oppose both the dysfunctional views of human arrangements that could develop in folk religion and the disorders of people who held considerable political or military power but had been seduced by force, greed, vanity, lust, or any of the other vices that were bound to bring social disaster in the long run.

The Daoists agreed with the Confucians that wise people, filled with the spirit of the golden past and attuned to the Way not only revered in that past but running the cosmos in the present, were the living repositories of tradition. They differed from the Confucians in their distrust of the efficacy of ritual, mores that would prop the distributions of power constituting the status quo, and convention. The Daoists found more paradox in the ways of the Way, and they thought that the sage had to be more individualistic. As well, he or she (the Daoists were minor champions of wom-

en's wisdoms) had to be more attuned to the patterns of nature, where the Way constantly gave instruction on how to live well. We are speaking of the philosophical Daoists, of course. The religious Daoists kept less distance from folk religion and more subordinated such masters as Laozi and Zhuangzi to it than they subordinated it to them.

The Buddhists never replaced the folk religionists, Confucians, or Daoists, philosophical or religious. Their tendency was, rather, to supplement, deepen, and occasionally challenge the indigenous ways. That is not to say that Buddhism did not make a deep impact on China. It did, especially in such areas as the philosophy of nature, meditation, and both the understanding and the ritualization of death. But the Chinese pattern was to extend a Confucian instinct about social relations so that Buddhist instincts might enrich it. Similarly, the tendency was to combine Buddhist philosophy with philosophical Daoism, so that Buddhism became simpler and more paradoxical, as it did in Chan schools.

This interpretation of the religious history of China suggests that, in studying the Chinese worldview, students do well to concentrate on the cooperation of the different major forces or strata. The way of regarding nature, society, the self, and ultimate reality that one finds in the typical Chinese man or woman was almost always an amalgam of folk, Confucian, Daoist, and Buddhist influences. These influences were not uniform or equal. A given tradition might play a stronger or weaker role in a given area (for instance, social outlook) or with a given person (for instance, the peasant woman Wang). But for the abstract that we can derive from the total mixture of influences, we have to take into account the constant contributions of all the major traditions in all of the major areas. Pay attention, then, to the amalgamated, syncretistic character of the Chinese worldview. Do not consider the various Chinese traditions competitors (though they were that on occasion) so much as complementary stimuli—pressures to make the typical Chinese person aware of other options, sensitive to further complexities.

Nature

All ancient societies lived deep in what we have called the cosmological myth, and China was no exception.[65] However, China did not have India's tendency to call sensory experience into question. Throughout its axial period, China's attitude was that nature is utterly real—more primordial than human beings. After the axial period, when Buddhism had a deep effect, native Chinese thought and the dharma were joined in more than a marriage of convenience. For instance, the Chan and Huayen schools translated the Mahayana philosophy of emptiness into a Chinese version of the theory that nirvana and samsara are not two. Furthermore, although Buddhist devotional sects among the masses drew attention to the heavenly Pure Land, they also described the Pure Land as a present reality. Overall, then, nature bulked large and unquestioned. The vast majority of Chinese doubted neither its reality nor its ultimacy. If there had been a question of subordinating one of the four dimensions of reality (nature, society, self, and divinity), nature would have been the last to go.

Physical reality took form through *Dao*. *Dao* was the most basic force holding nature together. To be sure, the *Dao* most to the fore here is that which humans can name. The nameless *Dao* (which to Laozi was the more real) was too vast, too primordial, too womblike for humans to grasp. It was so unlimited as to be somewhat beyond the world, so full or complete as to be beyond our comprehension.

So, it was the worldly Way—the cause of the seasons, the peculiarities of history, the laws of gravity and the tides—that dominated most Chinese reflection on nature. Most Chinese reflection on nature concerned manifest entities, patterns and forces that affected human beings. The other latent *Dao* was only the intuition of an intellectual, indeed of a mystical, elite. Not only could that *Dao* not be named, it could not be brought under human control. Consequently, it was the best candidate in pre-Buddhist Chinese thought for the mystery whose uncontrollability is our primary indication that something more powerful and basic than what we see is at the origin of things.

Dao, it follows, was both Logos and mother. As Logos, it was the reasonable pattern, the intelligence running through nature. As mother, it was the womblike source of all things. Neither being nor nonbeing, the maternal *Dao* existed in a realm of its own. Yet this transcendent realm was also the basis for all the other realms of nature. The fish, waters, clouds, trees, mud, dung, and other elements of observable reality existed by *Dao*. Both the manner in which they existed and the fact that they existed implied this ultimate. So *Dao* functioned as the within and the without. Not many Chinese reasoned in this somewhat relentless way, but their more poetic and circular descriptions take us to such conclusions. Nature had a sense and a

mystery, and this sense finally was owed to its mystery. The pregnant word *Dao* signified both.

Throughout Chinese history, *Dao* retained this richness. Confucians and Buddhists used it to express their understanding of nature, as did Daoists themselves. Frequently *Dao* was associated with heaven *(Tian)*, which often gave it a sacred aspect. Originally heaven was the overseer (a notion that the Chinese shared with Indians and Near Easterners). There was nothing that heaven did not notice and record. Heaven itself, though, never took on personal features among the Chinese. No father with a white beard, no Apollo with a dashing chariot, became its emblem. Neither the sun nor the moon solicited reverence as the primary form of heaven. If anything, the sky itself, broad and indistinct, was the focus of Chinese devotion.

Opposite to the sky was the earth. Yet the earth seldom was viewed maternally, as it was by many ancient peoples. The Chinese acknowledged the mysteries of vegetation, seasonal changes, the fallow and the productive, and they touched their newborn to the earth in recognition of their origin. But the maternal aspect of nature's bounty they attributed more to *Dao* than to the earth. Perhaps they were more attuned to pattern and flow than to dirt-bound production. (Or perhaps we are speaking mainly about the beliefs of poets and intellectuals, whose writings shape our impressions overmuch.)

In any event, Laozi, Zhuangzi, and the Buddhists consistently invested nature with an aura of ultimacy and preferred to bow before *Dao*. For instance, Zhuangzi's Great Clod is more than mother earth. Returning to the Clod at death keeps one in a universal rhythm. The Great Clod is the material system, the massive lump, that *Dao* turns. Similarly, Buddhist landscapers and gardeners went beyond mother earth to Suchness, buddha-nature, or emptiness for their inspiration. Although the Japanese developed the aesthetic resulting from this inspiration more fully, it first came from China.

Folk Views. More mundane matters—such as yin and yang, the five dynamic qualities, and the ghosts and helping spirits—absorbed the masses. These concepts rendered Chinese nature lively.[66] Of course, virtually all ancient peoples thought of nature as alive. Although the Chinese stressed the cult of ancestor spirits more than comparable peoples, such veneration was yet present among other peoples as well. Indian Buddhists, for instance, thought that the dead would turn malevolent unless the living venerated them.

Chinese folk religion is also distinctive (although, again, not unique) in its concern for the compass directions. The geomancy of *feng-shui* is a clear expression of Chinese emphasis on nature's four directions. Of course, other peoples were concerned with directions; Native Americans made a great deal of the four geographic directions, while early civilized peoples such as the Egyptians built their temples with great concern for their orientation toward the sun. However, China carried this concern to a high art. Even for the average person, the angle of the wind or the shape of the terrain was magically influential.

Chinese divination expressed another set of naturalistic assumptions. The *Yi Jing,* for instance, elaborated on the belief that yin-yang components shape human participation in nature's course of events. Like the African diviner who studied the patterns of chits in a magical basket, the Chinese fortune-teller believed that numbers and designs expressed nature's coherence. In popular Chinese religion, then, there was a primal sense that nature coordinates with mind. That sense did not develop to the point of gaining a control over nature, as it would in modern Western science and technology, but for Chinese diviners, astrologers, and even fortune-tellers, that sense had great mythic power.

Such a mythic mentality may largely derive from a deep appreciation of what might be. Anything that is not contradictory might be. Therefore, anything non-contradictory can, under the pressure of imaginative suggestion, be accepted as something that is or that soon will be. From faddish "cures" for cancer to the stock market, we can see the same dynamics at work in late twentieth-century America.

In using the *Yi Jing*'s patterns of broken and unbroken lines, Chinese diviners were moved by the powerful human tendency to blur the distinction between what might be and what is, between the imaginable and the real. The interest motivating mathematicians, physicists, novelists, and theologians is little different from this tendency.[67]

Case History: Classical Chinese Aesthetics. The traditional Chinese notions of beauty were so intimately involved with nature that we can consider both classical poetry and classical painting in a naturalist context. To be sure, classical poetry did not neglect the supernatural world, for one finds poems concerned with God, nature deities, Daoist "immortals," and ancestors. In addition, there were numerous poems concerned with family ties, friendship, love, social jus-

tice, war, and other human themes. But nature tended to be the encompassing orbit (for example, "God" was *Tian,* heaven) and the great source of inspiration.

In the earliest poetry, from the *Book of Poetry* (about 1100–600 B.C.E.), nature often offers analogies to human life. Thus the first poem in this classical collection speaks of the cries of ospreys on an island in a river, which remind the poet of a man longing for the love of a virtuous maiden. As the poem unfolds, the river becomes a backdrop for the shifting emotions of human love.

Another early theme was just the opposite. In poetry from the early centuries C.E., we can read of nature's distance from human ways. Where human beings feel things intensely, hoping and sorrowing, nature goes its way in indifference. Where human affairs are always changing and the human life span is brief, nature goes its way with little alteration, confident in its endlessness. Unlike metal or stone, human beings cannot be expected to endure. The poet finds this contrast poignant, even bitter: Why should human life be so fragile and fleeting?

Still a third theme of classical Chinese poetry is the personification of nature, according it feelings like the poet's own. Thus some lyrics of Li Yu (937–978) describe flowers in the woods losing their red bloom, paling because of chilly rains or strong night winds. The flowers are like rouge-stained tears asking the poet to stay and share nature's sorrow. Other notable Chinese poets indulged in this "pathetic fallacy," as John Ruskin called it. Conventional imagery, for instance, attributed to rivers a great grief, as though their spring rising were the effect of voluminous tears, or their endless flow were a ceaseless lament for the harshness human beings must endure.

A fourth way the classical corpus treats nature is more subtle and sophisticated. Seeming to depict a natural scene objectively, the poet actually evokes almost stylized emotions, through the conventional associations his naturalistic images would stimulate. Thus a ninth-century C.E. poem of Wen Ting describes a tower backed by a river, a moon gazing down on the sea, and mists along a seacoast punctuated only by two lines of migrating geese. Adding images of frontier sparseness, the poet insinuates the melancholy of the homesick traveler, alone while his family and friends have gathered at night. The Western reader can catch the general mood, but the Chinese reader would have been affected by such details as willows waving along the dike, because traditionally one gave a willow branch to a friend departing on a journey.

Like artists everywhere, the classical Chinese poets turned their materials this way and that, searching for the best inspiration. They felt little need to be "logical" and treated nature sometimes directly and at other times indirectly. Thus an eighth-century poem of Wang Chang-ling portrays nature subjectively, as a stimulus of emotions. The poem, "A Woman's Complaint," tells of a young wife, hitherto carefree, who first experiences regret when she climbs to the top of a tower on a spring day and catches sight of some willows along the road. They remind her of the gift she gave her husband, when he acceded to her urgings and went off to seek his fortune. Led by the sight of the willows, the woman enters a new land, the domain of regret. For the first time, she wonders whether her impetuous urging was wise. The poet's lesson seems to be that nature can nudge us along the painful passage to wisdom. The timeless powers that move the world can open us to quiet reflection through flowers and sunsets.

Perhaps the most important motif in the classical poets' view of nature, however, was that peace comes from submerging the self in nature. Here the influence of Daoism and Buddhism seems strongest. For example, a work of the eighth-century poet Wang Wei speaks of birds returning home at evening, having traveled the vast void of the sky. At dusk the sky and earth invite the mind, too, to come home from its travels. If the mind would merge with the earth and sky, it would find rest. One feels through the poem the natural whole that birds or the setting sun can reflect. The human spirit finds its best place, the poet seems to say, when it lets birds and sunsets unite it emotionally with nature's mystery.[68]

Classical Chinese painting was equally preoccupied with nature. Before the rise of landscape painting, which is probably the most lauded Chinese development, there was a concern with depicting figures, such as impressive Buddhas, and after the heyday of landscape painting there was a concern with birds and animals, grasses and flowers. But landscape painting holds the central panel in the Chinese triptych, so we do well to concentrate on landscape painting.

There is no evidence of landscape painting before the Jin dynasty (265–419). The first specimen of natural scenery, attributed to Gu Kaizhi, a famous figure-painter of the fourth century C.E., shows a mountain inhabited by wild beasts. The animals are disproportionately large, as though they might gobble up the mountain, but for the first time we come upon a Chinese mind able to detach itself from human concerns and contemplate the wilderness. Zong Ping, who succeeded Gu as the leader of the new movement, wrote an essay entitled "Preface to Landscape Painting," in which he expressed what was to be the guiding philosophy of this school: "The complete form of the mountain cannot be seen when the eye is quite close to it, but from a distance the eye can take in its whole compass, since the size of the mountain diminishes as it recedes from sight."[69] From this bit of common sense, the landscape artists drew the conclusion that one best deals with naturalistic scenes by stepping back to see them whole.

During the Tang dynasty landscape painting flourished. Both of its essential components—the composition of the whole and the brushwork detailing the parts—grew more skillful. The northern school favored rugged brush strokes, leading to a more severe style, while the southern school favored more delicate strokes, leading to a more graceful style. Thus a snow scene by Wang Wei of the southern school is rather misty, with fine bits of snow falling on thin bare branches. A little bridge crosses a cloudy stream, its pilings and railings whitened by snow. A tiny human figure approaches the door of a house apparently lighted for the evening. The man likely is looking forward to the cheerful fire but regretting having to leave the peaceful winter scene. Such poetic, imaginative emphases were typical of the southern Tang school.

Landscape painting reached its greatest heights during the Song dynasty. The fashion of painting richly colored landscapes developed, although a majority of the masters finally favored simple shadings of black ink. Gradually brush strokes became the distinguishing feature of the great masters, and color faded to insignificance, but there are some early paintings with beautiful rich colorings. The southern Song school gained most renown for its fusion of poetry and painting. Not only would the artist usually run a text down the side of the scroll, he would also blend the scene with the poetry so that sight and sound married perfectly. A small snow scene by Liu Songnian, for example, perfectly pictures the literary contents of its poem: mountains, a little bridge, lonely pavilions, and a desolate willow tree. The total effect is "poetic" rather than objective, a tug at the heart rather than an analysis by the eye. "Winter is beautiful but bitter," it seems to say. "Much of life's loveliness is bleak and cold." The artist presents the natural forms in considerable detail, conveying a great respect for nature's intricacies.

Figure 12 *Fishermen (handscroll detail) by Xuning, about 970–1051. Ink on silk; 82 in. long, 19 in. high. The picture stresses the vastness and permanence of a nature that dwarfs human beings and wraps them in emptiness. The Nelson–Atkins Museum of Art, Kansas City, Missouri (Nelson Fund)..*

Later southern Song landscapes moved away from this detail, preferring a mere hint of nature's intricacies. Thus their canvases grew sparse, with large areas of empty space. The artists would show only the topmost peaks of a mountain or a single spray of flowers. Since this southern Song development, *space* has dominated Chinese landscapes. Whether one considers this a triumph of Buddhist "emptiness," or a maturation of an inner artistic perception (an indirect way of suggesting nature's mystic whole while emphasizing its striking individual parts), it is singularly effective, pleasing the onlooker in both eye and soul. The eye is drawn to the perfectly executed flower or thin cloud, while the soul delights in leaving details,

busyness, behind so that it can simply contemplate. Communing with the *all* that runs behind, in, and through the details, the soul can aspire to "unknowing" facts and intuiting reality, as many mystics might have put it.

Thus a painting of Mi Feng entitled *Pine and Bower* has only several mountaintops, a tree, and a little hut. Half the picture is empty space, which might be clouds obscuring the bottom half of the mountains or a lake behind the little hut. There is no human presence except that suggested by the hut. The entire scene is tranquil: nature perfectly in balance, because left alone. Mi breaks the stereotype of southern delicacy, however, through a predilection for rugged natural features. This squares with a story told of him. Once he was walking along a forest path when he saw a large rock blocking his way. The rock was grizzled and oddly shaped, but his heart went out to it. So he knelt in the dust and embraced the rock, calling it "my elder brother." For this he got the nickname Mad Mi, but any good Buddhist or Daoist could understand his emotion. He developed a technique of "Mi dots" to help him express his love of strong particulars. Thus the mountains of *Pine and Bower* are wonderfully grainy, and the clouds have a thick consistency, as though unknowing were wrapping itself around the mind prior to enlightenment.

Nature in Buddhism.   Richard Mather has shown that the concept of nirvana only won acceptance in China after the Buddhists had modified it considerably.[70] At the outset, ultimate Buddhist reality seemed wholly contradictory to Chinese concreteness. Thus, Chinese Buddhists accomplished a rather thorough cross-cultural translation. They had predecessors in the Indian Mahayanists, who identified samsara with nirvana, but the Mahayanists were far more abstract than the Chinese. Indeed, Chan probably became the most successful of the sects rooted in Mahayana metaphysics because it most thoroughly domesticated nirvana. Little interested in words or speculations, Chan focused on meditation, by which one might experience nirvana. It also stressed physical work, art, and ritual that deemphasized dualistic thinking. This deemphasis is more familiar to Western readers in its Japanese (Zen) form, but it had a Chinese beginning.[71]

So the radical buddha-nature (whether as emptiness or as mind-only) found in Chan a natural form. It could be the essence of all physical things, so present that one need not flee the world nor even close one's eyes to experience it. Since meditation expresses this conviction through the bodily postures that one assumes, one has only to sit squarely in the midst of natural reality and focus on its is-ness. (Not incidentally, one does not close one's eyes. The proper focus is neither a direction within nor a withdrawal to fix on the passing mental stream. In Chan it is a gaze with eyes open toward the end of one's nose.) The objective is to see without reasoning the reality that is right here. Such seeing should not focus on particulars, or concern itself with colors and forms. Rather, it should appreciate reality's wholeness by not making distinctions. When such appreciation flowers, there is enlightenment: "I came to realize

clearly that Mind is no other than mountains and rivers and the great wide earth, the sun and the moon and the stars."[72]

Society

Historically, China used Confucianism as its binding social force, and Confucianism thoroughly subordinated individuals to the community. Consequently, the Chinese individual felt inserted not only into a nature more impressive than the self but also into a society greater than its parts. Furthermore, the great Confucian thinkers based their theory of ideal social relationships on legendary rulers of the past. Such rulers embodied the social *Dao*. Their way, then, was a paradigm that ordered society by exemplary morality. Somewhat magically, the virtue *(de)* that went out from the legendary kings and dukes brought those it touched into harmony, at least according to Confucianism.

The Confucian mythic history evidences the common ancient notion of sacred kingship. Because the ruler stands at the peak of the human pyramid, he can conduct heaven's governing power to earth. The Chinese king manifested this holy meditating role by offering sacrifices to the gods of heaven and earth. In pre-Confucian times, he sacrificed human beings.[73]

The imperial cult, consequently, was the keystone in the Chinese social edifice, and the Confucian notion of *li* (propriety) applied especially to the punctilious execution of its ceremonies. To know the music and ritual appropriate to different occasions was the mark of a high gentleman. In fact, from this cultic center radiated something religious that touched all social relationships. Since human activities related to heaven, they partook of cultic propriety. By maintaining a harmonious family, for instance, individuals contributed to the most important order, that between natural divinity and humanity.

The harmony that the Confucians encouraged, though it extended to all aspects of social life,[74] expressed itself most importantly in its rating of key human relationships. It rated men over women (and so pictured marriage not as a partnership but as the wife's servitude to the husband). It rated children (among whom the eldest son was the plum) distinctly inferior to the parents—so much so that obedience and service toward the parents (most importantly toward the father) dominated the lives of children.

Likewise, rulers were rated over subjects, masters over peasants, and, to a lesser extent, elder brothers over younger brothers.

In logical extension of their veneration of the past, the Chinese honored ancient ancestors more than more recent ones, and they rated children according to the order of their birth. Surely some parents loved a younger son more than an elder son or a gracious girl more than a mulish boy, but in determining the important matter of inheritance, age was the main standard. In these and many other ways, Chinese society looked backwards. The past was the age of paradigms; the elderly were the fonts of wisdom. The axial masters of Chinese political thought give little evidence of celebrating youth or brave new worlds.

Social space was similarly static. From the ruler's key connection to heaven, the social classes descended in clearly defined ranks with little egalitarian or democratic moderation. The Confucians especially felt that the rank of a person was important. One said quite different things to a fellow noble riding in a hunting carriage and the carriage driver. A person of breeding knew and respected such differences. If Confucius and Mencius themselves are representative, such a person was almost prickly about his social rights.

For example, the master would not visit just anyone, and for a pupil to come into town and not quickly pay a visit of homage was a serious slight. Somewhat like Plato, the Confucian master protected his dignity and honor. Perhaps surprisingly, the Confucians turned their insistence on moral worth into a partial break with the cosmological myth (and with sacred kingship). Implicit in their exaltation of virtue over external rank or status was a turn to the wisdom of the sage—a turn from cosmology to anthropology.[75]

Women's Status. Among the Confucians, a peasant or a woman, however virtuous, had a hard time gaining respect. In fact, of the three Chinese traditions, Confucianism was the most misogynistic. The woman's role in Confucianism was to obey and serve her parents, husband, and husband's parents. She was useless until she produced a male heir, and her premarital chastity and marital fidelity were more important than a man's. In some periods, obsession with female chastity became so great that society insisted on total sexual segregation.[76] No doubt some men genuinely loved their wives and treated them tenderly, but the Confucian view of marriage gave little place to romance.

Since a Chinese woman's destiny was early marriage, childbearing, and household duties, her education was minimal. She was not necessarily her husband's friend, confidante, or lover—males and courtesans could fulfill these roles. A Chinese woman was primarily her husband's source of sons. They were the reason for her marriage—indeed, for her sex. As a result, the ideal Chinese woman was retiring, silent, and fertile. Custom severely curtailed her freedoms, but never more cruelly than through foot binding. Mary Daly described this custom in graphic terms: "The Chinese ritual of footbinding was a thousand-year-old horror show in which women were grotesquely crippled from very early childhood. As Andrea Dworkin so vividly demonstrates, the hideous three-inch-long 'lotus' hooks—which in reality were odoriferous, useless stumps—were the means by which the Chinese patriarchs saw to it that their girls and women would never 'run around.' "[77] One should add that footbinding was not a universal practice, either historically or throughout all ranks of Chinese society. Wherever it occurred, though, it maimed a woman significantly. Nonetheless, there is anthropological evidence that many Chinese women overcame their submissive role by cleverly manipulating gossip so that abusive husbands or mothers-in-law would lose face.[78] Still, until the Communist takeover, women had no place in the official political system and did very well if they merely outwitted it.

The Daoists were kinder to women and to the socially downtrodden generally. They were responsible for curtailing the murder of female infants by exposure, and their more positive regard for female symbols as examples of how the *Dao* worked upgraded femininity.[79] This was not an unmixed blessing, since it involved the "strength" of the one who was submissive and the manipulative power of the one who got herself mounted. Still, by bestowing feminine or maternal attributes on the *Dao* itself, the Daoists made femininity intrinsic to ultimate reality.[80] Analogously, the Buddhist symbolism for ultimate reality and the admission of women to the *sangha* were boons.

Case Study: Women Warriors and Shamans. In Maxine Hong Kingston's *The Woman Warrior,*[81] one glimpses how the Chinese sense of women echoed in the twentieth century. As a child, Kingston heard from her mother innumerable stories about Fa Mu Lan, the woman warrior. Stretching the imagination that would later make her a fine writer, she pictured what it would be like to be Fa.

It would be like a little girl coming upon a little hut in a forest and having the door open. An old man and woman would come out carrying bowls of rice, soup, and a branch of peaches. They would offer the little girl a share of their meal, she would refuse out of politeness, but they would press her to honor them with her presence. After lunch the three would go for a walk, the little girl enjoying the lovely mountains and pines, the old couple walking so lightly their feet would not disturb so much as a pine needle. The old couple would invite the little girl to spend the night and she, fearing the ghosts of the forest, would thankfully agree. Being tucked into a little bed just her width, the little girl would hear the old woman say, "Breathe evenly, so that you do not fall out." The old couple would then raise the roof over the girl's bed, and she would fall asleep watching the moon and the stars.

The next day, the old couple would invite the girl to stay with them, so that they could train her as a warrior. "What about my family?" the girl would ask. Stirring the water in a drinking gourd, the old man would show the little girl her family discussing the honor of their daughter being invited to become a warrior. So she would agree and begin her strict training.

First, she would learn to be quiet. The couple would leave her by streams, that she might watch the animals that came to drink. If she were not absolutely quiet, she would scare them away. With time the squirrels would come and bury their hoardings near the hem of her skirt, taking her for part of the landscape.

Next would come years of strengthening. With time her body would be strong enough to run with the deer, to leap twenty feet into the air, to control even the dilation of the pupils of her eyes. Then she would be ready for her first test, surviving alone in the forest. Fasting, she would find out how much her body could endure, how sharp her senses could become, the energy that comes when the body grows pure. She would grow so intimate with the forest a rabbit would toss himself into her fire, making himself her meal. The trial in the forest would end with a vision of a man and woman made of gold dancing together, like the axis of the earth's turning. They would be lion dancers, all light. They would be angels with high white wings. They would become so bright they would make the girl's head swim, and she would faint. Later she would be able to see ordinary people as golden dancers, understanding all the meanings of their

movements. When she awoke from her dreams, the old couple would feed her hot soup and ask for an account of her adventures. They would be satisfied, and so set her onto the next phase of her training.

This would involve learning all about dragons. Tigers connote adolescent power, but dragons are the source of a mature wisdom. The mountains are but the heads of dragons. A person climbing a mountain is like a bug moving along the forehead of a great beast. The quarries in the mountain show the dragon's veins and muscles. The minerals are its teeth and bones. The soil is its flesh and the trees are its hairs. One can hear its voice in the thunder and feel its breath in the winds.

The girl's training would conclude with the martial arts, and then she would return home to her family, whose need of a champion would have grown desperate. Indeed, so strong would be their desire for revenge on their enemies, they would carve in the girl's back a whole series of oaths. When she recovered from this operation, she would get ready for battle. A white horse would come into the courtyard, as a magical sign the drama was to begin. Donning her armor and mounting the horse, the girl would begin gathering her army. When her troops met marauders and gangs of criminals, she would lead them forward, screaming a mighty scream and swinging two great swords over her head. From her mouth would come rousing songs urging her troops to victory. Wherever they went order would be restored.

Finally they would come to the capital in Beijing and prepare to face the wicked emperor who had caused all the hardship in the provinces, all the hunger and conscription of sons. So quickly that it would be anticlimactic, the woman warrior and her husband (she would have married during the campaign and brought forth a child) would behead the emperor, clean out the palace, and set on the throne a peasant who would preside over a new social order. Then they would journey along the Long Wall, chasing back the Mongols.

Still, the woman warrior would not yet have avenged her brother, whose conscription had caused her family's great sorrow. To gain this revenge she would have to slay the fat baron who had led her brother away. Finally she would confront the baron, tearing off her shirt and showing him the oaths inscribed in her back. While he stared at her breasts, shocked that the famous warrior was a woman, she would slash him across the face and cut off his head.

Then she would ride back to her family, and the whole village would celebrate a great festival.

Kingston's girlhood fantasies drew on a great treasury of Chinese folktales. The dragons, tigers, golden dancers, and warriors with which her brain seethed had delighted Chinese children for centuries. However, she wanted to draw closer to actual history, so she began to collect stories of her mother's life; but all her efforts seemed only to tie her more tightly to myth.

Her mother had trained as a doctor in China in the 1920s. Before the family's flight in 1939, her mother had been a person of prestige. The laundry the mother ran in San Francisco's Chinatown was a great comedown from her previous station. At night she would tell the children stories of her training to be a doctor, which involved much more than battles with textbooks. It involved battles with ghosts, for even in her time Chinese doctors kept one foot in the shamanist tradition. Though the medical schools were opening to Western science, they had not completely closed the door on ghosts.

Kingston's mother was older than the other medical students, having lied about her age. She therefore made fun of their reports that a ghost had occupied an abandoned dormitory room. When the other students challenged her for affecting unconcern, she offered to spend the night in the ghost's room. Her account of that night burned itself into her daughter's mind, and so was reconstructed years later, as a young Chinese-American author tried to fix herself and her mother to paper. The ghost of her mother's medical training came to stand for all the ghosts transplanted people must exorcise. To become American and modern, Kingston felt she had to conquer the incubi of her unconscious, which said that in Chinese scales no female, no matter how glorious a warrior, could ever balance a male.

Her mother was reading in the ghost's lair, slowly making herself sleepy. Her eyes drooped and she turned out the lamp. The darkness was so black it shocked her awake. All her nerves grew taut, like the time she had been caught in a snowstorm on a mountain. A rushing came at her from under the bed. Fear seized the soles of her feet, as something alive climbed the foot of the bed, rolled over her, and sat on her chest. It pressed against her, sapping her breath. "It is a sitting ghost," her mother thought. The more she pushed against it, the heavier it became. She grabbed the ghost's thick hair, which was like an animal's coat. She pinched its skin and tried to gouge its flesh with her fingernails. She searched for its eyes, to stab them, but it seemed to have no eyes. So she grew discouraged. The more she fought, the more her strength oozed away.

If only she could reach the knife lying on the lampstand. The ghost sensed her thoughts and spread itself over her arms. Rallying her spirit—the spirit that her daughter later found so indomitable—she began to hector the ghost:

> You will not win, greedy ghost. There is no pain I cannot endure. This school has big jars of alcohol. I will get some alcohol, put it in my bucket, spread it across the floor, set fire to it, and burn you out. You have made a big mistake, greedy ghost. I will track you all over the school and burn you out. What an ugly ghost you are. You must be one of the lower spirits. Now I am going to chant tomorrow's lessons. There are no such things as ghosts.

When she awoke in the morning, Kingston's mother told her classmates of her adventure. After class she gathered them all in the ghost's room and began the great burnout. In twos and threes, they arranged their buckets and jars of alcohol. Down poured the alcohol, up flared the flames, across went the rows of fire. Back and forth, they burned the room free of its ghost. "I told you, stupid ghost. Your end has come. There is no place for you in this school of medicine. You have to go—back to your dark haunts, back to the old villages, back to the depths of our minds."

When the smoke cleared and the mops stood idle, the room rested in peace. Under the bed where Kingston's mother had slept was a piece of wool, dripping with blood. They burned it in a bucket, and the stench was like a corpse exhumed for its bones.

In her inner rites of passage, Kingston could not tell which ghosts to laugh at, which ghosts to accredit. Her mother was a fabulous woman, a creature from a different age. Storyteller and shaman, warrior and healer, her mother was the tip of a mythic iceberg. How could a child of the new world manage such a mother's psyche? What could women's liberation say to a dragon ironing sheets?

Kingston's novel reminds the reader that none of us is only the person our social group reflects back to us. Each of us is also the person our imagination conjures up: the hero riding forth in dreams of the day, the ghost-slayer battling in dreams of the night. Daoists like Zhuangzi who rode the winds knew much about the spirit of fancy. Healers who tapped pulses and drove off devils imagined a better balance for bodies and souls. Writing her way through the labyrinth to her self, Kingston put Chinese characters on American paper. Her fingers typed an IBM Selectric, but her mind reproduced images of tattered scrolls. Our character and our images imprint one another. Much more than what we eat, we are what we imagine. Because we can imagine more than our society assumes, we are always somewhat free.

Buddhist Social Influence. Buddhism downplayed social differences in another way. By teaching that the buddha-nature is present in all reality, it said that equality is more basic than social differentiation. The monastic *sangha* institutionalized this equality. It would be naive to think that background or wealth played no part in monks' evaluations of one another, but the *sangha* was governed by a monastic code that underplayed wealth and severely limited monks' possessions.

Furthermore, during many periods in Chinese history, the *sangha* was genuinely spiritual. That is, its actual raison d'être was religious growth. In such times, the only "aristocracy" was determined by spiritual insight. For instance, though Hui-neng, who became the sixth Chan patriarch, was born poor (and, according to legend, brought up illiterate), his spiritual gifts mattered far more. Because he was religiously apt, a reading of the Diamond Sutra opened his mind to the Buddha's light. After enlightenment, his peasant origins became insignificant.

The Buddhist *sangha* also improved the lot of women. It offered an alternative to early marriage and the strict confinement of the woman's family role. In the *sangha* a woman did not have full control of her life, but she did often have more peer support and female friendship than she could have in the outside world. In fact, Confucian traditionalists hated Buddhist nuns for their influence on other women. By telling women there were alternatives to wifely subjection, the nuns supposedly sowed seeds of discontent.[82] Besides the jealousy of their Confucian and Daoist rivals, then, and the sometimes warranted outrage at their extensive landholdings, the Buddhists suffered persecution because they offered attractive alternatives to traditional Chinese family and social structures. The government frequently forced monks and nuns into lay life during a time of purge to force them back into traditional social patterns.

Thus, although persecution was not the norm, Buddhists and other effective religionists often felt the controlling hands of the state. Formally, there was little independent religious authority. In times of peace, Buddhists and Daoists were left to go their own ways. When they perceived any threat, however, the rulers clamped down and made it clear that religion was a function of an integrated Chinese culture, not something outside the culture that could set itself up as the critic of culture. As the Daoist revolutionary sects showed, the rulers had good grounds for their fears.

As a result, Chinese religion was what C. K. Yang has called "diffused."[83] Stronger by far than any institutional achievements was a pervasive sense of the supernatural. In good part because it propped the state against the potential rebellion that Daoism and Buddhism housed, Confucianism became the state orthodoxy. Daoism and Buddhism, by contrast, were always somewhat heterodox.[84]

Among the common people, an important function of religion was to shore up received culture and authority. Apart from advanced positions in Daoist and Buddhist thought, religion did not liberate the individual. In this sense, Chinese religion broke neither the cosmological myth nor what we might call the social myth (conceiving of the political community as being divine). Both nature and the state (or the local duchy during the many periods of fragmentation) existed before the individual and predominated over him or her.

Consequently, China had little sense that the human mind makes its own reality—little enlightenment, in the European sense. Thus it remained closer to nature and more socially unified than later Western religious society did. The Chinese defined themselves by their land and their group. Happy to be the center of the earth, the Chinese Empire regarded all outsiders as barbarians and less than fully human. Millennia of living within a shared myth of nature and society had wrought so strong a cultural identity that this attitude was almost invincible. That was both Confucianism's triumph and its limitation.

Self

By our stress on the primacy of nature and society, we have indirectly suggested the Chinese view of the self. Nevertheless, the Chinese experimented with various conceptions of the self, just as they experimented with gunpowder, acupuncture, and pottery. As Donald Munro has shown,[85] axial Chinese thought, both Confucian and Daoist, wrestled with the possibility that human beings are essentially equal (at least male human beings). The effect of this belief on the hierarchical structure of Confucianism is complex, but the Chinese concepts of *ren* and *li* (goodness and propriety) indicate that the Chinese sensed that all people have something to share as a basis for mutual respect.

In the structure of society, then, the self had some right to acknowledgment. Despite one's subordination to the whole (or, in many cases, one's near slavery), the common person found in such an author as Mencius a champion of the self's essential goodness. Mencius counseled princes to take their people's welfare to heart; his counsel was clearly more than a pragmatic bit of advice about how to avoid rebellions.

Furthermore, the Confucians exercised considerable care on the self's education, at least for the middle and upper classes. Their major motivation seems to have been societal needs (as opposed to the self's intrinsic dignity), but by stressing character formation, the Confucians had to probe what the self's substance and dignity were. They decided, with considerable prodding from Confucius himself, that the paramount human faculty was the inner mind. If one could act from this inner mind with clarity and dispassion, one could act humanely and civilly. The core of the Confucian view of the self, therefore, was a certain rationalism. Confucianism did not stress speculative reason (that which gives rise to abstract theory), since Confucianism was not concerned with the human capacity to illumine or be illumined by the Logos of nature, but it did stress practical reason or prudence. Laying aside passion and prejudice (which required self-control), the good Confucian could hope with experience to discern the appropriate and harmonizing course of action.

Either through reflection on history or further rumination on the mind, the Confucians eventually linked practical reason with the ancients' *Dao*. It was clear from the myths handed down that the foremost ancestors were people of composed, effective good sense, which enhanced their subjects' common good and even prosperity. Because they were not venal or petty, the ancestors were able to lead by example—by radiating the power of *ren*.

On further reflection the Confucians confirmed that the zenith of human achievement (which Confucius himself later came to epitomize) was such inner-directed action. In other words, the ideal human spirit feared no outer laws or sanctions. It was autonomous—it delighted in the good for its own sake. Though Confucius and Mencius both longed for public office, a major reason that neither ever achieved it was that neither would compromise his standards. This

uncompromising integrity became a lesson to disciples for centuries. When a devout Confucian observed an inhumane ruler, he felt more pity than envy.

The Daoist Self. The Daoists, who paid greater attention to the relationship between human consciousness and the cosmic *Dao,* produced a more paradoxical view of the self. They went against the Confucian standards of sagehood. Their masters were either cryptic eccentrics such as Zhuangzi or magical "immortals" possessing paranormal powers. The eccentrics' suspicion of human reason developed into a strong attack on logic and Confucian prudence. Logically, the *Zhuangzi*'s chapter on seeing things as equal suggests that the philosophical Taoists found conventional language and morality both arbitrary and relative.[86] Standard terms in Confucian discourse such as *great* and *small, good* and *bad* (which were also used in the Chinese linguistic analysis contemporary with Zhuangzi) turned out to be wholly relative. In fact, the Daoists cast doubt on the entire realm of discursive reason, which plods along from premise to premise and often misses the whole. If one could argue either side of a proposition, as lawyers always have tended to do, one clearly was not in the realm of ultimate concern.

For the philosophical Daoists, the realm of ultimate concern pivoted on *Dao.* They attempted to reach that realm by meditation and *wu-wei.* Consequently, they individualized the self more than the Confucians did. The Confucians, of course, realized that the talents of people differ, including the talent to reach the still inner reason from which humane action emanates. But the Daoists went beyond reason itself, encouraging each person to write his or her own script. What was important was that one write to the tune of the *Dao.* What the specific story was, how one chose to enact *Dao*'s inspiration, was secondary.

One of Daoism's greatest influences on Buddhism shows in Chan's acceptance of this individualism. Placing little stock in doctrines or formulas, the Chan master determined enlightenment by the pupil's whole bearing. The flash of an eye, the slash of a sword—a single gesture could indicate an enlightened being. One could even "slay the Buddha"—throw off all traditional guidance—if one had drawn near to the goal. To the unenlightened majority, one's actions and life would be strange. Quite literally, one would be eccentric. But if the *Dao* or buddha-nature really became the self's treasure, such eccentricity was but the near side of freedom.

The religious Daoists saw the self as a mortal physical body. Therefore, by the several "hygienic" regimes mentioned, they tried to prolong physical life. As a result, religious Daoists experimented with yogic practices, many of them in the vein of Indian *kundalini* or Tibetan Tantrism, both of which viewed the body as a repository of energy centers.[87] Depending on the particular interest of a religious Daoist group, the self might focus on breath or semen or some other quintessence.

Furthermore, most Daoists regarded the body as a warehouse of tiny gods, each in charge of a particular bodily part. In yogic exercise the adept was to visualize the god in charge of the spleen or the heart, and so gain health or blessing there. By their quests for immortality (in the sense of continued physical existence), then, the religious Daoists simultaneously underscored mortality and suggested that humans can defeat death. They did not distinguish an immaterial part of the self as the best candidate for such survival, but they did probe the relations between contemplative ecstasy and nature's apparent immortality.[88]

Karma and Selflessness. Through Buddhism, China received a heavy dose of belief in karma. That was most effective in the popular Buddhist sects, among which Pure Land headed the list, but it entered the general religious stream, influencing even those who rarely participated in Buddhist rites. Karma, of course, meant that the self was immersed in a system of rewards and punishments. All its actions, good or bad, had their inevitable effects. Past lives pressed upon the present, and the present was but a prelude to a future life. In popular Buddhism, this doctrine encouraged a sort of bookkeeping. Sometimes quite formally, with ledgers and numbers, Buddhists tried to calculate their karmic situation and plan out a better destiny. More generally, the concept of karma prompted the belief that the self's present existence was a trial that would be evaluated at death. How heavily this sense of trial pressed on the average person is hard to say. Combined with the rather lurid popular pictures of the several hells awaiting the wicked, karma probably sparked its share of nightmares.

The philosophical and meditative Chinese Buddhist sects accepted the traditional doctrine of *anatman*. So, the Chinese thinkers who followed Madhyamika or Yogacara speculation agreed that emptiness or mind-only implied an effort to rout the illusion of a permanent personal identity. To grasp buddha-nature and join the dance of reality, the individual had to annihilate samsaric misconceptions about the substantiality of the self. The Chinese appear to have been more concrete than the Indians in such efforts. That is, where the Indians often reasoned over the self very closely, trying by dialectics to understand the illusion of selfhood, the Chinese tried to get the self to see reality's totality. Such seems to be the intent of pictures that Tiantai and Hua-yen masters drew, as well as the intent of the more radical techniques of Chan. Bodhidharma's "just sitting" and "wall gazing," for example, were exercises designed to make clear that only buddha-nature is real.

Overall, these various Chinese religious views of the self made for considerable confusion and complexity. Despite Buddhist philosophical influence, the average person through Chinese history apparently did not doubt the reality of his or her self. The educational and governmental establishments in most periods were shaped by the Confucian ideal of a sober, restrained, altruistic personality. One aimed at discipline and grace, at becoming a source of wisdom. The force that shaped the Confucian self was political in the sense that living together with family members and fellow citizens rather than in isolation was the norm. Only the few artistic and religious professionals seem to have broken this pattern. For them Daoist or Buddhist contemplative solitude stressed the mystery of the self insofar as the self was where the *Dao* or buddha-nature most directly manifested itself. According to Laozi, one would find *Dao* by shutting the "doors" (the senses) and going within.

The conceptions of the self that were presented in the three high traditions blurred when they entered the common culture. Most of the people came to Confucianism, Buddhism, or Daoism from its folk side. So the Confucian scholar became a sort of wonder worker, the Buddhist *bodhisattva* glamorized holiness, and the Daoist "immortal" represented victory over death. From the ancient spirit world ancestors and ghosts said that being a conscious self meant participating in a cosmos that was alive, a system of heavens and hells that impinged on the present.

Ultimate Reality

China was only holistically, diffusely, aware of sacred powers and ultimate reality. At most, certain high points of Buddhist and Daoist speculation, and to a lesser extent of Confucian speculation, indicated a monism—a single, impersonal principle considered the inmost reality of all beings. As we have seen, the first stirrings of religious consciousness probably apotheosized (deified) the clan founder, making him the "face" of overwatching Heaven. As nature became better understood, however, heaven became less personal, more the general symbol of the vast sky. Earth, in association with a maternal *Dao,* took on overtones of a Great Mother, but with less of the humanity and intimacy that other cultures developed.

For most Chinese throughout history, nature has been the effective divinity. In other words, nature and divinity have run together. The physical world itself was something sacred and mysterious. This world intimated something beyond itself that was grasped by those who saw nature with mystic clarity, but the majority at best sensed this something beyond only vaguely. To sense clearly the *Dao* that cannot be named, one must reject the adequacy of all things nameable. Realizing that water, air, fire, wood, earth, yang, yin, and so on, do not explain the totality of heaven and earth, the mind senses that the ultimate is of a different order. It is without the limitations that characterize all the primal elements. As such, it must dwell in obscurity, too full or great or bright for mere human intelligence. Philosophical Daoism and Buddhism sometimes intimated that line of thought.

A muted reference to ultimacy probably plays in Confucius' laconic references to heaven. For the most part, the Master refrained from speculating about heavenly things. Like Alexander Pope, he believed that "the proper study of man is man." But Confucius' reverence toward the sacrifice to heaven suggests that, had such a modern Western notion been available to him, he would not have explained the sacrifice as a humanistic means of social bonding. Rather, he probably saw a link between the ancients' *Dao* and the way of sacred nature, and so viewed the sacrifice as humanity's chance to align itself with the power that most mattered, the power behind all life and all things.

Confucius made heaven the ultimate sanction for his ethical program. He believed that those who pay full court to the stove have no recourse when they fail. The true judge of success and failure must be more stable than a human creation. Against the Daoist belief that heaven treats all creatures as straw dogs, Confucius believed that heaven is the great champion of *yi* (justice). We go well beyond Confucius himself if we work this commitment to heaven into a theology or a theodicy (a vindication of God's justice). Clearly, however, the Confucians justified their calls to virtue by appealing to suprahuman standards. Indeed, the depth of Confucius' analysis of what is necessary for a

Figure 13 *Lohan* (arhat), *Liaojin dynasty, 900–1200 C.E. Pottery with three-color glaze; 40 in. high. This figure, found in the hills south of Beijing, has his hands in the* dhyana mudra, *a posture signifying deep meditation. The individuality of the* arhat's *quest for personal salvation (in contrast to the* bodhisattva's *concern for all beings) leads to a quite distinct portrayal. The Nelson–Atkins Museum of Art, Kansas City, Missouri (Nelson Fund).*

full humanity makes his overall program an invitation to explore the sacredness of the mystery of human potential.

Buddhism, of course, addressed ultimacy more squarely. In the philosophical mainstream, nirvana, buddha-nature, Suchness, or emptiness held sway. This mainstream suggested that the ultimate is the interconnected whole. For the idealists, the accent was on the mentality of the ultimate. In their view, the many things that we perceive by sense are fraudulent because only spirit or mind finally makes something be. For the less idealistic schools, material things and ideas were equally fraudulent. To accept the apparent plurality of either physical nature or consciousness was the folly of an unenlightened mind. The idealists were less concerned with physical nature than the nonidealists. By calling all dharmas empty, the followers of Madhyamika went directly to the rather radical (and potentially worldly or incarnational) point of the wisdom-that-has-gone-beyond. By contrast, those who followed Yogacara idealism stayed apart from the physical world mentally.

In popular Buddhism, such as Pure Land, some divinities had quite precise features. In its popular religion, then, Chinese Buddhism offered an access to aspects of ultimate reality that Confucianism barely indicated. (Daoism is more complicated: The *Dao* was a mother, and religious sects made Laozi into a cosmic principle.) The cult of Confucius himself qualifies this judgment somewhat, but overall the Buddhists offered the most personal concepts of divinity.

The beliefs of philosophical and religious Daoists, of course, must be distinguished. As we have seen, the philosophical Daoists, following Zhuangzi and Laozi, fixed on the cosmic Way. Often they seem to have invested it with divine attributes. For the philosophers, *Dao* was the source, the ultimate power, the model, and the prime value of the world. Inspiration from it, communion with it, and direction by it were the ways to wisdom, wholeness, and fulfillment.

Nonetheless, despite intuitions in Laozi that *Dao* is beyond the physical world, Daoist philosophers tended to equate *Dao* with nature. The naturalistic symbolism they preferred suggests this, as does their unconcern with immortality or an afterlife. If *Dao* had been independent of nature, union with *Dao* should have generated thoughts about escaping the cycle of birth and death. In India, for instance, the *nirguna* (unmanifest) Brahman and the Buddhist ultimate led to doctrines of *moksha* and nirvana as human release. For Zhuangzi and Laozi, natural harmony in the present was all-important, and they paid little heed to future enjoyment of some otherworldly states. Consequently, the divinity of *Dao* was preeminently the undergirding and direction it gave cosmic nature.

Reaching back to prehistory, the religious Daoists conceived of a pantheon of divine forces, often giving them picturesque names and features. Furthermore, the goal of religious Daoist practices was to prolong life, and so religious Daoists ventured into alchemy and yoga, as well as voyages to the Lands of the Blessed (the Immortals). What they shared with their philosophical counterparts, however, was a characteristically Chinese concern with the body. Their ideal was not an extinction of suffering humanity in nirvana, not a release in *moksha,* but a consolidation of vital powers so as to resist death. Their divinities, consequently, were gods who could help this process, or "immortals" (who probably spanned the often narrow gap between saints and gods) who had successfully accomplished such a consolidation. In either case, they offered followers encouragement and models.

How did Chinese divinity appear in the popular amalgamation? Through ritualistic, emotional, and shamanic points of entry.[89] The prevailing popular mind, which was primarily interested in warding off evil fortune and attracting good, and the great importance of ancestor veneration, gave ultimate reality a rainbow of colors. Ceremonies at the family hearth reaffirmed the clan by acknowledging the reality of its ancestors. Ceremonies in the fields, for building a new dwelling or for curing someone seriously ill, brought people face to face with spooky forces of life, luck, and disease. Shamans and mediums were the key figures, contacting spirits and ancestral souls. Diviners gave advice and told fortunes. The average person gathered talismans and totems, but also Buddhist and Daoist saints. The educated people patronized Confucius, but even they were open to other sacred figures who offered help. To say the least, then, the Chinese religious mind was syncretistic, and the study of folk religion, as recent studies suggest,[90] has to be very comprehensive.

However, most characteristic of China is its commitment to physical nature. It shares this with Japan and with many ancient peoples, but China most directed its various intimations of divinity toward nature. The *Dao,* the Chinese buddha-nature, the field of spirits—these far outweighed personal qualities. The Chinese divinity was the arc of the sky, the pulse of the earth, the life force itself.

SUMMARY: THE CHINESE CENTER

The clan and the Way held life together for most Chinese. The clan was the defining social reality, the psychological milieu in which the individual found his or her identity. Somewhat parallel to the way that Indian caste positioned a person in Hindu society, the clan positioned a person in Chinese society. However, the Chinese clan had a more pronounced historical dimension. The ancestors that one venerated in the household rites formed a golden chain back to better times. For the people as a whole, the best of times were the ages when the fabled nobility that Confucius and Mencius venerated had walked the land and embodied virtue. The way that they had lived was the benchmark against which traditional China measured itself. Their grace and reverence in executing the liturgical rites, their sense of restraint and propriety, and their freedom from all venality defined what humaneness or full development could be.

The Way therefore was something objective. One only walked it confidently, unswervingly, if one embraced it from the heart, but its general import was as much natural and social as personal. It was the way of the cosmos as well as the way of the clan. It moved in the heavens and the depths as well as in the individual heart. And it was a way that produced balance, harmony, and prosperity. When the yang and the yin forces were both given their due, the Way shone forth splendidly. When the people followed the lead of a virtuous leader and themselves lived virtuously, the mandate of heaven manifestly was in good hands. In office, the Chinese tried to bureaucratize the Way. What stability persisted through their millennia of political upheavals was in good part due to the consistency of the Confucian civil service. Taking pride in their high culture, traditional Chinese accounted themselves the center of the world. The *Dao* that formed their ancient culture ruled everywhere, but theirs was the land that had been most blessed with eyes to see and ears to hear.

In people's retirement, Daoist and Buddhist insights gave both the clan and the Way their poetry and metaphysics. If one backed away from the bureaucratic mind, accepted the lure of Zhuangzi and Laozi, the Way took on sharper angles, more vivid hues. It remained remarkably realistic, determinedly focused upon the commonsensical order of things. But it showed intriguing wrinkles of humor, elusive bends of fillip and paradox. So Zhuangzi carries across the thousands of years, speaking playfully to any generation that has kept some wit.[91] So Laozi remains a quite relevant political study, challenging all our established views of power and virtue. How, in fact, does the suc-

cessful natural organism survive and prosper? What, in reality, are the evolutionary and ecological virtues? As a matter of experience, how lasting or thorough is the victory that does not conquer the enemy's heart? In the best of personal times, when one does hear the Way in the morning, what is the contentment for which one would willingly die?

These are the sorts of questions that make a culture profound, concerned with ultimate realities or religion. Without them, a people's rites and social arrangements lack any special distinction, are matters of instinct and pheromones as much as matters distinctively human. China was fortunate in having Buddhists and Daoists who kept these questions throbbing. Through their influence on art, philosophy, and social ethics, they made the Way properly empty. Emptying the Chinese mind of the excesses to which its Confucian practicality tended, Daoists and Buddhists gave this great people inner space. So Chinese landscape paintings can haunt the beholder as few other artworks. So a lonesome, allusive poetry let thousands of gentlemen give voice to their inmost feelings.

This lonely, allusive persona sits awkwardly atop the teeming world of Chinese politics and clan intrigues, yet it does seem to distinguish the Chinese center. Something stoic and clear-eyed keeps the Chinese world less tangled than the Indian, the Chinese atmosphere less steamy. Those pictures of snowy mountain fastnesses can exert undue influence, but most of Chinese wisdom seems astringent and disciplined. Thus the Chan clarity of gaze, control of the emotions, and focused wholeness seem of a piece with the scenes of mountain snow. Thus silence seems quintessentially Chinese, a direct "word" from the center.

There is much irony in this word, much well-tested humor. The Way that collects us, giving us our vision and our depth, turns out to be sportive and unpredictable. To the sober-sided it is quite regular, but the sober-sided are more mummified than enlightened. To the sage, each day is fresh, each particular fights generalization. The sage does not master life by formulas and bureaus. The sage does not master life at all. Mastery is really discipleship, docility and constant attention. When a docile, empty mind meets a fluid, allusive way, things fall apart. There is no center fixed or certain. There is only a center moving, always being re-created, ever arranging itself in new yet ancient patterns, like a kaleidoscope. The way that can be told is not the real way. The real way is compressed in a glance, hinted in a gesture, sounded in the pure tones of an emptied life.

Discussion Questions

1. Sketch the outline of axial Chinese religion in terms of *Dao*.

2. What are the positive aspects of Chinese ritual propriety *(li)*?

3. What are the negative aspects of *wu-wei*?

4. Why were the ancestors such a potent symbol in popular Chinese religion?

5. Explain some of the likely assumptions and dynamics of Chinese divination.

6. If you meditate on the practice of foot binding, how do you picture Chinese social arrangements?

7. Why did philosophical Daoism long exist alongside religious Daoism, and how can one reconcile their different views of immortality?

8. Describe some of the leading motifs of Chinese aesthetics.

9. What were some of the most important influences that Buddhism had on China?

10. Is the Confucian hierarchical view of reality viable in the modern era? Why?

11. What did Laozi learn from the valley and the female?

12. What sort of a divinity did Confucius become?

13. Why did Mao Zedong reject the Confucian classics?

14. Why was China so taken with geomancy?

15. How did the religion of Chinese merchants differ from the religion of Chinese peasants?

Key Terms

Confucian classics: Confucius himself drew on several sources that became classical expressions of the golden age that he used to ground and illustrate his teachings. These sources included the *Book of History (Shu Jing),* documents purporting to record the words and deeds of ancient leaders; the *Book of Songs (Shi Jing)* an anthology of lyrics from the early feudal states and the court of Zhou; the *Book of Changes (Yi Jing),* a manual for divination; the *Springs and Autumns (Chunqui),* the annals of the state of Lu; and the *Canons of Ritual and Protocol (Li Jing),* three works on *li* (protocol). In addition, the Confucians came to revere four works as canonical expressions of the wisdom that the Master himself had inspired: the *Analects (Lun Yu),* sayings and dialogues of Confucius; the *Great Learning (Da Xue),* a short study of how cultivating perfection can contribute to the ordering of society; the *Doctrine of the Mean (Zhung Yung),* a somewhat metaphysical treatment of how the moral person is at the center of the universe; and the *Book of Mencius (Meng Zi),* a collection of sayings and dialogues of the foremost exponent of Confucian thought. Both the *Great Learning* and *Doctrine of the Mean* are excerpts from part (the *Li Ji*) of the *Canons on Ritual and Protocol.* Collectively, these nine works constituted the literary corpus that the Confucian literati strove to master.

Dao ("dow"): a Chinese term for the cosmic or moral Way or Path. Daoism most directly focused on understanding the Way and gaining harmony with it, but Confucianism also was interested in the Way, meaning both the traditions of the wise men of yore and the patterns encoded in nature. The *Dao* is perhaps the closest equivalent in native Chinese religion to the Western notions of God, the Logos, and the Law of Nature. Laozi spoke of the Way that was known, but also of the *Dao* bound to be unknown. The movement of the *Dao* explained the movement of the ten thousand things making up creation, and the movement of the *Dao,* as the philosophical Daoists interpreted it, was a not-doing *(wu-wei).* The female, infant, and valley better exemplified the Way than the male, the adult, and the mountain. Water was a better exemplar than rock, the uncarved block better than the finished piece of sculpture.

feng-shui: Chinese geomancy; the art of locating favorable sites for buildings, graves, and other constructions. *Feng-shui* assumes a premodern worldview in which directions, astral influences, the winds, and the waters are considered to have (animistic) powers significant for human beings' well-being, both bodily and spiritual. In effect, it is a divination of the forces, auras, and spirits of the lay of a particular land, to assure people considering inhabiting that land the most favorable siting of themselves (their beings as well as their buildings) upon it.

folk religion: the beliefs and practices of the common people, in contrast to the views of the intelligentsia and religious officials. Folk religion, virtually by definition, is somewhat inarticulate and unreflective, but it may be no less rich or even sophisticated for that. It embraces the cult of the saints honored in a given religious tradition, the full round of paraliturgical devotions and religious practices, and the simple everyday acts of piety, prayers of petition, and other practices that get unlettered believers through the day. Some generations ago folk religion received rather short shrift from scholars, who deprecated it as untutored, but with the advent of anthropological investigations many students of religion have realized that peasant ways often house amazingly persistent and profound views of both the particular religious tradition in which they occur and the basic problematic of human existence that religious mythology regularly has kept lively, persuasive, and beguiling.

li: the Confucian term for propriety, ritual, protocol, etiquette. *Li* was the virtue that ideally presided over social interactions, the gentleman's participation in public life and external affairs. It required knowledge of the traditional ceremonies and mores, discipline, and grace. Probably the origins of *li* lay in ancient ideas about ritual, especially that surrounding the king. If such ritual were properly performed, it was thought bound, or at least very likely, to bring such good effects as bountiful harvests and social rest. *Li* tended to encourage politeness and social sensitivity, including a keen awareness of the different social ranks. It supported a somewhat formal persona, with considerable care given to preserving dignity, appearance, and face. At its best, when fully animated by *ren,* it suggested that all public living ought to be artful and sacramental.

ren: the primary Confucian virtue of humaneness. *Ren* signifies human nature as it ought to be, full of fellow-feeling or even love. It is what makes social life attractive, what long study and practice ought to develop. Confucians have seen ritual, filial piety, and the other important virtues (powers of the mature character) as expressions of *ren* or ways to build up *ren.* Insofar as *ren* has run low, Confucianism has been liable to legalism, formalism, pedantry. *Ren* therefore has been the spirit without which much of the Confucian teaching would have been empty letters. The Mas-

ter himself probably reached the ideal measure of *ren* when, at seventy, what the Way (the call to live humanely) required and what his own heart desired were one.

reverence for ancestors: The traditional Chinese did not worship their ancestors, but they did reverence them greatly. Just as young people were to reverence their elders (who had not only given the young people existence but had lived long enough to be wise), so the present generation was to reverence its forebears. The previous generations had accomplished the essential task of handing on life and keeping humanity in existence. Moreover, in many periods of Chinese history the past seemed a more ideal time than the present, so one's ancestors were assumed to have been more fully human. Something sacred attached to the ties between the present generation and the past. The obligation of the present generation to keep its ancestors in mind, to offer them material gifts in token of a spiritual gratitude and remembrance, was so strong that it was a major reason for having children. People who did not procreate failed to supply a crucial link in the chain of remembrance. Certainly, this Chinese attitude expresses close ties with nature and nature's mysteries of death and birth. Certainly, it also bespeaks a profound appreciation of how much the present depends upon the past—of how formative tradition has to be. But it also represents a deliberate choice, best articulated by the Confucians, to keep alive a sense of history. Those who ignored the past, in the specific form of their ancestors, would be bound to live truncated lives. They would not appreciate the mysterious depths out of which their own flesh, to say nothing of their culture, had arisen. It was not superstition but a profound humanism that moved the best Confucians to place veneration of elders and ancestors at the center of Chinese social life. They were convinced that those who contemplated the wonders of family history and lineage would be little inclined to deface their own lives—to shame their ancestors and call into question the worth of their having passed human existence along to subsequent generations.

wu-wei: Daoist not-doing or active-inaction. *Wu-wei* epitomizes how the philosophical Daoists thought the Way acted. It shone in the water that wore away rock, the cook who realized the best way to prepare fish was to stir them as little as possible. The infant who wrapped the adult household around its finger, the ruler who got others to do his will by silent example or subtle persuasion—both were good imitators of the *Dao*. Opposed to *wu-wei* was *ba* (force). *Ba* might win temporary victories, but in the long run it was bound to bring violent reactions and so do more harm than good. Laozi and Zhuangzi urged the Chinese to return to simpler days, when there were fewer laws, fewer criminals, less education, less sophistication, and more simple vigor.

yang: the Chinese principle of nature that is positive, light, dry, and male. Yin-yang theory was a dualism that conceived of natural processes as shaped by the relative proportions of male and female principles each contained. Yang usually was considered the positive force and yin the negative. These judgments should not be taken in a moral sense, but rather like the plus and minus poles of a battery. Each was equally necessary for life and the ongoing circuits of the cosmos.

yin: the Chinese principle of nature that is negative, dark, wet, and female. In diet, ritual paraphernalia, and the like, yin had to be coordinated with yang, if one were to get health and good fortune. Yin-yang theory correlated with astrology, geomancy, exorcism, and natural philosophy. It had ties with theories of divination and functioned as a protoscience. The Chinese search for harmony and to hold opposites in creative tension meant that neither yin nor yang ought ever achieve a definite triumph. Both were to be accepted and cultivated, although patriarchal China preferred the yang side.

CHAPTER 4

JAPANESE RELIGION

Torii: Gate to Shinto shrines

HISTORY

The Ancient-Formative Period

According to ethnologists, the people we now call the Japanese perhaps are a mixture of an indigenous people (the Ainu) and peoples from the Asian mainland and the southern islands. This mixture is one clue to the composite character of Japanese religion as well as to the general tolerance that has historically marked Japanese culture. The native religion goes back to the Japanese prehistoric period, which lasted until the early centuries of the Common Era. Clay figurines that archeologists have excavated from this earliest Jomon period indicate a special concern with fertility.[1] As the hunting and gathering culture of the earliest period gave way to agriculture and village settlement, religious practices came to focus on agricultural festivals, revering the dead, and honoring the leaders of the ruling clans. According to the primitive mythology, which existed long before the written versions that date from the eighth century, such leaders were descendants of the deities—once again a version of sacred kingship.

However, the mythology and cult surrounding the ruling family were but part of the earliest Japanese religion. Research suggests that in the villages outside the leading families' influence, people probably conceived of a world with three layers. The middle is the realm of humans, where we have a measure of control, but the realms above and below, which spirit beings control, are far larger. The kami dwell in the high plain of heaven and are the objects of cultic worship; the spirits of the dead live below, condemned to a filthy region called Yomi.[2] (In some versions, the dead go to a land beyond the sea.) Apparently Yomi was especially important for the aristocrats' cult, which suggests not only a connection between folk and imperial religion but also indicates why Shinto came to stress ritual purification, especially from polluting contacts with the dead.

The Kami. The **kami** represented the sacred power involved in the principal concerns of prehistoric Japanese religion (kingship, burial of the dead, and ritual purification).[3] They were rather shadowy figures or spiritual forces who were wiser and more powerful than humans. From time to time, kami would descend to earth, especially if a human called them down and helped them assume a shape (in their own world the kami were shapeless). They were called down by means of *yorishiro*—tall, thin objects that attracted the kami. Pine trees and elongated rocks were typical *yori-*

	SHINTO	BUDDHISM
Main Source	Indigenous Japanese culture	Chinese schools
Main Ideas	Holiness of nature	Emptiness
	Importance of purity and beauty	Meditation
	Integrity of Japanese people (as a whole and in clans)	Monasticism
		Significance of death
Influence	Nationalistic ideology	Funerals
	National mythology	Discipline
	Aesthetics	Philosophy
	Marriage ceremony	Meditation
	Folk arts	Devotional faith

shiro, and they suggest that the kami had phallic connotations. To a lesser extent, rocks of female shape also attracted the kami, and relics from the great tombs of the third and fourth centuries—a profusion of mirrors, swords, and curved jewels—suggest that these artifacts also drew the kami. (Such objects became part of the imperial regalia as well as the special objects of veneration in shrines.) There were also kami on earth, and revered ancestors who assumed a status like that of kami, so not all kami came from heaven.

Because the kami held key information about human destiny, it was important to call them down into human consciousness. That occurred through the kami's possession of shamans or mediums. Most of the early shamans *(miko)* were women, and they functioned in both the aristocratic and the popular cults. Ichiro Hori has shown that female shamans persisted throughout Japanese history.[4] The *miko* were quite important to society. They tended to band together and travel a circuit of villages, primarily to act as mediums for contact with the dead but also to serve as diviners and oracles. They also ministered to spiritual and physical ills, which popular culture largely attributed to malign spirits. As a result, the *miko* developed both a poetic and a pharmacological lore. In composing songs and dances to accompany their ministrations, they contributed a great deal to the formation of traditional Japanese dance, theater, balladry, and puppetry.

Essentially, the kami were the sacral forces of nature and impressive aspects of social life. They impressed the Japanese ancient mind, as they impressed the ancient mind elsewhere, by their striking power. Sensitive individuals could contact them, but the kami remained rather wild and unpredictable. Later, Shinto shrines stressed natural groves of tall trees and founders of religious cults were often possessed by spirits. As the early mythology shows, however, the kami remained in charge.

As the eighth-century chronicles, the *Kojiki* and *Nihon-shoki,* have preserved it, Japanese mythology adapted to Chinese influences early on. For example, redactors regularly changed the Japanese sacred number 8 to the Chinese sacred number 9,[5] and they were influenced by the Chinese cosmogonic myths. The result was a creation account in which the world began as a fusion of heaven and earth in an unformed, egg-shaped mass that contained all the forces of life. Gradually the purer parts separated and ascended to heaven, while the grosser portions descended and became the earth.

Shinto Mythology. Chinese influence disappears when the chronicles come to the myths of the kami's origin and to the related question of how the Japanese islands came to be. The first kami god was a lump that formed between heaven and earth; he established the first land. Six generations later, the divine creator couple, Izanagi and Izanami, arose by spontaneous generation. They married and by sexual union produced the many kami, including the Japanese islands.

For instance, heaven commanded Izanagi and Izanami to solidify the earth, which hitherto had been only a mass of brine. Standing on a bridge between heaven and the briny mass, they lowered a jeweled spear and churned the brine. When they lifted the spear, drops fell, solidified, and became the first island. The couple descended to this island, erected a heavenly pillar (the typical shamanistic connector to heaven), and proceeded to procreate. The account of their interaction is both amusing and revealing:

> Now the male deity turning by the left, and the female deity by the right, they went around the pillar of the land separately. When they met together on one side, the female deity spoke first and said: "How delightful! I have met with a lovely youth." The male deity was displeased, and said: "I am a man, and by right should have spoken first. How is it that on the contrary thou, a woman, should have been the first to speak? This was unlucky. Let us go round again." Upon this the two deities went back, and having met anew, this time the male deity spoke first, and said: "How delightful! I have met a lovely maiden."[6]

This account influences the Shinto wedding ceremony to this day, tabooing the bride from speaking first (under pain of perhaps having a deformed child).

In tortuous logic, the myth describes the fate of the first two. Izanami died giving birth to fire, and Izanagi followed her to the underworld. Izanagi then produced many deities in an effort to purify himself of the pollution of the underworld. By washing his left eye he produced the sun goddess **Amaterasu,** and by washing his right eye he produced the moon god. When he washed his nose he produced the wind god Susanoo. In this story of descent to the underworld and divine creation, scholars see an expression of the aboriginal Japanese rites of purification and fears of death. The sun goddess, who became the supreme being of the Yamato clan, a powerful Japanese family, and the focus of the clan's cultic center at Ise, presided over the land of fertility and life. Opposing her was the domain of darkness and death. Rituals were performed to keep darkness and death from afflicting sunny fertility—harvests, human procreation, and so on. As Izanagi purified himself of death by plunging into the sea, the Japanese throughout their history have used salt as a prophylactic. People still scatter it around the house after a funeral, place it at the edge of a well, set a little cake of it by a door jamb, and even scatter it before the bulging sumo wrestler as he advances toward his opponent.[7]

In subsequent myths, Amaterasu and Susanoo have numerous adventures arising from the antagonism between the life-giving sun and the withering wind. These figures also demonstrate the Trickster and noble sides of the divinity found in nature. Susanoo, the Trickster, committed "heavenly offenses" that later became a focus of ritual purification: He broke the irrigation channels for the imperial rice field that Amaterasu had set up; he flayed a piebald colt and flung it into the imperial hall; and, worst of all, he excreted on the goddess's imperial throne. Unaware, she "went straight there and took her seat. Accordingly, the Sun Goddess drew herself up and was sickened."[8] These offenses reflect practical problems of an agricultural society (respecting others' fields), cultic problems (a sacrificial colt was probably supposed to be of a single color and not be flayed), and speculation on the tension between divine forces of nature.

From these and other materials in the earliest chronicles, it is clear that the ancient-formative period of Japanese history centered on natural forces, some of which were anthropomorphized. In the background were the kami, whom we may consider as foci of divine power. Anything striking or powerful could be a kami. To relate themselves to the natural world, the early Japanese told stories of their love for their beautiful islands (worthy of being the center of creation) and of the divine descent of their rulers. The fact that Amaterasu is a sun goddess suggests an early matriarchy, as does the fact that kingship on the Chinese model of a rule possessing the mandate of heaven (rather than by heredity) only came with the Taika reforms of 645 C.E. Shinto maintained the divinity of the emperor until the mid-twentieth century, when the victorious Western Allies forced the emperor to renounce his claims.

Buddhism

Buddhism infiltrated Japan by way of Korea during the second half of the sixth century C.E. It first appealed to members of the royal court as a possible source of blessing and good fortune. Also, it carried overtones of Chinese culture, which had great prestige. The Japanese rulers, in the midst of trying to solidify their country, thought of the new religion as a possible means, along with Confucian ethics, for unifying so-cial life. So, during the seventh century, emperors built shrines and monasteries as part of the state ap-paratus. In the eighth century, when the capital was at Nara, the Hua-yen school (called Kegon in Japan) es-tablished itself and began to exert great influence. The government ideologues expediently equated the em-peror with the Hua-yen Buddha Vairocana, and they made the Hua-yen realm of "dharmas not impeding one another"[9] a model for Japanese society. Kegon has survived in Japan to the present day and now has about 500 clergy and 125 temples.

The Medieval-Elaborative Period

Most commentators consider the move of the capital from Nara to Kyoto in 794 a pivotal event. Indeed, the Heian era (794–1185), when Mount Hiei in Kyoto was home to as many as 30,000 monks,[10] was a golden age whose memorials may still be found in Kyoto. Politi-cally, Japan passed from a centralized bureaucracy to feudalism. While the imperial court still held nominal power, in fact a few aristocrats, especially those from the Fujiwara clan, were responsible for the main polit-ical initiatives. With the loosening of centralized au-thority, Buddhists were freer to innovate, although they had to keep good relations with the leading clans.

The first decades of the Heian era saw the rise of two new schools of Japanese Buddhism, Tendai and Shingon. Dengyo Daishi (767–822), the founder of Tendai, went to China to learn about the latest forms of Buddhist doctrine and practice. Upon returning to Japan, he established a new monastic foundation on Mount Hiei. The school that Dengyo Daishi founded derived from the Chinese Dien dai sect. Dien dai taught a quite syncretistic outlook, laying special importance on the Lotus Sutra. It was especially interested in joining philosophical speculation to meditation. Dengyo Daishi broadened the syncretistic outlook by adding moral discipline and ritual to the program he wanted his monks to follow. He also gave Tendai a nationalistic aspect, believing that Buddhist practice would help protect the Japanese nation. The result was a well-rounded school in which just about any traditional Buddhist interest could be pursued. Dengyo Daishi struggled with the government to gain recognition for his group, but after his death his fol-lowers got a full go-ahead and could ordain monks. It is difficult to overemphasize the importance of the establishment of Tendai on Mount Hiei, because from

its ranks in the Kamakura era (1185–1333) came the leaders of the Pure Land, Zen, and Nichiren sects.

Shingon was founded by the monk Kobo Daishi (774–835), who, like Dengyo Daishi, went to China to find fresh inspiration. The term *Shingon* derived from the Chinese term for *mantra,* and the school that Kobo Daishi established in Japan amounted to a branch of Buddhist tantra. Through elaborate rituals, Shingon expressed deep metaphysical notions thought capable of achieving through cult a great, magical power. Kobo Daishi was a talented writer, so he was able to furnish Japan a full manual on esoteric Buddhism. Through his influence, mantras, mandalas, and *mudras* (ritual gestures) became influential religious vehicles. As well, they made a great impact on Japanese iconogra-phy and fine arts.

Both Tendai and Shingon were open to outside influences, so during the Heian period Shinto and Buddhism came into closer contact than previously had been the rule. For instance, there arose numerous *jinguji* (shrine-temples), where Buddhist rituals took place within the precincts of a Shinto shrine. Relat-edly, the idea arose that the kami were manifestations of the Buddhist *bodhisattvas*. Until the beginning of the Meiji era (1868), when there was an official reform aimed at cleansing Shinto, Tendai and Shingon fostered such a syncretism between Shinto and Buddhism.

Last, we should note that during the Heian era there arose the conviction that Buddhism was bound to devolve through several ages (on the order of the Indian kalpas), and that the present age was the low-est—a time when religious practice was especially dif-ficult. This eventually laid the foundation for the rise of various savior figures during the Kamakura era—for example, Amida Buddha, the merciful figure who presided in the Western Paradise so eagerly pursued by the Pure Land sects.[11]

Kamakura Buddhism.[12] In many scholars' opinion, the rise of the Pure Land, Nichiren, and Zen Buddhist sects during the Kamakura dynasty (1185–1333) pro-duced one of Japan's most distinctive religious achievements. Pure Land Buddhism, which focused on Amida, the *bodhisattva* of light, became the most in-fluential form of devotional Buddhism. It was popular-ized by evangelists such as Ippen (1239–1289), who encouraged songs and dances in honor of Amida. Ippen taught that devotion to Amida and the holy realm where Amida presided was "the timely teaching"

Figure 14 *Amida Buddha, late Heian to Kamakura dynasty, twelfth–thirteenth century. Gilded wood; 9 ft., 2 in. high. Amida Buddha, who presides over the Western Paradise, is shown here in a posture of deep meditation. The Nelson–Atkins Museum of Art, Kansas City, Missouri (Nelson Fund).*

suitable for a degenerate age. By practicing the *nembutsu* or recitation of "homage to Amida Buddha," followers could gain great merit or even full salvation (entry to the Pure Land). This prescription was simple, practicable, and available to all. It did not require deep philosophy or meditation, simply faith. The laity found Ippen's message very appealing.

As one of Ippen's devotional works makes clear, he encouraged followers of Pure Land with a steady stream of moralistic advice. Verse after verse, the work tells devotees to adore the Buddha, not ignore the Buddha's virtue, revere the three jewels, not forget the power of faith, devoutly practice the *nembutsu*, forget other religious practices, trust the law of love, not denounce the creeds of other people, promote a sense of equality, and avoid discriminatory feelings. They

were to awaken a sense of compassion, be mindful of the sufferings of other people, cultivate amiability, not display an angry countenance, preserve a humble manner, and not arouse a spirit of arrogance. It is as though Ippen found all the traits of a good character to flow from faith in Amida. Were the faithful to yearn for the bliss of the Pure Land and not forget the tortures of hell, they would lead wonderfully meritorious lives.

Honen (1133–1212) was more insistent on the singularity of the *nembutsu,* in effect separating Pure Land Buddhism from other sects and making the *nembutsu* the be-all and end-all of the Middle Way. Honen personally suffered persecution for his position and for his success in winning converts. In a letter written to the wife of the ex-regent Tsukinowa, Honen described the essentials that a convert to Pure Land would have to embrace. The gist of his exposition was that the *nembutsu* was the best way to rebirth in the Pure Land, because it was the discipline described in Amida's own vow to become a *bodhisattva* and open salvation to all creatures. Indeed, the earthly Buddha Sakyamuni entrusted the *nembutsu* to his disciple Ananda, that Ananda might make it Sakyamuni's main bequest to posterity. Finally, all the buddhas of the six quarters of the world endorsed the *nembutsu.* So while other religious practices, such as meditations or ritual ceremonies, had considerable value, only the *nembutsu* had the highest stamp of authority. What did it matter that some critics claimed the *nembutsu* was too easy, fit only for simpletons? Amida and Sakyamuni had endorsed it; would one rather stand with earthly critics or heavenly masters?

Shinran (1173–1262), Honen's most successful disciple, came to feel that the successful propagation of the *nembutsu* depended on the clergy's closer identification with the laity. He therefore urged breaking with the tradition of clerical celibacy and with the permission of Honen he himself took a wife. So strong was his conviction that salvation depends purely on the grace of Amida that he rejected practices such as monastic vows and disciplines as possible impediments to genuine faith. Whereas some conservative Pure Land preachers urged a continuous recitation of the *nembutsu,* Shinran thought that a single invocation of Amida Buddha, if filled with loving faith, would suffice for salvation. Shinran's hymns ring with this loving faith: Amida endlessly sends forth his pure, joyous, wise, universal light. It is brighter than the sun and the moon, illumining numberless worlds.

Sakyamuni came into the world only to reveal Amida's vow to help human beings and the primacy of faith in Amida's grace. By faith even the worst of sinners will come to Amida's mercy, as surely as all mountain water finally comes to the ocean. Eventually, Amida's faith in the disciple will make things right.

Pure Land has the effect of providing Japan a very appealing form of Buddhist devotionalism. The mercy of Amida rang true to the Japanese tendency to seek an ultimate reality who shows signs of maternal kindness. Nichiren (1222–1282) agreed with the Pure Land Buddhists that simple devotional forms like the *nembutsu* were desirable, but he found their stress on Amida unwarranted. For Nichiren the be-all and end-all of Buddhist faith was the Lotus Sutra. He considered this scripture the final teaching of Sakyamuni, in which his three bodies (historical, doctrinal, and blissful) came together in a marvelous unity. Other schools had overlooked one or more of these three aspects, slighting either the historical life of the Buddha, his existence as the dharma giving all reality its true form, or his existence as the perfection of salvation (the center of the abode of the blessed). Devotion to the Lotus Sutra assured that a balance would be restored. Thus Nichiren urged the practice of chanting homage to the Lotus Sutra. In rather uncompassionate style, he called Amida Buddhism a hell and Zen a devil. Today there are many subsects of Nichiren Buddhism that together make this school second only to Pure Land in popularity.

Zen. Two of the great pioneers who launched Chan on its illustrious career in Kamakura Japan, were Eisai (1141–1215) and Dogen (1200–53). Eisai studied Chan in China and then established himself in Kamakura, the new center of Japanese political power. His teaching won special favor among the hardy warlords who were coming to dominate Japan, and from his time Zen and the samurai (warrior) code had close bonds. For Eisai, mind was greater even than heaven. Buddhism, which concentrated on the mind, had known great success in India and China. Among the different Buddhist schools, the one founded by Bodhidharma especially stressed mastering the mind. From Bodhidharma's missionary ventures in China, Zen had made its way to Korea and Japan. Now it was time for Japan to capitalize on Zen's great potential.

By studying Zen, one could find the key to all forms of Buddhism. By practicing Zen, one could bring one's life to fulfillment in enlightenment. To outer appearances, Zen favored discipline over doctrine. Inwardly, however, it brought the highest wisdom, that of enlightenment itself. Eisai was able to convince some of the Hojo regents and Kamakura shoguns of this message and make them patrons of Zen, so he planted Zen solidly in Japan.

If Eisai proved to be a good politician, able to adapt to the new Kamakura times and to benefit from them, Dogen proved to be the sort of rugged, uncompromising character Zen needed to deepen its Japanese roots and gain spiritual independence. After studying at various Japanese Buddhist centers without satisfaction, he met Eisai and resolved to follow in his footsteps and visit China. After some frustration in China, Dogen finally gained enlightenment when he heard a Zen master speak of "dropping both mind and spirit" (dropping dualism). Returning to Japan, he resisted the official pressures to mingle various forms of Buddhism and would only teach Zen. Nonetheless, within Zen circles Dogen was quite flexible, teaching, for example, that study of the Buddhist scriptures (scholarship) was not incompatible with a person-to-person transmission of the truth (the guru tradition).

Within Zen circles, Dogen also distinguished himself for his worries about the use of koans. The Rinzai school of Chan that Eisai had introduced to Japan stressed the use of these enigmatic sayings as a great help to sudden enlightenment. In Dogen's opinion, the Chinese Soto school was more balanced and less self-assertive. He therefore strove to establish Soto in Japan, teaching a Zen that did not concentrate wholly on the mind but rather on the total personality. This led him to a practice of simple meditation *(zazen)* that ideally proceeded without any thought of attaining enlightenment and without any specific problem in mind. Disciplining the body as well as the mind, Dogen aimed at a gradual, lifelong process of realization.

In some of his "conversations," Dogen movingly expressed his great faith in the power of Zen Buddhism. Quoting Eisai, he spoke of a monk's food and clothing as gifts from heaven. The teacher is but an intermediary between the pupil and heaven. Heaven gives each of us what we need for our allotted life span, and we should not make a fuss over these things. The student should direct his gratitude to heaven, much more than to his master, opening himself to all of heaven's gifts. The greatest of heaven's gifts is truth, and it is the good fortune of monks to be able to pursue truth full time. The difficulties monks or any of us face in securing life's practical necessities should not obscure this central point. Such difficulties should merely make us serious, willing to sacrifice for being able to pursue the truth. If monks lived utterly leisurely lives under full patronage, they likely would grow lazy and selfish. If, on the contrary, they live in poverty, begging for their food or working the land, they likely will grow hardy in spirit.

Dogen's compassion was equal to his faith, for he also liked to tell his disciples the story of Eisai's decision to give some copper to a destitute man who had come to the monastery begging help for his wife and children. The copper had been destined to make a halo for a statue of the Buddha. When some of Eisai's monks complained that he had forgotten this lofty designation for the copper, Eisai agreed that ideally the copper would have gone into a halo for the Buddha's statue. But the Buddha's own example of spending himself for the sake of needy human beings had urged Eisai to be generous, sacrificing some of the monastery's goods for the lives of fellow human beings.

Both Pure Land and Zen made their great impressions on Japanese culture largely in terms of the goodness they encouraged. From its deep faith in the goodness of Amida Buddha, Pure Land taught the Japanese people Shinran's concern for sinners, outcasts, men and women tending to doubt their own worth. From its deep experiences of self-realization, Zen matured a gratitude for all of creation that easily became a great compassion for all creatures suffering pain. Situating themselves within the common Buddhist tradition, the Kamakura schools suggested that faith and insight, devotion and practical charity, are not antagonistic but complementary. If one goes deeply enough into faith, one reaches a gratitude that is almost identical with the gratitude that rushes forth in enlightenment. If one goes deeply enough into meditational insight, one reaches a gratitude that is almost identical with the wholehearted faith that Amida Buddha is utterly trustworthy and good. The legacy of the Kamakura schools, finally, was their depth. Shinran and Dogen were such heroes of the spiritual life that all subsequent Japanese aspirants to sanctity or wisdom saw in them clear models of the way.

Francis Cook has summarized the overall innovations that these Japanese masters introduced into Buddhism.[13] First, the Japanese tended not to adhere to traditional codes of conduct, whether for laity *(sila)* or for monks (Vinaya). Eventually, priests were able to marry, eating meat and drinking alcoholic beverages were allowed, and monks could have more than a spare robe. Second, Japanese Buddhism tended to move religious activity from the temple to the home. As a result, emphasis was shifted to the laity, and monks or priests were relegated to the care of temples and the performance of ceremonies (especially funerals). Caring for temples frequently came to be a family affair, as fathers passed a priesthood on to their sons.

Third, during the Kamakura period several sects promulgated the notion that one particular practice summarized Buddhism. In that they were to a degree reacting against the syncretism of the Shingon and Tendai sects. As we have seen, Honen made chanting Amida's name *(nembutsu)* the only way to be reborn in the Pure Land. Dogen thought that meditative sitting summarized everything essential. Nichiren, finally, insisted that chanting "homage to the Sutra of the Lotus of the True Law" was the way to identify with the Buddha.

Shinto. During the Kamakura period, Buddhism sometimes eclipsed Shinto, but the native tradition always lay ready to reassert itself. Whenever there was a stimulus to depreciate foreign influences and exalt native ones, Shinto quickly bounced back. Also, Shinto only defined itself in the seventh century, when Buddhism, Confucianism, and Daoism started to predominate. In defining itself, Shinto picked up something from Buddhist philosophy, Confucian ethics, and Daoist naturalism. The result was a nature-oriented worship with special emphasis on averting pollution. Furthermore, Shinto domesticated Buddhism as a religion of *kami-bodhisattvas,* and it modified Confucian social thought to include the emperor's divine right.

Earhart defines the medieval-elaborative period of Japanese history as the years 794 through 1600.[14] This stretches from the Heian era, when the court at Kyoto had a glorious culture, through the Kamakura and Muromachi eras, and ends with the fall of the Momoyama era. While Japan worked its changes on Buddhism, Shinto was liberally borrowing from the foreign traditions. Since it represented the oldest native traditions, the result was a great enrichment, or at least a great complication, of what constituted Shinto. From Buddhism, as noted, Shintoists developed the notion that the kami were traces of the original substances of particular buddhas and *bodhisattvas.* As a result, Buddhist deities were enshrined by Shintoists (and kami by Buddhists). So thoroughly did Buddhism and Shinto combine that Dengyo Daishi and Kobo Daishi, the founders of Tendai and Shingon, thought it natural to erect shrines to honor the kami of the mountains of their monastic retreats.

Figure 15 Torii *(sacred gateway) to National Shrine at Ise. The* torii *separates the sacred space of the shrine grounds from the profane space outside. Ise is the most venerable Shinto shrine, distinctive for the rough, unadorned character of its buildings. Photo by J. T. Carmody.*

From Shingon, Shintoists absorbed certain esoteric practices, such as using mandalas to represent the basic dualities of mind-matter, male-female, and dynamic-static.[15] Because of such dualism, people began to call Shinto "Ryobu," which means "two parts" or "dual." In one of its most dramatic actions, dualistic Shinto gave the Ise shrine an inner and an outer precinct to make two mandalas that would represent the two sides of Amaterasu. She was the sun goddess of the ancient traditions, but she was also Vairocana, the shining Buddha of Heaven.

Later in the medieval period, a number of Shinto scholars took issue with syncretism.[16] Some of them just wanted to upset the evenhandedness that had developed, so that the kami would predominate over the *bodhisattvas* or so that Amaterasu would predominate over Vairocana. Others wanted to rid Shinto of its accretions and return it to its original form. The most

important of these medieval Shinto reformers were Kitabatake and Yoshida, who worked in the fourteenth and fifteenth centuries. They drew from writings of Ise priests, who wanted to give Shinto a scripture comparable to that of the Buddhists. Another step in the consolidation of Shinto's position was the organizing of its shrines, which began in the tenth century and continued through to the twentieth. The resulting network provided every clan and village with a shrine to represent its ties with the kami.

Christianity. In the mid-sixteenth century Christianity came to Japan in the person of the charismatic Jesuit missionary Francis Xavier. It flourished for about a century, until the Tokugawa rulers first proscribed it and then bitterly persecuted it. The first Western missionaries made a great impact because Japan was used to religions of salvation. Pure Land

Buddhism, for instance, was then popular among the common people. By impressing the local warrior rulers (often by holding out prospects of trade with the West), the Christians gained the right to missionize much of Japan and made some lasting converts. Western artifacts fascinated the Japanese as well, and for a while things Western were the vogue.

However, before the missionaries could completely adapt Christianity to Japanese ways, the shoguns became suspicious that the missionaries had political and economic designs. The shogun Ieyasu (1542–1616) killed many who had converted to Christianity, and after his death Christianity's brief chapter in Japanese history came to a bloody close. Shusaku Endo's novel about the Christians' persecution, *Silence,*[17] caused a stir in the contemporary Japanese Christian community because of its vivid description of the trials (in faith as well as body) that the missionaries underwent.

Summary. At the end of the medieval period of elaboration (around 1600), then, five traditions were interacting. Buddhism brought Japan a profound philosophy and system of meditation that stressed the flux of human experience, the foundation of being, and death. In return, it was revamped to suit Japanese tastes and the interests of the diverse social classes: rulers for rituals, warriors for discipline, common people for devotional love and hope. Confucianism furnished a rationale for the state bureaucracy and for social relationships. It stressed formality and inner control, which especially suited merchants and government officials, and one can see its imprint in the Bushido Code, which prevailed during the Tokugawa period.[18] Daoism most influenced folk religion, while, as we have seen, Shinto developed a rationale for the kami and a strong shrine system. Christianity came to represent foreign intrusion, but since it converted perhaps 500,000 Japanese, it also satisfied a hunger for other ways to salvation. Probably the average person mixed elements from these traditions with folk beliefs to fashion a family-centered religion that would harmonize human beings with the forces—kami, *bodhisattvas,* and evil spirits—that presided over good fortune and bad.

The Modern-Reformative Period

During the Tokugawa shogunate (military dictatorship), which lasted from 1600 to 1867, Japan experienced peace and stability. The Tokugawa rulers expelled the Christian missionaries and severely limited contacts with the West. The biggest shift in the social structure was the rise of the merchant class, which went hand in hand with the growth of cities.

Regarding religion, the Tokugawa shoguns made sure that all traditions served the state's goals of stability. In the beginning of the seventeenth century those goals had popular support because the preceding dynasties had allowed great civil strife. Buddhists had to submit to being an arm of the state. Neo-Confucianism eclipsed Buddhism in state influence, perhaps because it was less likely to stir thoughts of independence or individualism. Shinto suffered some decline in popular influence but retained a base in folk religion. As well, Shinto generated a clearer rationale for separating from Buddhism.

Early during the Tokugawa period there arose a movement called *Kokugaku* ("National Learning"), designed to furnish Japan a more impressive native religious/cultural tradition. In terms of positive goals, the leaders of this movement wanted to improve historical learning about Japanese culture, thinking that scholarship about Shinto and other aspects of the native ways were in a deplorable state. Negatively, many of the leaders attacked the way that Japan had adopted Confucian and Buddhist ways. The tendency of the leaders of the Kokugaku movement was to schematize Japanese history into three phases. In the early period, a pristine native culture and spirit had flourished. During the middle period, foreign imports had contaminated Japanese culture. They hoped to make the modern period a time when the ancient native ways would be restored and their country would be purged of foreign contaminations.

In fact, the beginnings of this reform movement owed something to the Buddhist priest Keichu (1640–1701), who proposed aesthetic reforms that would return poetry to ancient forms, and who noted the differences between Shinto and both Buddhism and Confucianism. He showed special respect for the kami, claiming they were beyond human understanding, and generally provided some of the initial impetus to restore ancient Japanese traditions. A Shinto priest from Kyoto, Kada Azumamaro (1669–1736), contributed one of the first influential critiques of the synthesis between Confucianism and Shinto that had arisen, arguing that Shinto ideas were not well interpreted through such Confucian notions as yin and yang or the five basic elements constituting reality.

A second generation of Shinto reformists came with Kamo no Mabuchi (1697–1769) and Motoori

Norinaga (1730–1801), who sharpened the focus of Kokugaku to precisely religious matters. Mabuchi founded a school of "ancient learning" dedicated to reviving the Japanese spirit that had prevailed before the introduction of Buddhism and Confucianism. Norinaga edited the *Kojiki,* the chronicles that became regarded as the Shinto scriptures. His commentaries on the *Kojiki,* along with his other writings on such topics as the kami, and his poetry, gave the Shinto revival much more intellectual clout than it had had previously. Hirata Atsutane (1776–1843) represents a third generation of the Kokugaku movement. He was the most passionate advocate of Shinto religiosity, arguing that the way of the kami was superior to all other religious ways.

Despite their claim to be purifying Japanese religious traditions of the foreign accretions that had denatured them, the later reformers in fact drew on the Daoist philosophers Laozi and Zhuangzi. Atsutane even borrowed from Christianity, which the Tokugawa leaders had proscribed. The rationale for such borrowings seems to have been twofold. First, Shinto traditions themselves were proving too thin on theoretical matters to undergird the revival the reformers wanted. Second, Buddhism and Confucianism were the great rivals or enemies, so borrowing from such politically weaker traditions as Daoism and Christianity amounted to a minor evil.

In their attacks on Buddhism and Confucianism, the Shinto reformers argued that those traditions had arisen through human contrivance, while the way of the kami was natural—completely in accord with the dictates of heaven and earth. The Daoist notions of spontaneity and nonstriving *(wu-wei)* seemed to support the superiority of such naturalism and so were adapted to the argument on behalf of the superiority of Shinto. Norinaga used the further Daoist concept that things are self-explanatory (do not require a full chain of causes) to rebut Neo-Confucian ideas about the workings of nature that he felt had invaded the Shinto view of the world. He also explored medicine, his profession, with an eye to reviving ancient theories, which were quite empirical (concentrated on simple facts and cures), and to ousting the complex, more rarefied theories of the Neo-Confucians. The religious payoff Norinaga found in this contrast was a support for his view that one ought to give the kami complete obedience, respecting the mysteriousness of their ways and not poking into how they had arranged nature. Thus what he considered Shinto naturalism, bolstered by Daoist views (Chinese naturalism), seemed more properly religious (worshipful) than what had infiltrated Shintoism through Neo-Confucianism.

Some later Shinto scholars have argued that Norinaga also was shaped by Christian views of the Creator, but the clearer Christian influence appears in the works of Atsutane, who apparently incorporated materials from translations of books on Christian doctrine brought by Western missionaries to China such as Matteo Ricci (1552–1610). The missionaries had been searching for ways to show the superiority of Christianity to Confucianism and some of their arguments seemed relevant to Shinto attacks on Confucianism. As well, Atsutane adapted Christian notions of the Trinity and the last judgment to a theology of the nature and works of the kami. A third feature of his theology was its special emphasis on Japanese ancestor veneration, which he found superior to Chinese ancestor veneration because it was broader in its range of devotion (Japanese ancestor worship was dedicated not only to members of one's own clan but also to the great kami associated with the imperial family). This latter point was extremely important in the nineteenth-century Meiji restoration of the power of the imperial family, for it provided a basis for discrediting the Tokugawa leaders (who were shoguns, not members of the imperial line) and bolstering the sacredness of the restored royal line. The subsequent "divinization" of the Japanese emperor, which went hand in hand with the extreme nationalism of late nineteenth-century and early twentieth-century Japan, owed much to the last phases of the Kokugaku movement, when the kami had come to reoccupy the royal ancestral line, much as Shintoists believed they had done during the earliest period, before Japan had been tainted by foreign religious ways.[19]

The New Religions.   During the Tokugawa period the first "new religions" arose. They were eclectic packagings of the previous, medieval elements, and they gained their success by contrasting favorably with the highly formal, even static, culture that had prevailed in the early nineteenth century. The new religions usually sprang from a charismatic leader who furnished a connection with the kami—indeed, whom his or her followers took to be a kami. By personalizing religion and addressing individual faith, the new religions stood out from the dominant formalism and offered something attractively dynamic.

Since the government was pushing Shinto, the new religions tended to join the nationalistic trend. Tenrikyo and Soka Gakkai both owe as much to

Figure 16 *Moss Temple grounds, Kyoto. The sunlight filtering through the trees illumines and shades the rich vegetation into a wondrous variety of green colorings. The rocks and waters add a calming contrast, making for a sense of fertility and peace. Photo by J. T. Carmody.*

Buddhist as to Shinto inspiration, but other new religions found it useful to shelter under the nationalistic umbrella. Tenrikyo sprang from a revelation that its founder, Nakayama Miki, had in 1838.[20] She had been a devout Pure Land Buddhist, but while serving as a medium in a healing ceremony for her son, she felt a kami possess her—the "true, original kami Tenri O no Mikoto" ("God the Parent"). Thereafter, her religion had a distinctively shamanic character. Miki embarked on a mission to spread her good news, healing sick people and promulgating the recitation of "I put my faith in Tenri O no Mikoto." The Tokugawa authorities harassed her somewhat, but in time a large number of followers accepted her as a living kami. Her writings became the Tenrikyo scripture, her songs became its hymns, and her dances shaped its liturgy. Recalling the creation myth of Izanagi and Izanami, she built a shrine "at the center of the world," where she thought

the first parents had brought forth the land. The shrine had a square opening in its roof and a tall wooden column—ancient symbolism for the connection to heaven.

Miki's teachings stress joyous living. In the beginning God the Parent made human beings for happiness, but we became self-willed and gloomy. By returning to God the Parent and dropping self-concern, we can restore our original joy. The way to return is faith in God the Parent and participation in Tenrikyo worship. Earhart has suggested that Tenrikyo's success comes in part from its return to peasant values.[21] By stressing gratitude for (sacred) creation, social rather than individual good, hard manual work, and the like, this sect has generated great popular enthusiasm. By the end of the nineteenth century, Tenrikyo claimed more than two million members, testifying to the power of combining old, shamanistic elements with new organizational forms and liturgies. Tenrikyo even revived the ancient Shinto concern for purification by focusing on an interior cleansing of doubts and untoward desires.

Soka Gakkai derives from Makiguchi Tsunesaburo (1871–1944), who preached a new social ethic based on three virtues: beauty, gain, and goodness.[22] Makiguchi found Nichiren Buddhism attractive, so he worked out his ethics in terms of the Lotus Sutra: Beauty, gain, and goodness came from faith in the Lotus. During World War II the leaders of Soka Gakkai refused the government's request that all religionists support the military effort, arguing that compliance would compromise the truth of the Lotus Sutra (by associating Soka Gakkai with other Buddhist sects and with Shintoists). For this he went to prison. Makiguchi died in prison, but his movement revived after the war through the efforts of Toda Josei. By 1957, Toda had reached his goal of enrolling 750,000 families, largely through his fine organizational abilities, and his shrewd use of enthusiastic youths. As well, Soka Gakkai capitalized on the frustration of Buddhists committed to the Lotus Sutra but alienated by the bickering among the various Nichiren groups. In a time of national confusion, Soka Gakkai's absolutism (all other religious options were held to be false) carried great appeal. According to Soka Gakkai, commitment to the Lotus Sutra (and to itself) would dissolve all ambiguities.

Many observers have criticized Soka Gakkai for its vehement missionizing and its political involvement. It offers a "cellular" structure like that of Communists, a simple program for daily devotion, pilgrimages to the National Central Temple near Mount Fuji, and an extensive educational program. Under the name Nichiren Shoshu, it has exported itself to the West, and though Soka Gakkai has separated from its political arm (Komeito), the party continues to have considerable political effect.

The Bushido Code. The Bushido Code provides a good summary of the religious and ethical values that formed the Japanese character throughout the late medieval and early modern periods. Bushido was especially significant for gathering together the sense of honor most samurai warriors and their consorts held to be more precious than life itself. John Noss has said of Bushido:

Bushido did not consist of finally fixed rules. It was a convention; more accurately, it was a system of propriety, preserved in unwritten law and expressing a spirit, an ideal of behavior. As such, it owed something to all the cultural and spiritual forces of the feudal era. Shinto supplied it the spirit of devotion to country and overlord, Confucianism provided its ethical substance, Zen Buddhism its method of private self-discipline, and the feudal habit of life contributed to it the spirit of unquestioning obedience to superiors and a sense of honor that was never to be compromised.[23]

Bushido was the "way of the warrior," whether he was a **samurai** (warrior) in fact or only in spirit. For Japanese women, the Bushido concern for honor focused on chastity. Manuals instructed young girls who had been compromised how to commit suicide (with the dagger each girl received when she came of age), including details of how, after plunging in the blade, she should tie her lower limbs together so as to secure modesty even in death. When a powerful lord would not stop his advances, the noble Lady Kesa promised to submit if he would kill her samurai husband first. The lord agreed, and she told him to come to her bedroom after midnight and kill the sleeper with wet hair. Then she got her husband drunk, so that he would sleep soundly, washed her hair, and crept under the covers to await her fate.[24] This was not typical, but it is instructive.

Recent History. From the close of the Tokugawa period in 1867 to World War II, Japan was in transit to modernity. It abolished the military dictatorship and restored the emperor. It also changed from a largely decentralized feudal society into a modern nation organized from Tokyo. Japan made astonishing strides in education and culture, assimilating Western science and again opening itself to the outside world (at first under duress, due to Commodore Perry and the U.S. gunboats during 1853 and 1854, then voluntarily). Success in two major wars with China and Russia between 1895 and 1905 gave the Japanese great confidence, and the first third of the twentieth century was a time of increasingly strident nationalism. One of the main foci of this nationalism was what became state Shinto. Because of its chauvinist potential, some Japanese thinkers and politicians stressed the divinity of the emperor and the unique dignity of the Japanese people.

During this period Buddhism lost its official status as a branch of the government, Shinto was established as the state religion, and Christianity was reintroduced. In addition, more new religions appeared, which, like Buddhism and Shinto, took on nationalistic overtones.

For our interests the modern period, beginning with the Meiji Restoration (of the emperor) in 1868, is most significant because of the revival of Shinto. This was largely a political operation, designed to glorify the imperial family and to unify the country around its oldest traditions. Edwin Reischauer has described the widespread changes in secular life that the Meiji leaders introduced.[25] Japanese cities were revamped, and Western ideas of individual rights and responsibilities that are part of a modern state were brought in. H. B. Earhart provides documents of the propaganda that Meiji leaders generated to link the nation with religion and reestablish Japan's sense of divine mission.[26] "The Imperial Rescript on Education" (1890),[27] for instance, explicitly linked the imperial throne ("coeval with heaven and earth") with filial piety to make nationalism the supreme personal virtue. To bring their tradition up to date and do what their revered ancestors had done, the modern Japanese had only to be utterly loyal to the emperor. In fact, Joseph Kitagawa has argued that the Japanese notion of national community (*kokutai*) "incorporates all the major thrusts of individual and corporate orientation of the Japanese people to a sacral order of reality."[28]

Japan's defeat in World War II produced great national trauma, prompting the success of hundreds of new religions. Culturally, defeat meant a shattering of national pride; religiously, it meant a body blow to state Shinto. The Western conquerors, led by Douglas MacArthur, force-fed the Japanese democracy and the concept of individual liberties. On its own, Japan rebuilt with incredible speed, soon becoming the economic giant of Asia. The new constitution disestablished Shinto and allowed complete individual religious freedom. The older traditions, which people identified with the national self-consciousness of prewar times, were shattered, and the new religions rushed in to fill the void. In the past two decades or so, the older traditions have regrouped, especially Buddhism, but secularism has been a strong trend. Caught up in its technological spurt, Japan has seemingly put aside nationalistic and religious issues, preferring to let the traumas of the war heal by benign neglect.

Today the Japanese religious picture is quite complicated. The culture is secularistic, at least outwardly, but in the byways Buddhism and Christianity struggle to revive themselves. Confucian and Daoist elements remain part of the Japanese psyche, but in rather muted voice. Strangely, perhaps, it is Shinto—the ancient version rather than the state—that is the strongest religious presence. Divinity in nature, which Japanese religion has always stressed, continues in the shrines that connect present times to the aboriginal kami. The place of the emperor remains a touchy issue.

WORLDVIEW

How ought we to regard the relation between history and worldview in Japan? Perhaps the most profitable way would be to imagine the historical influences interacting with a strong ethnocentrism. As Confucian, Daoist, and Buddhist influences penetrated Japan, the Japanese people worked steadily to make them their own. Shinto arose, as the articulation of the native traditions, and the strong social cohesiveness of the Japanese gradually shaped how the new ways would color the old.

As in China, the different religious traditions seldom competed on the Western, individualistic model. By and large, people did not feel forced to choose between a wholehearted allegiance to Shinto or a wholehearted allegiance to Buddhism. Confucianism proved useful in expressing Japanese convictions about social relations. Daoism provided help in articulating native feelings about nature, in aesthetics, and also in expressing aspects of Buddhist philosophy. But the typical Japanese person felt free to pick and choose from the wealth of ideas and rituals that the several traditions offered. Any showdown that occurred tended to be between Shinto and Buddhist loyalties, and Shinto always had the great advantage of being intimately bound up with the symbolism of the royal family and the birth of the Japanese islands. The Confucian influence was more indirect or internal than imposed from without. Many more people thought about family life and social relations in Confucian terms than studied the Confucian classics or considered themselves disciples of Master Kong.

From the relative homogeneity of its people, Japanese religion could rely on many tacit assumptions. People long schooled to living closely together and taking pride in their beautiful land did not need to be lectured on consensus or veneration of natural beauty. Certainly, modern technology has shown that Japanese respect for nature is vulnerable; ecological problems are serious. Similarly, modern Western political ideas have posed significant challenges. But Japan's genius for taking foreign ideas, technology, and other accomplishments into itself and refashioning them to fit its own sense of peoplehood and social values has continued strong into the contemporary era. What seldom cracks is the ability of the people to work cooperatively, for a common good. In the case of religion, that has meant creating a digest of foreign influences that mixed well with Shinto convictions about the significance of beauty and the primacy of the Japanese people.

It should prove useful to focus on the ways that Japanese religion has not only offered the usual ministrations (ways of coping with death and other deep questions, ways of hallowing everyday life) but has also helped to energize the Japanese people. This is perhaps clearest in the case of Zen Buddhism, but one can probe for an energizing influence in the acceptance of other Buddhist schools, of Confucian convictions, of Daoist aesthetic notions, and even of Christian ceremonies (for weddings, for Christmas). The Shinto sense of being the people privileged to live on a beautiful string of islands has moved the Japanese to draw from other traditions what might enhance such a life—give it more vitality, increase its pleasures and decrease its pains. So, for example, the discipline that Zen Buddhism developed made it seem useful for more than personal enlightenment. Samurai warriors found in Zen a spiritual training to ground their martial arts and clarify their complete dedication to the service of their lord. Some contemporary industrialists have looked to Zen for a similar service, thinking that it could sharpen the attention of their workers and so improve efficiency.

Thus Japanese religion has been an important part of an energetic, creative culture—one more stimulated by the challenges of foreign influences, including those of Western modernity, than intimidated. The worldview that has developed in Japan, with considerable religious support, has canonized hard work and loyalty to one's kind (clan, fellow workers). It has been a worldview clearer than many others about the high survival value of social cohesiveness—the way that social cohesiveness keeps life relatively simple and keeps all significant ranks closed to outsiders.

Nature

From its earliest beginnings, Japanese religion has been enraptured by nature. Y. T. Hosoi has detailed prehistoric Japan's focus on the sacred tree;[29] Manabu Waida has described the rich mythology that surrounded the moon;[30] and ancient mythology, as we have seen, featured the sun goddess Amaterasu and the wind god Susanoo. Furthermore, we best describe the kami as nature forces (though they could also possess human beings), and the Japanese Buddhists' love for nature, which poets such as Saigyo and Basho dramatize, developed from a pre-Buddhist base. A closeness to nature, a love of natural beauty, an aesthetic geared to flowers and trees, seasons and vistas—these have been Japanese characteristics.

Japanese folk religion, which exerted a hardy influence, viewed nature with a peasant's eye. Nature was fertile and fickle, nourishing and devastating. The early myths reflect this paradoxical quality. The sun goddess was benevolent—a source of warmth, light, and the power to make things grow. The wind god was unpredictable, often destructive. Susanoo's punishment for his misdeeds belies a peasant hope that nature's order and benevolence will prevail. However, Susanoo and his like might have destructive outbreaks at any time; Japan has been a land of earthquakes, volcanoes, floods, and typhoons. Japan is a very beautiful land, but rugged and not easily tamed, and controlling the effects of nature has been a herculean task. Perhaps that accounts for the Japanese delight in gardens and groves—places where they have brought peace to nature.

As we noted in describing the Japanese innovations in Buddhism, this sort of delight showed in the Japanese embellishment of religious ceremonies. Not only do most temples have some sort of grounds, often quite lovely, but their liturgies employ flowers, incense, candles, and other adornments. Along with the Japanese stress on order and cleanliness, which goes back to ancient concerns for purification, a desire has grown to make living graceful. Buddhism has benefited from this desire, as the breathtaking Moss Temple and the Rock Garden Temple grounds show. In Shinto shrines, such as Ise, Heian, and Meiji, gardens, pools, fields of flowers, and lofty trees also reflect this desire.

The mode in which the Japanese have received these nature lessons, we suggest, has been "religio-aesthetic." Japan is not very concerned with a philosophy of nature in the Western sense. It does not analyze "prime matter" or nuclear particles. Its religion appears to move more by a sense of harmony. If the folk interest is nature's agricultural energies (and the powers responsible for sickness), the higher class interest is nature's ability to soothe. Sensing that the groves and gardens represent something primal, the warrior, merchant, and bureaucrat have returned to it to escape the human concerns that threatened to swamp them. By communion with nature, the samurai warrior could collect his spirit for a single-minded attack. By slipping away from his accounting, the merchant could anticipate a "retirement," which, in Japan as well as China, allowed more poetic, Daoist preoccupations. The same applies to the bureaucrat. Even Emperor Hirohito, who after World War II was merely a figurehead, specialized in marine biology. Somewhat inept in social situations, he came alive in his pools and gardens.

This interest in nature is religious in the sense that nature has regularly represented to the Japanese something ultimate. Thus, concern for nature has often been an ultimate concern—a stance before the holy. This stance seldom involved violent beliefs. The major prophetic figures do not tell tales of burning bushes or theologize out of mysteriously parted seas. Rather, the predominant mood has been peaceful.[31] Japanese religion tries to gain access to the core of the personality, where the personality touches nature's flow. It tries, probably semiconsciously, to let the moss and rocks work their influence. These objects can summarize existence, giving messages from mind-only. Such Buddhist ideas suggest emptiness—the strangely satisfying "no-thingness" that the spirit disgusted with ideas, the spirit more holistically inclined, often finds in open space or the sea.

The religious veneration of nature, or even the religio-aesthetic use of nature for soothing the soul, implies an impersonal ultimacy. Furthermore, it implies that humanity, as well as divinity, is more at one with nature than over or against it. Religion based on nature, in fact, tends to collapse humans and gods into nature's forces or nature's flows. As a result, Japan has not seen the world as created by a transcendent force. Rather, Japan has let nature somewhat suppress knowledge and love of divinity, subordinating them to energy and flow. Human beings have been encouraged not to exploit nature (though recent technological changes qualify this statement). Through most of Japanese history, one would prune or rake nature rather than lay waste to it, at least in part because human

beings did not have a biblical writ to fill the earth and subdue it.[32] Rather, they had a call to live with nature. Today we might hear that as a call to be ecological, grateful, and thus graceful.

This emphasis on nature relegated intellectual concerns to second place. Many Japanese monks have lived in mountain fastnesses, while relatively few have been theoreticians of divinity's word. The reasoning of theoreticians tends to be sharp, attacking, and dialectical. The reasoning of contemplative monks tends to be poetic, symbolic, and expressive. Those who ponder the "feminine" intelligence of Eastern cultures come upon this contemplative mind. Generally, Japan has sought the whole rather than the part, the movement rather than the arrest, the beauty as well as the utility. These are feminine characteristics only if *masculine* refers to only one sort of logic (the shortest distance between two points). If a culture moves more circuitously, Western men will likely call it feminine. We are fortunate to live in a time that challenges such stereotypes.

Case Study: Japanese Aesthetics.[33] Much of the Japanese effort to gain religious peace has expressed itself aesthetically, in artistic pursuits. Classical Japanese painting, for instance, tended to portray the physical world realistically, with great attention to details. It was not abstract or surrealistic. On the other hand, classical painting also was not photographically objective, but tended to use a flat, undistanced surface to express subjective perceptions of reality. A good example is a series of screens by Kano Naizen from the Momoyama period (1568–1600). The screens portray the arrival of Portuguese merchants and the conversion of some Japanese citizens by Christian missionaries. In one street scene the foreground presents the foreign priests and merchants mingling with the Japanese natives. In the background, a local shop and a pine grove are portrayed without depth, covered by golden mists. The effect is a standoff between time and eternity. The busy street scene with the newly arrived foreigners argues that times are always changing, novelty is nearly rampant. The golden mists, pine grove, and stylized shop argue that the more things change the more they stay the same. Novelty is but a small wrinkle on the surface of an ancient culture and a timeless nature.

Some of the oldest Japanese ceramics, the *haniwa* figurines from the fifth and sixth centuries C.E., display what became an almost standard Japanese love of simple, austere presentations. The *haniwa* figurines tend to have oval eyes and tiny mouths, as though they were timeless masks, suitable for the ceremonial dances that take us out of profane time. They are sober and archetypal, yet poised on the brink of motion (for the sacred dance is always occurring, always inviting us to join in). Some historians find Chinese influences in these early ceramics, but they express qualities that Japan soon made wholly its own. Buddhist influences brought an increased concentration on portrait sculpture in order to represent the Enlightened One. In the best of these representations, artists captured the Buddha's humanity, giving him the slightest trace of a smile, a bit of warmth and playfulness. Portrait sculpture of the Nara period (710–794) included monks among its subjects. Thus the sculpture of the famous blind monk Ganjin shows a holy man deep in meditation. The smile lines at the mouth and the corners of the eyes help to heighten his attractiveness. Though physically blind, he probably had great insight into human nature. Though concentrating on the timeless dharma, he probably had been molded to a timely humaneness, becoming a person we would like to know.

Zen masters of the Muromachi period (1392–1568) were instrumental in Japan's appropriation of the landscape techniques developed during the Chinese Song dynasty. This led to the *suiboku* style (ink on paper with splashed-ink wash). The conventions of the *suiboku* landscapes called for a vertical perspective, featuring craggy mountains or deep basins with lakes and canyons. Clouds or empty spaces tended to divide the pictures into three realms, reminiscent of the doctrine of the Buddha's three bodies. The lower level of the painting usually dealt with earthly and human concerns: a lake, a hermit's hut, several fishermen. The middle of the picture would have temples or pagodas suggesting paradise. At the top the picture would portray icy mountain peaks, to symbolize the perfection beyond all human imagining.

Working within this conventional form, a Zen master such as Sesshu (1420–1506) was able to introduce some striking originality. His *Winter Landscape,* for example, shows jagged mountaintops lost in clouds, a temple in the middle range, and near the base a traveler in a broad-brimmed hat. The traveler is lost in the immense landscape, quite vulnerable as he picks his way. Though this is all quite conventional, Sesshu has invested the painting with an electric energy. Using short, ragged lines, he has expressed the Zen sense that nature is tremendously alive. Thus the

impression is not of a soft, misty nature but of sharp angles, well-defined particulars. That this effect at the bottom is in tension with empty space at the top, which makes a white, heavenly vagueness, makes the picture an epitome of Zen philosophy. Emptiness accents particulars. Mystical absorption at the top should lead to vitality and decisiveness at the bottom.

Another interesting Japanese art form was the *ukiyo,* which means a picture of the "floating world." The hallmark of this style was the changeableness of things, the world's transiency. Yet whereas transiency had traditional Buddhist overtones of sadness, the *ukiyo* artists tended to be happy. The excitement of the latest gossip, the fun of seizing the day, ran through their work. One of their favorite subjects was Kabuki actors. In a celebrated series of portraits done by Toshusai Sharaku in 1794–95, the arresting feature is the actors' facial expressions. They show brilliant rage, triumph, coyness, defeat—all the emotions required on the Kabuki stage. The faces are heavily made up, and the total effect is to drive home the energy and pathos of the actor's life.

Japanese aesthetics also led to notable architecture, gardens, and rituals such as the tea ceremony. The traditional Japanese house was a model of simplicity, even austerity. It had straw-mat floors, sliding-screen walls, and very little furniture. The custom of removing one's shoes on entering the house suggested coming into a new, venerable space. The screen walls offered minimal protection against nature, but they were flexible enough to accommodate to quick changes of mood. In summer, the screens easily opened to the elements, eliminating the barriers between the family and nature.

During the Muromachi period Zen monastic influence made the style of the abbot's quarters attractive for laypeople's houses. The main room therefore came to center around a floor-level writing desk, and there would usually be an alcove for arranged flowers. A scroll usually would hang in the corner, the floors would be covered with *tatami* (straw mats), and the walls would be sliding paper doors and screens. Among the wealthy, who could afford large houses with many screens, there would be special arrangements for viewing the moon or the snow to best advantage. The Katsura imperial villa on the edge of Kyoto is a good model of such large houses designed for beautiful views.

For many Japanese, the most beautiful views have opened onto exquisite gardens. The Shinto roots of the gardening tradition stressed gnarled old trees and

Figure 17 *Teahouse of the Rock Garden Monastery. Photo by J. T. Carmody.*

large rocks in places set aside for the kami. When Chinese culture began to shape Japanese tastes, Daoist and Buddhist influences became important. Traditional Chinese gardens sought to reproduce the islands and grottoes of the Daoist immortals or the beauty of the Buddha's Pure Land. Chinese geomancy set many of the stylistic ideals, and harmony between yin and yang forces was a high requirement. Thus a large yang boulder would be counterbalanced by a low yin pool. Waterfalls represented life and bamboo represented strength.

Once again, Zen was the native Japanese development that most directly varied the Chinese model. In the case of gardening, Zen pushed the designs in a more abstract and asymmetrical direction. In the Zen scheme, gardens were not so much places for leisurely strolling as places for meditation. Translating many notions from Song landscape painting, the Zen gardeners stressed emptiness and the lack of human or emotional touches. So the Zen gardens tended to have no benches or wine cups. Instead of showy flowers they

stressed moss or rocks. The Ryoanji or Rock Garden Monastery of Kyoto, built around 1500, epitomizes this abstract style. There are no ponds or streams, only white gravel raked to resemble eddies—phenomenal reality playing on the surface of emptiness.

The tea ceremony was one of several rituals the Japanese developed to beautify each part of daily living. Often it would take place in the teahouse of a shrine garden (see Figure 17). Indeed, many Zen Buddhists came to consider the tea ceremony a sort of sacrament, symbolizing the grace, austerity, and concentration that good living requires. While the core of the ceremony was simply making and sipping whipped green tea, the teahouse, the utensils, and the manner of serving all played important parts. Ideally there would be lovely surroundings: a garden of great beauty, flowers, a *suiboku* painting or a scroll of elegant calligraphy. Aficionados paid special attention to the bowl in which the tea was served, and master potters often strove to produce simple, elegant tea vessels. Although the upper classes sometimes embellished the tea ceremony with ostentatious displays, the protocol developed by Sen no Rikyu, the greatest of the tea masters, stressed "poor tea": absolute simplicity and ordinariness.

Ideally the tea ceremony would take place in its own teahouse, usually a small structure apart from the main house. Failing that, it would occur in a special room within the main house. The goal in designing the teahouse was to achieve a simplicity both rustic and refined. At one end of the house usually was an alcove decorated with a hanging scroll and floral arrangements. Another usual feature was a small sunken fireplace for heating the tea kettle in winter. During summer months people would use a portable brazier. Bowing to enter the small, low door of the teahouse, guests would begin the ceremony in a spirit of humility.

The ceremony itself has usually consisted of the host bringing tea utensils into the room, offering the guests sweets, and then preparing and serving tea made of pulverized tea leaves stirred in hot water. Normally the tea one prepared was thin and frothy, but on occasion a heavier tea might be served. At times the ceremony would be preceded by a light meal, which made the tea the climax of a social and culinary occasion. After the consumption of the tea, guests often would inquire about the implements that had been used, for as noted these often were considered art objects.

The tea ceremony has long had special ties with Zen Buddhism. Zen monks of the Kamakura period drank tea to stay awake during their meditation periods. Later they made tea drinking part of their ceremony for honoring their founder Bodhidharma. By the fifteenth century the tea ceremony itself had become a much loved art form, if not a religio-aesthetic ritual, as well as a vehicle for friends to gather and discuss aesthetics in a congenial atmosphere.

At the beginning of the Tokugawa period, the ceremony was somewhat codified and simplicity became the approved note. The ideal was to achieve harmony between the guests and the implements being used; respect among the participants and for the implements; cleanliness (a Shinto note), which led to ritual washings before entering the teahouse; and tranquillity, encouraged by a slow, careful use of each article in the ceremony. Thus the tea ceremony itself became something of a religious "way"—a distinctively Japanese blend of aesthetics and religion.

Flower arrangement (*ikebana*) brought aesthetic refinement home to many Japanese family circles. In a sense, the goal of flower arrangement was to make a miniature garden, and so a miniature, domestic paradise. Like the tea ceremony, flower arrangement became a "way": an avocation both refreshing and disciplining. In flower arrangement the great virtues were simplicity, asymmetry, and form (color was secondary). The preferred forms were understated rather than obvious, subtle rather than bold. The ideal was to hint at a mysterious meaning and suggest old, somewhat formal ways. During the Tokugawa period (1600–1868) a threefold style developed. A high and a low branch on one side would represent heaven and human beings. A middle branch on the opposite side would represent earth. One would gain variety by changing the flowers, grasses, leaves, sticks, and other elements placed in these three positions. The result was a timeless pattern varied by new materials.

Throughout all their arts, the Japanese have tried to express and develop their sense of emptiness, form, the changeableness of human beings, and the primacy of nature. Rarely did a Japanese art form flourish without close ties to religion. In the tea and flower ceremonies, for instance, one is hard pressed to say where art leaves off and religious contemplation begins. A certain blankness signals the touch of Buddhist emptiness. A certain austerity signals the touch of Shinto antiquity, when life was close to nature, unemotional and strong.

Society

Women's Status. It is ironic that a culture that has had many stereotypically feminine refinements has been almost oppressively male dominated. Although there are traces of an early matriarchy and strong influences from female shamans and their successors in the new religions, women have regularly occupied a low position in Japanese society. Of course, women's influence in the traditional home and even the modern office is stronger than superficial sociology suggests.[34] Expert in the very refined Japanese tact, wives and mothers have found ways of influence despite their institutionalized powerlessness. As well, they have run the home and controlled the purse strings. Officially, however, Japan accepted Confucian notions of social relationships (no doubt because they fit traditional predilections), so the female was almost always designated as the underling.

The important religious roles played by females in Japanese history should be further discussed. Perhaps their phallic overtones made it fitting that the kami should possess females. Or perhaps shamanism offered the powerless a chance to gain attention and influence. Whatever the reasons, women were the prime contact with divinity in folk Shinto, despite strong menstrual taboos. As well, they were the prime contact with the spirits of the dead and so were central in maintaining the sense of the clan. The figurines from the prehistoric Jomon period suggest that women were originally considered awesome because of their power to give birth. The difficulty of the women's liberation movement in contemporary Japan suggests that the powers of women represented by these former roles have long been suppressed.

No doubt for a variety of reasons, the men dominating Japanese society have found it advantageous to place religion and femininity in opposition to warfare and business. As the recourse to nature (retirement) has been in contrast to things official, so the recourse to monasteries, female shamans, and even geishas has been in contrast to workaday life. In part, of course, this contrast links religion with recreation, art, and family life. (In modern Japan a man identifies as much with his job and company as with his family.) Thus, nature, religion, and women are considered surplus commodities and yet especially valuable ones: surplus in that they do not figure much in modern work, but valuable in that work alone does not constitute a complete existence.

Clan Emphasis. The modern stress on a man's work, identifying him with his corporation, is the result of the group structure of Japanese business. Consequently, the typical businessman takes much of his recreation with his fellow workers apart from his family. Considered in the context of Japanese religious history, this situation is somewhat anomalous. Earhart, for instance, has gathered documents that testify to the religious significance of family life,[35] showing the sense of clan that has predominated. (In fact, the modern corporation exploits this sense of clan loyalty.)

Moreover, a characteristic of the traditional family was concern with the dead. As in China, ancestor veneration was a significant portion of the average person's religious contacts with ultimate powers. Originally, the Japanese probably believed that the departed continued to hover around the places where they had lived. The Japanese tended to associate their ancestors with kami and *bodhisattvas* after these figures were introduced by Shinto and Buddhism. Therefore, in its

petitions and venerations, the clan reminded itself of its own identity (the function that some sociologists, such as Durkheim, have considered the main rationale for religion) and kept attuned to the natural forces of life and death.

Thus, the family tended to be the locus of daily worship, and the family shrine tended to predominate over the village or national shrine. Still, there was not a sharp division between the family clan and the national clan. The emperor was often considered the head not only of his own line but also of the entire Japanese people; the gods of Shinto mythology were the gods of the collective Japanese group; and national shrines such as Ise were the site of ceremonies performed on behalf of the entire nation.

Overall, Japan is not a place where A. N. Whitehead's definition of religion (what a person does with his or her solitude) is very helpful.[36] Although standing alone before a striking shrine such as the Golden Pavilion has shaped for many Japanese a sense of ultimacy,[37] group activities—at home, in war, or at work—have been crucial factors in developing such a sense.

The Confucian cast of much traditional Japanese social thought is evident from the first article of a constitution developed by Prince Shotoku in 604. The implication is that throughout the land, harmony—cooperation—ought to be the watchword:

Harmony is to be valued, and an avoidance of wanton opposition is to be honored. All men are influenced by partisanship, and there are few who are intelligent. Hence there are some who disobey their lords and fathers, or who maintain feuds with the neighboring villages. But when those above are harmonious and those below are friendly, and there is concord in the discussion of business, right views of things spontaneously gain acceptance. Then what is there which cannot be accomplished?"[38]

Ethics. This historical sense of clan was accompanied by certain ethical assumptions that were immensely influential in shaping the Japanese conscience. The medieval samurai felt that his life belonged to his feudal lord. If he failed his lord, by being defeated or less than fully successful, he was expected to offer to commit ritual suicide—to petition his lord for this "favor," so that he might mend the honor he had violated. In contemporary Japan, the individual worker is supposed to promote the honor of his bosses above all. He is to assume any failures by his group and to attribute any successes to the group's leader. Thus, the boss (or at most the group as a whole) always gets credit for a bright idea or increased productivity. If the worker does not rock the boat, the corporation will take care of all his needs until he dies.

Buddhism offered an alternative to the Japanese group orientation. Though the Buddha's own thought was quite social, as manifested by the *sangha,* his original message stressed the uniqueness of each individual's situation. It is true that each being possessed the buddha-nature (at least according to Mahayana Buddhism, which introduced the Buddha to Japan), and that this belief, coupled with the doctrine of no-self, led to a conception of the relatedness of reality. Practically, however, the Buddha made the existential personality the religious battleground. Only the individual could remove the poison of karma and rebirth; only the individual could pronounce the Buddhist vows for himself or herself, let alone live them out. However, early Japanese attempts to appropriate Buddhism were sponsored by the state, because the state leaders thought they might enlist its magical or ritual power.

In Japan Buddhism both kept some of its individualism and suffered a socialization. As Zen perhaps best shows, the *sangha* could gear itself to making free spirits. Its discipline could be odd, even cranky. At least, the Zen masters brim with spontaneity, venerating their tradition but often in iconoclastic ways. Yet Japan acculturated Buddhism. Indeed, Buddhism became a government agency, propping warlords and nationalistic ideology. Ultimately, Japan decided that Shinto served nationalism better than Buddhism, but that was not for Buddhism's lack of trying.

Self

Theoretically in Buddhism there was no self and so no barrier (for the enlightened) to union with nature or the group. Shinto defined the self less clearly than it defined nature or the group. Thus, when Confucianism brought an elaborate social protocol, the sense of self in Japanese religious consciousness was bound to be deemphasized.

In fact, Japanese religion does not emerge as a champion of freethinking. Compared with religion elsewhere, Japanese religion does not support individual initiative or responsibility to a significant degree. Except for Zen, Japan has told the individual that ful-

fillment is a matter of harmonizing with nature and society. For instance, the traditional Japanese artist does not agonize in the creative process like Western artists do. Japanese art has not been primarily for working out a self. We may doubt, therefore, that many Japanese artists have thought of their lives or work in terms of Patrick White's "vivisection" (of experience).[39]

More prominent has been the Daoist notion that the artist goes to the center of nature, where the Way rules, and from union with the Way spontaneously expresses a fleeting glimpse of reality.[40] The fall of a cherry blossom, the pattern of a scarf, the rumble of a mountain—those are the subjects that seize a classical poet such as Basho or a modern novelist such as Kawabata. In the tea ceremony, the No play, archery, or swordsmanship, the ideal is selflessness. Such activities, in fact, are but active forms of what the meditator pursues in *zazen.* Cast off the dichotomizing mind, the culture has said. Distinguish no more between your self and the world. Distinguishing makes for multiplicity and illusion. Buddha-nature is one. Full attainment, in the Japanese aesthetic religion, is the unitive mind, the mind lost in Mind.

Perhaps as a consequence of selflessness, the individual Japanese may appear ethically underdeveloped to the Westerner. Such a description can provide confusion, as well as misperception and offense. Still, a Western student has to begin with existing Western categories, even if they prove inappropriate. In Western ethics, the individual person judges right and wrong, largely because Greek philosophy and Israelite religion, the bases for Western culture, made the individual an intellectual and moral subject of revelation—in the Greek case, revelation from a nature or personal experience structured by reason (Logos); in the Israelite case, revelation from a willful God. By the time of the Enlightenment (the eighteenth century), the West had developed this patrimony to the point that the individual could be autonomous and ethics a matter of individual reasoning. Even though recent thought has found this view to be inadequate, it remains influential and at least partially true.

For instance, Western scholars of Shinto such as Bownas[41] and Blacker[42] go out of their way to underscore that its persistent concern with pollution had little to do with morality. Pollution did not pertain to the intentions of the actor, and no distinctions were made between accidental and deliberate violations. Merely to shed blood or encounter death was polluting. Consequently, the polluted person did not have to assume responsibility, to repent, or to renew the self morally. Essentially, both the pollution and the purification were external to the violator and amoral. Polluting acts occurred in the context of rather physical forces, akin to electricity or the shark's response to blood. (Buddhist teaching veered away from an amoral pollution, stressing personal responsibility. People with both Shinto and Buddhist loyalties therefore suffered some ambiguity.)

In the medieval period, the warrior or serf let his master be his will. The master held the power of life and death over the servant; morality was more a matter of loyalty to conscience. This deemphasis on conscience in personal life has persisted even in the modern period. As the honor accorded ritual suicide suggests, the individual has been subject to the social code in nearly all matters.

From medieval times, as we suggested earlier, an individual's proper bearing toward the group was loosely codified in Bushido, the warrior's way. Robert Bellah's study of Tokugawa religion suggests that Bushido discipline is largely the basis for the vitality of the modern Japanese economy, serving a purpose similar to what Protestant worldliness did for Western capitalism.[43]

The watchwords for the individual in Japanese religious history, then, were discipline and self-effacement. Fulfillment would come from submission to nature and service to the group, not from self-development or personal contact with God. The religious traditions, consequently, tended to help satisfy society's need for good workers and compliant citizens. Although this is true of religious traditions in most places, it stands out in Japan. The happy life that a new religion such as Tenrikyo holds out to its faithful is the result of reviving ancient concepts, including the submersion of the individual in the group. Soka Gakkai and other politically active religions stress service to the group.

Just as radical and Marxist political groups in the West offer their faithful a cause in which to lose themselves, the Japanese new religions have capitalized on the security that an individual feels in being part of a large group. In the clan, the nation, or the religious group, the Japanese individual has felt secure—safe from meaninglessness and partner to something large and compelling. All the beauty in Japanese culture, all the intelligence in Japanese technology, ought to incline us to study such "belonging" carefully.

Ultimate Reality

Japanese divinity, though complex, is essentially an impersonal collectivity of natural and clan forces. Although devotion to a particular kami, Buddha, or Daoist god qualifies this assertion somewhat (the people who place offerings at the "baby shrine" of the Bodhisattva of Mercy in Tokyo no doubt pray to an individual figure), the sharply defined personage that we associate with the God of Western religion hardly appears in Japan. The gods of Shinto mythology, for instance, have a quite finite knowledge, love, and power; they have not separated from the cosmos to make particular demands. (Particular kami do take over individuals such as Miki, the foundress of Tenrikyo, so we must qualify that statement, too.)

In the course of Japanese history, there have been numerous personal claims to divinity such as Miki's. In the thirteenth century, Nichiren was confident enough of his success in propagating Buddhist dharma to proclaim himself "Bodhisattva of Superb Action,"[44] taking advantage of the common doctrine about the buddha-nature residing in all living things. For the common populace, though, divinity did not reflect individual humanity. Its best representations were nature or the clan. Yet insofar as people always conceive of divinity through their sense of perfection or power (and through their revelatory experiences), even impersonal Japanese divinity occasionally touched the human qualities of knowledge and love.

The Buddhists best showed deep knowledge to Japan—the ultimate reality that shone in enlightenment. Insofar as Japan deified the Buddha, it deified glorious understanding. From enlightenment, further, one could reason that the buddha-nature was the basis for the world's intelligibility. It was what makes things be and what gives things meaning. It was also an active source, issuing all things from its womb. The generation of all things from buddha-nature was not the same as the "logical" creation that Hellenized Western religion developed, but it did correlate Buddhist ultimate reality with mind and understanding.

Love was another matter. The *bodhisattva* vow, of course, was based on great compassion, and all East Asia best loved the *bodhisattva* Kannon, the *bodhisattva* of mercy, to whom it looked for motherly care. Amida Buddha, dispensing mercy from the Pure Land, was another divine figure both personal and encouraging warm emotion. In keeping with the injunction to stop craving, though, love or compassion was not to stir desire, however noble. So one could work for the salvation of all beings in good cheer, believing that their present sufferings were no cause for raging against divinity's or even society's injustices. So the love of the *bodhisattva,* even when it entailed suffering, was of a different sort than the redemptive love (*agape*) of Western religion.[45] For Japan evil has been more an illusion than a disordered love or an idolatry. In the eons of time, in the vastness of *ku* (emptiness), present problems have been but fleeting. If one would abandon thinking about them and loose one's attachment to them, one could relate to them properly. Then death would lose its sting and suffering have no fangs.[46]

The Buddhists were by far the most acute Japanese philosophers; the conceptions of divinity in the other traditions were far less clear. For Japanese folk religion, which touched all but the most intellectual, divinity was quite piecemeal. Its representation was the local shrine or the house altar; neither negated the other, and neither denied the divinity of the shrines in the neighboring villages or of the altars in the next block. Folk religiosity therefore was quite tolerant—and quite confusing. It was relatively happy to multiply divinities without seeming necessity. A Shinto wedding, a Buddhist funeral, and a good many charms in between were the common custom. The gods of Shinto mythology, Daoist magic, and popular Buddhism but varied a sacredness felt to be quite near. For the few who hungered after simplicity, nature or the Buddhist void sufficed. Either could anchor spirituality in the present. Either could rouse wonder and make any time or space profound.

To the present, the times and spaces that are most wonderful, though, are the folk festivals and the popular pilgrim shrines. As the diary of a pilgrim to Ise puts it: "One does not feel like an ordinary person any longer but as though reborn in another world."[47] At special festivals or shrines, one passed a threshold (*limen*) and went from the ordinary to the sacred world. The diary of the Ise pilgrim describes this liminal experience in the aesthetic manner noted above: The pine groves have an unearthly shadow; the rare flowers that survived the frost carry a delicate pathos; most of the adornments in the shrine recall the ancient days, when religious life was honest, simple, and rough. The pilgrim notes the spray over the hills, the solitary woods that beckon to the meditative. He washes in the sea to gain outer purity and strives for a clean Shinto worship (with no Buddhist interference) to gain inner purity. Throughout, the physical beauty of Ise engrosses him.

Shinto Shrines.[48] To set off places where people might venerate the kami, the Japanese have long fashioned wooden shrines with encompassing groves. They have not designed the shrines for communal worship, but rather as simple sites where people might recite ritual prayers and make offerings to the kami. Unlike the Buddhist temples, the Shinto shrines originally did not contain statues. The official focal point of veneration usually was an old sword or mirror, which was considered to be the kami's resting place or "body." However, these ritual objects were seldom seen, even by the Shinto priests, so the general impression most visitors received was of a simple wooden pavilion where one might make a personal petition or venerate the kami in the course of a village celebration.

Usually the encompassing grove was almost as important as the wooden pavilion. The grove typically was of rectangular shape, and one entered it through a sacred archway or *torii.* At the entrance stood a well, where visitors were to take some water in a wooden dipper and purify their hands. At the entrance to many Shinto shrines two stone lions stood guard. Even today the tall trees create an atmosphere of quiet, which the trees' association with the kami turns in the direction of religious respect. The general appearance of both the grove and the shrine buildings is unadorned. Thus the grove's vegetation burgeons almost wildly and the shrine buildings usually are of rough wood. Exceptions occur, as in the red-painted Heian shrine of Kyoto, but even there the total effect is subdued, in flight from anything fancy or garish. The roofs of the large Heian buildings are shingled with natural materials, and the gardens behind the buildings are understated. As with the great shrine at Ise, the grove keeps a fairly dense appearance, probably so that the natural influences of the kami can seem to outweigh the cultural influences of human beings.

When visitors approach a main shrine, they usually clap their hands and ring a suspended bell to attract the gods' attention. They then bow, in reverence or prayer, and deposit their offerings in a money chest. Another building, at the innermost part of the shrine, is a sort of holy-of-holies, where the deities actually dwell. Laity have no access to this building, and the popular attitude has been that to peek into it, and observe the ritual objects that attract the kami, would be to court blindness or death. Buddhist influences caused some Shinto shrines to erect pictures of human beings or images of gods, but generally the "bodies" of the kami have been impersonal objects. In addition to the old swords and mirrors, stones, sacred texts, ancient scrolls, jewels, and balls of crystal have predominated. All these objects have associations with natural forces (or, on occasion, heroic human figures) thought to embody the kami. When the influence of Buddhist *bodhisattvas* came to color the Shinto notion of the kami, and so led to deifying especially loyal subjects of the emperors, the headgear, batons, weapons, clothing, writing implements, and other possessions of such deified subjects also became "bodies" of the kami.

Before the disestablishment of Shinto after World War II, the government classified shrines on twelve levels. At the head of the list was the Great Imperial Shrine at Ise. Below Ise came the various large government or national shrines, such as the Heian Shrine in Kyoto and the Meiji Shrine in Tokyo, and then the smaller local shrines. Not even on the list were the tens of thousands of little village or domestic shrines, at which a great deal of Shinto worship actually occurred. Before World War II there were about 111,000 official shrines and about 15,500 Shinto priests.

Two major themes sound in most pilgrims' accounts. One is the holiness of nature, and nature's superiority to our cultural gewgaws. If not interfered with, nature offers us a lush growth and quiet that can reorient our souls. The second major theme is the antiquity of the Shinto shrines and their traditions. Japanese told themselves: Ancestors have come to shrines such as this, prayed prayers such as these, for hundreds of years. Shinto has been the native Japanese way, the tradition that has made us who we are. Coming close to nature, doing as our ancestors have always done, we approach the sacred center of reality, where things work as they should.

SUMMARY: THE JAPANESE CENTER

Characteristically, the Japanese have shown a remarkable talent for taking other peoples' works and giving them a distinctive polish or perfection. This has happened recently with Western technology, and historically it has happened with non-Japanese religion. Most of the religious influences that Japan appropriated and perfected came from China. To its native Shinto orientations, Japan welded Confucian, Daoist, and Buddhist components. The result was an energetic, disciplined, elegant religious ideal. Aesthetic as well as philosophic, solitary yet bounded by clan psychologies, the Japanese way could take nationalistic and militaristic turns without completely losing sight of a beautiful center.

At the midmost portion of the Japanese imagination, a cherry blossom stands threatened by an unseasonable frost. Cool, refined, melancholic, this image says that the center of reality is an emptiness that incises natural details. In both the lonely novels of a Nobel laureate such as Yasunari Kawabata and the serene lectures of a Zen roshi such as Shunryu Suzuki, the center keeps particulars lean and alert, makes tea utensils objects of art.

The Japanese center that provokes such responses is not personal. The nature that gives serenity and proportion is not warm. No divine face waits to break through the emptiness of the Rock Garden. In the reflecting pond of the Golden Pavilion one sees only trees, pavilion, and sky. Buddha upon Buddha, the rows of statues in the Kyoto temples depersonalize as well as multiply the possibilities of enlightenment. Like the many haiku depicting different moments of spiritual arrest or insight, the buddhas diversify as much as they unify. Thus they make the unity of the buddha-nature cumulative: Since any being can flash forth the light of being, a single force of light, a uniform no-thingness, might remove the barriers between us and the rest of the world. When such barriers are removed, the central light can shine. Then our problems reduce to delusion, rather than to the Hindu illusion. The world itself is completely real and lightsome. Only our ignorance keeps us in the dark.

At the Japanese center, reality is polite. Cleanliness and formality, mediated through Shinto concerns with purity and the vital forces of nature, obtain. The rituals of the traditional religious year express different aspects of this vitality. For harvests, marrying, the New Year, and burials, different measures of Shinto and Buddhist beliefs color life's mystery fertile, familial, regenerative, or transmigratory. It is a beautiful land that the Japanese people celebrate. It is a cohesive national identity.

At the Japanese center throbs an amazing energy, coupled with a redoubtable discipline. Yet the center itself remains elusive. The shrines and statues cannot sum it up. It is a whole pictured by preference in peace. It is a flux stopped just long enough to become art. The center sheds much light on death. Death to the body can be as near as failure to serve one's lord perfectly. Death to the self can be as familiar as a popular sutra. Nature dies and is reborn so regularly that the death and rebirth of the personality seem quite fitting. Shame and honor revolve so inexorably that detachment is but common sense.

Detached, the Japanese personality stands a good chance of following up its affinities for beauty, of tending its gardens, and throwing its pots. Detached, the personality finds life's inequities more bearable. Rich and poor, male and female, honored and downcast are the ways things are. Things can change, but they do not have to change for there to be meaning, order, and a reasonable tradition. Reality may seem to be diverse, but in fact Japanese culture shows those who penetrate to the center that it has a remarkable unity.

The polite center judges all brutality harshly, but brutality had many inglorious seasons in Japan. For peasants, women, and ordinary people, it has been easy to be in the wrong place at the wrong time. Then the ruling powers have crushed people thoughtlessly, like a cart rolling over a bug. The consolations of nature never shroud the fact that nature itself can be very cruel. In a land of volcanoes and fierce storms, beauty and violence have often commingled. In a land of warriors and artists, discipline has had several faces. The Japanese center more lets these disparities be than reconciles them in some thicker mystery. Atonement and redemption are not the Japanese way. True, Shinran came to a profound sense of self-abandonment, in which he let the ultimate do its own chanting in his heart. But Shinran seems emotionally extraordinary, the warm exception proving the generally cool rule.

Warm and cool, raw and cooked—both sides of our dichotomies apply in most lands. The best one can do is speak of tendencies, generalities, proclivities—quite fallible impressions that the reader should test warily. We keep coming back to moments in quiet Japanese gardens, when rain gently dimpled the waters. The message then was primitive, ungilded by human contrivance, preferring rough timber and clean thatch. The message was: "Be attentive! Focus your gaze; give the wind and rain good hearing." There wasn't more than the wind and rain at the Japanese center. Quiet and sun added nothing essential. Any time one perceived the force of nature, whether the kami were gentle or the kami were wild, one perceived ultimate, defining reality. This was cool and raw, strong and beautiful, astringent yet ineffably peaceful.

Discussion Questions

1. In what sense is Shinto a fertility religion?
2. What seem to have been the primary psychodynamics of the new religions?
3. Analyze the feminine and masculine components in native Japanese culture.
4. How does the Japanese sense of shame differ from the Western sense of sin?
5. Does Japan make any hard distinctions between aesthetics and religion? Explain.
6. Where would you locate Confucian influence on Japan?
7. Explain how the tea ceremony could become a religious pathway.
8. What were the main Buddhist developments of the Heian period?
9. What was the significance of the Kokugaku movement?
10. How did the kami figure in the average Japanese person's life throughout history?

Key Terms

aesthetic: concerning the beautiful or artistic. In many religions it is hard to separate aesthetic values from the people's sense of what is fitting or filled with divine splendor.

Amaterasu: the sun goddess who has been the chief deity among the Shinto kami. The myths about Amaterasu place her in tension with such other natural forces as the wind and make her the ancestor of the Japanese ruling clan.

Bushido: the ethical and disciplinary code of Japanese samurai (warriors). Bushido was more cultural than expressly religious, but it drew on Confucian notions of responsibility to one's superiors and Buddhist (especially Zen) notions of the disciplined spirit. Those formed by the Bushido Code considered dishonor worse than death and offered their superiors (the lords for whom they fought and served) complete loyalty. For women, the Bushido Code stressed loyalty, fidelity, and above all chastity, creating a feminine parallel to the warrior's commitment to honor.

kami: the Japanese (Shinto) term for the gods or spirits. Traditionally one numbered the kami at 800,000, a round figure probably intended to suggest their profusion. Although most of the kami apparently originally were natural forces (wind, storm, sun; spirits of various striking local phenomena—tall trees, distinctive rocks), heads of the clan and other heroes also could be kami. Indeed, when Buddhism had made a great impact in Japan, the line between kami and *bodhisattvas* often vanished, leading to Buddhist saints being accounted kami and kami being considered *bodhisattvas*. The kami prompt reflection on why it is that people around the world seem to personify or animate the striking things in their natural and social orbits. With the rise of modern critical consciousness this tendency has atrophied, but one can see remnants of it in poets' talk about their muses and naturalists' descriptions of their love or awe for particular desert, mountain, or seaside sites.

nembutsu: an invocation ("Homage to Amida Buddha") central to the practice of Pure Land ("Jodo") Buddhism. The *nembutsu* combines characteristics of a typical Eastern mantra with characteristics of Christian prayer. As mantric, it offers the disciple a familiar, repetitive sound that can calm and direct consciousness, freeing it to sense reality as Buddhist devotionalism has found most useful. As similar to Christian prayer, it offers a personified focus, a divine being one can imagine (because of traditional iconography) and love. "Homage" is an awkward translation of something that combines reverent acknowledgment with submission, respect, and praise.

new religions: a name applied to largely Shinto sects that arose in Japan from the nineteenth century on. As a general phenomenon, the new religions clearly expressed a need for religious ways more vital than what were available by the end of the Tokugawa shogunate. Most of the founders of the new religious groups were charismatic personalities who felt taken over by a kami or called to restore old religious ways rooted in traditional village life. The loose lines between Buddhism and Shinto meant that Buddhist elements were not excluded, while a desire for warm ties with the divinity sometimes led to making the chief deity a parental god. Some of the new religions ran

afoul of the government, but others were apolitical and sought only a renewal of charismatic religious authority.

samurai: Japanese warriors of the feudal period who swore fealty to their lord under pain of death. The samurai became renowned for their courage, sense of honor, and discipline, as well as for their outbursts of cruelty and their share in the infighting of Japanese politics. Many samurai found Zen Buddhism congenial, since it seemed to offer a spiritual discipline to inform their life of dedication to their liege-lords. Despite the traditional Buddhist demand for noninjury *(ahimsa)*, the samurai developed swordsmanship, archery, and hand-to-hand combat as holistic disciplines. For women, the Bushido virtues of chastity and honor offered a parallel field for spiritual discipline.

torii: the sacred gateway that stands at the entrance to Shinto shrines. Most interpreters see the *torii* as dividing the sacred realm of the shrine from the profane outside world. Usually there is a well nearby, for purification, and visitors become more serious after having passed through the *torii* (though Shinto shrines are not grim places). The shrine itself is thought of as a domicile of the kami, who not only reside at a special holy building but also are present in the trees, the streams, and the other aspects of the natural beauty. Some say the *torii,* which has the form of two posts with a double horizontal lintel, represents perches for the birds *(tori),* in thanks for the help they gave the gods.

Zen: the Japanese name for the school of Buddhism that has most stressed meditation. In China this school went by the name Chan and was attributed to Bodhidharma, a meditation-master come from India. Zen has considered meditation to epitomize the Enlightened One's teaching and methodology. Historically it has had great influence in Japanese culture, shaping the ideals of the samurai and undergirding such practices as swordsmanship, floral arrangement, the tea ceremony, and gardening. Rinzai Zen has tended to seek sudden enlightenment, urging disciples to strive hard, try to crack their koans, and keep up a firm discipline of work, silence, and obedience. Soto Zen has been more relaxed, thinking that enlightenment should come gradually, as the ripening of an overall maturation in Buddhist faith and practice. Soto has also lessened the distinction between meditation and the rest of life, thinking that as one's practice developed one would always be cultivating one's innate buddha-nature and helping it manifest itself.

CONCLUSION: SUMMARY REFLECTIONS

A symbol of the concentricity of the natural, the social, the divine, and the personal that religious searches for the center reveal.

At the outset, we postulated that the religious life of humanity is a vast and diversified spectacle. Perhaps you now find that postulate only too well verified. The Eastern traditions alone make a tapestry of unmanageable proportions. We have tried to discern some of this tapestry's principal patterns. We have tried to present the information and the themes that might make such terms as "Hinduism" or "Buddhism" intelligible. Our final task is to review the whole and suggest its implications.

UNITY AND DIVERSITY

The unity of the phenomena we have studied is religion—the common quest for a way to the center. The diversity of the phenomena makes the religions—the distinctive traditional ways in which sizable numbers of people have worked at this quest together. Specifically, we have studied the Indian and East Asian traditional ways.

The quests are all deeply humanistic, in that they all focus intensely on human welfare. For instance, according to C. G. Jung,[1] the American Indian or African who greets the sun as a daily miracle performs

American Religious History: Twenty-five Key Dates	
1492	About 10 Million American Indians Living North of Rio Grande
1565	Roman Catholic Colony in New World
1619	Beginning of Black Slavery
1620	Mayflower Compact
1654	First Jewish Settlement in New Amsterdam
1683	William Penn Founds Philadelphia
1734	Great Awakening in New England
1776	Declaration of Independence Expresses Nonconformist, Enlightenment-Influenced Religious Outlook
1784	Death of Shaker Leader Ann Lee
1799	Creation of Russian Orthodox Diocese in Alaska
1801	Beginnings of Western Revivalism
1836	Founding of Transcendentalist Club in Concord, Massachusetts
1847	Bushnell's Christian Nurture
1848	Mormons Found Salt Lake City
1850	Oberlin College Grants First Theological Degree to a Woman
1863	Emancipation Proclamation
1866	Second Roman Catholic Plenary Council in Baltimore
1876	Mary Baker Eddy Founds Christian Science Association
1885	Columbia Platform of Reformed Rabbis
1890	Massacre at Wounded Knee
1901–1902	William James's Gifford Lectures, The Varieties of Religious Experience
1917	Rauschenbush's A Theology for the Social Gospel
1920–33	Prohibition
1935	Peak of Protestant Neo-Orthodoxy
1964	Civil Rights Act; Martin Luther King, Jr., Receives Nobel Peace Prize

deep psychic work. The Hindu who makes *puja* (worship) or whom bhakti (devotionalism) carries to Krishna constructs a world that makes sense and provides emotional comfort. The same is true of Buddhists who ponder koans, Daoists who try to confect the elixir of immortality, and Hasidic Jews who learn diamond cutting to preserve what they can of the old Orthodox life. In most times and places, the religions have supported or developed meaning unpretentiously, unobtrusively. For most people the traditions have worked subtly as sets of largely unquestioned assumptions.

Still, the traditions have varied in their subtleness. People who ate bean curd sensed the world differently from people who ate roasted lamb. The Prophet who recited, "There is no God but God," oriented Arabs away from the world that the Greek philosopher Thales saw when he exclaimed, "The world is full of gods." The recent introduction of social scientific and critical historical methods has made religious studies more empirically minded and so more sensitive to such variety. Thus, the differences among the religions have been in the spotlight.

Quite properly, we have seen that Hinduism and Buddhism are vast concepts. Indeed, they are quite abstract, for Hindus and Buddhists have lived out their dharma very differently depending on time, place, and

Figure 18 *Taj Mahal: Islam on Hindu soil. Photo by J. T. Carmody.*

station. Therefore, to talk about Hinduism or Buddhism requires finding common qualities among great diversity, such as a regard for the Vedas or the Buddha, for karma or Kuan-yin. Increasingly scholars debate whether there is a common quality among all the traditions, a common religion at the traditions' cores.

We believe that there is such a common quality or unity, and at various points we have described it as a common attraction toward mystery. Relatedly, we believe that the empiricism that misses such unity and mystery is at least an unwitting reductionism—an insistence that humanity is no more than as it behaves. Usually, that insistence indicates an impoverished imagination or interiority—an inability to intuit how two different behaviors (for example, yoga and ritual propriety) might be directed toward the same goal: sacredness, the really real.[2]

The tricky thing about meaning, which extroverted observers tend to miss, is that ultimacy or mystery is always but a step away. Still, distraction and

lack of reflection on the part of either the people under scrutiny or the scholars who are scrutinizing them are defenses that mystery easily breaks down. As Brahman, nirvana and *Dao*, ultimacy broke down the defenses against deep meaning in the peoples we have studied. Whether they wanted it or not (and usually they did), sacred mystery defined their world.

If one can see the sacred, it breaks through all the barriers that have divided our modern world. Perhaps the only traces of the sacred we can see are the anxieties on which the tranquilizer industry trades. Or perhaps we are able to appreciate it in the Nobel Prize–winning efforts of outstanding scientists and writers. Either way, with or without overt theology, ultimacy is always at hand. We may choose not to embrace it, not to call mystery our inmost vocation. However, as surely as we suffer and die, it will embrace us. All people by nature desire to know, Aristotle declared. Our mortal condition makes Aristotle's dogma existential: All people by nature desire to know the mystery from which they come and to which they go. All people are by nature set for religion.

Religion

The world *religion* refers to the inmost human vocation. By empirical fact as well as theoretical interpretation, *religion* pertains to all life that is reflective, that heads into mystery. Largely for that reason, the word *religion* was seldom uttered by the great teachers.[3] They rather spoke of meaning, the way to "walk," the traditional wisdom, the balance called justice, and the fire called love. Because they were embodied spirits speaking to other embodied spirits, they used familiar figures: mountains, rivers, widows giving alms. Furthermore, their speech led to common action: rhythmic prostrations, gutsy resistance to the emperor, helping a friend. All these actions, though, were religious.

People organized communities around the great teachers' speech and actions. The communities expressed their religion (their venture after meaning into mystery) in ways that Joachim Wach has labeled theoretical, social, and active.[4] That is, they made theologies, brotherhoods and sisterhoods, and liturgies and laws. Regularly, the communities lost the spirit of their founders, as succeeding generations repeatedly prized order more than charisma, control more than inspiration, and orthodoxy more than creativity. Just as regularly, reformers tried to find their way back to the original vision. In China it was "Back to the ancients." In the Christian West it was "Back to the Word."

The various traditions have shaped their peoples in endless ways. Some have spoken rather simply—Judaism and Islam, for instance. Others have made strange bedfellows and cultures more complex, such as the religions of China and Japan. Still, all traditions have used the past to decipher the present and to prepare for the future. All have received and handed on.

That handing on is what we mean by *tradition*.[5] None of us fashions meaning free of external influences. All of us receive a cultural inheritance, meager or rich, to which we add. We do this willy-nilly—by having children, teaching students, working with colleagues, supporting friends. Original sin is the dark side of such a sense of tradition. According to this concept, we all take our first breath in air that is polluted, in a game that is tilted against us. How polluted or tilted the world is has been a matter of vigorous debate. The only consensus seems to be that evil is a sad fact and that there is sufficient good to justify hope. The handing on therefore leads all the religions to revile evil and buttress hope—a process that can be called a concern for salvation.

For instance, ancient peoples banded together for evolutionary salvation—against the evil of extinction and in hope that the race would go on. Close to the earth, they thought in concrete terms, undifferentiatedly, telling stories of life and death. Life came from the fatherly sky and the motherly earth. Life was as possible, as renewable, as heavenly water and productive dirt. Death was breathtakingly near, but perhaps the dead were as seed falling in the ground. Perhaps they were but a link in the chain of generations. Or maybe they passed to a new form of life. As smoke passes from burning wood, so perhaps the subtle part of a person, the part that thinks and travels in dreams, could pass to a new state. In those ways, perhaps, ancient peoples fought for hope, tried to block out absurdity.

To suffer, lose, rejoice, or trust—such acts know no religious, ethnic, or national bounds. We all walk a way (if only a way to death) that we cannot name. We all seek (if only covertly) a path that is straight, a path that mystery blesses. If some of our predecessors have been Nordic berserkers, who heated up to feel mystery boil, others have been Eastern yogis, who so slowed themselves that they could be buried alive. If some of our predecessors have been erotics, convinced that the force of the way is sexual *shakti,* others have been lonely ascetics, convinced that meat clouds the spirit. There are few roads that no one has taken, few options that no one has tried. Though the options make all the difference for the individual, we can see from others where we might have gone. Indeed, that is a major reason why we study the humanities. There would be no basis for studying the humanities were there no unity called human nature. Likewise, there would be no religious studies were there no unity called religion.

Contending with nature, society, the self, and whatever ultimacy they have known, all human beings have mused about their sunrise and sunset. For all of them, the cosmos and the group have had effects, the self and ultimacy have beguiled. Without and within each person, the world has taken shape, changed, occasionally threatened to slip away. Since we are "synthetic" beings, whose incarnate spirits include the lowest matter and the heights of thought, we cannot escape religion's full span. Madness comes when the span tilts and the synthesis comes unglued. Boredom comes when we lose the span's tension, when imagination goes stale. In health, we find nature, society, and the self fascinating. In health, science, politics, and art are all essential, all deeply humanistic. If they become so specialized, so arcane, that their essential humanity is not apparent, we must speak of disease—of dysfunction, pathology, alienation.

Though disease has terrible power in our time, as nuclear arms and the prison systems show, it has always written arguments for despair. Parents who wept over dead children heard despair at Stonehenge, Gettysburg, and My Lai. Every woman raped, every man tortured, has heard voices within counseling her or him to abandon hope. Amazingly, though, human beings will not live by despair alone. Their very sense that the times are out of joint is a cry that there ought to be health.

Until we give up completely, we label health as normal. Disease, we say, is the lack of health. Evil, we say, is the lack of good—of proper order, right being, justice, and love. Indeed, so deep is our drive toward health that we cannot think of nonbeing and evil directly. They are irrational, absurd, and void. In their hope, then, the religions uncover more religion. In their hope, Marxists and religious believers can dialogue.

Meaning and Idiosyncrasy

The themes above are some of the constants that all the traditions carry. If they are general, it is because they pertain to all of humanity. In religious perspective, our human characteristics comprise a common condemnation (or consecration) to meaning. Thus, the differences among traditions are simply *how* their peoples have sought, conceived, and enacted meaning. That affirms, of course, that differences do differentiate.[6] It affirms that a Buddhist is not a Hindu and a Christian is not a Jew.

Because he or she is always dealing both with religion as a whole and with the individual religions, the student of religion must develop a peculiar balance. If she or he is blind to the unity behind all religions, the student will miss the deep humanity that the traditions can offer us. On the other hand, if the student sweeps all the information together, making all Buddhists anonymous Christians or all Christians renegade Jews, he or she will miss the grainy texture

that religion always has in people's lives. As is often the case, the ideal involves a duality: *both* cutting to the heart of the matter, where all human beings are siblings, *and* respecting the idiosyncrasies that differentiate people as nations, tribes, sexes, individuals, and traditional religionists.

The idiosyncrasies are mysterious. Why should the Buddha have proposed no-self? A first answer might be because no-self answered the question of suffering that the Buddha's personal life and the life of his Indian culture posed. Fine, but this is hardly an end to the matter. Why should death, disease, and putrefaction have troubled this particular prince so deeply? Presumably many other princes saw corpses without deciding to leave their palaces, wives, and children to adopt a life of asceticism; similarly, many other cultures experienced suffering. Why, then, did the Indians penetrate the psychology of suffering so profoundly? Why not the Babylonians, Chinese, Aztecs, or Mayans?

As those questions show, there is a limit to historical analysis. It can explain some of the differences among individuals or cultures, but their real origin lies beyond it. For the real origin of differences is the incomprehensible world order[7]—St. Paul's *mysterion*. We did not set the cosmic dust spinning. We don't know why it wove the combinations it did. Therefore, when we respect differences, we respect the totality of history and its mystery. We respect the ultimacy behind the facts, the often very brutal facts, that just this universal drama has played and no other.

Let us again try to be concrete. The Australian dream world, as scholars imperfectly reconstruct it from artifacts and interviews, reflects the peculiar landscape of the Australian continent. The aboriginal myths are similar to those of other areas that explain how the ancestors or demiurges fashioned the world, yet the aboriginal world is unique. The Australian use of the *tjurunga*, the sacred wooden boards, for instance, is distinctive. Other ancient peoples painted and carved, but none (that we know) with just the Australian concern for totemic ancestors. Or consider African peoples' use of masks. That, too, has analogies—with the American Indian use of *kachinas* and even the Greek use of theater masks. Yet in Africa masks relate to thought, such as Ogotemmeli's Dogon thought,[8] that speaks of man and woman, fox and ant hill, smithy and granary as the people of no other continent do. Again, the Chinese divination practice of *feng-shui* (geomancy) is like the complex basket divination of the Africans, yet they differ greatly. The two types of divination have the same purpose (to determine what will happen in nature and time), but they express it differently. *Feng-shui* would not seem appropriate in the Congo.

Differences, then, are real. We could develop that theme for Hinduism contrasted with Jainism or Buddhism, for Catholics contrasted with Orthodox or Protestants. How great differences are, how divergent they make their adherents' realities, is difficult to determine. Often it seems as much a matter of the analyst's temperament as of the adherents' realities. In the terms of a famous debate,[9] the analyst who has an *"esoteric"* (inner-directed) personality tends to stress the unity in the traditions, while the *"exoteric"* (outer-directed) personality tends to stress the diversity.

Esoteric types respond to innermost notions and innermost realities. For them, a common mystery is as real as distinctive facts, even more real. Therefore, esoteric types tend to the negative way—the Hindu *"neti, neti"* ("not this, not that"). They may downplay or even disparage the diverse ways that people have chosen to pursue the supreme value. In contrast, exoteric types respond to outer phenomena—to the actual births, hungers, murders, orgasms, and deaths that make people's lives colorful, intense, palpably real. They fear that moving away from such realities ignores the way things are.

Besides exoteric blood, sweat, and tears, ultimate reality does seem esoteric, pale and abstract. Looking closely, though, we find that esoterica have given religions most of their life. For instance, what would American Indian ceremonies—the Sun Dance, the vision quest, the potlatch (gift-giving feast)—have been without Wakan Tanka, the Great Spirit? What would the Egyptian pyramids have been without Osiris and Re? Those pale gods gave the ceremonies and massive stones their meaning. Apart from such meaning, exoterica are mute. The same applies in other traditions. Hindu bhakti festivals make no sense without a Krishna to play the flute, a Kali to wield the sword. Buddhist meditation depends on karma and nirvana. In the West, Jewish circumcision, the Christian Eucharist, and the Muslim *hajj* (pilgrimage to Mecca) depend on the covenant, redemption, and the eternal Word. In the lives of religious people, the exoteric is a body for the esoteric. We think it should be the same in the writings of religion scholars.

COMPARING THE EASTERN TRADITIONS

When we discussed some of the methodological perspectives scholars are using to study religion today, we tacitly assumed the diversity and complexity of the world religions. In principle, most contemporary methods are supposed to be "value-free," assuming that all traditions are equally human. In our view, this does not mean that a scholar must refrain from all value judgments. We see no need to pass by Hindu caste, Chinese footbinding, or American racism with nary a discouraging word. We do need to explain how the traditions in which they occur see such phenomena and to make no assumptions that Indians or Chinese or Americans are more or less virtuous than other human tribes.

In this spirit, we shall attempt a summary comparison of the four Asian traditions we have studied, assuming that they are equally human, equally complex, but trying to distill the unique character, advantages, and liabilities of each. This distillation is bound to reflect biases we do not fully appreciate, but so would any other comparison, as well as the decision not to make a comparison at all.

Placed side by side, Hinduism, Buddhism, Chinese religion, and Japanese religion are four asymmetrical traditions. Although each is dizzyingly complex, and arguably is complete unto itself, their dependencies on one another are unequal. Hinduism generated a great deal of Buddhism, and continues to share a great deal with it, because of their common Indian roots. It shares much less with Chinese and Japanese religions. Buddhism shares much more with Chinese and Japanese religions, because of being transplanted to China and Japan. In the case of China, Buddhism set its seal very deeply, but in turn it was influenced deeply by Daoism, and to a lesser extent by Confucianism. In Japan, Buddhism interacted with Shinto, receiving a further stimulus to focus on nature, and giving the Japanese love of nature a more profound philosophical underpinning. China and Japan themselves interacted, China having more cultural influence on Japan than Japan on China. Neither China nor Japan had a great cultural influence on India, but the lands between India and China often melded characteristics of the two. Thus Tibet, Burma, and Thailand sometimes seem to be midcountries, whose scripts, architectures, and religions have creatively blended Chinese and Indian elements.

Generally, India has been the great land of interiority and speculation. China has been the great land of exteriority and practicality. That does not mean India did not farm, fight, and organize political units. It does not mean China did not meditate, worship, and philosophize. It just means that when one searches for that elusive thing called a country's peculiar "genius," one does not point to India's political organization, nor to China's metaphysics. Despite all its wars and internal divisions, China has been the land of order and bureaucracy. Despite all its trade and kingdoms, India has been the land of karma and transmigration. Where China fingered the world like a piece of fine cloth, something to be delicately appreciated, India thought about the world like a mathematical problem or a dramatic plot, something to be grasped mentally. "Planting our feet solidly," the Chinese said, "let us make here a family structure, a cuisine, an aesthetic, a technology that allow us to live harmoniously with nature and one another." "Since the world of the senses is doubtful," the Indians said, "let us plant our feet lightly, and keep our spirits free. Pleasure and wealth are legitimate life-goals, but duty and salvation are higher."

Of course, these are simplistic comparisons—almost caricatures. In venturing to make them, we do not deny they can be terribly abused. Indeed, we are reminded of the Western "negative" tradition, which taught that God is more unlike than like even our true statements about him (or her, or it). There is a cultural analogue: If one could get down to specific villages and individuals, our comparisons might prove more untrue than true. From the vantage of a mental Goodyear blimp, however, the cultural contrasts we have made seem valid. India has been the more esoteric cultural basin, China the more exoteric.

The religious poles in this comparison would be philosophical Hinduism and Buddhism, on the esoteric side, and Confucianism, on the exoteric side. Devotional Hinduism and Buddhism, Daoism, and Shinto would occupy the intermediate ground. The cutting edge of Indian philosophy has been idealism—the priority of mind over matter. The cutting edge of Confucianism has been social realism—the priority of public affairs over private thoughts. In between, devotional Hinduism and Buddhism have worked the emotions and the imagination that mediate between human mentality and materiality. Daoism and Shinto have worked the mature spirits and human aesthetics that mediate between nature-centered humanity and political humanity. This does not mean that Indian philosophers did not have to consider economics and statecraft. It does not deny that Confucians made a place for meditation. It simply paints with the broad brush that "summary reflections" suggests, responding to those students who come to "summary reflections" hoping their teachers finally will risk a few generalizations.

Of the Asian traditions, to which should you go for a penetrating theory of nature? You should go to Hinduism or Buddhism for an analysis of how "nature" comes to us through the senses, and to Chinese or Japanese religion for directives on how best to enjoy natural beauty. For the foundations of natural science, you should go outside the Asian orbit, to Greek philosophy and Western revelation, since they were the main sources of the confidence in nature's intelligibility necessary for what we have come to call "natural science."[10]

To which Asian tradition should you go to for a penetrating theory of society? You should go to Confucianism and Daoism. Confucianism taught that only moral virtue will make any political unit healthy. The great Confucian key was the quality of a village's or a country's rulers. If such rulers were learned and good the village or country would prosper. To be learned, they had to know the ways of the ancients, the giants who first saw the lay of the political land. To be good, they had to attune themselves to the *Dao* of reality, disciplining selfishness, vanity, greed, and the other vices that kept people from walking the Way. The Way to social prosperity was "there," objectively available. If people had eyes to see and ears to hear, they could find it. But self-interest or seeking material profit so regularly blinded people's eyes or deafened their ears that most social units wobbled along or fell into the ditch. Until inner goodness (*ren*) joined with gracious protocol (*li*), social relations would continue to go badly.

Daoism agreed with much of this deeper Confucianism, but Daoism was appalled by the Confucian tendency to make stuffed shirts. When lesser spirits trumpeted the Confucian tunes about inner goodness and outer protocol, legalism and bureaucracy multiplied like cancers. For the Daoists, imagination was the crucial difference. Unless people stayed creative, their societies would bumble into dead ends or become impossibly boring. Only free spirits could keep the bureaucrats from driving everyone to drink. Only wit, irony, satire, and creative musing could keep politicians free to see the point. The point was justice, fair-dealing, and the way to justice was *wu-wei:* indirection, not-doing, the wink that's as good as a nod. Heavy-handedness, aggression, the lawyers' obsession with jots and tittles were the sure and rocky road to political disaster. People had to be lured, seduced, beguiled into cooperation. Unless you won their hearts and minds, you lost the long-range game. Because most would not grasp these rather obvious truths, China got generation after generation of wars and fatuous politicians.

To which Asian tradition should you go for a penetrating theory of the self? You should go to Hinduism or Buddhism. Their common font of wisdom is the centrality of detachment. If the human self is to become free, it must detach itself from layer after layer of illusion. Although Hinduism and Buddhism disagree about the final layer, Hinduism tending to retain a "self" and Buddhism tending to deny it, they agree that the individual is wrongly situated until he or she connects with the All. Whether the All is Brahman or nirvana, it is the only adequate context for human self-understanding. If we do not understand the mysterious envelope in which we are sealed, we do not understand our most basic characteristic.

In Western terms, the analogue that comes to mind is the Danish philosopher Søren Kierkegaard's view that the self is a relation relating itself to the Absolute. As a relation, my "I" is both a subject and an object: I can think about, reflect on, move myself. As a relation relating itself to the Absolute, my "I" moves its complex self toward God, whether it realizes this or not. For Kierkegaard, the great prod to grasping the human situation is sin, which shows itself in depression and despair. For Hinduism and Buddhism, the great prod is death, which shows itself in suffering and disease. Either way, the only solution is to realize, actualize, achieve what one is. Christian, Hindu, and Buddhist salvation all come from uniting the self with the All that lets the self be.

The Chinese and Japanese theories of the self have been more social and less profound. Behind that judgment, of course, is our conviction that social relations are less profound than the ontological (being) relation of the self to the Absolute. Many contemporary scholars would dispute this thesis, either speculatively or practically (either in their theories or the ways they choose to do their work). For them "the social construction of reality" makes all our selves intrinsically dependent on the cultures in which we live, move, and have our being. We have no language without our culture, no economics or politics. Language, economics, and politics more shape religion or metaphysics than they derive from religion or metaphysics.

There is a lot to be said for this thesis, but we do not think it finally wins the day. For all the massive influence of our cultures, we remain people who can move from language to language, religion to religion, economic system to economic system. Contrariwise, we can never move away from our relation to Brahman, nirvana, or God, because this relation is constitutive, built into the depths of reflective intelligence (selfhood).

To which Asian tradition should you go for a penetrating theory of ultimate reality? To devotional Hinduism or Zen. Devotional Hinduism, focused on Krishna or Shiva, spotlights the centrality of love. Binding the devotee to divinity with reasons of the heart, it makes religion a consuming passion. Zen Buddhism pivots on realizing one's pact with nirvana, one's intrinsic knowledge-nature. In silence, Zen sacramentalizes our ultimate enlightenment. The result can be a wonderfully gracious living, cool, serene, and artistic. Such living says that ultimate reality dances, paints, speaks itself forth in poetry. It says that ultimate reality is art, science, and ineffable light.

The Sage as Eastern Archetype

If asked to paint a picture of the ideal product the Asian traditions were trying to develop, we would entitle it *The Sage*. Whereas the nonliterate traditions have tended to pivot on the shaman and the Western traditions have originated from prophets, the Asian traditions have tended to pivot on the sage. To be sure, there have been shamans and prophets in India and East Asia, just as there have been sages in the West. But Buddha, Confucius, and Laozi—the three most influential Asian personalities—have all been more sagacious than prophetic. It will be useful, therefore, to reflect on the differences in the Asian traditions' understandings of sagehood and then on the message the Eastern sages offer students of the world religions today.

The Indian sage, Buddhist or Hindu, has tended to be a yogi. The *rishis* whose visions lay behind the Vedas, the Mahavira, and the Buddha, all disciplined the flesh and the mind to win enlightenment and liberation. The Indian archetypal figure won his great wisdom by penetrating the veil of maya or samsara, by intuiting the reality of Brahman or Suchness. The popular tradition might embellish this victory with miracles and myths, but its core was yogic meditation. Meditation was the method, wisdom was the substance, and morality was the fruit. Archetypally, intuition *(jnana)* or trance *(dhyana)* were the principal yogas. *Karma yoga* (acting without attachment) and *bhakti yoga* (devotion) were accommodations, perfectly valid and effective for salvation, but spun off from the quieter core.

In East Asia, the sage had a more social inclination. For both Confucius and Laozi, union with the *Dao* was a font of political order. One might say, therefore, that the East Asian sage was more prudent or ethical, the Indian sage more ontological. For example, there is little evidence that the Buddha aspired to political office. The world was burning; it would have been folly to plunge into worldly affairs. By contrast, Confucius greatly aspired to political office, or at least political counselorship. Like Plato, Confucius thought that good social order was the prime requisite and that good social order would come only when kings had sages for brains. From the demands of good social order, Confucius worked his way back to gentlemanliness, and then to *ren,* the heart of human nobility. By the time he was seventy, he could move nobly in all situations, letting his *ren* be the embodiment of the Way. Thus a certain mysticism shines through Confucius' last relations with the Way. He could hear the Way in the morning and in the evening die content because the Way had become his meat and drink, the other half of his heart and soul.

Laozi is initially more mystical than Confucius, but eventually just as political. For Laozi, all power *(de)* comes from union with the Way, for the Way runs nature and society alike. Therefore, the sage shuts the doors of the senses and places his spirit in the Way. Therefore, the sage advocates *wu-wei,* reveres the uncarved block. Backing away from social conventions and hackneyed speech, the sage is alert, poetic, and paradoxical. To the ordinary run of people, he is an eccentric, always trying to see the world afresh. Zhuangzi pushed this eccentricity further than Laozi, delighting in affronting the sobersided Confucians. Soaring with the great birds, he was not surprised that the little birds found him very odd.

The deeper Confucians and Daoists joined with the East Asian Buddhist philosophers to make the sage's wisdom worldly. In the final frames of the Zen teaching pictures called *Herding an Ox,* the enlightened person comes back into the marketplace, able to enjoy enlightenment in the midst of buying and sell-

ing, eating and drinking. Empty and gone beyond, the *Prajna-paramita* is as near as a blooming cherry blossom, as full as the rugged rocks. Wisdom swirls in the master's whipped green tea, whistles in the flight of the archer's arrow. The enlightened life is graceful, integrated, at home in the world. By the time the dharma reached the Pacific, the world was no longer burning. It had cooled in the mountains of the Song landscapes, lost its fever in the Shinto pools. So pacified, it looked outward as much as inward, found rest on the keen edge of body-mind. It grew to love subtlety and indirection, tactfulness and play. "There is no good and evil," the Zen disciple heard. "All jobs are worth doing well." What is is what is in front of us. After enlightenment, mountains are mountains and trees are trees.

It is hard to imagine Indian Buddhists and Hindus comfortable with this East Asian worldliness. In Delhi, Bombay, and Calcutta, life remains very steamy, burning with misery. The grass around Hindu shrines is seldom immaculate. The water buffaloes behind the Taj Mahal intrude an instructive dung and mud. Along with the blazing summer sun, they mock the sultan who thought the Taj would immortalize his lovely queen. The Taj will have crumbled long before the queen's soul has found rest.

Does the Eastern sage have a distinctive message for students of the world religions today? Perhaps so. If the students come from the West, they likely have been touched by the West's loss of confidence in wisdom. Western people who speak authoritatively about enlightenment, who persuasively incarnate the *Dao,* are few and far between. So, an increasingly influential argument has arisen. "Since so few wise people appear in our midst," the argument runs, "wisdom must be an endangered species, going the way of the dodo. Evolution must be in the hands of the technicians, the marines shouting 'can do!' " Swiftly and surely, the Eastern sages rebut this argument. Let Laozi occupy your mind a half-hour and the marines will lie high and dry. "What can you do?" Laozi politely asks. "What is the end of all your technique? If your graphs do not bring you beauty, your tanks do not win you peace, why all your plotting and piloting?"

The Eastern sages are sufficiently concerned with technique—in meditation, painting, ritual, and many other things—to make it clear that they are not opposed to engineering. They are merely opposed to calling a spade a pearl. A spade should be called a spade: an instrument for digging. With a spade, you may dig in the earth and come up with a goodly treasure. If

Figure 19 *Landscape attributed to Kano Motonobu (1476–1559). Ink and light color on paper; 20 × 13½ in. This picture shows the Japanese appropriation of the Chinese aestheticoreligious notion of emptiness. The Nelson–Atkins Museum of Art, Kansas City, Missouri. (Gift of Mrs. George H. Bunting, Jr.)*

spiritual drama that makes your community significant. To focus on your community's moving and shaking is to miss what your people might be.

You do not like these quirky phrases? Paradoxes put you off? Ah well, no Eastern sage ever promised you a garden of platitudes. If you want a good guru, an abbot who knows his business, you will have to knock and knock and knock again. Easy admittance means superficial discipline. Superficial discipline means shallow learning. Shallow learning means specious enlightenment, and so the sickening of the dharma. It is not cruelty that makes good gurus demanding. It is unusual kindness. In the spiritual life, you become what you do. In the spiritual life, outer persona and inner self must come closer and closer together.

"Consider yonder Bald Mountain," the sage Mencius said. "You know, once it was thick with trees. The mind of human beings is much the same. If they would nurture it, it would grow lush and very useful. But they neglect it, or abuse it, or hack it away without care, so it becomes barren and ugly, useless and an eyesore."

The *Dhammapada* begins: "Yesterday's thoughts make the self of today, and today's thoughts make the self of tomorrow. Our life is the creation of our mind." Is the *Dhammapada* passé? Have we found shortcuts to beautiful selfhood on our way to the mushroom cloud?

No. Many people in many nations now lament the lack of vision, the venality, the small-souledness in which they drown. But few Western people know that therapy is as near as the *Mencius,* as simple as the *Dhammapada.* You cannot have political vision if you never open your mind. You are bound to be venal and pusillanimous if you never feed your soul.

What doth it profit people if they can assemble any stereo and never hear the music of the spheres? What doth it profit people to place all their energies in the stock market? Stereos and the stock market have their place—all the Eastern sages allow them. What the Eastern sages do not allow them is primacy of place. If the *Dao* is in urine and dung, the *Dao* is in stereos and the stockmarket. But to hear the *Dao* in the morning and in the evening die content, one must vacate assembling and selling. The business of life is not business. The business of life is being. If we want to prosper significantly, we must be open, collected, and disciplined—"one-pointed" in soul and mind. It does not matter that many of our schools know nothing of such Eastern wisdom. The college catalogue is seldom a great book. Real learning occurs in dark

you want a pearl, especially one of great price, you will have to dive into the sea, go down deep to rebirth. It is his deep intelligence, his midmost mind, that gives Confucius his clout. Were he to work the surface only, merely to push and pull his facts, we could read Confucius like a newspaper. Similarly, it is *samadhi,* the deepest consciousness, that gives the yogi his freedom. Were he merely to sense or reason, we could watch him like daytime TV.

For the Indian and East Asian sages, the way up remains the way down. If you want to glimpse the heavenly *Dao* or consort with the glorified Buddha, you will have to return to yourself, find who you are, see your face before your parents were born. It is your inner space, your emptiness, that will make your house useful. To focus attention on your walls or roof is to miss your house's meaning. Similarly, it is its nights and painful passages. Wisdom to live by goes far below figures and facts.

"Leave off, Buddha and Zhuangzi," you may be saying. "Confucius, give us a break." "So sorry," the sages respectfully answer. "We thought you were asking Asia to gladden your heart."

If our hearts are ever to gladden, we must give them something to love. If we listen to the Eastern sages, we will give them natural beauty, social order, and personal depth. Day by day, one day at a time, we will try to make time graceful, to empty space for landscapes of peace. In emptiness we may possess our souls. In graceful time, the *Dao* may sing. If today you would possess your soul, you must empty it of what is tawdry. If today you would hear the *Dao,* you must attune your inner ear.

ON BEING AN AMERICAN CITIZEN OF THE RELIGIOUS WORLD

In general handbooks such as *The Historical Atlas of the Religions of the World, Historia Religionum, The Concise Encyclopedia of Living Faiths,* and *The Encyclopedia of Religion,* American religion does not receive 5 percent of the space. The first lesson that the world religions offer Americans, then, is that America is not as important as Americans tend to think. Our 400 years of religious experience are not much beside India's 5,000. If our 5 percent of the world's population and almost 35 percent of the consumption of the world's raw materials are disproportionate, we need all the help we can get to become less important.

We are not advocating the suppressing of patriotism. Few existing cultures are very old. Europeans or Asians who sniff because their cultures go back more centuries than ours are hardly less ridiculous than we. All nations need a perspective on world history. All nations need to see things "under the aspect of eternity."

For most Americans, religion has been Christianity, and Christianity has often pivoted on Jesus and the founder of their own church. In some cases the dark ages between those two personages stretch 1,800 years. For such people, Catholics are not considered Christians, and Orthodox are beyond the pale. True,

Approximate Membership Data on Major American Religious Groups (1986)

Adventists, Seventh Day	640,000
Baptists	27,000,000
Buddhists	100,000
Christian Church (Disciples of Christ)	1,132,000
Christian Churches and Churches of Christ	1,050,000
Church of Christ, Scientist*	250,000
Church of the Nazarene	516,000
Churches of Christ	1,600,000
Eastern Churches (Orthodox)	3,500,000
Episcopal Church	2,775,000
Friends United Meeting (Quakers)	100,000
Jehovah's Witnesses	700,000
Jewish congregations	5,000,000
Latter Day Saints (Mormons)	3,600,000
Lutherans	8,500,000
Mennonites	185,000
Methodists	13,500,000
Pentecostals	3,500,000
Presbyterians	3,300,000
Roman Catholics	52,250,000
Salvation Army	420,000
Unitarian Universalist Association	170,000
United Churches of Christ	1,700,000
Total: ca. 60% of population	142,000,000

*1936 data. Since 1936, American membership data have not been made public.

Source: *The World Almanac and Book of Facts 1987.*

Americans have modified this intolerance by coexisting with their neighbors. Almost all Americans, though, are quite provincial and need a deep breath of cosmopolitan air.

The root of provincialism is what Erik Erikson calls "pseudospeciation"—pretending that we are the only true human beings. In the past, that "we" has been Chinese, Japanese, and Eskimos. It has been Boston Brahmins and Oklahoma dirt farmers. It has been Catholics who would never darken a Protestant church door, Orthodox who would never visit a synagogue. Fortunately, we now know enough about the psychodynamics of pseudospeciation, largely through analyses of prejudice, to show that it has little to do with genuine religion. In fact, we now know that genuine religion directly opposes pseudospeciation.

In most cases, pseudospeciation stems from a combination of fear and self-interest. We fear the universal humanity, the radical equality, that a pluralistic world implies. It would force us to shed our shells; it would snatch away our platform for boasting. Similarly, we fail to grasp notions such as the Christian Church because it is to our advantage that "in Christ" there be male and female (Gal. 3:28). We fail to enact the notion of a union of all nations, because it is to our advantage to dictate prices to the world. Few of us are magnanimous willingly, textbook writers included.

If we Americans are to gain stature in religion's golden eye, we will have to become more realistic about time and space than we have tended to be. Throughout all time, most people have not been Americans, Christians, or whites, and any true God has blessed more lands than just ours. By today's standards, the colonial Puritans' "errand in the wilderness" was terribly naive. Those who launched it simply did not have our facts about human prehistory and human diversity. It was largely ignorance, then, that led them to locate salvation in New England. The same is true of those who proposed that America be God's new Israel. Sober students of American history wonder to what extent such notions were used to justify ravaging the Indians. Historians of religion stumble over the obvious fact that God's old Israel was perfectly well.[11]

If we deflate our egos, we may see things in better perspective. From the vantage point of an astronaut or the sun god Re, Americans have never been *the* holy people. Long before the whites, reds revered every striking American locale. Shortly after the whites, blacks became America's suffering servants. Unbeknownst to our pioneers, peoples in Asia were living lives of grace under pressure.

The only holy people, in religious perspective, are of the single race, the single species. All divisions make but partial stories. There is a dictum in religious studies that he or she who knows just one religion knows no religion. By that dictum Americans urgently need to study world religions; if only to determine our own identity, we need to know what others have been, what alternatives there were.

In addition, the world religions can suggest what in American religious experience has been distinctive.

This topic is immense, so we can only offer a few leads. First, the Reformation and Enlightenment had a marked effect on American religion. Together, they led to a peculiar blend of pietism and rationalism. Of course, pietism and rationalism have been present in other cultures. For instance, India embraced both bhakti and Vedanta; Islam embraced both Sufism and Law. In America, the mixture tended to set the Bible against the brain. Evolution and the Scopes trial of 1925 dramatized this tension. In colonial times, Calvinists made syntheses of biblical faith and intellectualism that pleased at least themselves. During the drafting of the Constitution, it appears that reason ousted piety—unless we should call the founding fathers pietistic.

One way of looking at American pietism and rationalism is aesthetic. William Clebsch has elaborated that point of view.[12] In his opinion, such representatively American thinkers as Jonathan Edwards, Ralph Waldo Emerson, and William James were most moved by the world's beauty. Another way of approaching American religion is to emphasize religious liberty. Sidney Mead has argued that the American experiment in religious pluralism proved as momentous as the establishment of Christianity in imperial Rome.[13]

Both these views owe much to the Enlightenment's advances on the Reformation. The Reformation established the principles of individual conscience and individual interpretation of scripture. The Enlightenment proposed that reason—nondogmatic thought common to all—should be the judge when individual interpretations shattered civic peace. In this new land, where individual opportunity was rich, reason sat in the official driver's seat.

In the matter of religious liberty through law, Americans made quantum leaps over their European forebears. There was much less than full political equality, as generations of blacks and women have underscored, but something novel was present that we have come to call pluralism. In religious terms, it was an attempt to live together as equals despite differences in creed. In secular terms, it was a search for a common sense to ensure economic and political cooperation. In theological terms, it conjured up natural theology—speculation about God apart from scripture or dogma. For Roman Catholics, the implications of American pluralism hit Europe only in the "Decree on Religious Liberty" of the Second Vatican Council, where the American model was accepted for the whole Church.

Despite its faults, America has done much that is commendable. In a world where the majority still seek basic human rights, including the right to religious liberty, America looks quite good. Even in the perspective of the world religions, our civic tolerance is remarkable.

At its most tepid, American religion has tolerated civic piety—mouthings on Memorial Day and the Fourth of July. However, it has also sponsored ecumenical debate, academic freedom, and political and religious dissent. The question now is whether pluralism is so inseparable from secularism that it condemns us to religious superficiality.[14]

Has our agreement to disagree about fundamentals relegated them to the private sphere? If religion is absent from the public places where we forge our national culture, our center may not hold. On the other hand, if religion is pursued only by the pious, genuine traditionalists will not want it to hold. Eric Voegelin has said that a crucial test of a culture is whether it enlists the best of its youth or alienates them. For both United States government and United States religion, that can be a hard saying.

We have become used to speeches telling us that our government has only to be as good as its citizens for America to prosper. In too many political assemblies, churches, and synagogues, that is a palliative, a placebo. It brings no health or distinction to the speaker or the audience. To a religious guru, it shows that the speaker ignores the human condition—the beginner's mind, the nature of enlightenment. Unreflective, unmeditative, the speaker cannot be terse, poetic, evocative; he or she can only pour forth the old, stale, placating language. Ignorant of ignorance and sin, the speaker sees no tragedy. Lacking rigor, stupid in the reasons of the heart, the speaker thinks hope is the same as good cheer.

Much the same is true of the audience, of ourselves. Not having gone down in spiritual death, we do not fly to the gods. Not set for spiritual combat, we do not resent that the seats are plush, the rhetoric easy. In part, that is because our culture tells us that only eggheads knit their brows and ponder. In part, it is because we are too lazy to live. In many cases it is a major accomplishment for us to endure ten minutes of silence.

From a religious perspective, the economic facts of American popular culture—the money we pay entertainers, athletes, and business executives—are absurd. Compared to what we pay the people who shape our nation's soul—the artists, scientists, nurses,

teachers, and mothers—they are spiritual madness, what Aeschylus called *nosos*. Compared to how we treat the world's starving, they are beyond belief. Two thousand years ago, the *Book of Mencius* began by condemning profit. Wise people would have taken that lesson and banked it. We, however, have built a culture on profit. It is what makes our headliners run. When will we see that they are usually running in circles?

People who say things that others do not want to hear, no matter how true such things may be, will suffer for their indiscretion. Socrates stands as the paradigm of their fate, and Socrates shows that in the political realm, prophets and sages are one. He also shows that prophets and sages cannot live for audience applause. They must do what they have to do, say what they have to say, because it is their truth, their good, their charge. Shamans, for further instance, must sing—because it relieves their sadness, because it makes them whole. Plato's "Seventh Letter" says that the philosophical soul must live by a love of the Good, that it can deny the Good only by denying its self. Religious people, creative people, humanity's benefactors have all found something more precious than human praise. Better, they have all been found by something more precious.

That something is the sacred, the numinous, the holy, the really real. It is Wakan Tanka, the *Dao*, buddha-nature, God. Commonly, it is the essence of any conviction significant in the ultimate order, in the world as it finally is. The world as it finally is is the one place where you get what you are. It is where someone may finally tell you, "If you do not believe in mystery, God, or the *Dao*, be honest about it." By being honest you will reap two benefits. First, you will not bring ultimate realities into further disrepute. Second, you will take the first step in the pilgrimage toward wisdom, which is acknowledging the truth.

A second step is no less simple or heroic. It is to love the truth that you acknowledge. That may be the truth that mystery is beautiful or the truth that the religions often cant. It may move you to sound the ram's horn or to void at the flag. The point is not so much the content as the act. The dynamic of human consciousness, on which any genuine wisdom takes its stand, is a movement from one's present light to wherever that light leads. "Lead kindly light," Cardinal Newman and others have prayed. Go to your light's source, Augustine and others have counseled. Your light shines in the darkness, and the darkness cannot overcome it—as long as you want to be human, as long as samsara is not your all.

Figure 20 The Sleep of Reason Produces Monsters, *by Francisco Goya, Spanish (1746–1828). Etching and aquatint; 7³/₁₆ × 4³/₄ in. The Nelson–Atkins Museum of Art, Kansas City, Missouri.*

Whatever is noble, whatever is good, whatever is honest—think on it, St. Paul said. Whatever is your current belief about American religion, face it and start to love it. If it is a solid truth, your personality will ripen, your social circle will take fire. If it is a rotten pseudo-truth, you will hear a call to turn and change your heart. In the spiritual life, the only disaster is avoidance. Because they will not face their own beliefs, whether solid or rotten, many stay half-asleep.

Awakened, human consciousness reveals its intrinsic religiousness by pursuing the light to where it is love. Worthy religious traditions and patriotism have nothing to fear from this pursuit. The pursuer does have some things to fear, but they pale in comparison with what there is to gain. In Eastern terms, the pursuer learns about ignorance: how much is samsaric in his or her starting "truth." In Western terms, the pursuer learns about sin: how difficult it is to follow only the light. Why we do not know the good we should know, why we do not do the good we should do—these are among our deepest mysteries. Only when you ponder them can you call yourself mature, let alone wise. Still, understanding these mysteries is the major therapy that any self needs. Understanding them is the heart of traditional political science.

However, the religions' dharma and prophecy illumine much more than ignorance and sin. Ultimately they lead to enlightenment and grace. Enlightenment happens: It is an empirical fact. Light floods some people, bringing them inexpressible joy. Similarly, grace happens: There are marvelous saints. They love God with whole mind, heart, soul, and strength. They serve sisters and brothers more than themselves.

In a dark and troubled time (that is, in any historical time), saints and enlightened people save our beleaguered hope. Just one of them is stronger than all the rubbish, all the valid ground for cynicism. For a single really holy, really religious, really humane person says that what we want and need is possible. We want and need light and love. Light and love are possible. By definition, light and love are buddha-nature and God. By saintly testimony, they are our center.

Discussion Questions

1. To what extent do the religions share a common attraction toward mystery?

2. What have been the principal strengths and weaknesses of American religion?

3. Write a brief definition of *religion* that takes into account the traditions' unity and the traditions' diversity.

4. What is the permanent lesson in the Eastern traditions' elevation of the sage?

5. On what grounds might one defend "profit"?

6. How have the Eastern religions fostered or defended pseudospeciation?

7. Why does the experience of enlightenment or grace tend to lessen greed?

8. How valid is it to study a religion without personally confronting its call for conversion?

9. What have been the benefits of civil religions?
10. What is the mystical dimension in every human life?

Key Terms

pseudospeciation: a term employed by the psychologist Erik Erikson to denote the tendency of people to deny the humanity of groups outside their own cultural circle. Erikson's point was the gap between psychology and biology at this point, as people who manifestly belong to the same biological species (who could, for instance, mate and reproduce) contrive to deny that the "others"—foreigners, aliens—are as human as their own kind. The extreme form of pseudospeciation is xenophobia—fear of foreigners to the point of hatred. Pseudospeciation thrived when peoples were isolated and so somewhat plausibly could keep their myths to the effect that creation had occurred in their neighborhood and they were the center of the earth. With the development of a planetary culture in recent decades, pseudospeciation stands revealed as more pathological than was first appreciated, and the religious contributions to pseudospeciation (bigotry, crusades, holy wars) stand revealed as dubious expressions of an estimable divinity.

NOTES

Introduction

1. Philip Kapleau, *The Three Pillars of Zen* (Boston: Beacon Press, 1967), pp. 189–291.

2. W. Richard Comstock, *The Study of Religion and Primitive Religions* (New York: Harper & Row, 1971), pp. 13–17.

3. See Erik Erikson's *Gandhi's Truth* (New York: Norton, 1969).

4. See Clifford Geertz, *The Interpretation of Cultures* (New York: Basic Books, 1973), pp. 412–453.

Chapter 1:
Hinduism

1. Troy Wilson Organ, *Hinduism* (Woodbury, N.Y.: Barron's, 1974), p. 40; see also Thomas Hopkins, *The Hindu Tradition* (Encino, Calif.: Dickenson, 1971), pp. 3–10; A. L. Basham, *The Wonder That Was India* (New York: Grove Press, 1959), pp. 10–30.

2. On the earliest history and religion of the Indian Aryans, see Mircea Eliade, *A History of Religious Ideas*, vol. 1, *From the Stone Age to the Eleusinian Mysteries* (Chicago: University of Chicago Press, 1978), pp. 186–199.

3. Organ, *Hinduism*, p. 51.

4. See Edward C. Dimock, Jr., et al., *The Literature of India: An Introduction* (Chicago: University of Chicago Press, 1978), pp. 1–2. Also Satsvarupta dasa Gosvami, *Readings in Vedic Literature* (New York: Bhaktivedanta Book Trust, 1977), pp. 3–4. For an overview of Vedic literature, see James A. Santucci, *An Outline of Vedic Literature* (Missoula, Mont.: Scholars Press), 1976.

5. On the polarity of the *asuras* and *devas* in Vedic religion, see F. B. J. Kuiper, "The Basic Concept of Vedic Religion," *HR*, 1975, *15*(2):111.

6. Stella Kramrisch, "The Indian Great Goddess," *HR*, 1975, *14*(4):235–265. As an introduction to the complexity of the Hindu order of the gods, see J. Bruce Long, "Daksa: Divine Embodiment of Creative Skill," *HR*, 1977, *17*(1):29–60.

7. See Organ, *Hinduism*, p. 66; and Brian K. Smith, "Gods and Men in Vedic Ritualism," *HR*, May 1985, *24*(4):291–307.

8. Hopkins, *Hindu Religious Tradition*, pp. 19–35; see also Joseph Henniger, "Sacrifice," *ER, 12*, 544–557. On the horse sacrifice, see Wendy Doniger O'Flaherty, "Horses," *ER*,

6, 464, and *Women, Androgynes, and Other Mythical Beasts* (Chicago: University of Chicago Press, 1980), pp. 149–166; Francis X. Clooney, S. J., "Jaimini's Contribution to the Theory of Sacrifice as the Experience of Transcendence," *HR*, February 1986, *25*(3):199–212.

9. Morton Klass, "Varna and Jati," *ER, 15*, 188.

10. Robert Ernest Hume, *The Thirteen Principal Upanishads* (New York: Oxford University Press, 1971), pp. 5–13.

11. Wendy Doniger O'Flaherty, *Karma and Rebirth in the Classical Indian Tradition* (Berkeley: University of California Press, 1980); William K. Mahoney, "Karman: Hindu and Jain Concepts," *ER, 8*, 261–266.

12. Hume, *The Thirteen Principal Upanishads*, pp. 362–365.

13. For a comparison of the Vedic and Upanishadic mystiques, see S. N. Dasgupta, *Hindu Mysticism* (New York: Frederick Ungar, 1959), pp. 3–57.

14. Mircea Eliade, *A History of Religious Ideas*, vol. 2 (Chicago: University of Chicago Press, 1982), pp. 84–88.

15. Heinrich Zimmer, *Philosophies of India* (Princeton, N.J.: Princeton University Press, 1969), pp. 227–234.

16. For a brief summary of Jainism, see Carlo Della Casa, "Jainism," in *Historia Religionum, II*, ed. C. J. Bleeker and G. Widengren (Leiden: E. J. Brill, 1971), pp. 346–371; see also A. L. Basham, "Jainism," in *The Concise Encyclopedia of Living Faiths*, ed. R. C. Zaehner (Boston: Beacon Press, 1967), pp. 261–266, and Colette Caillat, "Jainism," *ER, 7*, 507–514.

17. See Dasgupta, *Hindu Mysticism*, pp. 113–168; see also Norvin Hein, "A Revolution in Krsnaism: The Cult of Gopala," *HR*, May 1985, *25*(4):296–317.

18. Organ, *Hinduism*, p. 150; see also David R. Kinsley, *The Sword and the Flute* (Berkeley: University of California Press, 1975), pp. 1–78.

19. See John Stratton Hawley, "Thief of Butter, Thief of Love," *HR*, 1979, *18*(3):203–220.

20. See Kinsley, *Sword and the Flute;* see also Basham, *Wonder That Was India*, pp. 304–306; John Stratton Hawley, "Krsna," *ER, 8*, 354–387; and Friedhelm E. Hardy, "Krsnaism," ibid., 387–392.

21. Franklin Edgerton, *The Bhagavad Gita* (New York: Harper Torchbooks, 1964), p. 105; see also R. C. Zaehner, *The Bhagavad-Gita* (New York: Oxford University Press, 1973), pp. 1–41; Ann Stanford, *The Bhagavad Gita* (New York: Seabury, 1970), pp. vii–xxvii; Juan Mascaró, *The Bhagavad Gita* (Baltimore: Penguin, 1962), pp. 9–36; Gerald

James Larson, "The *Bhagavad Gita* as Cross-Cultural Process," *JAAR,* 1975, *43*(4):651–669; John B. Carman, "Bhakti," *ER, 2,* 130–134; and Alf Hiltebeitel, "The Two Krsnas on One Chariot," *HR,* August 1984, *24*(1):1–26.

22.   Wendy Doniger O'Flaherty, *Asceticism and Eroticism in the Mythology of Shiva* (New York: Oxford University Press, 1973), pp. 83–110; see also Stella Kramrish, *The Presence of Siva* (Princeton, N.J.: Princeton University Press, 1981), and "Siva," *ER, 13,* 338–341. For specimens of later Dravidian devotional Shaivism, see R. K. Ramanujan, *Speaking of Siva* (Baltimore: Penguin, 1973).

23.   Dimock et al., *Literature of India,* p. 2.

24.   See Sarvepalli Radhakrishnan and Charles A. Moore, ed., *A Sourcebook in Indian Philosophy* (Princeton, N.J.: Princeton University Press, 1957), pp. 184–189.

25.   On the "tripartite Indo-European ideology" (priests-warriors-farmers) that George Dumézil has found at the root of Aryan society, see Eliade, *History of Religious Ideas,* vol. 1, pp. 192–195.

26.   See Radhakrishman and Moore, *Sourcebook in India Philosophy,* pp. 193–223.

27.   Sudhir Kakar, "The Human Life Cycle: The Traditional Hindu View and the Psychology of Erik H. Erikson," *Philosophy East and West,* 1968, *18:*127–136; see also Basham, *Wonder That Was India,* p. 158.

28.   Basham, *Wonder That Was India,* pp. 177–188; see also Katherine K. Young, "Hinduism," in *Women in World Religion,* ed. Arvind Sharma (Albany: State University of New York Press, 1987), pp. 59–103.

29.   See Roy C. Amore and Larry D. Shin, eds., *Lustful Maidens and Ascetic Kings* (New York: Oxford University Press, 1981), pp. 74–86.

30.   See ibid., pp. 166–168.

31.   On the six orthodox schools, see Radhakrishnan and Moore, *Sourcebook in India Philosophy,* pp. 349–572; Zimmer, *Philosophies of India,* pp. 280–332 (Samkyha and Yoga), 605–614.

32.   See Zaehner, *Hinduism,* pp. 36–56; see also R. C. Zaehner, *Hindu and Muslim Mysticism* (New York: Schocken, 1969), pp. 41–63.

33.   Glenn E. Yocum, "Shrines, Shamanism, and Love Poetry," *JAAR,* 1973, *61*(1):3–17.

34.   See Zaehner, *Hindu and Muslim Mysticism,* pp. 64–85.

35.   On the Puranic Shiva, see Cornelia Dimmitt and J. A. B. van Buitenen, eds., *Classical Hindu Mythology* (Philadelphia: Temple University Press, 1978), pp. 59–146. On Shiva in the Tamil literature, see Glenn E. Yocum, "Manikkavacar's Image of Shiva," *HR,* 1976, *16*(1):20–41; Fred W. Clothey, "Tamil Religions," *ER, 14,* 261–268; David Shulman, "Terror of Symbols and Symbols of Terror," *HR,* November 1986, *26*(2):101–124; Stuart H. Blackburn, "Death and Deification: Folk Cults in Hinduism," *HR,* February 1985, *24*(3):255–274; Norman Cutler, "The Devotee's Experience of the Sacred Tamil Hymns," *HR,* November 1984, *24*(2):91–112.

36.   Organ, *Hinduism,* p. 288.

37.   See Zimmer, *Philosophies of India,* pp. 560–602; see also Kees W. Bolle, *The Persistence of Religion* (Leiden: E. J. Brill, 1965); Mircea Eliade, *Yoga: Immortality and Freedom* (Princeton, N.J.: Princeton University Press, 1970), pp. 200–273; and André Padoux, "Tantrism," *ER, 14,* 272–280.

38.   Ernest Wood, *Yoga* (Baltimore: Pelican, 1962), pp. 140–147; see also Eliade, *Yoga,* pp. 244–249; and Daniel Gold and Ann Grodzins Gold, "The Fate of the Householder Nath," *HR,* November 1984, *24*(2):113–132.

39.   For a brief survey of Sikhism, see Khushwant Singh, "Sikhism," in *Historical Atlas of the Religions of the World,* ed. I. al Faruqi and D. Sopher (New York: Macmillan, 1974), pp. 105–108; see also John Noss, *Man's Religions* (New York: Macmillan, 1974), pp. 226–235; and Khushwant Singh, "Sikhism," *ER, 13,* 315–320.

40.   However, see Cyrus R. Pangborn, "The Ramakrishna Math and Mission," in *Hinduism: New Essays in the History of Religions,* ed. Bardwell L. Smith (Leiden: E. J. Brill, 1976), pp. 98–119.

41.   See Organ, *Hinduism,* pp. 319–325; and Charlotte Vaudeville, "Kabir," *ER, 8,* 226–227.

42.   Nervin J. Hein, "Caitanya's Ecstasies and the Theology of the Name," in *Hinduism: New Essays in the History of Religions,* ed. Bardwell L. Smith (Leiden: E. J. Brill, 1976), pp. 15–32; Joseph T. O'Connell, "Caitanya's Followers and the Bhagavad-Gita," in *Hinduism,* pp. 33–52.

43.   See Edward C. Dimock, Jr., and Denise Levertov, trans., *In Praise of Krishna* (Garden City, N.Y.: Doubleday, 1967).

44.   Following are some representative works: Swami Prabhupada, *The Nectar of Devotion* (Los Angeles: Bhaktivedanta Book Trust, 1970); *Krishna: The Supreme Personality of Godhead,* 3 vols. (Los Angeles: Bhaktivedanta Book Trust, 1970). On the Hare Krishna movement, see J. Stillson Judah, *Hare Krishna and the Counterculture* (New York: Wiley, 1974).

45.   Radical feminist Mary Daly has exposed the full horror of suttee; see Mary Daly, *Gyn/Ecology* (Boston: Beacon Press, 1979), chap. 3.

46.   For brief selections from the leading Indian voices of the past century, see Ainslee T. Embree, *The Hindu Tradition* (New York: Vintage, 1972), pp. 278–348.

47.   See Walker G. Neevel, Jr., "The Transformations of Sri Ramakrishna," in *Hinduism: New Essays in the History of Religions,* ed. Bardwell L. Smith (Leiden: E. J. Brill, 1976), pp. 53–97.

48.   Mohandas K. Gandhi, *An Autobiography: The Story of My Experiments with Truth* (Boston: Beacon Paperbacks, 1957), p. 349.

49.   Erik H. Erikson, *Gandhi's Truth* (New York: Norton, 1969), pp. 376–397.

50.   Joan Bondurant, *Conquest of Violence,* rev. ed. (Berkeley: University of California Press, 1965).

51. See Adrian C. Mayer, *Caste and Kinship in Central India: A Village and Its Region* (Berkeley: University of California Press, 1960), pp. 99–102; also Thomas B. Coburn, "Hindu Goddesses," *HR*, May 1988, *27*(4):412–414.

52. Gerald D. Berreman, *Hindus of the Himalayas: Ethnography and Change,* new extended ed. (Berkeley: University of California Press, 1972), p. 89.

53. James M. Freeman, "The Ladies of Lord Krishna: Rituals of Middle-Aged Women in Eastern India," in *Unspoken Worlds: Women's Religious Lives in Non-Western Cultures,* ed. Nancy A. Falk and Rita M. Gross (New York: Harper & Row), 1982, pp. 110–126; and Daniel Gold, "Comprehending Indian Devotional Love," *HR*, May 1987, *26*(4):401–421.

54. See Sudhir Kakar, *Shamans, Mystics and Doctors* (New York: Alfred A. Knopf, 1982), pp. 53–88.

55. V. S. Naipaul, *India: A Wounded Civilization* (New York: Vintage Books, 1978), pp. 42–43.

56. Basham, *Wonder That Was India,* pp. 74–231.

57. Kuiper, "Basic Concept of Vedic Religion"; see also Bruce Lincoln, "The Indo-European Myth of Creation," *HR*, 1975, *15*(2):121–145.

58. Basham, *Wonder That Was India,* p. 153.

59. Zaehner, *Hinduism,* p. 102.

60. Vern L. Bullough, *The Subordinate Sex* (Baltimore: Penguin, 1974), pp. 230–231.

61. See Ellison Banks Findley, "Gargi at the King's Court: Women and Philosophical Innovation in Ancient India," in *Women, Religion and Social Change,* ed. Y. Y. Haddad and E. B. Findley (Albany: State University of New York Press, 1955), pp. 37–58.

62. See Basham, *Wonder That Was India,* pp. 186–188.

63. Noss, *Man's Religions,* p. 188. On the role model that the *Mahabharata* described for women in Draupadi, see Nancy Auer Falk, "Draupadi and the Dharma," in *Beyond Androcentrism,* ed. Rita M. Gross (Missoula, Mont.: Scholars Press, 1977), pp. 89–114. For a sensitive fictional treatment of the modern Indian woman, see Kamala Markandaya, *Nectar in a Sieve* (New York: Signet, 1954).

64. Bullough, *Subordinate Sex,* p. 232.

65. Reference in Organ, *Hinduism,* p. 387.

66. Charles S. J. White, "Mother Guru: Jnanananda of Madras, India," in *Unspoken Worlds: Women's Religious Lives in Non-Western Culture,* ed. Nancy A. Falk and Rita M. Gross (New York: Harper & Row, 1980), p. 23.

67. Ibid., p. 27.

68. See Organ, *Hinduism,* p. 29.

69. A popular version is that by Swami Prabhavananda and Christopher Isherwood, *How to Know God* (New York: Mentor, 1969). The commentary is from the viewpoint of Vedanta, whereas Patanjali's own philosophy was Samkhya. See also Georg Feuerstein, "Patanjali," *ER, 11,* 206–207.

70. Basham, *Wonder That Was India,* p. 160.

71. See David Kinsley, "The Portrait of the Goddess in the Devi-mahatmya," *JAAR,* 1978, *46*(4):489–506.

72. A good reminder that most Hindus have not directly known or followed the high literary tradition is found in Philip H. Ashby, *Modern Trends in Hinduism* (New York: Columbia University Press, 1974), pp. 7–24; see also Brian K. Smith, "Exorcising the Transcendent: Strategies for Defining Hinduism and Religion," *HR*, August 1987, *27*(1):32–55.

73. Wendy Doniger O'Flaherty, *The Origins of Evil in Hindu Mythology* (Berkeley: University of California Press Paperback, 1980), p. 5.

74. Ibid., p. 375.

75. Kinsley, *The Sword and the Flute* (note 16), pp. 111–112.

76. V. S. Naipaul, *India: A Wounded Civilization* (New York: Vintage, 1978).

Chapter 2:
Buddhism

1. Richard H. Robinson and Willard L. Johnson, *The Buddhist Religion* (Encino, Calif.: Dickenson, 1977), p. 13; see also Trevor Ling, *The Buddha* (London: Temple Smith, 1973), pp. 37–83; Mircea Eliade, *A History of Religious Ideas,* vol. 2 (Chicago: University of Chicago Press, 1982), pp. 72–86.

2. Edward Conze, *Buddhist Scriptures* (Baltimore: Penguin, 1959), p. 34.

3. Conze, *Buddhist Scriptures,* pp. 48–49; see also Lowell W. Bloss, "The Taming of Mara," *HR*, 1978, *18*(2): 156–176.

4. Robinson and Johnson, *Buddhist Tradition,* p. 28.

5. Ibid., p. 31; see also Edward J. Thomas, *The History of Buddhist Thought* (New York: Barnes & Noble, 1951), pp. 58–70; Henry Clarke Warren, *Buddhism in Translations* (New York: Atheneum, 1973), pp. 202–208.

6. See William Theodore de Bary, ed., *The Buddhist Tradition* (New York: Vintage, 1972), pp. 15–20; see also Edward Conze, *Buddhism: Its Essence and Development* (New York: Harper Torchbooks, 1959), pp. 43–48; I. B. Horner, "Buddhism: The Theravada," in *The Concise Encyclopedia of Living Faiths,* ed. R. C. Zaehner (Boston: Beacon Press, 1967), pp. 283–293; Taitetsu Unno, "Eightfold Path," *ER, 5,* 69–71.

7. See Winston K. King, *In the Hope of Nibbana: Theravada Buddhist Ethics* (La Salle, Ill.: Open Court, 1964).

8. Texts on wisdom, morality, and meditation are available in Stephen Beyer, *The Buddhist Experience* (Encino, Calif.: Dickenson, 1974); see also Conze, *Buddhist Scriptures.*

9. Edward Conze, *Buddhist Meditation* (New York: Harper Torchbooks, 1969); see also Nyanaponika Thera, *The Heart of Buddhist Meditation* (London: Rider, 1969); Winston L. King, "Meditation: Buddhist Meditation," *ER, 9,* 331–336.

10.   John Bowker discusses this rather creatively; see Bowker, *The Religious Imagination and the Sense of God* (Oxford: Clarendon Press, 1978), p. 244; see also Willis Stoesz, "The Buddha as Teacher," *JAAR,* 1978, *46*(2):139–158.

11.   We have adapted Henry Clarke Warren's presentation of the Fire Sermon. See his *Buddhism in Translations* (note 5), pp. 351–353.

12.   See I. B. Horner, "The Teaching of the Elders," in *Buddhist Texts through the Ages,* ed. Edward Conze (New York: Harper Torchbooks, 1954), pp. 17–50. Also Warren, *Buddhism in Translations,* p. 392; Charles S. Prebish, ed. *Buddhism: A Modern Perspective* (University Park: Pennsylvania State University Press, 1975), pp. 16–26, 49–53; Conze, *Buddhism: Its Essence and Development,* pp. 58–69; Beyer, *Buddhist Experience,* pp. 65–73.

13.   On the laity, see Conze, *Buddhism: Its Essence and Development,* pp. 70–88.

14.   See Conze, *Buddhist Scriptures,* pp. 182–183.

15.   See Robinson and Johnson, *Buddhist Religion;* Lowell W. Bloss, "The Buddha and the Naga," *HR,* 1973, *13*(1):36–53.

16.   See Prebish, *Buddhism: A Modern Perspective,* pp. 29–45; see also Edward Conze, *Buddhist Thought in India* (Ann Arbor, Mich.: Ann Arbor Paperbacks, 1967), p. 121; Janice J. Nattier and Charles S. Prebish, "Mahasamghika Origins: The Beginnings of Buddhist Sectarianism," *HR,* 1977, *16*(3):237–272.

17.   Robinson and Johnson, *Buddhist Religion,* p. 77; see also John S. Strong, "Gandhakuti: The Perfumed Chamber of the Buddha," *HR,* 1977, *16*(4):390–406.

18.   Robinson and Johnson, *Buddhist Religion,* p. 81.

19.   Mircea Eliade, *Yoga: Immortality and Freedom* (Princeton, N.J.: Princeton University Press, 1969), pp. 162–199; see also S. N. Dasgupta, *Hindu Mysticism* (New York: Frederick Ungar, 1959), pp. 85–109.

20.   Conze, *Buddhist Meditation,* pp. 100–103.

21.   Winston L. King, *Theravada Meditation: The Buddhist Transformation of Yoga* (University Park: Pennsylvania State University Press, 1980), pp. 126–127.

22.   For general overviews of Mahayana, see Edward Conze, "Buddhism: The Mahayana," in *The Concise Encyclopedia of Living Faiths,* ed. R. C. Zaehner (Boston: Beacon Press, 1967), pp. 296–320; *Buddhist Texts,* pp. 119–217; Erik Zürcher et al., "Buddhism," *ER, 2,* 414–435; Nakamura Hajime, "Buddhism, Schools of: Mahayana Buddhism," ibid., 457–472.

23.   Edward Conze, *Buddhist Wisdom Books* (New York: Harper Torchbooks, 1972), p. 77. See also Donald S. Lopez, Jr., "Inscribing the Bodhisvatta's Speech," *HR,* May 1990, *29*(4):351–372.

24.   See Joanna Rodgers Macy, "Perfection of Wisdom: Mother of All Buddhas," in *Beyond Androcentrism,* ed. Rita M. Gross (Missoula, Mont.: Scholars Press, 1977), pp. 315–333.

25.   Conze, *Buddhist Wisdom Books,* pp. 101–102.

26.   Our exposition depends on Edward Conze's translation and study in *Buddhist Wisdom Books* (note 23).

27.   See Conze, *Buddhist Thought in India,* pp. 238–244; see also Prebish, *Buddhism: A Modern Perspective,* pp. 76–96; T. R. V. Murti, *The Central Philosophy of Buddhism* (London: Allen & Unwin, 1955).

28.   See Conze, *Buddhist Thought in India,* pp. 250–260; Prebish, *Buddhism: A Modern Perspective,* pp. 97–101; Thomas, *History of Buddhist Thought,* pp. 230–248.

29.   Juan Mascaró, trans., *The Dhammapada* (Baltimore: Penguin, 1973), p. 1.

30.   D. T. Suzuki, trans., *The Lankavatara Sutra* (London: George Routledge, 1932).

31.   Conze, *Buddhist Thought in India,* pp. 270–274; Robinson and Johnson, *Buddhist Tradition,* pp. 116–127; Thomas, *History of Buddhist Thought,* pp. 245–248; David Snellgrove, "The Tantras," in Edward Conze, ed., *Buddhist Texts through the Ages* (New York: Harper Torchbooks, 1954), pp. 221–273; Conze, *Buddhism: Its Essence and Development,* pp. 174–199; Alex Wayman, "Buddhism, Schools of: Esoteric Buddhism," *ER, 2,* 472–482.

32.   Hellmut Hoffmann, *The Religions of Tibet* (London: Allen & Unwin, 1961); Herbert V. Guenther, *Treasures of the Tibetan Middle Way* (Berkeley: Shambhala, 1976).

33.   Beyer, *Buddhist Experience,* pp. 258–261; Eliade, *Yoga,* pp. 249–254.

34.   Robinson and Johnson, *Buddhist Religion,* p. 120.

35.   Herbert Guenther, trans., *The Life and Teachings of Naropa* (New York: Oxford University Press, 1971), p. 43; see also W. Y. Evans-Wentz, ed., *Tibet's Great Yoga Milarepa* (New York: Oxford University Press, 1969), p. 93.

36.   See Beyer, *Buddhist Experience,* pp. 174–184, 225–229, 258–261.

37.   Stephan Beyer, "Buddhism in Tibet," in *Buddhism: A Modern Perspective,* ed. Charles Prebish (University Park: Pennsylvania State University Press, 1975), pp. 239–247; Herbert Guenther, "Buddhism: Buddhism in Tibet," *ER, 2,* 406–414.

38.   Hoffmann, *Religions of Tibet.*

39.   Evans-Wentz, *Milarepa.*

40.   On modern times, see David L. Snellgrover, "Tibetan Buddhism Today," in *Buddhism in the Modern World,* ed. Heinrich Dumoulin (New York: Macmillan, 1976), pp. 277–293.

41.   See *Tibetan Book of the Dead,* trans. Francesca Freemantle and Chogyam Trungpa (Boulder: Shambhala, 1975).

42.   Alexandra David-Neel, *Magic and Mystery in Tibet* (New York: Dover, 1971), pp. 5–9.

43.   There are major qualifications to this statement, of course. On Hinduism in Southeast Asia, see Robinson and Johnson, *Buddhist Tradition,* pp. 129–136; on Hinduism in Indonesia, see Clifford Geertz, *Islam Observed* (Chicago: University of Chicago Press, 1968), pp. 29–43.

44.   Melford Spiro, *Buddhism and Society* (New York: Harper & Row, 1970), pp. 209–214.

45. Charles S. Prebish, *American Buddhism* (North Scituate, Mass.: Duxbury Press, 1979), p. 164; Robert S. Ellwood, "Buddhism: Buddhism in the West," *ER, 2,* 436–439.

46. See Lama Govinda, *The Psychological Attitude of Early Buddhist Philosophy* (New York: Samuel Weiser, 1969), pp. 77–142.

47. For instance, Spiro found that the goal of Burmese Buddhists was not nirvana but a better rebirth; see Spiro, *Buddhism and Society.*

48. On the Buddhist shaping of Chinese folk religion, see Daniel L. Overmyer, "Folk-Buddhist Religion: Creation and Eschatology in Medieval China," *HR,* 1972, *12*(1):42–70. On Thai Buddhist cosmology, see Frank Reynolds and Mani B. Reynolds, trans., *Three Worlds According to King Ruang* (Berkeley: University of California Press, 1982).

49. Denise Lardner Carmody, *Women and World Religions,* 2d ed. (Englewood Cliffs, N.J.: Prentice-Hall, 1989), pp. 67–92; I. B. Horner, *Women Under Primitive Buddhism* (New York: Dutton, 1930).

50. See Nancy Falk, "An Image of Woman in Old Buddhist Literature. The Daughters of Mara," in *Women and Religion,* rev. ed., ed. J. Plaskow and J. A. Romero (Missoula, Mont.: Scholars Press, 1974), pp. 105–112.

51. Frank Reynolds, "The Two Wheels of Dhamma," in *The Two Wheels of Dhamma,* ed. Bardwell L. Smith (Chambersburg, Pa.: American Academy of Religion, 1972), pp. 6–30; Bardwell L. Smith, "The Ideal Social Order as Portrayed in the Chronicles of Ceylon," in *Two Wheels of Dhamma,* ed. Smith, pp. 31–57.

52. King, *Hope of Nibbana,* pp. 176–210.

53. Eric Voegelin, *Anamnesis: Zur Theorie der Geschichte und Politik* (Munich: R. Piper, 1966), pp. 179–222. This portion is not available in Gerhart Niemeyer's translation of *Anamnesis* (Notre Dame, Ind.: University of Notre Dame Press, 1978). However, it first appeared under the title "The Mongol Orders of Submission to European Powers," in *Byzantion,* vol. XV (1940/41), pp. 378–413.

54. See Jane Bunnag, *Buddhist Monk, Buddhist Layman* (Cambridge: Cambridge University Press, 1973); see also Spiro, *Buddhism and Society,* pp. 396–421. On the more spiritual ties among members of the community, see Richard Gombrich, " 'Merit Transference' in Sinhalese Buddhism," *HR,* 1971, *11*(2):203–219.

55. King, *In the Hope of Nibbana,* pp. 277–284.

56. G. P. Malalasekera, "Theravada Buddhism," in *Historical Atlas of the Religions of the World,* ed. I. al Faruqi and D. Sopher (New York: Macmillan, 1974), p. 172.

57. John B. Cobb, Jr., "Buddhist Emptiness and the Christian God," *JAAR,* 1977, *45*(1):11–25.

58. Yoshito S. Hakeda, trans., *The Awakening of Faith* (New York: Columbia University Press, 1967).

59. Philip Kapleau, *The Three Pillars of Zen* (Boston: Beacon Press, 1967), p. 207.

60. E. F. Schumacher, *Small Is Beautiful* (New York: Harper Colophon, 1973), pp. 50–58.

61. D. T. Suzuki, *Zen Buddhism* (New York: Anchor Books, 1956), pp. 157–226. On the Daoist influence, see Chang Chung-yuan, *Creativity and Taoism* (New York: Harper Colophon, 1970).

62. The famous Zen ox-herding pictures display the progress toward this freedom. See Kapleau, *Three Pillars of Zen,* pp. 301–313.

63. See Nagarjuna and Sakya Pandit, *Elegant Sayings,* trans. Tarthang Tulku (Emeryville, Calif.: Dharma Publishing, 1977), pp. 38–39.

64. Chogyam Trungpa, "Foreword," in *Buddhism: A Modern Perspective,* ed. Charles S. Prebish (University Park: Pennsylvania State University Press, 1975), p. ix; see also Malcolm David Eckel, "Gratitude to an Empty Savior," *HR,* August 1985, *25*(1):57–75.

65. John Bowker has discussed this matter in the illuminating context of information theory; see Bowker, *Religious Imagination,* pp. 244–307.

66. *Saddharmapundarika,* V:1, 5, 6; in *Buddhist Texts through the Ages,* ed. Edward Conze (note 12), p. 139.

67. See note 66.

68. William Johnston, *The Mirror Mind* (New York: Harper & Row, 1981), pp. 40–41; see also Judith A. Berling, "Bringing the Buddha Down to Earth," *HR,* August 1987, *27*(1):56–88.

Chapter 3:
Chinese Religion

1. Karl Jaspers, *The Origin and Goal of History* (New Haven, Conn.: Yale University Press, 1953), p. 2.

2. Arthur Waley, trans., *Monkey* (New York: Grove Press, 1958).

3. Laurence G. Thompson, *The Chinese Religion: An Introduction,* 3rd ed. (Belmont, Calif.: Wadsworth, 1979), pp. 3–15; Joseph Needham, *Science and Civilisation in China,* vol. 2 (Cambridge: University Press, 1969), pp. 216–345; Schuyler Cammann, "Some Early Chinese Symbols of Duality," *HR,* February 1985, *24*(3):215–254.

4. David N. Keightley, "The Religious Commitment: Shang Theology and the Genesis of Chinese Political Culture," *HR,* 1978, *17*(3–4):213.

5. Hans Steininger, "The Religions of China," in *Historia Religionum, II,* ed. C. J. Bleeker and G. Widengren (Leiden: E. J. Brill, 1971), pp. 479–482; Daniel L. Overmyer, "Chinese Religion: An Overview," *ER, 3,* 257–289.

6. *Chuang Tzu,* sec. 6; see Burton Watson, trans., *Chuang Tzu: Basic Writings* (New York: Columbia University Press, 1964), pp. 76, 81.

7. Thompson, *Chinese Religion: An Introduction,* 3rd ed. (Belmont, Calif.: Wadsworth, 1979), pp. 22–24; Needham, *Science and Civilisation,* pp. 354–363.

8. Arthur Waley, *The Nine Songs: A Study of Shamanism in Ancient China* (London: Allen & Unwin, 1955).

9.   Eliade, however, stresses the Chinese shaman's magical flight. See Mircea Eliade, *Shamanism* (Princeton, N.J.: Princeton University Press, 1972), pp. 448–457.

10.   On the ritualistic side of early Chinese shamanism, see Jordan Paper, "The Meaning of the 'T'ao-T'ieh,' " *HR,* 1978, *18*(1):18–41.

11.   Anna Seidel, "Buying One's Way to Heaven," *HR,* 1978, *17*(3–4):419–431; see also Stephen F. Teiser, "Ghosts and Ancestors in Medieval Chinese Religion," *HR,* August 1986, *26*(1):47–67; and Catherine Bell, "Religion and Chinese Culture: Toward an Assessment of 'Popular Religion,' " *HR,* August 1989, *29*(1):35–57.

12.   Donald W. Treadgold, *The West in Russia and China,* vol. 2 (Cambridge: University Press, 1973), pp. 20–26.

13.   Quoted in Thompson, *Chinese Religion,* 3rd ed., pp. 32–33; see also Whalen Lai, "Symbolism of Evil in China," *HR,* May 1984, *23*(4):316–343.

14.   Mircea Eliade, *A History of Religious Ideas,* vol. 2 (Chicago: University of Chicago Press, 1982), pp. 3–6.

15.   Arthur Waley, trans., *The Analects of Confucius* (New York: Vintage, 1938), pp. 27–29.

16.   A. C. Graham, "Confucianism," in *The Concise Encyclopedia of Living Faiths,* ed. R. C. Zaehner (Boston: Beacon Press, 1967), p. 367; Wing-Tsit Chan, "Confucian Thought: Foundations of the Tradition," *ER, 4,* 15–24; Laurence G. Thompson, "The State Cult," ibid., 36–38.

17.   Laurence G. Thompson, ed., *The Chinese Way in Religion* (Encino, Calif.: Dickinson, 1973), pp. 139–153.

18.   Wing-Tsit Chan, *A Source Book in Chinese Philosophy* (Princeton, N.J.: Princeton University Press, 1963), pp. 84–94.

19.   Ezra Pound, *Confucius* (New York: New Directions, 1969), p. 219.

20.   W.A.C.H. Dobson, trans., *Mencius* (Toronto: University of Toronto Press, 1963), p. 131.

21.   Lee H. Yearley, "Mencius on Human Nature," *JAAR,* 1975, *43*:185–198.

22.   See Eric Voegelin, *Order and History,* vol. 4 (Baton Rouge: Louisiana State University Press, 1974), pp. 272–299.

23.   On Xunzi, see Chan, *Chinese Philosophy,* pp. 115–135; Sebastian de Grazia, *Masters of Chinese Political Thought* (New York: Viking, 1973), pp. 151–181. On Mozi, see Chan, *Chinese Philosophy,* pp. 211–217; de Grazia, *Chinese Political Thought,* pp. 216–246.

24.   Arthur Waley, *Three Ways of Thought in Ancient China* (Garden City, N.Y.: Doubleday, 1956), p. 205.

25.   On this period, see Werner Eichhorn, *Chinese Civilization* (New York: Praeger, 1969), pp. 43–85; H. G. Creel, *The Birth of China* (New York: Reynal and Hitchcock, 1937), pp. 219–380.

26.   Graham, "Confucianism," p. 370; Wing-Tsit Chan, "Confucian Thought: Neo-Confucianism," *ER, 4,* 24–36.

27.   See Chan, *Chinese Philosophy,* pp. 588–653.

28.   This appears in Rodney L. Taylor, "The Centered Self: Religious Autobiography in the Neo-Confucian Tradition," *HR,* 1978, *17*(3–4):266–283.

29.   Thaddeus Chieh Hang T'ui, "*Jen* Experience and *Jen* Philosophy," *JAAR,* 1974, *42*:53–65.

30.   Adapted from Thompson, *Chinese Way,* pp. 144–153.

31.   Adapted from Thompson, *Chinese Religion,* 3rd ed., pp. 3–15.

32.   H. G. Creel, *What Is Taoism?* (Chicago: University of Chicago Press, 1970), pp. 37–47; Farzeen Baldrian, "Taoism: An Overview," *ER, 14,* 288–306.

33.   Thomas Merton, *The Way of Chuang Tzu* (New York: New Directions, 1968).

34.   Arthur Waley, trans., *The Way and Its Power* (New York: Grove Press, 1958).

35.   Waley stresses the mystical; Wing-Tsit Chan's *The Way of Lao Tzu* (Indianapolis, Ind.: Bobbs-Merrill, 1963) stresses the pragmatic.

36.   Denise Lardner Carmody, "Taoist Reflections on Feminism," *Religion in Life,* 1977, *44*(2):234–244.

37.   Holmes Welch, *Taoism: The Parting of the Way* (Boston: Beacon Press, 1966), pp. 35–49.

38.   For a sketch of a utopia that is Daoist in spirit if not in origin, see Ernest Callenbach, *Ecotopia* (New York: Bantam, 1977).

39.   *Tao Te Ching,* chap. 5, in *The Way and Its Power* (New York: Grove Press, 1955), p. 147; Chan, *Lao Tzu,* p. 108, note 2, says: "Straw dogs were used for sacrifices in ancient China. After they had been used, they were thrown away and there was no more sentimental attachment to them."

40.   Current scholarly opinion, however, associates religious Daoism with preaxial religion. See *Encyclopedia Britannica* 15th ed., s.v. "Taoism," "Taoism, History of"; N. Sivin, "On the Word 'Taoist' as a Source of Perplexity," *HR,* 1978, *17*(3–4):303–330.

41.   Werner Eichhorn, "Taoism," in *The Concise Encyclopedia of Living Faiths,* ed. R. C. Zaehner (Boston: Beacon Press, 1967), pp. 389–391; Welch, *Taoism,* pp. 151–158.

42.   Welch, *Taoism,* pp. 130–135; K'uan Yu, *Taoist Yoga* (New York: Samuel Weiser, 1973).

43.   Kristofer Schipper, "The Taoist Body," *HR,* 1978, *17*(3–4):355–386.

44.   Edward H. Schafer, "The Jade Woman of Greatest Mystery," *HR,* 1978, *17*(3–4):393–394.

45.   Chang Chung-yuan, *Creativity and Taoism* (New York: Harper Colophon, 1970), pp. 169–238; Albert C. Moore, *Iconography of Religions* (Philadelphia: Fortress, 1977), pp. 170–180; Raymond Dawson, *The Chinese Experience* (New York: Scribner's, 1978), pp. 199–284.

46.   C. Wei-hsun Fu, "Confucianism and Taoism," in *Historical Atlas of the Religions of the World,* ed. I. al Faruqi and D. Sopher (New York: Macmillan, 1974), p. 121.

47. For overviews, see R. H. Robinson, "Buddhism: In China and Japan," in *The Concise Encyclopedia of Living Faiths,* ed. R. C. Zaehner (Boston: Beacon Press, 1967), pp. 321–344; C. Wei-hsun Fu, "Mahayana Buddhism (China)," in *Historical Atlas of the Religions of the World,* ed. I. al Faruqi and D. Sopher (New York: Macmillan, 1974), pp. 185–194. Space forbids consideration of the history of Buddhism in the many other Asian lands that it influenced. For treatments on this subject, see Charles S. Prebish, ed., *Buddhism: A Modern Perspective* (University Park: Pennsylvania State University Press, 1975). On contemporary issues, see Heinrich Dumoulin, ed., *Buddhism in the Modern World* (New York: Macmillan, 1976); Erik Zürcher, "Buddhism: Buddhism in China," *ER, 2,* 414–421.

48. On Buddhist beginnings in China, see Arthur F. Wright, *Buddhism in Chinese History* (Stanford, Calif.: Stanford University Press, 1959), pp. 21–41. Also Kenneth K. S. Ch'en, "The Role of Buddhist Monasteries in T'ang Society," *HR,* 1976, *35*(3):209–230.

49. See Heinrich Dumoulin, *A History of Zen Buddhism* (Boston: Beacon Press, 1969), pp. 52–136; see also Bernard Faure, "Bodhidharma as Textual and Religious Paradigm," *HR,* February 1986, *25*(3):187–198.

50. Richard H. Robinson and Willard L. Johnson, *The Buddhist Religion* (Encino, Calif.: Dickenson, 1977), p. 161. For a full discussion of this sutra, see Philip B. Yampolsky, *The Platform Sutra of the Sixth Patriarch* (New York: Columbia University Press, 1967); see also Wing-Tsit Chan, *The Platform Sutra* (New York: St. John's University Press, 1963). Interesting background is Alex Wayman, "The Mirror as a Pan-Buddhist Metaphor-Simile," *HR,* 1974, *13*(4):251–269.

51. Dumoulin, *History of Zen Buddhism,* p. 88; Yampolsky, *Platform Sutra,* pp. 23–121.

52. Beatrice Lane Suzuki, *Mahayana Buddhism* (New York: Macmillan, 1969), pp. 63–65; T. O. Ling, *A Dictionary of Buddhism* (New York: Scribner's 1972), pp. 15–16.

53. Wright, *Buddhism in Chinese History,* p. 70.

54. See ibid., p. 72.

55. James J. Y. Liu, *Essentials of Chinese Literary Art* (North Scituate, Mass.: Duxbury Press, 1979), p. 17.

56. C. K. Yang, *Religion in Chinese Society* (Berkeley: University of California Press, 1970), pp. 265–272; Alvin P. Cohen, "Chinese Religion: Popular Religion," *ER, 3,* 289–296.

57. Steininger, "Religions of China," p. 486.

58. See Thompson, *The Chinese Way,* pp. 231–241; Donald E. MacInnes, *Religious Policy and Practice in Communist China* (New York: Macmillan, 1972). See also Yang, *Religion in Chinese Society,* pp. 341–404.

59. Stuart Shram, *Mao Tse-tung* (Baltimore: Penguin, 1967), p. 23.

60. Elisabeth Croll, ed., *The Woman's Movement in China* (London: Anglo-Chinese Educational Institute, 1974).

61. Robert Jay Lifton, *Revolutionary Immortality: Mao Tse-tung and the Chinese Cultural Revolution* (New York: Vintage, 1968).

62. Mao Tse-tung, *Poems* (Peking: Foreign Language Press, 1976).

63. *World Christian Encyclopedia,* ed. David B. Barrett (New York: Oxford University Press, 1982), p. 234.

64. Ibid., p. 231. Figures have been rounded.

65. N. J. Giradot, "The Problem of Creation Mythology in the Study of Chinese Religion," *HR,* 1976, *15*(4):289–318; see also his "Myth and Meaning in the *Tao Te Ching:* chaps. 25 and 42," *HR,* 1977, *16*(4):294–328.

66. Alvin P. Cohen, "Concerning the Rain Deities in Ancient China," *HR,* 1978, *17*(3–4):244–265.

67. See Helmut Wilhelm, *Change: Eight Lectures on the I-Ching* (New York: Pantheon, 1960).

68. This section is adapted from Liu, *Essentials of Chinese Literary Art,* pp. 4–24.

69. Chiang Yee, *The Chinese Eye: An Interpretation of Chinese Painting* (Bloomington: Indiana University Press, 1964), p. 152. We are indebted to Chiang throughout this section. See also Bernard Faure, "Space and Place in Chinese Religious Traditions," *HR,* May 1987, *26*(4):337–356.

70. Richard Mather, "Buddhism Becomes Chinese," in *The Chinese Way,* ed. Laurence G. Thompson (Encino, Calif.: Dickenson, 1973), pp. 77–86.

71. Dumoulin, *History of Zen Buddhism,* pp. 52–136.

72. Philip Kapleau, *The Three Pillars of Zen* (Boston: Beacon Press, 1967), p. 205.

73. Steininger, "Religions of China," pp. 482–487; Creel, *Birth of China,* pp. 204–216.

74. See Arthur F. Wright, ed., *Confucianism and Chinese Civilization* (New York: Atheneum, 1964).

75. This is a major theme in Peter Weber-Schafer, *Oikumene und Imperium* (Munich: P. List, 1968).

76. Vern L. Bullough, *The Subordinate Sex* (Baltimore: Penguin, 1974), p. 249; Teresa Kelliher, "Confucianism," and Barbara Reed, "Taoism," in *Women in World Religions,* ed. Arvind Sharma (Albany: State University of New York Press, 1987), pp. 135–159 and 161–181.

77. Mary Daly, *Gyn/Ecology* (Boston: Beacon Press, 1979), chap. 4. The reference to Dworkin is to her *Woman Hating* (New York: Dutton, 1974), p. 103.

78. Margery Wolf, "Chinese Women: Old Skills in a New Context," in *Woman, Culture, and Society,* ed. M. Z. Rosaldo and L. Lamphere (Stanford, Calif.: Stanford University Press, 1974), pp. 157–172.

79. Denise Lardner Carmody, *Women and World Religions* (Nashville: Abingdon, 1979), pp. 66–72.

80. Ellen Marie Chen, "Tao as the Great Mother and the Influence of Motherly Love in the Shaping of Chinese Philosophy," *HR,* 1974, *14*(1):51–63.

81. Maxine Hong Kingston, *The Woman Warrior: Memories of a Girlhood among Ghosts* (New York: Alfred A. Knopf, 1977).

82. See Nancy Schuster, "Striking a Balance: Women and Images of Women in Early Chinese Buddhism," in *Women, Religion and Social Change*, ed. Y. Y. Haddad and E. B. Findley (Albany: State University of New York Press, 1985), pp. 87–112.

83. Yang, *Religion in Chinese Society*, p. 294.

84. Max Weber, *The Religion of China* (New York: Free Press, 1968), pp. 173–225.

85. Donald J. Munro, *The Concept of Man in Early China* (Stanford, Calif.: Stanford University Press, 1969).

86. A. C. Graham, "Chuang Tzu's Essay on Seeing Things as Equal," *HR*, 1969, *9*:137.

87. Chang, *Creativity and Taoism*, pp. 123–168.

88. In her article "Is There a Doctrine of Physical Immortality in the Tao Te Ching?" (*HR*, 1973, *12*(3):231–249), Ellen Marie Chen argues that Laozi did not propose immortality. She also argues against the Daoist character of *The Secret of the Golden Flower* because it is Confucian in emphasizing the yang principle (p. 246, note 22). For the psychodynamics of *The Golden Flower*, see C. G. Jung, "Commentary," in Richard Wilhelm, trans., *The Golden Flower* (New York: Harcourt, Brace & World, 1962), pp. 81–137.

89. On the original peasant mentality, see Marcel Granet, *The Religion of the Chinese People* (New York: Harper & Row, 1975), pp. 37–56.

90. David C. Yu, "Chinese Folk Religion," *HR*, 1973, *12*:378–387. On the complexity of so small an item as a Daoist talismanic chart, see Michael Saso, "What Is the Ho-t'u?" *HR*, 1978, *17*(3–4):399–416.

91. See Kuang-ming Wu, *Chuang-Tzu: World Philosopher at Play* (New York: Crossroad/Scholars Press, 1982).

Chapter 4:
Japanese Religion

1. Johannes Maringer, "Clay Figurines of the Jomon Period," *HR*, 1974, *14*:128–139.

2. Carmen Blacker, "The Religions of Japan," in *Historia Religionum, II*, ed. C. J. Bleeker and G. Widengren (Leiden: E. J. Brill, 1971), p. 518.

3. H. Byron Earhart, *Japanese Religion: Unity and Diversity*, 2nd ed. (Encino, Calif.: Dickenson, 1974), pp. 11–16.

4. Ichiro Hori, *Folk Religion in Japan* (Chicago: University of Chicago Press, 1968), pp. 181–251. See also Carmen Blacker, *The Catalpa Bow* (London: Allen & Unwin, 1975); and Joseph M. Kitagawa, "Japanese Religion: An Overview," *ER, 7*, 520–538; Alan L. Miller, "Japanese Religion: Popular Religion," ibid., 538–545; Matsumae Takeski, "Japanese Religion: Mythic Themes," ibid., 545–552.

5. G. Bownas, "Shinto," in *The Concise Encyclopedia of Living Faiths*, ed. R. C. Zaehner (Boston: Beacon Press, 1967), p. 349.

6. Ryusaku Tsunoda et al., *Sources of Japanese Tradition*, vol. 1 (New York: Columbia University Press, 1964), pp. 25–26.

7. Bownas, "Shinto," p. 357. For other folk themes, see Alan L. Miller, "Of Weavers and Birds," *HR*, February 1987, *26*(3):309–327; Alan L. Miller, "Ame No Miso-Ori Me (The Heavenly Weaving Maiden)," *HR*, August 1984, *24*(1):27–48; and Robert S. Ellwood, "A Cargo Cult in Seventh-Century Japan," *HR*, February 1984, *23*(3):222–239.

8. Ibid.

9. For an introduction to Hua-yan metaphysics, see Francis H. Cook, *Hua-yen Buddhism* (University Park: Pennsylvania State University Press, 1977).

10. Richard J. Robinson and Willard J. Johnson, *The Buddhist Religion* (Encino, Calif.: Dickenson, 1977), p. 175.

11. Francis H. Cook, "Heian, Kamakura, and Tokugawa Periods in Japan," in *Buddhism: A Modern Perspective*, ed. Charles S. Prebish (University Park: Pennsylvania State University Press, 1975); Tamaru Noriyoshi, "Buddhism: Buddhism in Japan," *ER, 2*, 426–435.

12. The section adapts materials from Tsunoda et al., *Sources of Japanese Tradition*, vol. 1. pp. 184–260.

13. Francis H. Cook, "Japanese Innovations In Buddhism," in *Buddhism: A Modern Perspective*, pp. 229–233.

14. Earhart, *Japanese Religion*, pp. x–xi.

15. Ibid., p. 73.

16. See Tsunoda et al., *Sources of Japanese Tradition*, pp. 261–276.

17. Shusaku Endo, *Silence* (Rutland, Vt.: Tuttle, 1969).

18. Robert N. Bellah, *Tokugawa Religion* (Boston: Beacon Press, 1970), pp. 90–98.

19. See Ishida Ichiro, "Kokugaku," *ER, 8*, 360–362; Hirai Naofusa, "Shinto," *ER, 13*, 280–294; Allan G. Grapard, "Japan's Ignored Cultural Revolution," *HR*, February 1984, *23*(3):240–265; whole issue *HR*, February 1980; *27*(3), on Shinto.

20. See Blacker, *Catalpa Bow*, pp. 130–132.

21. Earhart, *Japanese Religion*, p. 112.

22. Ibid., pp. 114–117.

23. John B. Noss, *Man's Religions*, 5th ed. (New York: Macmillan, 1974), p. 324.

24. Denise Lardner Carmody, *Women and World Religions* (Nashville: Abingdon, 1979), p. 84.

25. Edwin O. Reischauer, *Japan Past and Present*, 3rd ed. rev. (Tokyo: Tuttle, 1964), pp. 108–141.

26. H. Byron Earhart, ed., *Religion in the Japanese Experience: Sources and Interpretations* (Encino, Calif.: Dickenson, 1974), pp. 201–210; see also Tsunoda et al., *Sources of Japanese Tradition*, vol. 2 (New York: Columbia University Press, 1964), pp. 131–210.

27. Earhart, ed., *Religion in the Japanese Experience,* p. 204.

28. Joseph Kitagawa, "The Japanese *Kokutai* (National Community): History and Myth," *HR,* 1974, *13*:209–226.

29. Y. T. Hosoi, "The Sacred Tree in Japanese Prehistory," *HR,* 1976, *16*:95–119.

30. Manabu Waida, "Symbolisms of the Moon and the Waters of Immortality," *HR,* 1977, *16*:407–423; Manabu Watanabe, "Religious Symbolism in Saigyo's Verse," *HR,* May 1987, *26*(4):382–400.

31. See Blacker, *Catalpa Bow,* and Hori, *Folk Religion in Japan,* for the shamanistic exceptions to this statement.

32. See Lynn White, Jr., "The Historical Roots of Our Ecological Crisis," in *Ecology and Religion in History,* ed. David and Eileen Spring (New York: Harper Torchbooks, 1974), pp. 15–31. The other articles in this volume suggest the sort of qualifications one would expect in discussing Japanese ecology. See especially Yi-Fu Tuan, "Discrepancies between Environmental Attitude and Behaviour," pp. 91–113.

33. This section adapts materials from Robert S. Ellwood, Jr., *An Invitation to Japanese Civilization* (Belmont, Calif.: Wadsworth, 1980), pp. 95–125; see also "Tea Ceremony," in *The New Encyclopaedia Britannica,* vol. II (Chicago: Encyclopaedia Britannica, 1987), pp. 596–597; Theodore M. Ludwig, "The Way of Tea: A Religio-Aesthetic Mode of Life," *HR,* August 1974, *14*(1):28–50; and Richard B. Pilgrim, "Intervals (*Ma*) in Space in Time," *HR,* February 1986, *25*(3):255–277.

34. On contemporary professional and business life in Japan, see Ichiro Kawasaki, *Japan Unmasked* (Rutland, Vt.: Tuttle, 1969); Nobutaka Ike, *Japan: The New Superstate* (Stanford, Calif.: Stanford Alumni Association, 1973); for further sociological insight, see Chie Nakane, *Japanese Society* (Berkeley: University of California Press, 1972); and Liza Dalby, *Geisha* (Berkeley: University of California Press, 1983).

35. Earhart, ed., *Religion in the Japanese Experience,* pp. 145–159.

36. Alfred North Whitehead, *Religion in the Making* (New York: Meridian, 1960), p. 16.

37. Yukio Mishima has brought this lovely Zen temple into recent Japanese religious consciousness. See his *The Temple of the Golden Pavilion* (Rutland, Vt.: Tuttle, 1959).

38. "The Seventeen-Article Constitution of Prince Shotoku," *Sources of Japanese Tradtion,* vol. 1, p. 48.

39. Patrick White, *The Vivisector* (New York: Viking, 1970).

40. Chang Chung-yun, *Creativity and Taoism* (New York: Harper Colophon, 1970).

41. Bownas, "Shinto."

42. Blacker, "Religions of Japan"; see also Denise Lardner Carmody and John Tully Carmody, *How to Live Well: Ethics in the World Religions* (Belmont, Calif.: Wadsworth, 1988), pp. 160–181.

43. Bellah, *Tokugawa Religion,* pp. 107–132, 178–197; Winston Davis, "Pilgrimage and World Renewal: A Study of Religion and Social Values in Tokugawa Japan," *HR,* November 1983, *23*(2):97–116, and February 1984, *23*(3):197–221.

44. Mircea Eliade, *From Primitives to Zen* (New York: Harper & Row, 1967), pp. 452–454.

45. Considering Shinran as a *bodhisattva* would force us to adjust this judgment. See Robert N. Bellah, "The Contemporary Meaning of Kamakura Buddhism," *JAAR,* 1974, *42*:7–9.

46. See Shunryu Suzuki, *Zen Mind, Beginner's Mind* (New York: John Weatherhill, 1970), pp. 92–95, 102–104.

47. Earhart, *Religion in the Japanese Experience,* p. 25.

48. This section adapts materials from Earhart, ed., *Religion in the Japanese Experience,* pp. 19–26.

Conclusion

1. C. G. Jung, *Memories, Dreams, Reflections* (New York: Vintage, 1963), p. 235.

2. In our view, Mircea Eliade shows that persuasively; see his *Shamanism* (Princeton, N.J.: Princeton University Press/Bollingen, 1972); *Yoga* (Princeton, N.J.: Princeton University Press/Bollingen, 1970).

3. See Wilfred Cantwell Smith, *The Meaning and End of Religion* (New York: Mentor, 1964); on the rise of the term *religio* with Cicero, see Eric Voegelin, *Order and History,* vol. 4 (Baton Rouge: Louisiana State University Press, 1974), pp. 43–48; Winston L. King, "Religion," *ER, 12,* 282–293.

4. See Joachim Wach, *The Comparative Study of Religions* (New York: Columbia University Press, 1961).

5. Three recent works that illumine religious traditioning are Huston Smith, *Forgotten Truth: The Primordial Tradition* (New York: Harper & Row, 1976); E. F. Schumacher, *A Guide for the Perplexed* (New York: Harper & Row, 1977); Peter Slater, *The Dynamics of Religion* (New York: Harper & Row, 1978).

6. This is a theme in John Bowker, *The Sense of God* (Oxford: Clarendon Press, 1973).

7. See Voegelin, *Order and History,* vol. 4, pp. 330–335.

8. See Marcel Griaule, *Conversations with Ogotemmeli* (New York: Oxford University Press, 1965).

9. Huston Smith, "Frithjof Schuon's *The Transcendent Unity of Religion:* Pro," and Richard C. Bush, "Frithjof Schuon's *The Transcendent Unity of Religion:* Con," *JAAR,* 1976, *44*:715–719, 721–724.

10. See Stanley Jaki, *The Road of Science and the Ways to God* (Chicago: University of Chicago Press, 1978).

11. On religious interpretations of American destiny, see Conrad Cherry, ed., *God's New Israel* (Englewood Cliffs, N.J.: Prentice-Hall, 1971).

12.   William A. Clebsch, *American Religious Thought* (Chicago: University of Chicago Press, 1973).

13.   Sidney Mead, *The Lively Experiment* (New York: Harper & Row, 1976); R. Laurence Moore, *Religious Outsiders and the Making of Americans* (New York: Oxford University Press, 1986); *The Bible in America,* ed. Nathan O. Hatch and Mark A. Noll (New York: Oxford University Press, 1982).

14.   On American pluralism, see *Soundings,* 1978, *61*(3), entire issue; also Denise Lardner Carmody and John Tully Carmody, *The Kingdom of Many Mansions* (New York: Paragon, 1990).

ANNOTATED BIBLIOGRAPHY

Introduction

Barrett, David, ed. *World Christian Encyclopedia*. New York: Oxford University Press, 1982. A full survey of demographic data and future probabilities for all the major religious traditions.

Carmody, Denise Lardner. *Women and World Religions*, 2nd ed. Englewood Cliffs, N.J.: Prentice-Hall, 1988. A survey of female images and roles in the major religious traditions that describes what being religious as a female has meant in the past and means today.

Carmody, Denise Lardner, and Carmody, John Tully. *Religion: The Great Questions*. San Francisco: Harper & Row, 1983. A comparative study of the major traditions in terms of their positions on the central existential questions of evil, the good life, and so on.

Eliade, Mircea. *The Sacred and the Profane*. New York: Harcourt, Brace & World, 1959. A concise statement of Eliade's view that human beings try to find meaning by making sacred the primary realities of their lives.

Hall, T. William, general editor. *Introduction to the Study of Religion*. San Francisco: Harper & Row, 1978. A team of scholars from Syracuse University tackles the major conceptual topics.

Hick, John H. *Philosophy of Religion*, 3rd ed. Englewood Cliffs, N.J.: Prentice-Hall, 1983. A good survey of the main problems and concepts involved in the study of religion.

Kitagawa, Joseph. *The History of Religions*. Atlanta: Scholars Press, 1988. Essays by a disciple of the masters who formed the discipline known as the history of religions.

Lovin, Robin W., and Reynolds, Frank E., ed. *Cosmogony and Ethical Order*. Chicago: University of Chicago Press, 1985. Studies dealing with how numerous religious traditions have tried to root their ethical systems in the order given at the birth of the physical world.

Smart, Ninian, and Hecht, Richard D., eds. *Sacred Texts of the World: A Universal Anthology*. New York: Crossroad, 1982. A good collection of primary sources on all the traditions that we treat.

Smith, Jonathan Z. *To Take Place*. Chicago: University of Chicago Press, 1988. Essays preliminary to a theory of ritual.

Stewart, David, ed. *Exploring the Philosophy of Religion*. Englewood Cliffs, N.J.: Prentice-Hall, 1988. A reader of selections from primary sources in the history of Western thought about religious experience, God, faith, religious language, evil, and death.

Whaling, Frank, ed. *The World's Religious Traditions*. New York: Crossroad, 1986. Essays in honor of Winfred Cantwell Smith, a pioneer in elucidating the function of religious traditions, which examine both what "tradition" has tended to mean in the major world religions and how scholars now tend to approach the study of religious traditions.

Wilson, John F. *Religion: A Preface*. Englewood Cliffs, N.J.: Prentice-Hall, 1982. A short overview of the problems and traditions that one must consider in studying world religion—weak on the East but good on modernity.

Chapter 1: Hinduism

Basham, A. L. *The Wonder That Was India*. New York: Grove Press, 1959. A readable and comprehensive study of Indian life before the coming of the Muslims.

Eck, Diana L. *Banaras, City of Light*. New York: Alfred A. Knopf, 1982. A study of a holy city that is a microcosm of Hinduism.

Eliade, Mircea. *Yoga: Immortality and Freedom*. Princeton, N.J.: Princeton University Press, 1970. A classical study of the presuppositions and main features of the various yogic quests to defeat space and time.

Erikson, Erik H. *Gandhi's Truth*. New York: Norton, 1969. A psychoanalytic study of the modern founder of militant nonviolence.

Hawley, John Stratton, ed. *The Divine Consort*. Berkeley: University of California Press, 1982. A colorful study of the major divine wives in Hindu mythology.

Hopkins, Thomas J. *The Hindu Religious Tradition*. Encino, Calif.: Dickenson, 1971. A brief and solid survey of the major religious developments.

Kinsley, David R. *Hinduism*. Englewood Cliffs, N.J.: Prentice-Hall, 1982. A brief introduction that offers a cultural perspective on Hindu history and thought.

McLeod, W. H. *The Sikhs*. New York: Columbia University Press, 1989. A historical study of Sikh traditions and culture.

Markandaya, Kamala. *Nectar in a Sieve.* New York: Signet, n.d. (originally 1954). A simple novel of Indian women caught in the crumbling of traditional culture.

O'Flaherty, Wendy Doniger. *Siva: The Erotic Ascetic.* New York: Oxford University Press, 1973. A study of a major Hindu god that illustrates the many different weights and symbolic associations a Hindu deity can carry.

O'Flaherty, Wendy Doniger. *Women, Androgynes and Other Mythical Beasts.* Chicago: University of Chicago Press, 1980. Studies in Hindu symbolism associated with fertility, vitality, and sacredness.

Stanford, Anne, trans. *The Bhagavad Gita.* New York: Seabury, 1970. A fairly readable verse translation of India's most influential book.

Younger, Paul, and Younger, Susanna. *Hinduism.* Niles, Ill.: Argus, 1978. A very brief, well-illustrated sketch of Hindu traditions, ideas, and practices.

Chapter 2:
Buddhism

Conze, Edward, et al., eds. *Buddhist Texts through the Ages.* New York: Harper Torchbooks, 1964. A good selection of representative primary sources, dealing with most of the major Buddhist sects.

Conze, Edward. *Buddhist Thought in India.* Ann Arbor: University of Michigan Press, 1967. A fairly demanding study of the origin of Buddhist philosophy in Indian dialectics.

King, Winston. *In the Hope of Nibbana: Theravada Buddhist Ethics.* La Salle, Ill.: Open Court, 1964. A solid survey of the framework and content of Theravada ethics, both individual and social.

Nyanaponika, Thera. *The Heart of Buddhist Meditation.* London: Rider, 1969. A thorough study of the Buddha's way of mindfulness that reflects Theravada traditions.

Rahula, Walpola. *What the Buddha Taught,* rev. ed. New York: Grove Press, 1974. A fine exposition, focusing especially on the Four Noble Truths, with selected important texts.

Robinson, Richard H., and Johnson, Willard L. *The Buddhist Religion.* Encino, Calif.: Dickenson, 1977. A comprehensive survey of Buddhist religion throughout the world.

Suzuki, Shunryu. *Zen Mind, Beginner's Mind.* New York: Weatherhill, 1970. A lovely and penetrating vision of Zen by a contemporary master.

Swearer, Donald K. *Buddhism.* Niles, Ill.: Argus, 1977. A good brief sketch of the teachings, history, and practice of Buddhism. Well illustrated.

Tucci, Giuseppi. *The Religions of Tibet.* Berkeley: University of California Press, 1980. A well-regarded investigation of both pre-Buddhist and Buddhist religious thought and practices in Tibet.

Welch, Holmes. *The Practice of Chinese Buddhism, 1900–1950.* Cambridge, Mass.: Harvard University Press, 1967. A valuable window onto the state of Chinese Buddhism (especially monastic life) prior to the anti-religious crackdown of the Maoists.

Zwolf, W., ed. *Buddhism: Art and Faith.* New York: Macmillan, 1986. A lavishly illustrated study based on collections in the British Museum.

Chapter 3:
Chinese Religion

Bush, Richard C. *Religion in China.* Niles, Ill.: Argus, 1977. A brief presentation of Chinese religion as a "stream" with several contributing "currents." Well illustrated.

Chan, Wing-Tsit, ed. *A Sourcebook in Chinese Philosophy.* Princeton, N.J.: Princeton University Press, 1963. The standard one-volume anthology of translated texts, covering the full historical range of pre-Communist Chinese culture.

Eber, Irene, ed. *Confucianism: The Dynamics of Tradition.* New York: Macmillan, 1987. A collection of essays showing how Confucianism responded to various historical challenges.

Giradot, Norman J. *Myth and Meaning in Early Taoism.* Berkeley: University of California Press, 1983. A good analysis of Daoist beginnings.

Jordan, David K., and Overmyer, Daniel L. *The Flying Phoenix: Aspects of Chinese Sectarianism in Taiwan.* Princeton, N.J.: Princeton University Press, 1986. A systematic study of modern Chinese popular sects that brings out the shamanic and folk-religious motifs.

Lagerwey, John. *Taoist Ritualism in Chinese Society and History.* New York: Macmillan, 1987. A study of the roots and intricacies of Daoist ritual.

Maspero, Henri. *Taoism and Chinese Religion.* Amherst: University of Massachusetts Press, 1981. A collection of essays by a pioneering Western scholar that show the Daoist concern for cultivating immortality.

Pound, Ezra. *Confucius.* New York: New Directions, 1951. An idiosyncratic but stimulating translation of major Confucian texts.

Roberts, Moss, ed. *Chinese Fairy Tales & Fantasies.* New York: Pantheon, 1979. A good collection of folktales that often show how Confucian, Daoist, or Buddhist ideas shaped the popular Chinese imagination.

Thompson, Laurence G. *The Chinese Way in Religion.* Encino, Calif.: Dickenson, 1973. A good collection of original sources that represent the span of Chinese religion.

Thompson, Laurence G. *The Chinese Religion: An Introduction,* 3rd ed. Belmont, Calif.: Wadsworth, 1979. An overview of the major components of Chinese religious culture.

Waley, Arthur, trans. *The Way and Its Power.* New York: Grove Press, 1958. A readable version of China's most beguiling classic.

Wright, Arthur F. *Buddhism in Chinese History.* Stanford, Calif.: Stanford University Press, 1959. A straightforward survey of Buddhism's fortunes in the major historical periods.

Chapter 4: Japanese Religion

Anesaki, Masaharu. *History of Japanese Religion,* 2nd ed. Rutland, Vt.: Tuttle, 1963. A standard overview providing a good general introduction.

Bellah, Robert N. *Tokugawa Religion.* Boston: Beacon Press, 1970. A somewhat demanding sociological analysis of Japanese religious culture on the verge of modernity.

Earhart, H. Byron. *Japanese Religion: Unity and Diversity,* 2nd ed. Encino, Calif.: Dickenson, 1974. An exposition of Japanese religious development from prehistoric times to the present.

Earhart, H. Byron. *Religion in the Japanese Experience.* Encino, Calif.: Dickenson, 1974. A good collection of texts that represent the many aspects of Japanese religion.

Ellwood, Robert S., and Pilgrim, Richard. *Japanese Religion: A Cultural Perspective.* Englewood Cliffs, N.J.: Prentice-Hall, 1985. A useful introduction focusing on social and cultural issues.

Franck, Frederick, ed. *The Buddha Eye.* New York: Crossroad, 1982. An anthology of writings by members of the recent Kyoto school, one of the most influential modern circles of Buddhist philosophy.

Hoover, Thomas. *The Zen Experience.* New York: New American Library, 1980. Studies in the thought of major Chinese and Japanese masters.

Hori, Ichiro. *Folk Religion in Japan.* Chicago: University of Chicago Press, 1968. A somewhat specialized study whose richness of detail, especially on shamanism, makes it of interest to the nonspecialist.

Kapleau, Philip, ed. *The Three Pillars of Zen.* Boston: Beacon Press, 1967. A clear view of the practice of Zen in modern Japan.

Nakamura, Hajime. *Ways of Thinking of Eastern People.* Honolulu: University of Hawaii Press, 1964. An interesting study of the cultural assumptions and mind-set that provides a basis for comparing Japanese religion with those of India, China, and Tibet.

Smith, Robert J. *Ancestor Worship in Contemporary Japan.* Stanford, Calif.: Stanford University Press, 1974. A study of postwar Japanese veneration of ancestors and attitudes toward the dead.

Tsunoda, Ryusaku, et al., eds. *Sources of Japanese Tradition,* two volumes. New York: Columbia University Press, 1964. A good anthology of important texts throughout Japanese religious history.

Conclusion

Ahlstrom, Sydney. *A Religious History of the American People.* New Haven, Conn.: Yale University Press, 1972. A massive, authoritative treatment of American religion from precolonial times to the end of the 1960s.

Carmody, Denise Lardner, and Carmody, John Tully. *Exploring American Religion.* Mountain View, Calif.: Mayfield, 1988. An introductory overview dealing with history, worldview, and recent trends.

Carmody, Denise Lardner, and Carmody, John Tully. *The Kingdom of Many Mansions.* New York: Paragon, 1990. An analysis of how major ideas from Puritan, Enlightenment, and pragmatic sources worked out in both the mainstream of American history and the margins.

Daedalus, Volume 111, Number 1 (Winter 1982). A collection of essays by leading scholars who try to interpret the current significance of religion, both in the United States and on the world scene.

Daedalus, Volume 117, Number 2 (Spring 1988). A discussion among educators about the current function of religion and religious studies in American higher education.

Johnston, William. *The Inner Eye of Love.* New York: Harper & Row, 1978. Shows the contemplative foundations of religion, with special reference to Christianity and Buddhism.

Moore, R. Lawrence. *Religious Outsiders and the Making of Americans.* New York: Oxford University Press, 1986. Chapters on the history of the process by which many groups, either sectarian or marginal to the cultural mainstream, were Americanized.

Neville, Robert C. *Soldier, Sage, Saint.* New York: Fordham University Press, 1978. Typological studies of some of the dominant religious personalities.

Voegelin, Eric. *Order and History,* Vol. 5, *In Search of Order.* Baton Rouge: Louisiana State University Press, 1987. A brief, demanding, but brilliant conclusion to Voegelin's epic study of how human beings have pursued the structures of history and consciousness.

INDEX OF
NAMES AND PLACES

INDEX OF SUBJECTS